THE UK CONSTITUTION AFTER MILLER

The judgment of the UK Supreme Court in R (*Miller*) v *Secretary of State for Exiting the European Union* is of fundamental legal, constitutional and political significance. The Supreme Court's judgment discussed the relative powers of Parliament and the Government, the relationship between Westminster and the devolved legislatures, and the extent to which the UK's membership of the EU had changed the UK constitution, both prior to and even after departure. It also provided further evidence of the emerging role of the UK's Supreme Court as a constitutional court, despite the lack of a codified constitution in the UK.

This edited collection critically evaluates the decision in *Miller*, providing a detailed analysis of the reasoning in the judgment and its longer-term consequences for the UK constitution through the period of Brexit and beyond. The case is used as a lens through which to evaluate the modern UK constitution and its potential future evolution. Whatever form Brexit may eventually take, the impact that EU membership and the triggering of Brexit has already had on the UK's constitutional settlement is profound. The book will be of great value to anyone interested in the effect of the *Miller* case and Brexit on the UK's constitution.

The UK Constitution
after *Miller*

Brexit and Beyond

Edited by

Mark Elliott, Jack Williams and Alison L Young

·HART·
OXFORD · LONDON · NEW YORK · NEW DELHI · SYDNEY

HART PUBLISHING

Bloomsbury Publishing Plc

Kemp House, Chawley Park, Cumnor Hill, Oxford, OX2 9PH, UK

HART PUBLISHING, the Hart/Stag logo, BLOOMSBURY and the Diana logo are
trademarks of Bloomsbury Publishing Plc

First published in Great Britain 2018

A catalogue record for this book is available from the British Library.

Library of Congress Cataloging-in-Publication data

Names: Elliott, Mark, 1975- editor. | Williams, Jack (Barrister), editor. |
Young, Alison L., editor.

Title: The UK constitution after Miller : Brexit and beyond / edited by Mark Elliott,
Jack Williams and Alison L Young.

Description: Oxford, UK : Hart Publishing, 2018. | Includes bibliographical
references and index.

Identifiers: LCCN 2018011666 (print) | LCCN 2018012292 (ebook) |
ISBN 9781509916429 (Epub) | ISBN 9781509916405 (hardback : alk. paper)

Subjects: LCSH: Treaty-making power—Great Britain. | Prerogative, Royal—Great Britain. |
European Union—Great Britain. | Miller, Gina, 1965—Trials, litigation, etc. | Great Britain.
Department for Exiting the European Union,—Trials, litigation, etc.

Classification: LCC KD4452 (ebook) | LCC KD4452 .U39 2018 (print) |
DDC 342.41—dc23

LC record available at https://lccn.loc.gov/2018011666

ISBN: HB: 978-1-50991-640-5
        ePDF: 978-1-50991-641-2
        ePub: 978-1-50991-642-9

Typeset by Compuscript Ltd, Shannon
Printed and bound in Great Britain by TJ International Ltd, Padstow, Cornwall

To find out more about our authors and books visit www.hartpublishing.co.uk.
Here you will find extracts, author information, details of forthcoming events
and the option to sign up for our newsletters.

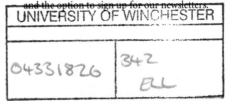

FOREWORD

The simple binary issue placed before the United Kingdom's voters in the 2016 referendum—to remain in the European Union or to leave it—opened up a cleft which is unlikely ever to heal. On one view, setting aside the hubristic political misjudgement which brought it about and the commerce in political mendacity which it licensed, the outcome has been an act of collective folly for which our children and grandchildren will not forgive us. On another view, the UK is at last on the road to freedom from foreign domination and alien immigration, able now to forge its own destiny as a world trading power.

I happen to hold the first view. But one's personal view of Brexit has little or nothing to do with what this book is about, even if authorial partisanship leaks through many of the fissures in its chapters. For scholarship is not neutral: academics, like judges, embark on an inquiry with some sense of where they hope or expect that it will lead. Their minds may be open, but they are not blank.

There are at least two striking things about Gina Miller's claim that any decision to give notice of withdrawal from the EU treaty was legally one for Parliament and not for Ministers. The first is that the litigation was completely unnecessary: once permission was granted to proceed, nothing would have been more straightforward than to put the issue beyond doubt by placing a Withdrawal Bill before Parliament—as of course eventually happened.

The second—and we come now to the essays in this book—is that there is more than one mode of judicial reasoning. It may be cerebral; it may be intuitive; it may be both. The cerebral mode, at least in its platonic form, proceeds from facts to law to conclusion. This is a paradigm, however, which assumes that both facts and law are clear, or at least are ascertainable with confidence. The minority in the Supreme Court considered that *Miller* was such a case, and they find commendation and support among the contributors. Intuitive reasoning is frequently more potent, but correspondingly more difficult to articulate. It proceeds typically from postulated conclusion to law to facts. The paradigmatic question is: can this be right? It is arguably how the Divisional Court and the majority in the Supreme Court went about deciding the case.

There is nothing unlawyerly or intellectually dishonest about such a process. There can be few judges who have not stood back from a logically impeccable draft judgment, looked at the conclusion and asked themselves: can this be right? I have certainly done so, and been satisfied that my initial conclusion could not stand. More importantly, some of the historic judgments of the common law have taken this course. You can debate which fall into this category, but there can be little doubt that the great judgment of Pratt CJ in *Entick v Carrington* does: notwithstanding clear authority in favour of ministerial powers of search and seizure, Pratt concluded that it simply could not be right—that it was intuitively unacceptable—that such powers were sanctioned by common law.

The contrast between the majority and minority judgments in *Miller* is, I think, of this kind. The majority view may lack the crystalline logic of the minority. But it falls back on something which its authors take to be more fundamental: the centuries-long process of restricting the use by Ministers of the Royal Prerogative to bypass Parliament, and the role of the courts in securing this cornerstone of a modern democracy. This may sound politically charged—as Lord Reed cautioned it was—but it is what the rule of law is about. It is one thing to say, as can today increasingly be said, that Ministers are themselves subject to judicial review if they abuse their prerogative powers; it is another to ensure that Parliament is not simply circumvented by them.

In the end, in one sense, it did not matter: a laconic and practically unopposed Withdrawal Bill handed the Prime Minister the discretionary power the courts had denied her. In a more important sense, however, it has mattered a great deal. The abuse directed by the *Daily Mail* at the Lord Chief Justice, the Master of the Rolls and a Lord Justice of Appeal, for holding that withdrawal was a matter for the legislature, faded when the Supreme Court, whose supremacy the Brexit campaign had been vocally promoting, agreed with them. It has meant something that the Supreme Court has been able, so far, to fly above the storm.

The legal arguments remain massive and are not going to be easily resolved. This is not least because the legal issues and the political critiques tend to be joined at the hip: there is now in substance a pro-Brexit and an anti-Brexit jurisprudence. Both the lawyers and the law students who will spend many years picking their way through the issues and arguments to be found in these pages would do well to keep this in mind as they ponder the future meaning of parliamentary supremacy.

Stephen Sedley
Former Lord Justice of Appeal and Visiting Professor of Law
Oxford
January 2018

CONTENTS

LIST OF CONTRIBUTORS

Gordon Anthony is Professor of Public Law at Queen's University Belfast and was Junior Counsel for Mr Agnew and others in the Reference from Northern Ireland in *R (Miller) v Secretary of State for Exiting the European Union* [2017] UKSC 5.

Eirik Bjorge is a Senior Lecturer in Law at the University of Bristol.

Paul Craig is Professor of English Law at the University of Oxford and a Professorial Fellow of St John's College, Oxford.

Richard Ekins is an Associate Professor at the University of Oxford and a Tutorial Fellow in Law at St John's College, Oxford.

Mark Elliott is Professor of Public Law at the University of Cambridge and a Fellow of St Catharine's College, Cambridge.

Graham Gee is Professor of Public Law at the University of Sheffield.

David Howarth is Professor of Law and Public Policy at the University of Cambridge and a Fellow of Clare College, Cambridge.

Sir John Laws is a former Lord Justice of Appeal in the England and Wales Court of Appeal.

Aileen McHarg is Professor of Public Law at the University of Strathclyde.

Anne Twomey is Professor of Constitutional Law at the University of Sydney.

Jack Williams is a barrister at Monckton Chambers and was counsel for one of the interested parties in *R (Miller) v Secretary of State for Exiting the European Union* [2017] UKSC 5.

Alison L Young is the Sir David Williams Professor of Public Law at the University of Cambridge and a Fellow of Robinson College, Cambridge.

1

The *Miller* Tale: An Introduction

MARK ELLIOTT, JACK WILLIAMS AND ALISON L YOUNG

I. Prologue

A. Substantive Background

On 23 June 2016, a referendum was held under the European Union Referendum Act 2015, which asked: 'Should the United Kingdom remain a member of the European Union or leave the European Union?' The view of the majority of those who participated in the referendum was that the United Kingdom (UK) should leave the European Union (EU).[1] Article 50 of the Treaty on European Union ('Article 50') provides the mechanism for a Member State to withdraw from the EU. Materially it provides:

1. Any Member State may decide to withdraw from the Union in accordance with its own constitutional requirements.
2. A Member State which decides to withdraw shall notify the European Council of its intention ...

The question in *R (Miller) v Secretary of State for Exiting the European Union*[2] ('*Miller*') concerned the UK's 'own constitutional requirements' for giving effect to that decision and triggering the Article 50 process: did the UK Government already possess competence to notify the European Council of the UK's intention to leave under Article 50(2) by use of the foreign affairs prerogative, or was an Act of Parliament necessary to authorise such notification?

As is often the case with the UK's uncodified constitution, answering the apparently simple question generated by this competence dispute (between the executive and the legislature) turned out to be a far from straightforward matter. Indeed, it gave rise to one of the most politically controversial and intellectually contested constitutional cases of recent times, thanks to the fundamentally

---

[1] 51.9% of those voting agreed that the UK should leave the EU. Majorities in Gibraltar (95.8%), Northern Ireland (62%) and Scotland (55.8%) voted to remain in the EU.
[2] *R (Miller) v Secretary of State for Exiting the European Union* [2017] UKSC 5, [2017] 2 WLR 583.

significant nature of the legal, constitutional and political issues that were at stake in *Miller*. This litigation represented not only a key milestone in relation to the process of the UK's withdrawal from the EU, but also afforded the UK courts an opportunity to address a range of key issues relating to the operation of the UK constitution and the way in which it interacts with the EU legal system.

This edited collection takes the judgments of the Divisional Court and the Supreme Court in *Miller* as a point of departure for the purpose of taking stock of, and assessing the likely direction of travel of, the contemporary UK constitution. While the *Miller* case is therefore central, this book is not exclusively about the case; rather, the case serves as the launching pad for a wide-ranging analysis of the modern constitution. This introductory chapter, however, provides an overview of the issues giving rise to the *Miller* case, tracks the stages of the litigation itself, summarises the judgments of both the Divisional Court and Supreme Court, and provides a synopsis of the longer-term implications and consequences for the UK constitution that are then addressed, in turn, in successive chapters.

B. Procedural Background

The European Union Referendum Act 2015 did not say anything about what should happen if the majority of votes were cast in favour of the UK's leaving the EU. As such, as a matter of domestic law, it was an advisory referendum. The 2015 Act thus stands in contrast to the Parliamentary and Voting Constituencies Act 2011 and section 1(2) of the Northern Ireland Act 1998, under both of which referendums (depending on the outcome) may result in legal obligations being imposed upon Ministers. The availability of this 'binding' model was well known to Parliament before enactment of the European Union Referendum Act 2015,[3] but Parliament chose to legislate for a referendum the outcome of which would not legally require the Government to take, or to refrain from taking, a particular course of action.

The referendum itself was therefore not the 'decision' for the purpose of Article 50(1). Nor was there anything in the 2015 Act itself to suggest that the holding of the referendum amounted to the taking of a decision that Parliament would, if it wished to do so, be legally incapable of overriding or reversing. None of this, however, determined where authority *did* lie for the triggering of the Article 50 process. As the Court of Appeal held in *Shindler v Chancellor of the Duchy of Lancaster*,[4] the EU referendum 'contains part' of the UK's 'constitutional

---

[3] See, eg, the House of Commons Library Briefing Paper (No 07212, 3 June 2015), which stated that '[The Bill] does not contain any requirement for the UK Government to implement the results of the referendum, nor set a time by which a vote to leave the EU should be implemented. Instead, this is a type of referendum known as pre-legislative or consultative, which enables the electorate to voice an opinion which then influences the Government in its policy decisions … The UK does not have constitutional provisions which would require the results of a referendum to be implemented.'

[4] *Shindler v Chancellor of the Duchy of Lancaster* [2016] EWCA Civ 469.

requirements' for the purposes of Article 50(1). The *Miller* case concerned the remaining requirements.

The litigants in *Miller* argued that it would be unlawful for a Government Minister to notify the European Council of a decision of the UK to withdraw from the EU under Article 50 without statutory authority. Their motives for doing so are surmised to be various: to assist the halting of Brexit altogether (by providing the opportunity for MPs and Lords to vote against any authorisation to notify); to delay the triggering of Article 50 to give the country time either to re-consider, or at least to prepare for negotiations before the Article 50 two-year-to-exit clock began ticking; to constrain the Government's negotiating hand (by providing the opportunity for MPs and Lords to prescribe limitations or conditions on the notification to leave the EU in any Act authorising notification); to protect against the loss of rights; and, quite simply, to uphold what they considered to be the proper functioning of the UK's constitution, with parliamentary sovereignty at the core and the executive subject to parliamentary control. Whatever the motives of the individuals bringing the claims or one's political view of such motives—both of which are materially irrelevant to the underlying legal issues—the question for the courts was a purely legal one, as to the respective allocation of competence in the UK constitutional order between the Government and Parliament.[5]

Letters before claim were sent to the Government on 1 July 2016, on behalf of Gina Miller (and, at that time, other potential co-claimants whose identities were confidential), on 8 July, on behalf of Grahame Pigney and others (self-styled as 'the People's Challenge'), and on 7 and 11 July, on behalf of AB and a child. Mr Deir Tozetti Dos Santos had already filed a claim and published a draft skeleton argument, without having fully complied with the judicial review pre-action protocol. On 15 July, a group of expatriates applied for permission to intervene. Each group[6] alleged that the Government did not possess any relevant prerogative power to trigger Article 50, and averred that statutory authorisation was required before the UK Government could do so. The proposed defendant, at this point in time, was the Chancellor of the Duchy of Lancaster, there being no Secretary of State for Exiting the European Union at this stage.

The matter came before the Divisional Court (Sir Brian Leveson and Cranston J sitting) on 19 July 2016 for directions. Such directions hearings are usually mundane affairs, but there was unprecedented interest in, and attendance at, this one—so much so that the participants and spectators were advised to move from the assigned court room in the Royal Courts of Justice to the largest one next door in order to accommodate the already large legal teams and interested members of the press and public.

Whilst, at this time, only one claim had formally been issued (that of Mr Dos Santos), the Court nonetheless ordered that Ms Miller's (then, future) claim be

---

[5] Cf Richard Ekins and Graham Gee's contribution in ch 11 of this volume.

[6] Together, all these parties will be referred to as 'the claimants' in relation to the Divisional Court proceedings and 'the respondents' in relation to the Supreme Court proceedings.

designated as the lead claim, and that the other parties had, at their discretion, permission to have their separate claims joined, or to become interested parties or interveners in the Miller claim. Mr Dos Santos ultimately opted to continue his claim, becoming the second claimant, whilst, for reasons of procedural convenience and cost, others decided to join as interested parties or interveners, rather than as claimants. This decision was taken on an explicit mutual understanding— articulated at the directions hearing—that there was no real practical disadvantage in so doing, save that submissions were not to be duplicative. This at least partially explains the intriguing list of names and formal statuses to be found in the judgments that were subsequently issued.[7] There may, indeed, have been others but for the vitriolic abuse many potential claimants received at the pre-action stage, something the Court was particularly quick to condemn and caution against, both orally at the directions hearing and in its Order dated 26 July 2016:

> UPON the Court expressing its grave concern on receiving reports that parties and prospective parties to these proceedings, and their legal representatives, have been the subject of abusive conduct by a minority of the members of the public which may be criminal and/or in contempt of court, and indicating that the Court will be prepared to deal with such conduct severely if it interferes with the bringing or conduct of this litigation.

A strict timetable was laid down by the Court in its Order following the directions hearing. The Government, now in the form of the Secretary of State for Exiting the European Union, was to reply to the pre-action letters by 25 July; the lead claimant, Ms Miller, was to serve and file her written skeleton argument by 14 September (with each of the interested parties and interveners to file and serve additional written skeleton arguments by 21 September); and the Government was to respond substantively by 30 September. The substantive hearing was listed for 13, 17 and 18 October 2016 on account of the Court's availability and a judicial determination not to be accused of delaying the political process. The Order noted that

> it is not the present intention of the United Kingdom Government ... to make notification under Article 50(2) of the Treaty on European Union before the end of 2016 ... the intended Miller claim (including any other claims joined to it), including any appeal ... should, subject to the Supreme Court, be finally determined before the end of 2016.

For similar reasons, the Court already envisaged a 'leapfrog' appeal to the Supreme Court (ie missing out the usual Court of Appeal stage),[8] and informal conversations were taking place with the Supreme Court's staff so that the matter could be

---

[7] The parties before the Divisional Court were, then, all private parties save for the Secretary of State for Exiting the European Union. The devolved Governments were not formally involved until the Supreme Court stage. What might not have been widely known, however, is that the Welsh and Scottish Governments both had counsel in attendance on noting briefs. Legal representatives for clients from Northern Ireland were also observers.

[8] Pursuant to the Administration of Justice Act 1969, s 12. The Order stated that 'The Court shall make arrangements to liaise with the Supreme Court concerning the possibility of a certificate being granted ... for a leapfrog appeal, so that (in the event such a certificate is granted) any such appeal could, subject to the Supreme Court, be heard and determined before the end of 2016.'

concluded by the end of 2016 in line with the Government's then intention not to trigger the Article 50 process before the start of the New Year.

The Divisional Court, once constituted, was essentially (though not formally) a Court of Appeal bench, and a strong one at that. It consisted of the Lord Chief Justice, the Master of the Rolls and Lord Justice Sales. The rest of this chapter analyses the substantive decision reached by the Divisional Court and the aftermath of that Court's decision (section II), followed by a description of the events and submissions at the Supreme Court stage (section III), a discussion of noteworthy features of the *Miller* litigation (section IV), and, in section V, an overview and summary of the substantive implications of the case, which are discussed more thoroughly by the authors of each of the chapters in this book. The chapter concludes in section VI with a brief forward-looking discussion situating the *Miller* case in its wider context in the Brexit process.

II. *Miller* in the Divisional Court

A. Submissions of the Parties

In contrast to the somewhat convoluted position advanced by the Government in the Divisional Court—a position that we sketch below—the claimants' central argument was clear and attractively presented. It is difficult to improve (in terms of summarising this argument) upon the formulation adopted by Lord Pannick QC, counsel for the lead claimant. He likened notification under Article 50(2) to the firing of a bullet from a gun: the trigger is pulled by the act of notification, and the bullet eventually hits the target, causing the EU Treaties to cease to apply to the UK. Contained within this metaphor was a chain of reasoning that had every appearance of being—and which the Divisional Court plainly considered to be— irresistible. On this view, then, once the exit process was triggered by the giving of notice under Article 50(2), the default consequence of that process was that the EU Treaties would cease to apply two years later, yielding vast changes to the law applicable in the UK: changes that would include the removal from individuals of a wide array of legal rights.

The question then became whether the prerogative could be used to remove legal rights or otherwise change domestic law, to which, it was argued, the answer was 'no'. On this analysis, it was contended that it would be lawful for the Government to trigger Article 50 only if it had statutory authority to do so, because (as the Court put it, summarising the claimants' primary contention) 'the Crown's prerogative powers cannot be used by the executive government to diminish or abrogate rights under the law of the United Kingdom'.[9] Nor, said the

---

[9] *R (Miller) v Secretary of State for Exiting the European Union* [2016] EWHC 2768 (Admin), [2017] 1 All ER 15, [74].

claimants, could the Government show any statutory authority that enabled it to trigger Article 50. Moreover, the claimants argued that even if they were wrong that general principles of constitutional law precluded the removal of rights that derived from EU law and exercisable in domestic law, any possibility that might otherwise have arisen of using the prerogative to that end was removed by the European Communities Act 1972 ('ECA'), properly construed.

In contrast, lying at the heart of the Government's position was its conviction that it already had prerogative authority to trigger Article 50, and that there was therefore no need for Parliament to legislate so as trigger, or to empower the Government to trigger, the exit process. As Oliver Letwin put it on 5 July 2016, speaking in his capacity as Chancellor of the Duchy of Lancaster and the Minister with caretaker responsibility for handling the fallout from the referendum pending the appointment of a new Prime Minister:

> It is entirely a matter for the new administration to take how to conduct the entire negotiations, and obviously part of that decision is about when to trigger Article 50 … I am advised that the government lawyer's view is that it clearly is prerogative power. No doubt that will be heard in court.[10]

Following this early indication of its line, the Government's position as to the legal issues was revealed more fully when it published its first written case—or 'detailed grounds of resistance'—at the end of September 2016, a step that it was prepared to take only when required to do so by a court order. In its written case, the Government took the view that the giving of notice under Article 50(2) amounted to nothing more than 'an administrative step on the international law plane'.[11] This audacious suggestion, which attempted to reduce notification to a bureaucratic sideshow, rested on the proposition that the main event—that is, the taking of the 'decision' to leave the EU for the purpose of Article 50(1)—had *already* taken place. As the Government saw it, notification was merely 'the procedural implementation of the decision to withdraw'—a decision that had been 'articulated in the outcome of the referendum'.[12] But an obvious difficulty with this view is that while the taking of a 'decision' in the Article 50(1) sense requires the relevant Member State to notify the European Council under Article 50(2), it is the giving of that notification, as distinct from the taking of the decision, that sets in train the exit process, the default consequence of which is that the EU Treaties cease to apply to the withdrawing state two years after notification. To characterise the giving of notice as a purely administrative matter was thus to attempt to heavily disguise what was, in reality, an act that would have momentous legal, constitutional, political and economic consequences.

We note in passing that the Government's reliance upon the distinction between the taking of the decision and notification of it highlights an issue that was never

---

[10] Available at http://parliamentlive.tv/Event/Index/46df4956-a397-4fc2-ad0a-20f70fb08e65.

[11] Government's detailed grounds of resistance, para 8(2), available at https://www.bindmans.com/uploads/files/documents/Defendant_s_Detailed_Grounds_of_Resistance_for_publication.PDF.

[12] ibid, para 9.

fully resolved in the *Miller* litigation: namely, when and by whom the underlying decision to withdraw from the EU was taken.[13] Indeed, this issue was obscure even in the Government's written case—which is surprising, given the analytical weight the point had to bear in the light of the Government's line of argument. For instance, having argued that the decision had been 'articulated in the outcome of the referendum', the Government went on to appear to suggest in its written case that the combination of the European Union Referendum Act 2015 and the outcome of the referendum meant that the *Government* was 'entitled to decide that the UK should withdraw from the EU',[14] albeit that this was a line that the Government did not press in oral argument: by that point, the Government had accepted it did not contend that the 2015 Act provided any relevant statutory authority.[15] In any event, whatever uncertainty might have surrounded the issue of when and by whom the 'decision' was taken, the matter was surely put beyond doubt by the legislation enacted in the wake of the Supreme Court's judgment in *Miller*, the European Union (Notification of Withdrawal) Act 2017, authorising the giving of notification under Article 50(2) (as discussed further in section V).

The Government further argued that Parliament had not legislated so as to curtail the foreign affairs prerogative in this context, meaning that it remained available for the purpose of giving notification under Article 50(2). In adopting this position, the Government took the view that its prerogative authority could be restricted by statute only *expressly*, and argued that nothing in the ECA was inconsistent with the use of the prerogative for the purpose of effecting withdrawal from the EU. In putting forward the latter argument, the Government maintained that while the ECA 'might be said to *assume* that the UK remains a member of the EU', it contains no provision that '*requires* the UK to remain a member'.[16] On this view, the fact that withdrawal would result in there being 'no [EU law] rights etc upon which s 2(1) [of the ECA] would bite'[17] posed no problem, because the purpose of that provision was not to vouchsafe that there would be such rights, but merely to give domestic effect to whatever rights, if any, might derive from any relevant UK Treaty obligations at any given time—a line of argument that would later go on to be advanced by the Government more rigorously before the Supreme Court, albeit that it would be found persuasive only by the dissentients. Meanwhile, in what appeared to form part of a belt-and-braces strategy, the Government simultaneously (initially at least) contended that the European Union Referendum Act 2015 supplied positive, if implicit, authorisation for the triggering of Article 50, on account of the fact that (as the Government saw things) Parliament, when enacting that legislation, had granted the Government permission 'to give effect to the

---

[13] For discussion of this issue, see M Elliott and AL Young, 'On whether the Article 50 decision has already been taken', *Public Law for Everyone*, 9 October 2016.

[14] Government's detailed grounds of resistance (n 11), para 12(3).

[15] *Miller* (n 9), [105].

[16] ibid, [32].

[17] ibid, [34].

result' of the referendum.[18] The Government's position thus appeared to be that the 2015 Act supplied positive authority for the triggering of Article 50, albeit that (according to the Government's analysis of the ECA) no such authority was in the first place required.

Yet further arguments were advanced by the Government in its written case, including the surprising proposition that a decision to notify the European Council under Article 50(2) was a 'polycentric' one engaging 'matters of high, if not the highest, policy', thus rendering the matter non-justiciable.[19] But this argument overlooked the fact that while considerations of justiciability (and deference) might limit the appropriateness of judicial review of the *exercise* of extant prerogative powers, it is much harder to see why such matters should have any purchase when courts are asked to rule on the logically prior question of the *existence* of such authority: a question that raises issues only of law.[20] Sensibly, the Government did not press this view, and by the time the case was argued orally, it had been 'agreed on all sides that this is a justiciable question which it is for the courts to decide', the Court choosing to emphasise that it was 'only dealing with a pure question of law'[21]—not that that spared the Court, in the wake of its judgment, from the excoriating and ill-informed media onslaught to which we refer more fully in section II.D.

B. The Northern Ireland Litigation: *McCord and Agnew*

While the *Miller* case was being litigated before the Divisional Court in London, parallel proceedings were underway in Northern Ireland, where *Re McCord and Agnew* was heard between 4 and 6 October 2016 by Maguire J.[22] To the extent that these proceedings duplicated issues that were being considered in *Miller*, Maguire J stayed consideration of them. He did, however, rule on the questions that arose in *McCord and Agnew* that were specific to Northern Ireland's constitutional arrangements. Maguire J handed down judgment shortly after the Divisional Court had concluded the oral hearing in *Miller*, but before the Divisional Court had given judgment. Whereas the Divisional Court would go on to rule against the Government, Maguire J, restricting himself to the Northern Ireland-specific issues, found in favour of the Government.

The key argument advanced by the claimants was that it would be unlawful for the prerogative to be used to serve notice under Article 50(2), because any prerogative power that might otherwise have been exercisable to that end had been

---

[18] ibid, [12(2)].

[19] ibid, [15].

[20] For a contrasting analysis, see Richard Ekins and Graham Gee's contribution in ch 11 of this volume. See also Lord Carnwath's classification of frustration arguments as concerning the exercise and not the existence of prerogative powers.

[21] *Miller* (n 9), [5].

[22] *Re McCord and Agnew* [2016] NIQB 85, [2017] CMLR 7.

excluded by the Northern Ireland Act 1998, read with the Good Friday Agreement. In essence, the argument was that ongoing UK membership of the EU was one of the constitutional premises underpinning Northern Ireland's contemporary constitutional arrangements, such that EU membership and the 1998 Act were 'inextricably interwoven' with one another.[23] This argument, however, did not persuade the Court, which indicated that it would need clear evidence before concluding that legislation had displaced the prerogative, the question being 'whether the prerogative has become unavailable by reason of any necessary implication arising out of any of the statutory provisions read in the light of their status and background'.[24] In applying this test, Maguire J set considerable store by what he did—and did not—consider to be the consequences of serving notice under Article 50(2). In particular, to characterise the taking of that step as 'the *beginning* of a process which ultimately will *probably* lead to changes in UK law'.[25] However, he considered it important that '[o]n the day after the notice has been given, the law will in fact be the same as it was the day before it was given', and that '[t]he rights of individual citizens will not have changed'.[26] Being unpersuaded that giving notice under Article 50(2) would produce specific legal changes that would run counter to the 1998 Act, Maguire J went on to consider whether it would produce relevant changes of a more diffuse nature. But he concluded, applying similar reasoning, that it would not. It could not be said, concluded Maguire J, that any 'constitututional bulwark ... would be breached' simply by virtue of triggering Article 50,[27] the point being (on this view) that notification would not immediately or necessarily produce such consequences. None of these things would happen (if they were to happen at all) 'by reason of the step of notification per se', the 'reality' being that 'it remains to be seen what actual effect the process of change subsequent to notification will produce'.[28]

Thus, as we shall see, a fundamental difference between Maguire J's analysis and that of the Divisional Court (and, subsequently, the majority in the Supreme Court) lies in the former's willingness to downplay the legal and constitutional significance of triggering Article 50, on the ground that it is impossible to know, at the point in time when the withdrawal process is initiated, whether it will actually lead to withdrawal and, if it does, what the precise consequences of withdrawal will be for relevant purposes. In contrast, the Divisional Court and the majority in the Supreme Court focused not on the fact that we *could not be certain* of what would happen at the point of triggering Article 50, but on the fact that it was plain that the *default consequence* of initating the exit process is wholesale departure from the EU by dint of the EU Treaties ceasing to apply after two years.

---

[23] ibid, [87] (Maguire J).
[24] ibid, [103] (Maguire J).
[25] ibid, [105] (emphasis added).
[26] ibid.
[27] ibid, [106].
[28] ibid, [107].

The Court considered a number of further issues in *McCord and Agnew*, not all of which need be rehearsed here. Among other things, however, Maguire J concluded—in relation to a matter that would later surface in the Supreme Court—that if, contrary to his conclusion on the main point, legislation authorising the triggering of Article 50 were in fact needed, there would be no requirement under the Sewel Convention, as it applies to Northern Ireland, for the consent of the Northern Ireland Assembly. Once Maguire J's judgment was handed down in Northern Ireland, back in the Divisional Court proceedings in London, one of the sets of interested parties[29] filed and served brief submissions updating the Divisional Court on the Northern Irish litigation and suggesting ways in which that judgment did (and did not) affect the proceedings before the English Court.

C. Judgment of the Divisional Court

Judgment was given, unanimously in favour of the claimants, by the Divisional Court on 3 November 2016, just two weeks after the substantive hearing.[30] This was a remarkable turnaround. There was a real sense of anticipation in Court on the morning of 3 November, even for the legal teams: contrary to the usual practice, and in recognition of the extreme political sensitivities raised by the case, no draft judgment had been sent in advance to counsel for the parties. Although the Divisional Court's attention had been drawn to the decision in *McCord and Agnew*, it observed that, to the extent that Maguire J's judgment touched upon matters that intersected with those under consideration by the Divisional Court, the case in Northern Ireland 'appears to have been argued based on the premise that such issues were primarily for determination by us'.[31] Moreover, the Divisional Court was unpersuaded by Maguire J's view that (as the Divisional Court paraphrased it) 'notification under [Article 50] will only "probably" ultimately lead to changes in United Kingdom law', observing that he had adopted this view 'without knowledge it had been accepted before us on all sides that it necessarily *will* have that effect'.[32] The Divisional Court thus did not consider that *McCord and Agnew* resulted in its having anything other than a clear run at the issues that it had considered.

To say that the Divisional Court was underwhelmed by the Government's arguments would be something of an understatement. Indeed, it regarded the Government's position to be 'flawed' at a 'basic level',[33] and concluded that

---

[29] Namely, Pigney and others, who had a Northern Ireland client amongst their number and who had agreed not to pursue certain devolution submissions in London on the understanding that they were being dealt with by the Northern Ireland High Court, while reserving the right to do so.

[30] The Court also certified that, for the purposes of s 12 of the Administration of Justice Act 1969, 'the relevant conditions have been fulfilled and a sufficient case for an appeal to the Supreme Court … has been made out to justify an application for leave to bring such an appeal'.

[31] *Miller* (n 9), [104].

[32] ibid (emphasis added).

[33] ibid, [85].

the ECA denied the executive any prerogative authority to give notice under Article 50(2) simply by considering, and finding wanting, the Government's own submissions, before it got on to the business of examining the claimant's principal contention.[34] The Court's approach was plainly coloured by what it (rightly) considered to be the fundamental propositions of constitutional law that were implicated by *Miller*. It placed great emphasis upon the principle of parliamentary sovereignty—and in particular upon the implications of that principle for the executive's prerogative power. Thus, said the Court, the Crown 'has only those prerogative powers recognised by the common law', 'their exercise only produces legal effects within boundaries so recognised' and '[o]utside those boundaries the Crown has no power to alter the law of the land, whether it be common law or contained in legislation'.[35] The Court went on to emphasise that 'subordination of the Crown (ie the executive government) to law is the foundation of the rule of law in the United Kingdom'.[36]

It was with these foundational propositions firmly in mind that the Court turned to assess the Government's central argument: that the ECA was to be understood as giving domestic effect to EU law rights only to the extent that the UK's Treaty obligations required, and that the ECA should be further understood as having left it to the Government, through the exercise of its prerogative power, to determine whether such obligations should be extinguished via the UK's departure from the EU. It was at this point that what was, in some senses, the central conundrum of the case had to be confronted. The ECA, of course, was actually silent as to who had the authority to trigger Article 50 (not least because Article 50 was not even a glimmer in future treaty-drafters' eyes when the ECA was enacted in 1972). The question therefore became what should be made of the ECA's silence—a question the answer to which inevitably turned upon the presumptions that were to be brought to bear upon the statute. The Government contended that the ECA should be construed as leaving its prerogative power intact, unless 'the claimants could point to an intention on the part of Parliament as expressed in the 1972 Act to remove the Crown's prerogative power to take action to withdraw the United Kingdom from the [EU] Treaties once they were ratified'.[37] The Court, however, fundamentally disagreed, holding that the Government's position turned the usual, and proper, approach to statutory interpretation on its head. Given that a fundamental constitutional principle—'that, unless Parliament legislates to the contrary, the Crown should not have power to vary the law of the land by the exercise of its prerogative powers'[38]—was in play, it was for the Government to show that Parliament had intended to subvert that principle by leaving the executive with prerogative power to withdraw the UK from the EU and thereby

---

[34] ibid, [95].
[35] ibid, [25].
[36] ibid, [26].
[37] ibid, [80].
[38] ibid, [84].

effect far-reaching changes to domestic law. And that, the Court concluded, the Government could not do. Parliament, by passing the ECA, had 'intended to legislate so as to introduce EU law into domestic law ... in such a way that this could not be undone by exercise of Crown prerogative power'.[39] In the light of this conclusion, the Court, allowing the claimants' application for judicial review, declared that the Secretary of State did not have power under the Crown's prerogative to give notice pursuant to Article 50 for the UK to withdraw from the EU.[40]

D. Aftermath of the Divisional Court's Judgment

The Divisional Court's ruling produced a feeling amongst the claimant parties that this result was a 'game changer'. The Government had been rather 'bullish' to begin with, and many commentators expected the Government to win, thinking that the claimants might stand more of a chance in the Supreme Court. There was generally, we think, some underestimation and surprise at how strong the claimants' arguments were. Some lines of argument had not been fully anticipated by either commentators or the Government. Whilst this chapter does not purport to provide a full political analysis of the events, we sense that at this stage there was a feeling that the judgment had real political implications, changing the views of many members of the press and public and, importantly, MPs, thereby increasing calls for parliamentary involvement, now bolstered by the support of a unanimous judgment. This was reflected in some of the headlines found on the front pages the day after judgment was given in *Miller*. The *London Evening Standard* chose 'Judges' Brexit Blow to May', *The Guardian* selected 'Turmoil for May as judges rule that Parliament must decide Brexit' and the *Independent* decided on 'The verdict that rewrites the rules of Brexit'.

Not all the reaction was positive, however. The day after judgment was delivered saw a flurry of newspaper headlines, many of them highly critical. The *Daily Express* declared that 'three judges yesterday blocked Brexit. Now your country really does need you ... WE MUST GET OUT OF THE EU'. The *Sun* featured a picture of Gina Miller, with the headline 'Who do EU think you are?' The *Daily Telegraph* ran pictures of the three High Court judges who heard the *Miller* decision in the High Court, with the headline 'The Judges versus the people'; only to be outdone by the *Daily Mail* with its now (in)famous 'Enemies of the People' headline accompanying its colour photos of Thomas LCJ, noted as a 'europhile', Sales LJ, described as once having worked with Tony Blair, and Sir Terrence Etherton, described as an openly-gay former Olympic fencer. Whatever one's view of the substantive merits of the outcome, or political views as to the merits of Brexit, these sorts of headlines and commentary are shocking.

---

[39] ibid, [92].
[40] ibid, [111].

The Government's response to the judgment of the Divisional Court—that is, to appeal—came as no real surprise, though some had queried whether it might decide not to: there were dangers associated with such a course of action, namely the risks of a stronger precedent concerning the use of prerogative powers, the increase in delay and cost (rather than simply proposing an Article 50 Notification Bill), and the possibility of the devolved Governments intervening (and securing a more formal, legal place for the Sewel Convention). Nonetheless, appeal the Government did, and the Supreme Court was quick to respond, announcing on 8 November that permission had been granted to appeal from the decision of the Divisional Court (leapfrogging the Court of Appeal), with the hearing listed for 5 to 8 December 2016. The Court also confirmed that the appeal would be heard by the then 11 Justices of the Supreme Court.[41] This in itself is unique, although one can certainly understand the reason for so doing—there could then be no accusations of the panel composition affecting the result or of any bias. The Supreme Court recognised that it was going to be in the spotlight. On the opening day of the four-day oral hearing, Lord Neuberger was at pains to emphasise that no party had asked any of the Justices to recuse themselves, no doubt a subtle response to media accusations that Lady Hale should step aside on the basis of comments which she had made during a lecture a few weeks earlier.[42]

III. *Miller* in the Supreme Court

After some procedural complications,[43] the Northern Ireland matters were also referred to the Supreme Court to be joined with the *Miller* litigation. The Supreme Court case was therefore an appeal by the UK Government against the Divisional Court's judgment, and an appeal by the unsuccessful claimants in Northern Ireland against Maguire J's judgment in the Northern Ireland High Court. Another novelty at the Supreme Court level was the involvement of the devolved Governments of Scotland and Wales in favour of the respondents in the *Miller* litigation (ie the claimants at first instance), and the Attorney-General for Northern Ireland in favour of the appellant, the UK Government.[44]

For the most part, the arguments mirrored those that had been provided in the Divisional Court. The Government continued to argue that there was a prerogative

---

[41] Notice published on the Supreme Court's website, available at https://www.supremecourt.uk/news/permission-to-appeal-decision-08-november-2016.html.

[42] Lady Hale, 'The Supreme Court: Guardian of the Constitution?', Sultan Azlan Shah Lecture 2016, Kuala Lumpur, available at https://www.supremecourt.uk/docs/speech-161109.pdf.

[43] See ss 12–16(1A) of the Administration of Justice Act 1969; ss 42–43 of the Judicature (Northern Ireland Act) 1978; and s 2.1.2.3 of Practice Direction 1 of the Supreme Court.

[44] Lawyers for Britain Limited were also granted permission to file written submissions not exceeding 10 pages by Order of the Supreme Court, dated 25 November 2016. These were in favour of the respondents (ie the claimants).

power to trigger Article 50. The respondents continued their argument that the prerogative could not be used. To the extent that the Supreme Court heard new arguments, they mainly concerned devolution. Three such arguments should be mentioned. First, that the impact of leaving the EU on the devolution legislation provided a further justification for why the Government did not have a prerogative power to trigger Article 50. Second, that if legislation were needed then a legislative consent motion would be required. Third, that the consent of the devolved legislatures would be needed even if the prerogative could be used to trigger Article 50.

In order to understand the legal arguments presented to the Supreme Court, it is helpful to examine first those concerning the correct legal principle to apply in order to determine whether the Government had the prerogative power to trigger Article 50. Second, the application of the relevant legal principle to the facts of the case will be investigated. Third, consideration will be given to the issues surrounding whether the consent of the devolved legislatures would be required, either as regards legislation used to empower the Government to withdraw from the EU Treaties, or in relation to the use of the prerogative to trigger Article 50.

A. Submissions of the Parties

There was no disagreement between the parties as to the existence of the foreign affairs prerogative power, nor as to the inclusion within this general prerogative power of a specific power to withdraw from treaties. The issue arose as to the relevant legal principle to be applied in order to determine whether the prerogative power could be used to trigger Article 50. For the Government, the legal principle to be applied stemmed from *De Keyser's Royal Hotel*.[45] This is the conventional authority governing the relationship between prerogative powers and legislation. It holds that, to the extent that legislation and prerogative powers regulate the same area, legislation abrogates the prerogative. In such circumstances, the Government must use a statutory power found in legislation as opposed to using prerogative power. As it was clear that the ECA did not provide a specific statutory power to the Government to withdraw from the EU Treaties, this meant, on the Government's case, that there was no legislation regulating either the general prerogative power to withdraw from Treaties, or the specific prerogative power to withdraw from the EU Treaties. As such, the prerogative power had not been abrogated by legislation and the Government could use the prerogative to trigger Article 50.[46]

However, the argument of Miller, dos Santos, and various of the interested and intervening parties, was that a different set of legal principles applied.

---

[45] *Attorney-General v De Keyser's Royal Hotel Ltd* [1920] AC 508.
[46] Skeleton Argument of the Secretary of State for the European Union, paras 54–61, available at https://www.supremecourt.uk/news/article-50-brexit-appeal.html.

These principles stemmed from the Bill of Rights 1689/Claim of Rights Act 1689, *The Case of Proclamations*[47] and a series of cases relied upon in support of the claim that prerogative powers cannot, for example, frustrate legislation or remove domestic rights.[48] *The Case of Proclamations* was used to support the existence of the legal principle that a prerogative power cannot modify domestic law, either legislation or common law. This principle is supported by the wording of the Bill of Rights 1689. Article 1 of the Bill of Rights states that 'the pretended power of suspending of laws or the execution of laws by regall authority without consent of Parlyament is illegall', with Article 2 asserting that 'the pretended power of dispensing with laws or the execution of laws by regall authoritie as it hath beene assumed and exercised of late is illegall'. Similar prohibitions are found in the Claim of Rights 1689 in Scotland, which states that 'all Proclamationes asserting ane absolute power to Cass annull and Dissable lawes … are Contrair to Law'. As such, the starting point was, on the respondents' cases, not to determine whether the ECA provided for a specific power to withdraw from the EU Treaties, but rather to inquire as to whether the ECA was an example of a law which would be modified were the UK to withdraw from the EU. If this were the case then the general prerogative power to regulate foreign affairs would not extend to include the power to trigger Article 50. The only way in which this argument could be rebutted would be if it were possible to show that the ECA nevertheless provided that its provisions could be modified. As this was not the case, the prerogative could not be used to trigger Article 50.[49]

The frustration argument operated in a similar manner. The general prerogative power to withdraw from treaties could not be used to frustrate legislative provisions. In *Laker Airways*, the Minister was prevented from using the prerogative to revoke the designation of Laker Airways as an airline provided for routes between the UK and the USA, as to do so would render useless the statutory licence that Laker Airways had been granted to fly these routes.[50] In *Fire Brigades Union*, the Minister could not use the prerogative to introduce a new compensation scheme for those injured as a result of crimes, as to do so would frustrate a statutory provision which required the Minister to consider when to introduce a statutory compensation scheme set out in legislative Schedule.[51] In a similar manner, it was argued that to use the prerogative power to trigger Article 50 would frustrate the ECA and other legislative provisions, particularly the European Parliamentary

---

[47] *The Case of Proclamations* (1610) 12 Co Rep 74.

[48] *Laker Airways Ltd v Department of Trade* [1977] QB 643; and *R v Secretary of State for the Home Department, ex parte Fire Brigades Union* [1995] 2 AC 513.

[49] Skeleton Argument of Miller, paras 66–69; Skeleton Argument of Grahame Pigney and others, paras 12–23; Skeleton Argument of the Lord Advocate (Scottish Government), paras 51–62; and Skeleton Argument of Agnew, paras 81–91. All of the Skeleton Arguments are available at https://www.supremecourt.uk/news/article-50-brexit-appeal.html.

[50] *Laker Airways* (n 48).

[51] *Fire Brigades Union* (n 48).

Elections Act 2002. As such, it would not be possible for the Minister to use the prerogative to trigger Article 50.[52]

B. Application of the Law

One of the main arguments of Miller, dos Santos, and the interested and intervening parties (to varying extents) turned upon the fact that the default effect of triggering Article 50 would be the eventual modification of the ECA, specifically as regards the removal of rights incorporated into domestic law through the Act. The ECA incorporates EU law into domestic law. Therefore, withdrawal from the EU would lead to the inevitable loss of rights, duties, privileges and immunities from EU law incorporated into UK law through the ECA.[53] This meant, on the claimants' case, that the foreign relations treaty prerogative—which does not extend to modifying domestic law or removing domestic rights—could not be used. The hearing before the Supreme Court was heard on the assumption that, once triggered, Article 50 was non-revocable.[54] As such, the process established under Article 50 meant that the UK would leave the EU either with no agreement, or with a withdrawal agreement, after a two-year negotiation process with the EU.[55] The only other possible outcome would be an extension of the negotiation period were all parties to agree, which would delay, but not prevent, the inevitable conclusion that the UK would no longer be a member of the EU.[56]

The Counsel General for Wales,[57] the Lord Advocate for Scotland,[58] counsel for Agnew,[59] and counsel for Pigney and others (one group of interested parties) also argued that using the prerogative power to trigger Article 50 would have an impact

---

[52] Skeleton Argument of Miller (n 49), paras 20–43; and Skeleton Argument of Grahame Pigney and others (n 49), para 26.

[53] Skeleton Argument of Miller (n 49), paras 44–66; Skeleton Argument of Grahame Pigney and others (n 49), paras 30–47.

[54] *Miller* (n 2), [26]. The reversibility of Article 50 is a matter of EU law. The assumption which the Supreme Court was asked to (and did) make was subject to considerable academic debate prior to the Supreme Court hearing. The assumption was, however, contended for by all the parties, including by the Government. One can only surmise that the reasons for this were, on the claimants' side, that the irreversibility of Article 50 brought to life the definite consequences in terms of loss of citizens' rights (thereby bolstering their legal submissions in relation to the limitations of prerogative powers to affect such rights), and, on the Government's side, for political grounds, not wishing to be seen to go against the 'will of the people'. In any event, see, further, Jack Williams' contribution in ch 2 of this volume, for an explanation as to why, in his view, the assumption regarding Article 50 was irrelevant to the core issue and reasoning adopted by both the Divisional Court and the Supreme Court, ie that the conclusion reached by both courts, and the reasoning utilised in the judgments, is sustainable even if Article 50 is reversible.

[55] Article 50(3).

[56] ibid.

[57] Skeleton Argument of the Counsel General for Wales, paras 20–57, available at https://www.supremecourt.uk/news/article-50-brexit-appeal.html.

[58] Skeleton Argument of the Lord Advocate (Scottish Government) (n 49), paras 38–49.

[59] Skeleton Argument of Agnew (n 49), paras 33–77.

on devolution legislation. Specifically, it would have an impact on the law-making powers of the devolved legislatures in Wales, Scotland and Northern Ireland. None of the three devolved legislatures has the power to enact legislation which is contrary to EU law. Withdrawal from the EU would mean that this restriction on legislative powers would be removed. However, it was argued not only that this would be contrary to *The Case of Proclamations* and the Bill of Rights 1689 and the Claim of Rights 1689, but in addition that this was not permitted by the devolution legislation itself, which provided a specific means of changing the devolution settlement through Orders in Council,[60] or where new legislation was enacted.

The Government's main response to this argument was to dispute that the ECA incorporated EU law into domestic law in such a manner as to mean that EU rights, powers, liabilities and obligations were examples of domestic rights. Rather, the argument was made that section 2(1) ECA was an ambulatory provision, which incorporated EU rights into domestic law as they arose from time to time. As such, the prerogative powers could be used to modify those rights that were incorporated into domestic law through the ECA. Just as the prerogative could be used to join the EU, and to modify the rights, powers, liabilities and obligations flowing into domestic law through the ECA, so the prerogative could also be used to withdraw from the EU Treaties. This would not be to modify domestic rights, as these rights were conditional on EU membership. They were not statutory rights in the same manner as other rights established by UK legislation.[61]

In addition, the Government disputed the analogy between the triggering of Article 50 and the firing of a gun, first proposed by Lord Pannick QC in argument before the Divisional Court. It was not the case that triggering Article 50 would inevitably lead to a situation in which rights would be removed without legislative intervention. This was because there was, by default, a two-year interval between the triggering of Article 50 and the UK's exit from the EU. During that time, the Government intended to initiate legislation to repeal the ECA, as well as enacting other withdrawal-related legislation. As such, it would be future legislation, and not the mere use of the prerogative to trigger Article 50, that would be used to remove any rights incorporated into UK law through the ECA.

The argument based on the extent of the prerogative focused on the assertion that the default effect of triggering Article 50 would frustrate the purpose of the ECA (which, it was said, was to ensure the UK's membership of the EU), render it a nullity (because its key provisions would have no relevant EU rights etc upon which to bite) and remove individuals' rights. In order to reinforce the respondents' argument, attention was paid to the importance of the ECA. Not only was the legislation of constitutional importance, and an example of a

---

[60] Scotland Act 1998, s 30; Government of Wales Act 2006, s 95; Northern Ireland Act 1998, s 6.

[61] Skeleton Argument (Supplementary) Secretary of State for Exiting the European Union (devolution issues), paras 4–37, available at https://www.supremecourt.uk/news/article-50-brexit-appeal.html.

constitutional statute, but in addition it incorporated a wide range of rights into UK law.[62] Moreover, directly effective EU law has primacy over domestic law, such that legislation which contradicts directly effective provisions of EU law can be disapplied. In addition, its importance can be seen in the devolution legislation, which, as noted, prohibits the devolved legislatures and administrations from legislating or acting contrary to EU law. The importance of the ECA was drawn upon to reinforce the contention that the prerogative could not be used to frustrate its provisions or render it devoid of purpose.

These arguments were further afforced by reference to additional provisions of constitutional law. In particular, attention was paid to the principle of parliamentary sovereignty.[63] To allow the prerogative to be used to affect the ECA would be akin to allowing the executive to override the will of the legislature. This would be contrary to the principle of parliamentary sovereignty. In addition, the principle of legality was referenced. The principle of legality is best understood as a principle of interpretation. Legislation is interpreted against a background of constitutional principles. More precisely, broad legislative provisions are interpreted in a manner to ensure that they do not override fundamental principles of the common law. If specific words are required in legislation to override fundamental principles of the common law, it follows by analogy that the ECA, which incorporates fundamental EU rights into UK law, cannot be affected by the use of the prerogative to trigger Article 50.

The Government's main objection was as to the interpretation of the ECA. It argued that the purpose of the ECA was to ensure that the UK fulfilled its obligations in international law flowing from its membership of the EU. As such, it was not the case that the purpose of the ECA would be frustrated were the UK to leave the EU. Rather, the purpose of the Act could still be fulfilled, in the sense that it would continue to ensure that the UK discharged whatever Treaty obligations it had, the difference being that it would have no such obligations.

C. Devolution Issues

One set of arguments relating to devolution issues was used to strengthen the respondents' arguments that the prerogative could not be used to trigger Article 50. This was through reinforcing the impact of withdrawal from the EU on the devolved settlements, set out in the Scotland Act 1998, the Northern Ireland Act 1998 and the Governance of Wales Act 2006 (all as amended by future legislation). None of the devolved nations can legislate contrary to EU law. To leave the EU would modify this statutory definition of their powers.

---

[62] Skeleton Argument of Miller (n 49), paras 31–43; Skeleton Argument of Pigney (n 49), paras 58–58 and para 67.

[63] See the Skeleton Argument of Deir Tozetti Dos Santos, available at https://www.supremecourt.uk/news/article-50-brexit-appeal.html. For further discussion on the implications of *Miller* for the meaning of parliamentary sovereignty, see Mark Elliott's contribution in ch 10 of this volume.

Two further arguments were raised as regards the impact on the devolved legislatures, which merit more detailed consideration. First, the argument was made that, if legislation were required to empower the Government to trigger Article 50, this legislation would require a legislative consent motion.[64] Second, the argument was made that, even if the prerogative could be used to trigger Article 50, there would nevertheless be a requirement to obtain the consent of the devolved legislatures prior to exercising the prerogative power.[65]

The arguments in favour of a legislative consent motion concerned the application of the Sewel Convention. The Sewel Convention, understood narrowly, requires that, although the Westminster Parliament can legislate in areas that have been devolved to Scotland, Wales or Northern Ireland, it will not normally do so without obtaining the consent of the devolved legislature or legislatures concerned. Counsel for Agnew and the Government of Wales, and the Lord Advocate argued that the Sewel Convention also applied more broadly to situations where Westminster legislated to alter the devolved competences. As triggering Article 50 and leaving the EU would alter those competences, a legislative consent motion would be needed as regards any legislation enacted to empower the Government to trigger Article 50. The argument of the Lord Advocate was reinforced by section 2 of the Scotland Act 2016, which inserted a new subsection, section 28(8), into the Scotland Act 1998.[66] This subsection confirms that 'it is recognised that the Parliament of the United Kingdom will not normally legislate with regard to devolved matters without the consent of the Scottish Parliament'.

The Government argued both that the Sewel Convention did not apply and that, even if it did apply, as a convention it was not capable of being enforced by the courts. The Government preferred the narrower interpretation of the Sewel Convention, which only applies when Westminster legislates on a devolved matter. The triggering of Article 50, however, is not within the scope of devolved powers. Foreign affairs generally, and specifically the nature of the relationship between the UK and the EU, is not a devolved matter, being reserved to the Westminster Parliament. Moreover, even if the Sewel Convention did apply, conventions are not capable of legal enforcement. Although courts can recognise the existence of conventions, they cannot enforce them by imposing a legal obligation to adhere to a convention.[67]

Two arguments were provided to explain why, even if legislation was not required, nevertheless the consent of the devolved legislatures was required before using the prerogative to trigger Article 50. First, Article 50 refers to the ability of a

---

[64] Skeleton Argument of the Lord Advocate (Scottish Government) (n 49), paras 68–84; Skeleton Argument of Agnew (n 49), paras 120–45.

[65] Skeleton Argument of the General Counsel for Wales (n 57), paras 71–92; and Skeleton Argument of the Lord Advocate (Scottish Government) (n 49), paras 18–22.

[66] For further discussion on these matters, see Aileen McHarg's contribution in ch 7 of this volume.

[67] Skeleton Argument (Supplementary) Secretary of State for Exiting the European Union (devolution issues) (n 61), paras 4–37.

Member State to withdraw from the EU 'in accordance with its own constitutional requirements'.[68] Constitutional requirements should be interpreted broadly to include not just legal but also other constitutional requirements. This would include constitutional conventions. As such, given the impact of triggering Article 50 on the devolution settlement, the Sewel Convention should be counted as a constitutional requirement and consent must be sought before triggering Article 50 by the use of a prerogative power. Second, it was argued that the existence and exercise of prerogative powers were governed by the common law. As such, there were good reasons for the common law to develop a principle to ensure that the prerogative could not be used to modify the devolution settlement without the consent of the devolved legislatures.

The Government countered both arguments. First, it rejected the idea that 'constitutional requirements' would include non-legal rules.[69] As such, the Sewel Convention could not be a 'constitutional requirement' for the purpose of Article 50(1). Second, the Government argued that there were no provisions of the common law that would require consent before the use of the prerogative power to modify devolved powers.[70]

D. Judgment of the Supreme Court

Judgment was handed down on 24 January 2017—again, a relatively quick and unusual turnaround. The handing down was, like that of the Divisional Court, an event in itself, as the vast majority of legal counsel had not seen judgment beforehand (with the exception of leading counsel for the two main respondents and the Government). The Supreme Court concluded, by a majority of eight Justices to three, that the Government did not enjoy a prerogative power to trigger Article 50. As such, it upheld the Divisional Court's conclusion, though this time with dissentients. In addition, all 11 Justices of the Supreme Court concluded that a legislative consent motion was not required given that conventions are not capable of legal enforcement.[71]

The following brief account of the reasoning of the majority in reaching these conclusions (and why the minority Justices disagreed) raises more questions than it provides answers. Whilst it gives a flavour of the legal argument and an outline of the nature of the dispute between the parties and the conclusions in the Supreme Court, it does not purport to provide a detailed evaluation of the relative strengths and weaknesses of these arguments, or their relative importance.[72]

---

[68] Article 50(1) Treaty on European Union (TEU).

[69] Skeleton Argument (Supplementary) Secretary of State for Exiting the European Union (devolution issues) (n 61), para 38.

[70] ibid, para 39.

[71] *Miller* (n 2).

[72] For more detailed overviews by two of the present authors, see M Elliott, 'The Supreme Court's Judgment in *Miller*: in search of constitutional principle' (2017) 76 *Cambridge Law Journal* 257; and AL Young, '*R (Miller) v Secretary of State for Exiting the European Union*: Thriller or Vanilla?' (2017) 23 *European Law Journal* 280.

This is a conscious choice. The contributions in this collection all reflect on the decision in *Miller*, each providing its own evaluation of the reasoning of the Supreme Court and its impact on the UK constitution. We have deliberately chosen contributors who represent a spectrum of views on the merits of the Supreme Court's decision, ranging from those who strongly agree with the majority opinon, those who support the minority opinion and those who, whilst accepting the outcome of the case, are critical of the process through which this conclusion was reached.

Although there was disagreement over the outcome, all 11 Justices of the Supreme Court purportedly agreed that the relevant legal principles governing the existence and effect of a relevant prerogative stem from *The Case of Proclamations*, the Bill of Rights 1689, the frustration principle and *De Keyser's Royal Hotel*. As such, all agreed that general prerogative powers, and particularly the foreign affairs treaty prerogative, did not extend to include an ability to modify domestic law, either in legislation or in the common law.[73] This also meant that prerogative powers could not be used to modify rights.[74] Further, prerogatives could not frustrate legislation.[75] The only main disagreement over the relevant legal principles stemmed from the classification of the frustration principle. Whilst the other 10 Justices of the Supreme Court regarded this as a further element of the determination of the scope of prerogative powers, Lord Carnwath (dissenting) classified this as a control over the exercise, or abuse, of a prerogative power as opposed to its existence or extent.[76]

In order to understand how the majority reached their conclusion, it is helpful to first set out the main argument of the minority, provided in the judgment of Lord Reed.[77] Lord Reed accepted the argument of the Government that triggering Article 50 would not, on the facts, modify domestic law. This stemmed from his interpretation of the ECA. In particular, he focused on the dualist nature of the UK and on the wording of the ECA. As is well known, and recognised in *Miller* by both the majority and the minority, the UK adopts a dualist position in relation to international law.[78] As such, although the executive can enter into and withdraw from treaties, the provisions found in treaties to which the UK is a party do not apply in domestic law until they have been incorporated into domestic law, normally through an Act of Parliament or through executive action taken under a statutory power that authorises the Government to incorporate specific aspects of international law into domestic law. This is the case, for example, with EU law.[79]

Lord Reed concluded that the ECA established an ambulatory provision in order to incorporate EU law into UK law, which was conditional on the acts of the

---

[73] *Miller* (n 2), [44]–[46] and [50].

[74] ibid, [69]–[73].

[75] ibid, [51].

[76] ibid, [266].

[77] ibid, [179]–[197].

[78] For further discussion on the international law dimensions of *Miller*, see Eirik Bjorge's contribution in ch 4 of this volume.

[79] ECA, s 2(2).

UK executive on the international plane. This is found in section 2(1) of the Act, which provides that

> [a]ll such rights, powers, liabilities, obligations and restrictions from time to time created or arising by or under the Treaties and all such remedies and procedures from time to time provided for by or under the Treaties, as in accordance with the Treaties are without further enactment to be given legal effect or used in the United Kingdom shall be recognised and available in law, and be enforced, allowed and followed accordingly …

Lord Reed focused on the way in which this section incorporates EU law as it arises 'from time to time'. As such, the section makes it clear, on this view, that the provisions incorporated into domestic law are those arising from the UK's international law obligations under EU law as they change over time, depending on executive action. In short, the rights are conditional on the UK's membership of the EU, and their content changes according to changes in the UK's international law obligations. This means that the rights incorporated are not the same as domestic rights. Rather, they are conditional on the UK's membership of the EU. If the UK leaves the EU then these rights are no longer part of UK law. To leave the EU would not modify domestic rights. Rather, it would remove the condition precedent on which EU rights are based. The ECA would continue to incorporate into UK law those provisions which the UK was required to incorporate given its membership of the EU. However, once the UK leaves the EU, the provisions which the UK was required to incorporate would be removed.[80]

The majority of the Supreme Court, in a jointly written decision given by Lord Neuberger, the then President of the Supreme Court, rejected this interpretation of the ECA. The majority focused more on the constitutional importance of the UK's membership of the EU, in particular the way in which the provisions of directly effective EU law have primacy over UK law, such that legislation which contravenes the provisions of directly effective EU law can be disapplied. The majority agreed that the ECA acted as the conduit through which EU law flowed into UK law. However, they also concluded that EU law was a new source of law—law enacted by the EU institutions. In addition, although the majority accepted, in part, the possible ambulatory nature of section 2(1) of the ECA, they disagreed with Lord Reed's conclusion that this meant that EU law was not domestic law. Instead, they concluded that there was a difference between the alteration of the content of the rights, powers, liabilities, obligations and restrictions incorporated into UK law through the enactment of EU law, and the withdrawal from the EU treaties which would remove all EU law. To withdraw from the EU would alter domestic law by removing rights that had been incorporated into UK law. It would render the legislation futile, frustrating its purpose of ensuring the UK's membership of the EU.

---

[80] *Miller* (n 2), [184]–[194]. For support of the ambulatory thesis as described in this paragraph, see also M Elliott, 'The Supreme Court's Judgment in Miller', available at https://publiclawforeveryone. com/2017/01/25/analysis-the-supreme-courts-judgment-in-miller/; and Elliott (n 72). For counter arguments to the ambulatory thesis described in this paragraph and in the judgment of Lord Reed, see Jack Williams' contribution in ch 2 of this volume.

In addition, given the constitutional importance of the ECA, it was clear that such a modification required legislation; a change of such constitutional importance could not be enacted by the executive alone and required parliamentary authorisation.[81]

In addition to the reasons given by Lord Reed for disagreeing with the conclusion of the majority, Lord Carnwath provided a further argument. He rejected Lord Pannick QC's analogy that triggering Article 50 was similar to firing a gun. It was not the case that triggering Article 50 would lead to the removal of EU rights from UK law. Rather, in the two-year time period there was time for legislation to be enacted to remove these rights from UK law; indeed at the time of the *Miller* decision the Government had announced its intention to enact a 'Great Repeal Bill'—now known as the European Union (Withdrawal) Bill 2017–19—which would repeal the ECA.[82]

As regards the devolution issue, the Supreme Court only provided its account of why a legislative consent motion was not required. The majority judgment, with all 11 Justices of the Supreme Court agreeing on this point, acknowledged that there were examples of legislative consent motions having been obtained for legislative provisions which had altered the distribution of powers between Westminster and the devolved legislatures. Nevertheless, even though the Sewel Convention could apply, it was not the role of the courts to enforce the Convention. Conventions were enforced through political and not legal means. Moreover, to enforce the Sewel Convention would require the Court to question proceedings in Parliament, in breach of Article 9 of the Bill of Rights 1689. Nor was this position altered by the reference to the Sewel Convention in section 2 of the Scotland Act 2016. Rather, as the legislation 'recognised' the Convention, the section was best interpreted as expressing an intention to entrench the Sewel Convention as a convention, rather than as creating a legally enforceable statutory obligation.[83]

IV. Noteworthy Aspects of the Litigation

A. Public Engagement: The Boons of Open Justice

Aside from the substance of the decision and its implications, one thing the *Miller* case will be remembered for is the high level of engagement with the case, at every stage, from members of the public and the academic community. The result of the UK's referendum on EU membership was announced on 24 June 2016. By 27 June, the first blog post (by Nick Barber, Tom Hickman and Jeff King) had appeared on

---

[81] *Miller* (n 2), [74]–[93].
[82] ibid, [262]–[267].
[83] ibid, [149].

the UK Constitutional Law Association's blog, highlighting an issue as to whether the prerogative enabled a member of the executive to trigger the Article 50 process.

It is easy to forget, then, in light of the impressive transparency and public access arrangements that followed in both the Divisional Court (with transcripts published daily) and the Supreme Court (with live video broadcasts of the submissions plus published transcripts), that initially the Government opposed publication of its detailed grounds of resistance and other parties' skeleton written arguments to the extent that they referenced or referred to the Government's arguments. On 22 September 2016 (ie during the preparations for the Divisional Court's hearing), Pigney and others (one set of interested parties) were the first to publish their final skeleton argument, appropriately redacted as requested by the Government. At the same time as doing so, the group applied to the Divisional Court for clarification of its Order made in July, as they believed that the Government could (and should) make its case available so that the general public could understand its position. On 27 September, Mr Justice Cranston amended the Order to provide that 'the parties are not prohibited from publishing (1) the defendant's or their own detailed grounds; (2) their own skeleton arguments'. The judge observed that 'Against the background of the principle of open justice, it is difficult to see a justification for restricting publication of documents which are generally available under the Rules.'

All other parties duly followed suit and published their written materials unredacted. Indeed, by the Supreme Court stage, the Court itself was publishing all the parties' written arguments and collating them on a designated 'hub' page for the case.[84]

Such publication of written arguments (and then active dissemination thereof) is unusual, even in high-profile litigation. The usual rule is that such court documents only become publicly available (by request) once they are entered into the court's file and referred to in open court. It is fair to comment that the academy enjoyed the opportunity: the high level of engagement with the legal issues and arguments as presented to the courts by the litigants was unprecedented. Every line of argument was scrutinised and discussed in at least a handful of new blog posts each day in the build up to the litigation. This level of scrutiny was, we are sure, a blessing and a curse—a blessing in that a treasure trove of imaginative and detailed lines of argumentation was thereby at the finger-tips of the legal teams (and courts), enabling them to deploy them or refine their own arguments; but a curse for the juniors and judicial assistants having to read each new publication (adding to the 22,000 pages of written materials before the Supreme Court), or for those counsel whose submissions were not as well received.

Perhaps more importantly, however, this high level of engagement and interaction between practitioners and academics led to rich debates and discussions, which ultimately fed into the preparations for the hearings and the counsel submissions and judicial questions at the hearings themselves. Indeed, the contribution of the

---

[84] https://www.supremecourt.uk/news/article-50-brexit-appeal.html.

academic community to the case cannot in any way be overestimated. A vivid example of this is the shift in the Government's legal arguments between the Divisional Court level and the Supreme Court level to take into account, for example, arguments about the ambulatory and conditional nature of the ECA and double taxation treaties, which originated in online blog posts.[85] The *Miller* case is most likely the first UK case to include the citation of blogs in written arguments and judgments: indeed, the Supreme Court expressly praised the blogosphere in its judgment: 'The very full debate in the courts has been supplemented by a vigorous and illuminating academic debate conducted on the web (particularly through the UK Constitutional Law Blog site).'[86]

Whilst in our view overwhelmingly positive in the *Miller* litigation, nevertheless, the extensive interaction between the academy and practice, in a fashion never seen before, does raise interesting ethical questions. For example, to what extent is it proper to comment, via a short and quickly produced blog, on individual barristers' oral submissions, by name, particularly between hearing and judgment, when to do so could—though technically should not—influence the determination of the dispute, without opportunity for rebuttal? To what extent should academics involve themselves in the production of submission arguments (unaccredited); and if they do, what confidentiality and professional boundaries are in place? What weight should be given to academic blogs by the courts? To what extent should legal academics present political arguments in public? There are no easy answers—and we do not pretend either to have extensively outlined the issues or to have begun answering them—but we suspect that many have learnt a great deal about the role of, and pressures at, the Bar, which, with clients seeking a particular result and tactical considerations in play, mean that not every argument can, or will, be developed. At the same time, we expect that many practitioners involved in the litigation equally learnt a great deal from the academics who contributed to the debates.

B. Crowdfunding

Not only were arguments occasionally crowdsourced. Another novel aspect of the case was the use of crowdfunding on a large scale. Grahame Pigney and others (one group of interested parties), for example, crowdfunded over £300,000 via

---

[85] J Finnis, 'Terminating Treaty-Based UK Rights', *UKCLA Blog* (26 October 2016), available at https://ukconstitutionallaw.org/; J Finnis, '*Brexit* and the Balance of our Constitution', Sir Thomas More Lecture, Lincoln's Inn (1 December 2016), available at https://www.lincolnsinn.org.uk/images/pdf/education/Sir%20Thomas%20More%20Lecture%20-%20Professor%20John%20Finnis%20Text.pdf; M Elliott, 'On why, as a matter of law, triggering Article 50 does not require Parliament to legislate', *Public Law for Everyone* (30 June 2016), available at https://publiclawforeveryone.com/2016/06/30/brexit-on-why-as-a-matter-of-law-triggering-article-50-does-not-require-parliament-to-legislate/; M Elliott and H J Hooper, 'Critical reflections on the High Court's judgment in *R (Miller) v Secretary of State for Exiting the European Union*', *Public Law for Everyone* (7 November 2016), available at https://publiclawforeveryone.com/2016/11/07/critical-reflections-on-the-high-courts-judgment-in-r-miller-v-secretary-of-state-for-exiting-the-european-union/.

[86] *Miller* (n 2), [274].

the online platform, Crowdjustice, which is a website specifically set up to help raise funds for litigation. In exchange for donations, those signed up received regular updates via email, and a commitment to publish all legal pleadings and the like. This relatively new development may, to some extent, cover for losses in legal aid funding, or provide new opportunities for public interest groups to raise funds for issues that affect a large number of people, or generally raise public interest issues that would otherwise be unfunded. It is notable that since the *Miller* litigation, a number of other crowdfunding groups have been set up in relation to Brexit-related issues, namely, for the challenge of the non-disclosure of Government impact assessments and to trigger the Scottish courts to refer the question of the unilateral reversibility of an Article 50 notification to the European Court of Justice. Again, interesting questions arise out of this developing practice: to what extent, for example, should those who have donated be privy to legal advice about the risks and prospects of success before blindly contributing to a cause?

C. The Nature of Constitutional Adjudication

Two later chapters (by Richard Ekins and Graham Gee, and Alison Young respectively) discuss the implications of the *Miller* judgment on the nature of constitutional adjudication. At this juncture it is appropriate to make only the following comments. The case gives an insight into how major constitutional cases with political impact will be tried. The Supreme Court is increasingly in the public and media gaze. For instance, there were substantial numbers of journalists and reporters both outside and inside court at the hearings; constitutional academics were even called upon to give live commentary and updates on TV and radio. Even the largest court room was unable to fit all those wishing to spectate (and, indeed, all the legal team members, some of whom had to watch on livestreams in other court rooms). Nevertheless, the Court was acutely aware of the broader political arena in which it was necessarily operating, albeit that it refrained from entering that arena as far as possible. For example, despite a resolution by the House of Commons on 7 December 2016 (ie during the hearing), calling on Ministers to give an Article 50 notification by 31 March 2017, the Court held that that could not

> affect the legal issues before this court. A resolution of the House of Commons is an important political act. No doubt, it makes it politically more likely that any necessary legislation enabling ministers to give Notice will be enacted. But if, as we have concluded, ministers cannot give Notice by the exercise of prerogative powers, only legislation which is embodied in a statute will do. A resolution of the House of Commons is not legislation.[87]

Perhaps aware of political ramifications for individual Justices (particularly in light of the media reaction after the Divisional Court's judgment), only one majority

---

[87] *Miller* (n 2), [123].

judgment, written and assented to by all the majority Justices, was issued. This is an increasing trend in Supreme Court judgments, the aim presumably being to simplify judgments. It is arguable, however, that the desire in *Miller* to speak with one voice in a relatively accessible fashion may, paradoxically, have served to obscure the majority's reasoning, thereby giving rise to some of the controverseries surrounding the judgment that are discussed in this book.

V. Implications of *Miller*

The Divisional Court and the Supreme Court were both keen to emphasise that the questions they had to consider were not political but purely legal ones. Nevertheless, the implications of the judgment were, at least in the short term, intensely political, not least because the Government had to introduce a Bill into Parliament to authorise the initiation of the Article 50 process. The Bill progressed rapidly and unscathed through the House of Commons, and was passed at third reading 494 to 122 votes. The Bill's passage through the House of Lords was more eventful, with two amendments being made: to protect the EU citizenship rights of those living in the UK, and requiring parliamentary approval of any agreement between the UK and the EU at the end of the withdrawal process. However, when the Bill returned to it, the Commons voted against the Lords' amendments, and in the end the Bill was enacted in an unamended form, receiving Royal Assent on 16 March 2017. Section 1 of the European Union (Notification of Withdrawal) Act 2017 simply states:

    (1)   The Prime Minister may notify, under Article 50(2) of the Treaty on European Union, the United Kingdom's intention to withdraw from the EU.

    (2)   This section has effect despite any provision made by or under the European Communities Act 1972 or any other enactment.

Even if, prior to the enactment of this legislation, no 'decision' had been taken for Article 50(1) purposes, the 2017 Act is surely evidence of Parliament's having implicitly made or endorsed that decision, or of its having authorised the Prime Minister to do so. Against the background of the litigation, the resolution in Parliament during the litigation and the terms of debate concerning the Bill, the notion[88] that the notification issued by the UK to the European Council on 29 March 2017 is invalid because no 'decision' to withdraw has (yet) been taken in a way that conforms to the UK's 'own constitutional requirements' within the meaning of Article 50(1) TEU seems hard to sustain. Whether that decision is inherently conditional (as a matter of domestic law on account of parliamentary sovereignty) or revocable (as a matter of EU law) are different matters.

---

[88] See, eg, the crowdfunding pitch for a new claim at https://www.crowdjustice.com/case/a50-chall-her-e50/.

Apart from requiring the parliamentary legislative process to be followed, *Miller* thus had no substantive effects in terms of halting, or significantly delaying, or conditioning the UK's withdrawal from the EU. If these were any of the claimants' ultimate aims then the litigation itself did not achieve them.[89] The *Miller* case does, nevertheless, have significant and long-term effects on the nature, and our understanding, of the contemporary UK constitution. Regardless of the immediate political consequences that the *outcome* of the case produced, the *reasoning and nature* of the judgments in *Miller* have significant implications that will be relevant well after Brexit, and in non Brexit-related areas. It is with those broader constitutional implications that this book is concerned.

VI. Contributions to this Volume

This book begins with an analysis of the impact of the *Miller* decision on prerogative powers. In Chapter 2, Jack Williams examines the reasoning of the Supreme Court, explaining how the decision clarifies the manner in which UK law controls prerogative powers. He argues that the decision demonstrates that control over prerogative powers is not limited to control over the exercise of justiciable prerogative powers or determining the degree to which statutory powers regulate the same matter previously regulated by the prerogative, such that the prerogative power has been abrogated. Instead, Williams argues that there are four elements of the control over prerogative powers, which he refers to as the 'four E's': existence; extent; exclusion; and exercise. First, courts can determine whether a purported prerogative power exists, through an examination of the common law and historical record. Second, the court can determine the extent of the prerogative power. When doing so, the court pays attention to legal principles that delimit the very nature and scope of prerogative powers themselves. For example, prerogative powers cannot be used to modify domestic law, to remove common law or statutory rights, or to suspend or dispense with legislation. These first two controls are necessarily prior to the third and fourth controls. It is not possible to determine whether legislation has excluded the prerogative before one has determined the existence and extent of the prerogative that legislation is purported to have excluded. Third, prerogative powers cannot be used to exclude legislation. Williams argues that this extends beyond the situation in *De Keyser's Royal Hotel* to include the limitation of using prerogative powers to frustrate legislation. Lastly, to the extent a relevant prerogative exists, courts can review the exercise of such

---

[89] The litigation itself could never, of course, have achieved such matters in and of itself. It did, though, give Parliament the opportunity to consider and address such matters—an opportunity taken up by a minority of MPs and the majority of the Lords, but ultimately rejected by a majority of MPs in the House of Commons.

(justiciable) prerogative powers. Williams defends his approach from other analyses of the decision, as well as explaining how this framework was used in the *Miller* decision. In doing so, he is highly critical of the ambulatory thesis adopted by the minority Justices in *Miller* and those who criticise the result of the case.

Our discussion of prerogative powers moves on from an analysis of legal controls over the prerogative to an assessment of the impact of *Miller* on prerogative powers more generally. In Chapter 3, Anne Twomey explains how aspects of the *Miller* decision failed to clarify some areas of prerogative powers. In particular, the decision failed to recognise the existence of legislative as well as executive prerogative powers, which calls into question the Supreme Court's broad assertions concerning the inability of prerogative powers to change domestic law. In a similar manner, Twomey argues that it is important to recognise that the relationship between prerogative powers and common law rights is more subtle than the mere assertion that prerogatives cannot alter common law rights. The prerogative forms part of the common law. As such, there can be instances in which the common law 'accommodates' the exercise of prerogative powers, including to the extent of modifying rights and interests to avoid potential conflicts. While the Supreme Court recognised this subtlety, it is perhaps lost amongst its broad assertions, which could lead to a potential future misunderstanding of prerogative powers. Twomey's contribution also investigates the impact of the *Miller* decision on the prerogative power to withdraw from treaties, concluding that unless *Miller* is interpreted narrowly, requiring legislative authority because of the constitutional impact of withdrawal from the EU, the Supreme Court's decision could have too great a negative impact on treaty-making powers. Twomey also notes that the *Miller* decision could have a serious negative impact if applied in Australia, where the executive has a long-recognised ability to expand Commonwealth legislative power through the ratification of treaties. As such, Twomey concludes that *Miller* is best understood as reaching its conclusions given the very particular and specific constitutional circumstances. To understand *Miller* more broadly would significantly reduce the use of prerogative powers that play an important role in most constitutions, often accompanied by significant political scrutiny over their use.

Eirik Bjorge's contribution (Chapter 4) follows on from Anne Twomey's argument, considering the judgment's international law-related implications and the relationship between international law and domestic law. Bjorge argues that the ratio of *Miller* is a classic assertion of dualism. If the prerogative cannot be used to trigger Article 50, that is because of the position, agreed to by all the Justices of the Supreme Court, that only Parliament, and not the executive, can remove rights. Where disagreement arose was as to whether triggering Article 50 would remove rights. However, Bjorge also recognises that the broad provisions concerning the relationship between domestic and international law provided at the beginning of the judgment may paint a misleading picture of the place of international law in domestic law.

Bjorge argues that the conclusion in *Miller* is based, in part, on the assumption that, whilst treaties can bind in international law, they are not capable of creating rights and obligations in domestic law unless and until they have been incorporated into domestic law. However, Bjorge questions the extent to which this assumption holds true in English law, pointing to situations in which the courts have been prepared to base their judgments on treaty principles not according to whether the treaty has been incorporated, but according to whether the treaty affected, or extinguished, private rights. These exceptions, and the approach in *Miller*, question the extent to which the UK's adoption of dualism is based upon an understanding of parliamentary sovereignty, perhaps instead illustrating a form of dualism based on the need to protect individual rights from intrusion by the executive. If we base dualism on parliamentary sovereignty then treaties have no impact in domestic law until they are incorporated into domestic law through legislation. If the basis of dualism is the protection of individual rights from executive intrusion then it is possible for treaties to be enforced even if not implemented by Parliament, where to do so would protect individual rights from executive erosion.

Although *Miller* may suggest a move to a focus on the protection of individual rights, Bjorge concludes that it provides no specific answer that would offer definitive support for either of these justifications of dualism. It asserts the connection between dualism and parliamentary sovereignty in its general account of the law; yet the Court's specific focus appears to be the protection of individual rights. As such, the legacy of *Miller* for international law is unclear—its potential unfulfilled until the English courts are required to determine specifically whether unincorporated treaties can be relied upon in English law.

This volume then turns to consider more specific questions concerning the relationship between EU and UK law. In Chapter 5, Paul Craig considers the impact of *Miller* on that relationship, and begins by considering the pre-Brexit position. The conceptual frame through which EU law was accommodated in the UK was, in Craig's view, a mixture of legislative and common law *pragmatism*, coupled with statutory and judicial reserve grounded on *normative principle*. He concludes that *Miller* represents 'continuity with the status quo' rather than a reconceptualisation of EU law within the UK legal order. First, the majority's judgment demonstrates *pragmatism* in its conceptualisation of EU law within the UK legal order: while the ECA was the formal basis for EU law in the UK, the substantive reality was that where EU law applies in the UK, it is the EU institutions which are the relevant source of that law, since they made the rules that the ECA then incorporated into UK law. The *normative* dimension of *Miller* built on the conception of constitutional statutes: while the triggering of Article 50 would not in itself repeal the ECA, withdrawal would deprive it of substance, since we would no longer be party to the EU. The majority in *Miller* believed that this consequence should not ensue without parliamentary authorisation. In the second part of his contribution, Craig examines the relationship between UK and EU law in the period between triggering Article 50 and exit from the EU. During this period, the UK remains fully bound by EU law, such that the Court of Justice of the European Union retains its status as the ultimate authority on issues of EU law that are central to any withdrawal agreement and future trade agreement between the UK and the EU. Lastly, Craig explores the possible relationship between UK and EU law post-Brexit. Craig concludes that the legal and political reality is that the control and choice wielded by the UK concerning the future relationship between UK and EU law ranges on a spectrum. At one end of the spectrum, the UK has maximum (albeit not absolute) control in the terms of domestic legislation. Here, Craig explores the terms of the European Union (Withdrawal) Bill 2017. At the other end of the spectrum, there are many matters where the UK only retains partial control over the relationship between UK and EU law in important areas such as regulatory and trade provisions, including equivalence provisions. In these areas, domestic legislation will be constrained.

In Chapter 6, David Howarth also considers the relationship between EU and UK law. He focuses on how EU law rights and obligations acquired legal force in the UK, by inquiring into the viability of two competing metaphors. In doing so, he questions one of the most basic premises that underpinned the way in which the *Miller* case was argued and decided. Howarth's first metaphor treats section 2(1) of the ECA as a 'power cable'. On this view, EU law rights and obligations are 'powered' at the EU end of the cable, meaning that they continue to work in UK law only for as long as the cable is plugged in, in (let us say) Brussels. The effect of withdrawal—and of the EU Treaties no longer applying—would be to switch off the power at its (European) source, depriving EU law (as it operates in the UK) of its essential energy supply, and causing EU law rights and obligations to cease to apply. It was the power cable theory that formed one of the foundations of the claimants' case in *Miller*. Nor did the Government question that theory, choosing instead to argue that the ECA anticipated the possibility of the Government's using its prerogative power to flick the 'off' switch. Howarth contrasts this power cable theory with a second view, according to which the ECA serves as a 'bridge'. On this analysis, EU law is transported across the English Channel by the ECA— the metaphorical bridge—and is then plugged into the UK legal system. According to this view, departure from the EU has more modest effects. While nothing more can move across the bridge, that which has already crossed it remains where it is: in the UK, plugged into the domestic system and fully operational. As Howarth points out, whereas the power cable theory is relatively monist, the bridge theory is fundamentally dualist—and in that sense, is the more consistent of the two theories with the UK's constitutional tradition.

Howarth argues that the bridge theory forms the better fit with the language of section 2(1) of the ECA, as well as with section 18 of the European Union Act 2011. He further argues that adopting the power cable theory can be said to result in the unpalatable conclusion that the European Union (Notification of Withdrawal) Act 2017 gave the Prime Minister a power to extinguish vested legal rights, leading to an 'obnoxious' form of retroactivity. The bridge theory, in contrast, produces no such results, because legal rights and obligations that have already crossed the bridge remain available after Brexit. Nevertheless, Howarth acknowledges that the Supreme Court in *Miller* clearly adopted the power cable theory when it treated the EU institutions as the source of EU law as it applies in the UK. He does not, however, go as far as to argue that what he considers to be the Court's failure to adopt the better of the two theories led it to reach the wrong result. He suggests, for instance, that the conclusion at which the majority arrived might be supported by the bridge theory on the ground that in creating the bridge in the first place, Parliament could be taken to have intended traffic, in the form of EU law, to cross it, and that the bridge's closure was therefore properly a matter for parliamentary legislation, not prerogative action. Howarth concludes by considering the potential implications of the Supreme Court's having proceeded on what he regards as the wrong theoretical basis. Perhaps the most significant, and troubling, is the equanimity (as Howarth puts it) with which the 2017 Act was met, which might be taken by future governments as a precedent for the constitutional acceptability of handing Ministers wide powers to eliminate extant legislation.

Although devolution-related arguments were given short shrift by the Supreme Court, the implications of *Miller*—and of Brexit more generally—for the UK's territorial constitution are potentially highly significant. It is with such matters that Aileen McHarg is concerned in Chapter 7—the first of two contributions on the devolution-related aspects of the case. McHarg concentrates on *Miller*'s treatment of the Sewel Convention, particularly as regards its impact on Scotland. She first examines the scope of the Sewel Convention, recognising its policy and its constitutional arms. The former refers to the Convention's application to instances when Westminster legislates in a manner that is within the devolved competences, and the latter to situations where Westminster legislates to alter the devolved legislative or executive competences. McHarg provides a detailed evaluation of whether the Sewel Convention should have applied to the European Union (Notification of Withdrawal) Act 2017, which authorised the UK Government to notify the UK's intention to withdraw from the EU, concluding that there exists sufficient evidence of past practice and sufficient constitutional justification for the constitutional arm of the Sewel Convention to have applied to this legislation. McHarg then evaluates the refusal of the Supreme Court to determine the scope of, or to enforce, the Sewel Convention in the *Miller* decision. She is critical of the Supreme Court's approach, concluding that it was not obvious that the Sewel Convention was legally irrelevant, particularly in the light of the argument that the 'constitutional requirements' noted in Article 50 could extend to conventional as well as legal requirements. McHarg is also critical of the Supreme Court's overly narrow approach to conventions more generally. She refers to previous examples of when courts have been willing and able to determine the scope of conventions, as opposed to limiting their inquiry as to the convention's existence. This leads to her criticism of the Supreme Court's overly narrow approach to the relationship between law and conventions, referring to instances in which courts have in the past been willing to enforce conventions indirectly, if not directly. The overly narrow approach is not just limited to the Supreme Court's interpretation of the Sewel Convention, but also extends to its reading of section 2 of the Scotland

Act 2016. McHarg argues that this overly narrow approach has damaged the delicate relationship between Westminster and the devolved legislatures, both in terms of devaluing the importance of the Sewel Convention as a convention and in terms of the damage it may have done to the perception of the Supreme Court as a neutral arbiter in disputes between Westminster and the devolved nations.

In Chapter 8, Gordon Anthony evaluates the impact of *Miller* on Northern Ireland, focusing on the decisions of *Agnew* and *McCord*, whose appeals were joined with *Miller* in the Supreme Court. Anthony argues that, given the conclusion of the Supreme Court that the prerogative could not be used to trigger Article 50, the decision in *Miller* left more questions concerning devolution unanswered than answered. The Supreme Court's focus on the issues raised in *Miller* is problematic, signalling a potential u-turn from the recognition in *Robinson v Secretary of State for Northern Ireland*[90] of the specific constitutional importance of the Northern Ireland Act 1998, particularly given its connection to the Belfast Agreement. Anthony is also critical of the failure of the Supreme Court to engage fully with issues arising from the Sewel Convention, again explaining how this leaves the perception of the downgrading of the interests of the devolved legislatures. Whilst the devolved legislatures may perceive the UK as a sovereign country with power devolved to its component nations, this is not the perception of Westminster; the Supreme Court's orthodox account of sovereignty appears to reinforce this picture. Anthony's contribution then turns to an evaluation of the provisions of the European Union (Withdrawal) Bill, focusing in particular on the extent to which the Bill—by prohibiting the Northern Ireland Assembly from legislating contrary to retained EU law—effectively redistributes power to Westminster. Anthony also recognises the further asymmetry that may arise given the special nature of Northern Ireland, the only component nation of the UK which has a land border with another EU Member State. He further evalutes the implications of the recent Phase One Agreement, regarding the position of Northern Ireland. Anthony suggests that a better solution may be to adopt a model of federalism in the UK, whilst recognising that in the immediate future, it is important to ensure that proper consent is obtained from the Northern Ireland Assembly if Brexit is to proceed smoothly, without the ensuing risk of further fracturing the delicate union between the component nations of the UK.

The volume then turns to address the implications of the *Miller* case in relation to wider principles of UK constitutional law. In Chapter 9, Sir John Laws focuses on constitutional statutes—a category of legislation in whose development Sir John was himself instrumental through his well-known judgment in *Thoburn v Sunderland City Council*.[91] One of Sir John's aims is to consider the extent of the use to which the notion of constitutional statutes was—and was not—put

---

[90] *Robinson v Secretary of State for Northern Ireland* [2002] UKHL 32, [2002] NI 39.
[91] *Thoburn v Sunderland City Council* [2002] EWHC 195 (Admin), [2003] QB 151.

by the courts that heard the *Miller* case. He proceeds on the basis that the ECA is a constitutional statute, and that, as such, it is immune from implied repeal. He also notes that the majority in the Supreme Court acknowledged that the ECA plays an important role in securing the domestic effect in the UK of EU law. But he concludes that the majority judgment does not itself directly rely on the ECA's status as a constitutional statute, and that this may have led it into analytical error (even if it did not cause it, ultimately, to make what Sir John would have regarded as the wrong decision). Thus, while Sir John observes that the majority said that *the primacy of EU law* means that it cannot be implicitly displaced, he argues that this is to misunderstand both the true legal position and the role played by the concept of constitutional legislation in making sense of that position. On Sir John's view, it is (contrary to the majority in the Supreme Court) not the primacy of EU law that shields it from implied repeal, but the fact that EU law is given domestic effect by a constitutional statute that is itself (on this analysis) immune from implied repeal.

More broadly, Sir John is critical of the way in which both the majority and Lord Reed dealt with the question of what should be understood to be the *source* of EU law as it applies in the UK—and in particular what role the ECA should be understood to play in that regard. Sir John argues that the contrasting positions adopted by the majority and Lord Reed on this issue—pitting the EU institutions against the ECA—'obscure more than they reveal', and form a 'distraction' from the essential question, namely: 'How far should our constitutional law allow the executive to make or unmake domestic law?' Ultimately, Sir John concludes that the majority—in denying the executive the power to give notice under Article 50(2)—answered that question correctly within the context of the *Miller* case. But he argues that in arriving at what he considers to be the right answer, the majority's reasoning might have benefitted from greater reliance on the concept of constitutional legislation. In particular, he suggests that if the ECA is a constitutional statute by dint of conditioning the legal relationship between the individual and the state in a general, overarching manner, then it necessarily alters the law of the land in some fundamental way—and that that, on its own, should be sufficient to disqualify the executive from interfering with the arrangements it has put in place. However, his caveats concerning the majority's reasoning notwithstanding, Sir John is in no doubt that it reached the right result, and welcomes the fact that as well as preventing what would, on his view, have been an improper administrative incursion into Parliament's proper domain, *Miller* illustrates and confirms the courts' role as guardians of the constitution.

In Chapter 10, Mark Elliott analyses the implications of *Miller* for parliamentary sovereignty, focusing on how the approach of the Supreme Court regarding the interplay between the primacy of EU law and the UK Parliament's legislative supremacy can best be understood as demonstrating the inherently pragmatic and flexible approach of the UK constitution. The UK constitution, it is argued, prefers to answer questions as and when they arise, providing practical solutions, rather than providing a deep and detailed analysis of constitutional principles.

This approach is illustrated by what Elliott refers to as the two bookend cases to address this issue, *Factortame (No 2)*[92] and *Miller*.

Elliott proposes that there are three possible approaches to resolving the conundrum of the primacy of EU law and the supremacy of UK legislation. First, the UK could adopt a position of intransigence, refusing to accept the primacy of EU law. A second (and at the other extreme) view fully accepts the primacy of EU law because this is required by EU law itself, which has either 'overwhelmed' or 'inundated' the domestic system. Between these poles lies a third, intermediate position, which recognises an element of accommodation between these two more extreme views. This middle view acknowledges the primacy of EU law but in a manner that is determined by UK law. This intermediate view itself is a broad church, providing a series of potential reconciliations. *Factortame* and *Miller* make it clear that the first option is not a possibility, both providing solutions which accorded at least some primacy to EU law. This leaves the choice between the second and third approaches.

Elliott recognises that *Miller* appears to provide support for the view that EU law has primacy over UK law because this is a requirement of EU law. In particular, the judgment of the majority focuses on the unique nature of the EU Treaties. However, this interpretation is hard to reconcile with the Supreme Court's conclusion that membership of the EU, and the ECA, had not altered the rule of recognition. As such, we are left with the conclusion that, to the extent that primacy is accorded to EU law, this stems from requirements of UK law. However, there is a range of possible ways in which this reconciliation could have occurred. First, it could be through the provisions of the ECA, this being seen as providing for a modification or suspension of implied repeal for EU law. Yet this is hard to argue given a lack of specific provision in the ECA to this effect. Moreover, *Miller* appears to suggest that, to the extent that the ECA has a unique status, this turns as much on its classification as a constitutional statute as it does on the precise wording of its provisions. Second, this may occur through the common law, which recognises some legislation as constitutional and, therefore, immune from implied repeal. However, this argument also fails to reflect the true nature of the UK constitution. It requires a binary distinction between 'constitutional' and 'ordinary' legislation, and between implied and express repeal. Neither of these distinctions operate in a binary manner in practice.

Elliott concludes that *Miller* provides further illustration of the subtle and complex nature of the UK constitution, with its interplay between the role of the courts and Parliament. Whilst the preference for pragmatic resolution of specific problems may mean that judgments appear to be under-theorised, this also illustrates the flexible manner in which the UK constitution accepts and applies a hierarchy of norms, even though this may not always be clearly expressed. The UK constitution is one which prefers 'constructive ambiguity over conceptual clarity'.

---

[92] *R v Secretary of State for Transport, ex parte Factortame Ltd (No 2)* [1991] 1 AC 603.

In Chapter 11, Richard Ekins and Graham Gee turn their attention to the political context and consequences of the *Miller* decision. They argue that it is impossible to fully comprehend *Miller* if the decision is divorced from its political context—a move by the political elite to delay an unexpected and unwanted outcome from the Brexit referendum. Their contribution first charts the reaction to the Brexit referendum, noting the attempts of the political and legal elite both to question the use of referendums to decide such matters and to utilise the narrative of constitutional crisis. Gee and Ekins argue that both criticisms are unfounded. The Brexit question was a legitimate issue to put to a referendum, and its outcome did not give rise to a constitutional crisis. Second, they explain the political motivations behind the *Miller* litigation. Whilst they recognise that this may have been the only realistic course of action for those wishing to delay the referendum, they are critical of the litigation, believing this to be based on 'cleverly crafted' but ultimately 'legally unsound' reasons. Their third section supports this conclusion, setting out their argument as to why Lord Reed's dissenting judgment provided the more legally persuasive argument. In particular, they focus on the use, by the majority, of adopting a 'realistic' interpretation of the ECA, which they regard as evidence of a decision which focused on what the majority believed to be constitutionally proper, as opposed to what was legally sound.

Ekins and Gee argue that the majority Justices of the Supreme Court strayed from their proper constitutional role, which is to maintain the rule of law through an interpretation of the wording of the ECA. In doing so, the Court exchanged political controls over the exercise of prerogative powers for legal controls. They argue that, whilst we may understand why the Supreme Court felt able to act as the guardian of the constitution, particularly given that to do so would fit a proposed narrative of protecting Parliament from the executive, it is nevertheless important to recognise the political background to the *Miller* decision if we are to ensure its proper legacy. In particular, given the potential for future legal actions surrounding the triggering of Article 50, it is important to recognise the particular political context and specific constitutional setting of the *Miller* decision. Whilst the Brexit referendum is not an example of a constitutional crisis, to fail to recognise the political context of, and the weaknesses of the legal arguments which determined, the *Miller* decision could lead to a potential future constitutional crisis caused by the increasing politicisation of the legal process, as more litigation is undertaken for political motives.

This volume concludes, in Chapter 12, with Alison Young's contribution exploring the implications that the *Miller* case may have for the future of constitutional adjudication in the UK. Young takes as her starting-point the majority's handling of the argument that 'the 1972 Act is the source of EU law'.[93] The majority

---

[93] *Miller* (n 2), [61].

conceded that this could—'[i]n one sense'—be said to be so, 'in that, without that Act, EU law would have no domestic status'.[94] However, the majority immediately went on to say that 'in a more *fundamental* sense and, we consider, a more *realistic* sense, where EU law applies in the United Kingdom, it is the EU institutions which are the relevant source of that law'.[95] First, Young interrogates what the Court might have meant by these notions of 'fundamental' and 'realistic' readings of the ECA. While she acknowledges that this is not wholly clear, she argues that this language signifies an approach on the part of the Court whereby it is concerned with an interpretation of the ECA that is sensitive to the perceptions of those who have and rely upon rights and obligations under EU law, as distinct from a more legalistic approach.

Second, Young goes on to argue that although the Supreme Court's reasoning adopted a relatively deductive (as opposed to inductive) approach—in the sense that the Court was prepared to reason down from broad constitutional principles rather than reasoning up, and incrementally, from other cases—the case is not novel in this regard, the more deductive approach being discernible in other apex-level judgments in the UK.

Third, the contribution explores issues arising from the fact that the Court in *Miller* can be understood to have adjudicated on a 'moot' constitutional issue, in the sense that it considered the legal issues in advance of the occurrence of the contested legal act—that is, the notification of the European Council under Article 50(2). Again, however, Young suggests that this approach is not novel, and that its adoption, in appropriate circumstances, represents sound constitutional policy rooted in a precautionary principle that serves to anticipate constitutional problems and to avoid the instability that might be occasioned by the absence of such anticipatory intervention.

Fourth, Young considers the approach to the question of whether the Sewel Convention applied, arguing that here—in contrast to its approach to some of the other issues with which it was faced—it was relatively *unwilling* to adopt a 'fundamental' or 'realistic' approach. The contribution concludes by considering whether the (in general) more 'fundamental', 'realistic' and (sometimes) anticipatory approach to constitutional adjudication that *Miller* epitomises requires procedural innovation. In this regard, Young raises the question of whether thought should be given to a 'reference procedure'—akin to those that are found in, for instance, the Canadian, French and South African constitutions—which might accommodate 'abstract constitutional review' better than regular claims for judicial review are capable of doing.

---

[94] ibid.
[95] ibid (emphasis added).

VII. A Brief Look Ahead

The *Miller* case may have been the first major piece of litigation concerning Brexit,[96] but it will not be the last. The *Miller* case merely concerned the beginning of the Article 50 process: how, consistent with domestic constitutional require-ments, the process of departure from the EU was to be initiated. Many unresolved and contentious issues remain, of both a legal and a political character.

Drawing inspiration from the front cover of this volume, the key question at the heart of *Miller* merely concerned the decision to open the door: questions remain as to how far that door should be opened, whether it can or should be closed again, and what lies behind that door. What the contributions to this volume demon-strate is that the initial process of opening the door has itself raised fundamental legal questions for the UK's domestic constitutional framework, spanning from the nature of prerogative powers, through to the nature of parliamentary sover-eignty and representative democracy, the relationship between international and domestic laws, the separation of powers and the respective roles of the branches of the UK constitution, the territorial constitution and devolution arrangements, and the nature of constitutional adjudication. The contributions address those questions and themes, assessing the implications of the *Miller* case for our under-standings of the workings of the contemporary UK constitution. The judicial res-olution of those questions in *Miller* has had significant and no doubt long-lasting implications and effects on that constitutional framework, regardless of whatever 'type' of Brexit (if any) is eventually effected. The *Miller* case will be at the centre of almost all topics in any UK constitutional law course for generations to come. We hope that the contributions contained in this book will contribute to under-standing the ever-evolving and contentious debates concerning the flexible entity that is the UK constitution, both during Brexit and beyond.

---

[96] In addition to the prior case of *Shindler* (n 4).

2

Prerogative Powers After *Miller*: An Analysis in Four E's

I. Introduction

R (Miller) v Secretary of State for Exiting the European Union[1] ('*Miller*') has generated considerable academic commentary and disagreement. This collection is testament to that. Some of this commentary has been vehemently critical, with one academic even accusing the majority's judgment of being 'intellectually lackadaisical'.[2] I disagree with that critical assessment. The majority judgment in *Miller* reaffirms a well-established, though in parts recently forgotten or misunderstood, framework for assessing and reviewing prerogative powers. The judgment then correctly (though, at times, somewhat haphazardly) applies this framework to a novel scenario, that of the United Kingdom (UK) triggering the process of leaving the European Union (EU) under Article 50 of the Treaty on European Union (TEU).

This chapter begins (in section II) by setting out the analytical framework by reference not only to *Miller*, but also to all the key authorities on prerogative powers in the UK constitution. This framework will be applicable long after the *Miller* case and Brexit. In section III, the framework is then defended against various possible alternatives and critiques found in the commentary on *Miller*. Lastly (in section IV), the framework is applied to the circumstances of the *Miller* case. Here, the minority judgments in *Miller* and the critical academic commentary are subjected to a detailed review (and critique). Ultimately, it will be seen that

* The author is grateful for comments from Mark Elliott and Alison Young on an earlier draft, and also indebted to the many conversations with his co-counsel and instructing solicitors during the *Miller* case. He hopes this chapter captures 'the vibe of the thing'.

[1] *R (Miller) v Secretary of State for Exiting the European Union* [2017] UKSC 5, [2017] 2 WLR 583.
[2] M Elliott, 'The Supreme Court's judgment in *Miller*: in search of constitutional principle' (2017) 76 *CLJ* 257.

the majority's judgment truly is, as it professes to be, founded on 'the ordinary application of basic concepts of constitutional law'.[3]

II. The Analytical Framework: The Four E's

A. Overview

The effect of the *Miller* case is to demystify the nature and limitations of prerogative powers by reclarifying the full panoply of tools available when a court reviews such powers. The majority judgment achieves this by refocusing the metaphorical telescope to reveal the full framework of control, thus reminding us, in particular, that there are more questions to ask in relation to prerogatives than simply whether one has been excluded by a statute, as famously was held in *Attorney-General v De Keyser's Royal Hotel Ltd*.[4]

Instead, *Miller* re-reveals that a prior necessary exercise is to conduct an assessment of the very existence of, and then nature and scope of, the specific prerogative power in question. As Lord Bingham stated in *R (Bancoult) v Secretary of State for Foreign and Commonwealth Affairs (No 2)*:[5]

> When the existence or effect of the royal prerogative is in question the courts must conduct an historical enquiry to ascertain whether there is any precedent for the exercise of the power in the given circumstances. 'If it is law, it will be found in our books. If it is not to be found there, it is not law': Entick v Carrington (1765) 19 State Tr 1030 ...[6]

By recognising this exercise and conducting a detailed assessment of it, the majority in *Miller* adjust a myopic focus on only one form of controlling the prerogative (that found in *De Keyser's*). Instead, the majority judgment reveals that challenges to the use of purported prerogative powers can take one of four forms (what I shall call 'the four E's'): first, an examination of whether a prerogative power *exists*; second, assuming one does exist, the *extent* of that prerogative power (ie whether it is of a sufficient nature and scope to extend to the relevant circumstances and intended usage envisaged by the executive); third, an examination of whether any such prerogative power has been *excluded* by a statute or statutory provision (whether expressly or by necessary implication); and fourth, assuming that a

---

[3] *Miller* (n 1), [82].

[4] *Attorney-General v De Keyser's Royal Hotel Ltd* [1920] AC 508 ('*De Keyser's*').

[5] *R (Bancoult) v Secretary of State for Foreign and Commonwealth Affairs (No 2)* [2008] UKHL 61 ('*Bancoult*').

[6] ibid, [69]. See also *Council of Civil Service Unions v Minister for the Civil Service* [1985] AC 374 ('*The GCHQ case*'), 408 ('the courts will inquire into whether a particular prerogative exists or not, and, if it does exist, into its extent'); and *Burmah Oil Co (Burma Trading) Ltd v Lord Advocate* [1965] AC 75, 101 ('the proper approach is a historical one: how was it used in former times and how has it been used in modern times').

sufficient prerogative exists and has not been excluded by primary legislation, an examination of the *exercise* of that prerogative on grounds of, for example, irrationality, procedural impropriety or disproportionality. An applicant can bring judicial review proceedings on the basis of any one, or combination, of these four categories of control. In this section each is discussed in turn.

B. Existence

Whilst the exploration of whether a prerogative power exists is, in principle, a modest and limited form of judicial review, it is nevertheless a necessary inquiry. Whether a prerogative power exists is a surprisingly harder question to answer than it should be, in part because of its historical origins. As Professor Wade stated in his 1980 Hamlyn lectures, 'it is worth finding out what it really is'.[7] He was critical of many reported cases in which, in his view, 'no genuine prerogative power was in question at all'.[8] In Wade's opinion, the prerogative's 'etymology means that it should be some special power possessed by the Crown over and above the powers of an ordinary person, and by virtue of the Crown's special constitutional position'.[9] For this, he relied upon Blackstone, who stated that the prerogative must be 'singular and eccentrical', only comprising

> those rights and capacities which the King enjoys alone, in contradistinction to others, and not to those which he enjoys in common with any of his subjects; for if once any one prerogative of the Crown could be held in common with the subject, it would cease to be a prerogative any longer.[10]

And yet the modern authorities have followed Dicey's definition that the prerogative is 'the residue of discretionary power left at any moment in the hands of the Crown'.[11] Indeed, Wade himself acknowledged that authority was against him even in 1980: '[t]he truth seems to be that judges have fallen into the habit of describing as "prerogative" any and every sort of government action which is not statutory. It may be, also, that the responsibility for this solecism can be loaded onto that popular scapegoat, Dicey.'[12]

Whichever theoretical view one prefers, the debate points to the potential fruitfulness of retrieving the history books to explore whether history and practice does support the existence of a purported prerogative power in the first place. For present purposes, it also serves to demonstrate the use, in terms of transparency and checking the executive, of a catalogue of such (ill-defined) powers considered

---

[7] HWR Wade, *Constitutional Fundamentals* (London, Stevens & Sons, 1980) 46.
[8] ibid.
[9] ibid, 47–48.
[10] Sir William Blackstone, *Commentaries on the Laws of England*, vol 1 (1st edn facsimile, 1765) 239.
[11] See *Miller* (n 1), [47].
[12] Wade (n 7), 49.

to be exercisable under the prerogative in the modern day. A listing of prerogative powers is, indeed, the right exercise to undertake. For whilst it is common
to speak of 'the' prerogative, in truth prerogative power is a catalogue of specific
rights rather than a general power,[13] thus necessitating a specific exploration of the
exact prerogative power in question. The Select Committee on Public Administration in 2004 listed the 'principal' prerogative powers exercisable by Ministers[14] as
follows:[15]

(a)   The making and ratification of treaties.
(b)   The conduct of diplomacy, including the recognition of states, the relations (if any)
       between the United Kingdom and particular Governments, and the appointment
       of ambassadors and High Commissioners.
(c)   The governance of British overseas territories.
(d)   The deployment and use of the armed forces overseas, including involvement in
       armed conflict, or the declaration of war. (The Royal Navy is still maintained by
       virtue of the prerogative; the Army and the RAF are maintained under statute.)
(e)   The use of the armed forces within the United Kingdom to maintain the peace in
       support of the police.
(f)   The Prime Minister's ability to appoint and remove Ministers, recommend disso-
       lutions, peerages, and honours (save for the four Orders within The Queen's own
       gift), patronage appointments (eg in the Church of England), and the appointment
       of senior judges.
(g)   Recommendations for honours by the Foreign and Commonwealth Secretary and
       the Defence Secretary.

       ...

(i)   The grant and revocation of passports.
(j)   The grant of pardons (subject to recommendations by the Criminal Cases Review
       Commission) and the Attorney-General's power to stop prosecutions.

---

[13] See, eg, DS Berkowitz, 'Reason of State in England and the Petition of Right, 1603–1629' in
R Schur (ed), *Straatsräson: Studien zur Geschichte eines Politischen Begriffs* (Berlin, Duncker &
Humblor, 1975) 178: 'Whatever progress the crown and its adherents made in modernizing the theory
of royal power in the continental mode, it was apparent that the common law opposition still thought
of the prerogative as a catalogue of specific royal rights and not as a general, abstract, and unlimited
authority.'

[14] This chapter is concerned only with the executive prerogative powers exercised by Ministers in
the name of the Crown, as opposed to the Crown's personal discretionary powers which remain in
the Sovereign's hands. These personal prerogative powers include: the rights to advise, encourage and
warn Ministers in private; to appoint the Prime Minister and other Ministers; to assent to legislation;
to prorogue or to dissolve Parliament; and (in grave constitutional crisis) to act contrary to or without
Ministerial advice.

[15] Select Committee on Public Administration, *Taming the Prerogative*, 4th report of 2003–04, HC
422, para 9. As for (a) in the Select Committee's list, one can also include, post-*Miller*, the withdrawal
from treaties (save where that act itself would change domestic law or remove domestic rights). Further, one must now read the ratification of treaties as subject to the provisions in the Constitutional
Reform and Governance Act 2010, pt 2. I have removed the Committee's (h), 'The organisation of the
civil service', from its list as the Constitutional Reform and Governance Act 2010 put the Civil Service
on a statutory footing, save for the Secret Intelligence Service and Security Service: ss 1(2) and 3(4).

These prerogative powers, like all such powers, are 'a relic of a past age',[16] and derive from ancient rights and privileges enjoyed by the sovereign. The catalogue cannot be enlarged.[17] Today, the powers are seen as 'part of the common law',[18] and so it is for the courts to decide whether or not a particular prerogative power exists, and if so, the extent of that power.

C. Extent

There are three inherent delimitations on the extent of prerogative power generally by its nature.[19] First, prerogative power cannot be used to change domestic law. Second, prerogative power cannot generally be used to remove domestic rights. Third, prerogative power cannot be used to suspend or dispense with Acts of Parliament.[20]

i. Domestic Law

First, the prerogative 'does not enable ministers to change statute law'.[21] The same is true of the common law.[22] This is a principle of long standing: in *The Case of Proclamations*, Coke CJ held that prerogative power 'cannot change any part of the common law, or statute law or customs of the realm'.[23] It has been continuously upheld since: for example, in *The Zamora* the Privy Council stated that, even during wartime,

> [t]he idea that the King in Council, or indeed any branch of the Executive, has power to prescribe or alter the law to be administered by Courts of law in this country is out of harmony with the principles of our Constitution ... No one would contend that the prerogative involves any power to prescribe or alter the law administered in Courts of Common Law or Equity.[24]

And Lord Hoffmann, in *Higgs v Minister of National Security*, held that

> The rule that treaties [made under the prerogative] cannot alter the law of the land is but one facet of the more general principle that the Crown cannot change the law by

---

[16] *Burmah Oil Co (Burma Trading) Ltd v Lord Advocate* [1965] AC 75, 101 (Lord Reid).

[17] *British Broadcasting Corporation v Johns* [1965] Ch 32 (Diplock LJ): 'It is 350 years and a civil war too late for the Queen's courts to broaden the prerogative.'

[18] *The GCHQ case* (n 6), 407C.

[19] Though care should always be taken to conduct an historic enquiry in the assessment of the specific prerogative power in question. As discussed in the main text, prerogative power is, in truth, a catalogue of specific rights rather than a general power.

[20] The third is, in truth, an aspect of the first two.

[21] *Miller* (n 1), [50].

[22] *Bancoult* (n 5), [44].

[23] *The Case of Proclamations* (1611) 12 Co Rep 74 at 75. See also *Miller* (n 1), [44]–[45].

[24] *The Zamora* [1916] 2 AC 77, 90.

the exercise of its powers under the prerogative. This was the great principle which was settled by the Civil War and the Glorious Revolution in the 17th century.[25]

The prerogative can, however, change the facts to which the law applies.[26] For example, the prerogative power to declare war or expand the territorial scope of the sea both have legal consequences.[27]

ii. Domestic Rights

A second distinct, 'albeit related', delimitation[28] is that the prerogative power does not extend to affecting or removing common law rights enjoyed on the domestic plane.[29] For example, in relation to the foreign affairs treaty prerogative, Lord Oliver, in *Rayner (Mincing Lane) Ltd v DOT*, stated that

> the Royal Prerogative, whilst it embraces the making of treaties, does not extend to alter-ing the law or conferring rights upon individuals or depriving individuals of rights which they enjoy in domestic law without the intervention of Parliament … [A treaty] is res inter alios acta from which [individuals] cannot derive rights and by which they cannot be deprived of rights or subject to obligations.[30]

What the prerogative grants, however, the prerogative can remove. Thus, certain prerogative powers by their very nature can alter domestic rights where it is inherent in the prerogative power itself that it can affect the rights and duties of others,[31] for example a prerogative power to decide the terms of service of

---

[25] *Higgs v Minister of National Security* [2000] 2 AC 228, 241.

[26] *Miller* (n 1), [53].

[27] See *Post Office v Estuary Radio* [1968] QB 740, which held that the executive has the prerogative power to establish the territorial boundaries of the state. Where the executive has exercised that power, it may so certify to the court, which will be bound by the executive's certificate, because the matter is within the executive's competence. The executive, however, has no power by certificate to determine the law; the alteration of the boundaries of the state on the plane of international law does not affect the substantive content of the law of the land. The extent of the UK's territorial sea is now established by the Territorial Sea Act 1987 and Orders in Council made under the Act.

[28] For detailed discussion of this delimitation (and a rejection of arguments that such a delimita-tion does not exist), see C McLachlan, 'The Foreign Affairs Treaty Prerogative and the Law of the Land', *UKCLA Blog* (14 November 2016), available at https:/ukconstitutionallaw.org/; T Poole, 'Losing our Religion? Public Law and Brexit', *UKCLA Blog* (2 December 2016), available at https://ukconstitution-allaw.org/; and G Phillipson, 'The *Miller* Case, Part 1: A Response to Some Criticisms', *UKCLA Blog* (25 November 2016) available at https://ukconstitutionallaw.org. For an alternative analysis to that presented in this chapter and in these three blog posts, see Anne Twomey's contribution in ch 3 of this collection. The examples that Twomey gives to support the proposition that the prerogative *can* affect domestic rights can be explained away on the respective grounds that they concern situations of the prerogative changing the facts to which the law applies (rather than the law/rights themselves); they concern situations where the underlying right or relationship is governed by the prerogative rather than the common law, such that the prerogative can, in turn, alter that right or relationship; or they concern situations relating to non-nationals.

[29] *Miller* (n 1), [83]. See also ibid, [56] and [133].

[30] *Rayner (Mincing Lane) Ltd v DOT* [1990] 2 AC 418, 500B–C ('*The Tin Council case*'). See also *Walker v Baird* [1892] AC 491, 497 (Lord Herschell); and *Johnstone v Pedlar* [1921] AC 262, 273.

[31] *Miller* (n 1), [52].

Crown servants.[32] This is a limited exception and cannot be read more widely to undermine the general proposition.

iii. Bill of Rights 1688

The description of the delimitations of prerogative powers given above may not have always been an accurate reflection of the courts' practice at all points in British history (though the declaratory theory of the common law would posthumously declare that what 'is' always 'was'). For example, in *The Case of Ship-money*,[33] Finch CJ held that 'No act of Parliament can bar a king of his regality', and James I (of England) in his speech to the judges in the Star Chamber in 1616, stated with some success:

> Encroach not upon the Prerogative of the Crown for they are transcendent matters, and must not be sliberely carried with over-rash willfulness … deal not with it, till you consult with the King or his council … that which concerns the mystery of the King's power is not lawful to be disputed … the absolute Prerogative of the Crown is no Subject for the tongue of a Lawyer.[34]

The real turning point for the growing muscularity of the common law, ever evolving (some might say discovering) the delimitations of such executive powers, was undoubtedly 1688. James II (of England), emboldened by a decision of an unduly submissive court in *Godden v Hales*,[35] where the (hand-picked) Court upheld a dispensation from the King to Sir Edward Hales excusing him from taking religious oaths and fulfilling certain obligations in the Test Acts, had set aside statutes at his pleasure. He had, for example, granted suspension of penal laws relating to religion in the Declarations of Indulgence in 1687 and 1688. These actions were a partial cause of the 'Glorious Revolution' of 1688, leading to the downfall of James II (of England) and James VII (of Scotland) from his two thrones, and, of present interest, to the enactment of the Bill of Rights 1688.[36]

---

[32] *The GCHQ case* (n 6). The Constitutional Reform and Governance Act 2010 put the Civil Service on a statutory footing, save for the Secret Intelligence Service and Security Service: ss 1(2) and 3(4).

[33] *The Case of Ship-money* (1637) 3 St Tr 825, 1235. A trader sued the mayor for having wrongfully imprisoned him for refusing to pay ship money on the basis that the tax was unlawful, having been levied by the Crown without parliamentary sanction. The Court reject his claim.

[34] James I, 'Speech to Star Chamber of 20 June 1616' in JP Somerville (ed), *Political Writings* (Cambridge, Cambridge University Press, 1994) 212–14.

[35] *Godden v Hales* (1686) 11 St Tr 1165. See AW Bradley, 'Relations between Executive, Judiciary and Parliament: an evolving saga' [2008] *PL* 470 for a critical analysis of the, cursorily-reasoned, judgment. The result would be otherwise nowadays.

[36] In England, the terms of this Bill were accepted by the incoming joint monarchs, William and Mary, and approved by the House of Lords and the remnants of Parliament; it was later confirmed by the post-revolution Parliament too. In Scotland, the Scottish Parliament enacted the Claim of Right 1689. Its provisions closely align with those in the English Bill of Rights with certain tweaks; for present purposes, one pertinent example is the distinction between suspending and dispensing powers was not made, but all proclamations asserting an absolute power to 'cass, annul or disable laws' were nevertheless declared illegal. Nothing turns on the different formulations.

The Bill of Rights expressly prohibits the use of the prerogative in circumstances where its exercise would 'suspend' or 'dispense' statutory law. Articles 1 and 2 of the Bill of Rights respectively read:

Dispensing Power.

That the pretended Power of Suspending of Laws or the Execution of Laws by Regall Authority without Consent of Parlyament is illegall.

Late dispensing Power.

That the pretended Power of Dispensing with Laws or the Execution of Laws by Regall Authoritie as it hath beene assumed and exercised of late is illegall.[37]

The Bill of Rights is a constitutional statute.[38] It is best seen predominantly as a legal evolution rather than a revolution, that is, as declaratory of the proper, pre-existing delimitations of prerogative powers properly understood. As we have seen, the *Case of Proclamations* pre-dated the Bill of Rights 1688 by some 77 years. As Holdsworth stated, Coke's decision in the *Case of Proclamations* 'permanently settled' the matter, though 'It was not till after the Great Rebellion that these principles were recognised by all parties as finally settling the law on this point.'[39] Following the Glorious Revolution, the cases, according to Holdsworth, 'show that, as against the Crown, the supremacy of the common law was fully established, and that it was both an impartial and efficient protection of the liberties of the subject against the claims of the prerogative'.[40] As Brennan J held in the Australian case of *A v Hayden (No 2)*, 'Whatever vestige of the dispensing power then remained [pre-Bill of Rights], it is no more.'[41]

Three relatively modern authorities demonstrate the importance of the Bill of Rights. First, in *The King v The London County Council*[42] a local authority granted a licence on terms that demonstrated that it would not enforce section 1 of the Sunday Observance Act 1780. Scrutton LJ held in trenchant terms:

One is rather tempted to inquire whether the Theatres Committee of the London County Council have ever heard of the Bill of Rights. James II lost his throne, and one of the causes of it was that he took upon himself to dispense with the operation of Acts of Parliament, without the consent of Parliament. ... I take it that the London County Council is in no better position than James II and that laws cannot be dispensed with by the authority of the London County Council, when they cannot by royal authority.[43]

Second, in *Fitzgerald v Muldoon*[44] the New Zealand Prime Minister made a press statement announcing that a statutory superannuation scheme would no longer

---

[37] See also the preamble to the Bill of Rights.
[38] See *R (HS2 Action Alliance Ltd) v Secretary of State for Transport* [2014] UKSC 3, [2014] 1 WLR 324, [58]–[70] and [207].
[39] WS Holdsworth, *A History of English Law*, vol IV (London, Methuen, 1922–38) 296–97.
[40] ibid, vol VI, 268.
[41] *A v Hayden (No 2)* [1984] HCA 67.
[42] *The King v The London County Council* [1931] 2 KB 215.
[43] ibid, 228–29.
[44] *Fitzgerald v Muldoon* [1976] 2 NZLR 615, 622–23.

be applied, pending the passage of legislation to confirm this policy. A declaration was granted by the Court that this was illegal by virtue of articles 1 and 2 of the Bill of Rights, as 'in so doing [the Prime Minister] was purporting to suspend the law without consent of Parliament. Parliament had made the law. Therefore the law could be amended or suspended only by Parliament or with the authority of Parliament'.[45] The Prime Minister's public announcement constituted 'by regall authority' as the statement was made in the course of official duties.[46] Furthermore, the defence that there was no breach of the Bill of Rights because there was no assertion in the press statement that the Act was being lawfully suspended was rejected; it was enough that 'it was implicit in the statement ... that what was being done was lawful and had legal effect'.[47] Finally, the declaration of illegality was granted even though the Government had a clear intention to introduce legislation and there were 'high probabilities' that Parliament would be summoned within months to implement what the Prime Minister had said in his public announcement.[48]

Third, in *R (Nicklinson) v Director of Public Prosecutions*[49] the applicant sought a declaration that the respondent should give an assurance that it would be lawful for a person to assist with his suicide in order to give effect to Article 8 of the European Convention on Human Rights. Lord Sumption utilised the Bill of Rights to hold that no such undertaking could be given, as to do so would require the respondent to dispense with and suspend laws as laid down by Parliament in the Suicide Act 1961. This would be an act of executive discretion that, in effect, would 'exceed the bounds of constitutional propriety'.[50]

D. Exclusion

i. De Keyser's

It is well-established that prerogatives which are found to exist only do so to the extent that Parliament has not legislated contrary to them. As was held in *De Keyser's*, the prerogative is excluded whenever legislation overlaps with it. This has been expressed in a number of different ways—as 'ousting' the prerogative,

---

[45] ibid, 622.

[46] ibid.

[47] ibid, 623.

[48] ibid.

[49] *R (Nicklinson) v Director of Public Prosecutions* [2014] UKSC 38, [2015] AC 657.

[50] ibid, [241]. Lord Sumption further stated: 'The second limitation is a point of principle. The pursuit of clarity and precision cannot be allowed to exceed the bounds of constitutional propriety and the rule of law itself. The Code and associated guidelines may be "law" in the expanded sense of the word which is relevant to article 8.2 of the Convention. But they are nevertheless an exercise of executive discretion which cannot be allowed to prevail over the law enacted by Parliament. ... As Lord Bingham observed in *R (Pretty) v Director of Public Prosecutions* [2002] 1 AC 800, para 39, the Director has no power to give a "proleptic grant of immunity from prosecution". This is not just a limitation on the statutory powers of a particular public official. It is a constitutional limitation arising from the nature of the function which he performs'.

'abrogating' it, placing it 'in abeyance' and 'abridging' it. Nothing hinges on which phrase is used. 'Exclusion' is preferred on the basis that it encompasses all these ideas, without the incorrect connotation that the prerogative itself is somehow abolished by the statute.

The reasoning behind this rule is well explained by Lord Atkinson in *De Keyser's*:

> It is quite obvious that it would be useless and meaningless for the Legislature to impose restrictions and limitations upon, and to attach conditions to, the exercise by the Crown of the powers conferred by a statute, if the Crown were free at its pleasure to disregard these provisions, and by virtue of its prerogative do the very thing the statutes empowered it to do. One cannot in the construction of a statute attribute to the Legislature (in the absence of compelling words) an intention so absurd ... when such a statute, expressing the will and intention of the King and of the three estates of the realm, is passed, it abridges the Royal Prerogative while it is in force to this extent: that the Crown can only do the particular thing under and in accordance with the statutory provisions, and that its prerogative power to do that thing is in abeyance ... after the statute has been passed, and while it is in force, the thing it empowers the Crown to do can thenceforth only be done by and under the statute, and subject to all the limitations, restrictions and conditions by it imposed, however unrestricted the Royal Prerogative may theretofore have been.[51]

A few further observations are necessary. First, in order for the restriction to apply, there does not need to be a precise overlap between the statutory power and the prerogative. Instead, 'a prerogative power will be displaced in a field which becomes occupied by a corresponding power conferred or regulated by statute'.[52] Second, the prerogative may be wholly or only partially excluded or restricted; the question of the extent is a matter of statutory construction. Third, the prerogative can be excluded or restricted either by express words in the statute or by implication. Lord Parmoor in *De Keyser's* stated:

> The principles of construction to be applied in deciding whether the Royal Prerogative has been taken away or abridged are well ascertained. It may be taken away or abridged by express words, by necessary implication, or, as stated in Bacon's Abridgement, where an Act of Parliament is made for the public good, the advancement of religion and justice, and to prevent injury and wrong.[53]

As Paul Craig has pointed out,[54] the section of Bacon's Abridgement upon which Lord Parmoor draws is one concerned with whether a statute binds the Crown even though not particularly named therein. Bacon's answer was 'yes' in the three categories of statutes he uses. Bacon further qualifies this answer by stating that statutes were to be construed according to their subject matter and not to be extended further than the legislature had intended, such that general words might

---

[51] *De Keyser's* (n 4), 539.
[52] *Miller* (n 1), [48].
[53] *De Keyser's* (n 4), 575.
[54] P Craig, '*Miller*, Structural Constitutional Review and the Limits of Prerogative Power' [2017] PL 48.

not oust the King's prerogative.[55] In my view, the best interpretation of this series of events is that the third item in Lord Parmoor's list is a sub-set of the 'exclusion by implication' type of control: in the case of 'ordinary' statutes (not, in modern parlance, involving the protection of rights), the test for whether a prerogative is excluded is either by express words, or by *necessary* implication; whereas for statutes concerned with the protection of rights (and, perhaps, those which are termed, by the common law, as constitutional statutes), the test for exclusion is either by express words, or by *implication*, such that the courts would be more readily prepared to find such an implicit exclusion in such instances.[56] Some support for this is found in *R v Secretary of State for the Home Department, ex parte Northumbria Police Authority*, in which Croom-Johnson LJ acknowledged that 'the Crown cannot act under the prerogative if to do so would be incompatible with statute'.[57] However, in concluding that no such incompatibility arose, the Court was influenced by the fact that the prerogative was being used for the public good rather than (as in *De Keyser's*) to attempt to undercut the statutory safeguards which were beneficial to the public.

ii. Frustration

There is a second form of exclusion control. Ministers 'cannot frustrate the purpose of a statute or a statutory provision … by emptying it of content or preventing its effectual operation'.[58] Examples are *Laker Airways Ltd v Department of Trade*,[59] where it was held that Ministers could not exercise a prerogative power at the international level to revoke the designation of Laker Airways under an aviation treaty as that would have rendered a licence granted under a statute useless, and *R v Secretary of State for the Home Department, ex parte Fire Brigades Union*,[60] where it was held that Ministers could not exercise the prerogative power to set up a scheme of compensation for criminal injuries in such a way as to make a statutory scheme redundant, even though the statute in question was not yet in force.[61]

It is important to make a number of observations about this frustration control to avoid its misapplication. First, the principle is a sub-set of exclusion control, rather than part of extent control, because it is an external constraint (originating from statute) placed on the prerogative, which does not alter the very nature of the prerogative power but instead limits what it can achieve whilst the statute exists. This distinguishes it from extent control, which, as discussed further

---

[55] ibid.

[56] This would accord with the principle of legality.

[57] *R v Secretary of State for the Home Department, ex parte Northumbria Police Authority* [1989] QB 26, 44.

[58] *Miller* (n 1), [51].

[59] *Laker Airways Ltd v Department of Trade* [1977] QB 643, 718–19 and 728 ('*Laker*').

[60] *R v Secretary of State for the Home Department, ex parte Fire Brigades Union* [1995] 2 AC 513.

[61] This has similarities with *Fitzgerald* (n 44).

in section III, is an *ab initio* delimitation on the very nature and extent of the prerogative concept itself which remains evermore.

Second, the principle is distinct from exercise control because it is not a discretionary factor in an assessment as to whether any exercise of the prerogative is abusive (or irrational, etc). Instead, the Supreme Court clarified in *Miller* that the prerogative 'cannot' ever frustrate the purpose of a statute or its operation whilst that statute exists; it is a limitation on the legal powers and competence of the executive.[62]

Third, whilst the principle is a sub-set of exclusion control, it is nevertheless distinct from the *De Keyser's* line of authorities addressed in section II.D.i.[63] Both the majority and minority in *Miller* were aligned on this point. As Lord Reed, dissenting, stated, the cases of *Laker* and *Fire Brigades Union* were 'based on a different principle' from *De Keyser's*. This has important consequences. Whilst the two serve the same background value, namely Parliamentary supremacy, they do so in slightly different ways. The *De Keyser's* sort of cases exclude the prerogative directly (either expressly or by necessarily implication) in circumstances where the statute occupies the same field as, or corresponds to, a prerogative which regulated an activity beforehand. The frustration line of cases is an extension of this logic, but does not depend on the same prerogative in the same field (or regulating the same activity) being in play; instead, any prerogative cannot function to frustrate a statute's operation or purposes. In this second case, the statute excludes the prerogative indirectly.

E. Exercise

Once it has been established that a relevant prerogative power exists and has not been excluded by a statute, a final challenge can be made to the lawfulness of any exercise of that power. Both discretionary powers conferred under prerogative legislation[64] and the prerogative itself are reviewable.[65] Space precludes a detailed analysis of the nature of exercise control by the courts, but suffice it to say that exercises of prerogative powers are, in principle, reviewable 'on ordinary principles

---

[62] See further Lord Denning's judgment in *Laker* (n 59), 707: 'To my mind such a procedure [relying on prerogative power] was never contemplated by the statute. The Secretary of State was mistaken in thinking that he could do it ... He misdirected himself as to his powers'.

[63] For a detailed discussion of the distinction between cases such as *De Keyser's* (n 4), on the one hand, and cases such as *Fire Brigades Union* (n 60) and *Laker* (n 59) on the other, see Phillipson (n 28); R Craig, 'Casting Aside Clanking Medieval Chains: Prerogative, Statute and Article 50 after the EU Referendum' (2016) 79 *MLR* 1041; and R Craig, 'A Simple Application of the Frustration Principle: Prerogative, Statute and *Miller*' [2017] *PL* (Brexit Special Issue 2017) 25.

[64] *The GCHQ case* (n 6), 410 (Lord Diplock): 'I see no reason why simply because a decision-making power is derived from a common law and not a statutory source, it should for that reason only be immune from judicial review.'

[65] *Bancoult* (n 5), [35] (Lord Hoffmann).

of legality, rationality and procedural impropriety in the same way as any other executive action'.[66] It is sometimes claimed that some prerogative powers are non-justiciable.[67] This is incorrect. In truth, there is no such thing as a non-justiciable prerogative power *per se*.[68] Instead the standard of this review is likely to depend upon the subject matter and issues raised: matters of high policy (particularly foreign affairs)[69] are likely to receive highly deferential treatment from the courts, whereas questions concerning individual liberty (for example, the exercise of the prerogative of mercy[70]) are likely to receive more exacting examination. This reflects the usual practice in substantive judicial review across the board.

III. Defending the Four E's Framework Against Possible Challenges

A. Muscularity: Too Stringent?

The first criticism of the 'four E's' framework applied in *Miller* is that it leads to what Elliott calls 'unwarranted muscularity' and 'ill-focused constitutional assertiveness'.[71] This might be thought to follow, in particular, on the basis of bringing to the fore the extent category, which expands the inherent red-line parameters around what the prerogative powers can ever achieve, thereby reducing the scope for the executive's ever being able to rely on such powers regardless of the absence of any conflicting statute.

The first response to this, of course, is that the *Miller* judgment was not creating, for the first time, the extent category of control. Rather, it was applying it to novel circumstances. The 'four E's' framework has always been applicable. Whilst modern cases and thinking about the control of prerogative power have over-emphasised the exclusion by statute category of control, the truth is that prerogative powers have always had inherent delimitations on their very nature and scope. The *Miller* case has simply demystified the full framework for when a court

---

[66] ibid.

[67] This claim can be made on the basis of Lord Roskill's dictum in *The GCHQ case* (n 6), 418, that 'Many examples were given during the argument of prerogative powers which as at present advised I do not think could properly be made the subject of judicial review.' See also *R v Jones* [2006] UKHL 16, [2007] 1 AC 136, [65]; and *R (Abbasi) v Secretary of State for Foreign and Commonwealth Affairs* [2002] EWCA Civ 1598.

[68] M Elliott, *Administrative Law: Text and Materials*, 4th edn (Oxford, Oxford University Press, 2017) 123–28; and TRS Allan, *Constitutional Justice* (Oxford, Oxford University Press, 2011) 177. See also the Supreme Court in *R (Barclay) v Secretary of State for Justice* [2014] UKSC 54, [2015] AC 276, [58].

[69] *R (Sandiford) v Secretary of State for Foreign and Commonwealth Affairs* [2014] UKSC 44, [2014] 1 WLR 2697.

[70] *R v Secretary of State for the Home Department, ex parte Bentley* [1994] QB 349.

[71] Elliott (n 2), 257–59.

reviews such powers, including an analysis of the existence and extent of any pre-rogative power in the first place. As Lord Camden held in *Entick v Carrington*:

> [A Minister] is bound to shew by way of justification that some positive law has empow-ered or excused him. The justification is submitted to the judges, who are able to look into the books; and see if such a justification can be maintained by the text of the statute law, or by the principles of common law. If no such excuse can be found or produced, the silence of the books is an authority against the defendant, and the plaintiff must have judgment.[72]

This exercise is a far cry from 'unwarranted' or 'ill-focused'.

A more substantive response recognises that the full panoply of controlling the prerogative is justified. Proper review of prerogative powers—including an assessment of their claimed existence and extent—reflects the fact that prerogative powers are anachronistic: such powers have not been democratically conferred and are ill-defined, and as a result it is harder for Ministers to be held to account for their exercise (both legally and politically). Elliott himself recognises this: the 'basic problem', he says elsewhere, 'is that it is extremely difficult for Parliament to hold Ministers to account for decisions taken under the prerogative ... [T]his lack of transparency is also problematic in terms of judicial review of decisions taken under the prerogative'.[73] There has long been parliamentary and public commen-tary on the need to ensure executive accountability to Parliament by limiting the existence and exercise of prerogative powers, particularly in respect of important decisions affecting citizens' fundamental rights.[74] The same sentiment has been endorsed across the political spectrum, including indeed by the Secretary of State for Exiting the European Union.[75]

This is normatively justified.[76] Prerogative powers that contain important func-tions and whose exercise may entail major consequences, including going to war or leaving the EU, should be made through, or under the blessing of, the primary constitutional partner in the UK constitution—Parliament. Further, the courts

> should take a hard look at new assertions of prerogative power ... Representative democ-racy is served thereby, since if the government finds that it cannot cope without an asserted executive power, Parliament may at any time be asked to give impregnable statu-tory authority to the government for the power that it wishes to exercise.[77]

---

[72] *Entick v Carrington* (1765) 19 St Tr 1030, 1066.

[73] M Elliott and R Thomas, *Public Law*, 3rd edn (Oxford, Oxford University Press, 2017) 157.

[74] See, eg, the Green Papers *Governance of Britain* (CM 7170, July 2007) at 15, 16 and 19; and *The Governance of Britain—War Powers and Treaties: Living Executive Powers* (CM 7239, October 2007).

[75] David Davis MP (HC Deb 22 June 1999, vol 333, cols 930–31): 'There are three primary aspects of government where parliamentary scrutiny and control are either absent or inadequate. They are: first, the exercise of unfettered Executive power, largely under Crown prerogative ... [I]t strikes me as extraordinary that Parliament has no say not only in the decisions, but in who makes them ... Execu-tive decisions by the Government should be subject to the scrutiny and approval of Parliament in many other areas. Much of them arise under Crown prerogative—which, in truth, in modern Britain is a euphemism for the prerogative of the Prime Minister.'

[76] See Poole (n 28).

[77] AW Bradley 'Police powers and the prerogative' [1988] *PL* 298, 302.

None of this is to doubt the efficacy of the executive being the ultimate actor, or the pragmatic points Lord Carnwarth, in particular, stressed in *Miller*.[78] This is why the review of the exercise of the prerogative powers is, in many instances, deferential. But whilst the executive may indeed be the proper implementer, the courts have a proper role to play in assessing the initial competence to so act, and assessing the source from where that alleged power is claimed to derive. Whether the executive can act on account of powers sourced from historic prerogatives of the Crown, or whether ultimate authority lies with the legislature is a materially relevant enquiry, not without normative implications. One needs to have prior views about whether a competence exists and its extent, regardless of whether one ultimately agrees that it ought to be the executive that acts.

B. Constitutional Scale: An Additional Constraint?

Separately, it has been argued that there is an additional head of control, supposedly recognised for the first time in *Miller*, that prerogative power cannot be used to make major changes in the UK constitution.[79] This rests on a misreading of the majority judgment in *Miller*, relying on passages that are either normative *justifications* for the relevant principles (rather than a separate principle), or which are in the different context of assessing whether pre-existing legislation can be interpreted, by implication, as allowing the executive to effect major or fundamental changes to the UK's constitutional arrangements. (The scale of change, by the executive, is in any event a relevant interpretative tool in assessing what Parliament intended through silence.)

Nevertheless, the allegation can readily be dismissed on substantive grounds: the relevant head of control is that the prerogative cannot alter domestic law (ie extent control). It follows, *a fortiori*, that a *large* amount of domestic law or important domestic law cannot be altered. *Miller* cannot therefore be attacked on grounds that it supposedly introduces a novel head of controlling the prerogative; it does not. The scale argument is a straw man. For the same reasons, it is wrong to suggest that there is a separate category of control of undermining a constitutional statute.[80] The foreign relations treaty prerogative cannot, by its nature, affect any statute, constitutional or not.

C. Exclusion: Is it a Separate Category?

In contrast to the 'four E's' approach, Paul Craig has suggested that there are only 'three principal stages of analysis when considering the prerogative'—existence,

---

[78] *Miller* (n 1), [249].
[79] Elliott (n 2), 258.
[80] Cf Craig (n 54), 68.

extent, and manner of exercise.[81] This is achieved by treating what I have labelled as exclusion control as part of a broader category of extent control. In Craig's view, extent control captures all the limits placed on an admitted prerogative. Whilst the simplicity of wrapping exclusion control in with extent control may be attractive in the colloquial sense that any form of controlling the prerogative is, of necessity, limiting its extent, in my view the two categories are distinct and there are doctrinal advantages to separating them.

First, extent control and exclusion control are conceptually distinct. Concepts have inherent parameters in terms of what they can ever possibly achieve or do. A child, for example, by its very human nature cannot fly of its own accord, regardless of its parents' forbiddance or wishes. This is both an internal restriction (internal to the very nature of the concept or object in question) and an *ab initio* restriction (present from creation). Further, and of necessary consequence, such inherent parameters are ever-present: such restrictions cannot somehow be removed, that is, a parent who has hitherto forbidden the child from flying cannot by removing this restriction or stating otherwise successfully either create a power for humans to fly or expand the child's own abilities.[82] As historically derived powers originating from the Crown, the prerogative powers' inherent extents are determined, when called into question, by the common law.[83] That inherent extent is not dependent on statute, an altogether different originating source in the UK constitution. The label 'extent control' is intended to encompass these delimitations as described in this paragraph. A classic example of extent control is the *foreign* relations treaty prerogative—by its very nature it cannot alter *domestic* law or rights. The clue is in the name.

Exclusion control, on the other hand, works entirely differently. The *De Keyser's* line of authority, for example, examines whether a statute has excluded, or displaced, the prerogative—for the duration the statute is in force—by providing for something which had hitherto been doable under the prerogative. In this instance, the statute trumps the prerogative in the sense that the executive cannot depend upon the latter. The statute therefore works as an *ex post facto* limitation, or restriction, on a pre-existing prerogative power. It is *ex post facto* because it necessarily comes after an assessment of the existence and nature and scope of the relevant prerogative power. It is external because the restriction derives from a different origin, statute, as opposed to the very concept itself. It is temporary because the statute can itself be repealed. Exclusion control, then, is a 'limitation' in the sense used in this chapter: but for the statute in question, the prerogative could, in principle, have been used for the intended purpose (unlike if it were 'delimited' in the sense used in this chapter).

---

[81] ibid, 49.

[82] For convenience, in this chapter I label these sort of internal/*ab initio*/ever-present restrictions as 'delimitations' as opposed to 'limitations', the latter intended to signify a shift in context to discussion of a (possibly) temporary restriction imposed by another norm *ex post facto*.

[83] See, further, P Allott, 'The Courts and the Executive: Four House of Lords Decisions' (1977) 36 *CLJ* 255, 265–66.

Second, treating exclusion control as part of extent control also encourages doctrinal errors, which risks confused or incorrect reasoning. Treating exclusion control as part of extent control encourages one simply to assume the existence of such a pre-existing prerogative power and start by assessing whether Parliament has excluded it. This is a logically incorrect starting point, which distracts from a prior question of whether there actually was at any time a prerogative power of a relevant nature and scope. That assessment concerning the extent must come first, and is distinct from an analysis of whether such a power has been excluded by a statute—how can one properly assess whether something has been excluded or curtailed without an appreciation of what is said to exist? The nature and relevance of parliamentary intent is also different. For exclusion control it is the starting point—did Parliament intend to oust or override a prerogative, and to what extent? For extent control, it is a secondary consideration—the prerogative cannot by its own nature change domestic statutory law, so the material question becomes whether a particular statutory provision, properly construed in light of what Parliament intended for it to mean or apply to, be affected? Conflating the two stages risks conflating the different sorts of questions asked at each stage.

Particularly on the basis that Craig and I agree on the outcomes of all the relevant cases, it might be thought that the debate concerning whether there are three distinct categories or four is merely taxonomic. As will be seen in section IV, however, the conceptual distinctions matter, and the risks of these doctrinal errors (which a conflation of different categories of control increases) are well borne out by the minority judgments in *Miller* and the academics who support them, in particular their reliance on what I shall later label as 'the ambulatory thesis'.

IV. Application: Leaving the European Union

A. The Majority in *Miller*

Article 50 TEU states that a Member State 'may decide to withdraw from the Union in accordance with its own constitutional requirements', and then must notify the European Council of that intention to withdraw from the EU. The default effect is that the Treaty on the Functioning of the European Union and the TEU ('the EU Treaties') expire for the benefit of that state after two years. What were the UK's 'own constitutional requirements' for such a decision and notification? The judgments of the majority and minority judges in *Miller* that answer this question are discussed at length in Chapter 1 of this collection.[84] It is nevertheless important at this juncture to give an overview of the structure of the Court's judgment.

---

[84] See ch 1, section III.

The majority adopted, in substance if not in name, the 'four E's' approach. After establishing that a relevant prerogative power, the foreign relations treaty prerogative, existed,[85] the Court moved on to determining the extent of that prerogative power. The Court explored the delimitations of prerogative powers generally, and the foreign relations treaty prerogative specifically, in determining that such executive powers cannot affect domestic law[86] or, separately, domestic rights,[87] and cannot frustrate the purpose of a statute or statutory provision by effectively emptying it of content.[88] As such, the third category of control (exclusion by statute *De Keyser's* style) and the fourth (control of the exercise of such prerogative power) became unnecessary for the majority once the Court found that domestic law and rights would be affected if Article 50 were triggered.[89] As the Court stated,

> rather than the Secretary of State being able to rely on the absence in the [European Communities Act 1972] of any exclusion of the prerogative power to withdraw from the EU Treaties, the proper analysis is that, unless that Act positively created such a power in relation to those Treaties, it does not exist.[90]

The Court could not find such positive (statutory) authorisation in any of the relevant statutes, from the European Communities Act 1972 ('the ECA') to the European Union Referendum Act 2015.[91] With neither a prerogative power nor a pre-existing statutory power enabling it to act,[92] the consequence was that the Government had to seek fresh statutory authorisation from the 'constitutionally senior partner', Parliament, before a Minister could notify the European Council of the UK's intention to leave the EU pursuant to Article 50.[93]

B. The Minority in *Miller*: The Conditionality of the ECA

The majority's conclusions have been subject to fierce academic criticism, notably from Professors Elliott and Finnis, who prefer the minority's approach. Under this approach, no statutory authorisation was required to trigger the Article 50 process as the executive already enjoys a relevant prerogative power. Lord Reed gave the leading minority judgment. His judgment (and the academics who support him)

---

[85] *Miller* (n 1), [34] and [54].

[86] ibid, [44]–[45].

[87] ibid, [40]–[57], [83] and [133].

[88] ibid, [51].

[89] ibid, [60]–[89].

[90] ibid, [86]. The use of the word 'exist' in the last sentence should not be over-analysed; in context, it is short-hand for 'a prerogative power *of the extent alleged by the Government* does not exist'.

[91] ibid, [79], [104], [106], [118]–[121] and [171].

[92] For the contrary argument that Parliament had already provided sufficient statutory authority for the triggering of Article 50 TEU, see K Ewing, 'Brexit and Parliamentary Sovereignty' (2017) 80 *MLR* 585; and Craig (n 63).

[93] *Miller* (n 1), [90].

rests on what I shall call the 'ambulatory thesis'. This thesis can be distilled from the following dictum from Lord Reed:

> [The ECA] is inherently conditional ... on the UK's membership of the EU. The Act imposes no requirement, and manifests no intention, in respect of the UK's member-ship of the EU. It does not, therefore, affect the Crown's exercise of prerogative powers in respect of UK membership ... If Parliament chooses to give domestic effect to a treaty containing a power of termination, it does not follow that Parliament must have stripped the Crown of its authority to exercise that power ... As in the 1972 Act as originally enacted, Parliament has created a scheme under which domestic law tracks the obliga-tions of the UK at the international level, whatever they may be ... If Parliament grants rights on the basis, express or implied, that they will expire in certain circumstances, then no further legislation is needed if those circumstances occur.[94]

In essence, the thesis suggests that the ECA is a passive conduit, which leaves an unfettered discretion to the executive to negotiate the content of EU law and also to determine whether it will continue to apply in the domestic sphere at all.[95] Triggering Article 50 would not, on this view, infringe domestic laws or rights, on the basis that the obligation to give effect in domestic law to EU rights only applies whilst the Treaties apply to the UK. Moreover, but importantly, whether the Trea-ties apply to the UK is, on this view, conditional on the actions of the executive alone. If, in exercise of prerogative (executive) powers, the UK withdrew from the EU, there would then be no rights to which effect would be given through the ECA conduit.[96]

There are, however, a number of flaws with the ambulatory thesis, first as a mat-ter of application on its own terms, and second as a matter of principle.

i. Errors of Application

First, the thesis can be challenged on its own terms. As a matter of construction, the ECA is not conditional or contingent in the necessary manner. To understand why this is the case, it is important to note that a provision can be ambulatory in two ways:

1. Legislation may give effect to rights under such international agreements as the executive may, from time to time, enter into and exit from ('Type 1 ambulatory').

2. Alternatively, legislation may give effect to a specified international agree-ment, but the precise contents of the rights flowing from that defined treaty may evolve from time to time ('Type 2 ambulatory').

---

[94] ibid, [177] and [204].

[95] See further J Finnis, 'Terminating Treaty-based UK Rights', *UKCLA Blog* (26 October 2016), available at https://ukconstitutionallaw.org/; J Finnis, 'Terminating Treaty-based UK Rights: A Sup-plementary Note', *UKCLA Blog* (2 November 2016), ibid; and J Finnis, 'Intent of Parliament Unsoundly Constructed', *Judicial Power Project Blog* (4 November 2016), available at http://judicialpowerproject. org.uk/.

[96] *Miller* (n 1), [187], [190], [191], [197], [200], [216] and [217].

Depending on its statutory structure and language, a domestic implementing statute could in theory be ambulatory in either, both or neither of these senses. For
the minority's thesis to function, it requires the statute to be Type 1 ambulatory.

The only possible reading of the language of section 2 of the ECA, however,
is that the rights given effect by it are ambulatory only in the Type 2 ambulatory sense.[97] Lord Reed's conclusion that the ECA allows (or presupposes) that the
executive may revoke the European Treaties without parliamentary authority is
inconsistent with the language and nature of the Act. First, section 1(2) provides a
definitive list of 'the Treaties', which may only be varied by statutory amendment
or by Order in Council made under section 2(2) (and which are subject to Part I
of the European Union Act 2011). Second, section 2(1) gives effect to 'such rights
[and] powers ... created by or under the Treaties, and all such remedies and procedures from time to time provided for by or under the Treaties'. That is different
from a provision giving effect to 'such Treaties from time to time provided for, and
the rights, powers, remedies and procedures under them'. It is significant that the
words 'from time to time' come after 'the rights' (etc), and not after the phrase 'the
Treaties'. Third, the section refers to 'all' such rights (etc) rather than just some of
them, suggesting parliamentary expectation of at least something existing.

On the language used in the statute, therefore, the Treaties under which rights
may be conferred are defined by the terms of the statute itself and are envisaged by
Parliament to be fixed. It is only the rights and powers (etc) provided under these
Treaties which the statute envisages may vary from time to time, by operation of the
EU legal process. But those powers may not be exercised by a Minister so as to extin-
guish the existence of the Treaties whose continued existence the statute assumes.
Further, to do so would be contrary to Parliament's purpose expressed through the
statute. The purpose of the ECA was to establish UK membership of the EU and to
provide for the implementation of EU law in national law. Again, this can be seen
from the actual wording of the ECA. That purpose is clear from the long title of the
Act and the side heading of section 2. The long title shows that the purpose of the
Act is to *enlarge* the EU by making the UK a member. Section 2 is described in its
side heading as being concerned with the 'general implementation' of the Treaties.[98]

As such, on a technical analysis, the ambulatory thesis fails for the ECA on its
own terms. It is Type 2 ambulatory only.

ii. Errors of Principle

Second, even if it could be established that the ECA were Type 1 ambulatory
in some broader manner, the ambulatory thesis would still encounter trouble-
some issues of principle. The thesis suffers from what I shall call a 'core fallacy'.

---

[97] And even then, subject to the provisions of s 3 of the European Union Act 2011.
[98] These are both well-established permissible aids to interpretation. See *Black-Clawson International Ltd v Papierwerke Waldhof-Aschaffenburg* [1975] AC 591, 647F; *Ealing London Borough Council
v Race Relations Board* [1972] 2 WLR 71, 361; and *In Re Phelps* [1980] Ch 275, 281C.

The ambulatory thesis (which, it must be recalled, is an interpretive device aimed at construing an Act in a manner which leads to a relevant prerogative power remaining) serves an overriding objective—to prove that a *prerogative* power remains which is exercisable by the executive. But prerogative powers are not derived from a statutory origin. As historically derived powers originating from the Crown, the inherent extent of prerogative powers is determined, when called into question, by the common law. That inherent extent cannot be expanded by statute.[99] The fact that, separately, Parliament may envisage provisions or rights which it has created or authorised in domestic law being moulded, affected or destroyed (by virtue of being contingent upon a set of facts no longer pertaining or otherwise) is entirely irrelevant to the enquiry.

Instead, when arguing for a prerogative power,[100] the starting point in the analysis is not construing the statute to see whether it permits itself to be affected or envisages such; the starting point is instead a recognition that the foreign relations treaty prerogative power cannot, by its very nature, extend to changing domestic law or domestic rights. This quickly moves onto a consideration of whether such domestic law and rights would, in fact, be affected or lost. This is the material question—whether domestic law would, in fact, be altered or whether domestic

---

[99] It can, of course, be *restricted* by statute, though only for the lifetime of the statutory restriction. The executive's powers can be *expanded* in the (loose) sense that Parliament can authorise a Minister to do something which it could not under a prerogative power, but this is not expanding the *prerogative* power itself; it is the creation of a *statutory* power, which overrides any prerogative whilst it is in force. Executive power can also be expanded (in the loose sense) by the legislature's removing a pre-existing statutory restriction or provision which previously excluded the prerogative. But this is not the legislature expanding the inherent extent of any prerogative power itself; it is simply removing the (statutory) shackles. An Act could, expressly or by necessary implication, remove common law limitations to the prerogative of the sort under exercise control, and, in that sense, 'expand' a prerogative power (though this is not, in a strict sense, an expansion of the nature of the *prerogative* itself, just how that prerogative can be exercised). What an Act could not do, however, is remove the inherent *de*limitations of a prerogative power (and thereby expand the concept of a prerogative power, as opposed to creating a statutory power). As such, it would be a doctrinal error to suggest that a statute could, either expressly or by necessary implication, remove the delimitation that the foreign relations treaty *prerogative* cannot change domestic law or remove domestic rights. It is notable that neither John Finnis, nor Mark Elliott or Lord Reed argues that the ECA, or the ambulatory thesis, works in this way to expand the inherent extent of the prerogative—instead, on what I call the 'more charitable interpretation', they argue that the delimitation is not engaged because domestic laws and rights would not be affected: see, eg, Elliott (n 2), 271: 'The axiom that the prerogative cannot be used to change domestic law does not bite directly upon EU law if it is not, in the first place, domestic law.'

[100] The case would be different if one were arguing for a (pre-existing) *statutory* power to withdraw from an international agreement. Yet neither Mark Elliott, nor John Finnis or Lord Reed suggests that there is such a statutory power to leave the EU Treaties; all expressly utilise the ambulatory thesis in the context of arguing for a *prerogative* power. That said, at one point Lord Reed does suggest that the ambulatory thesis works in a manner that 'the rights are not revoked by the Crown's exercise of prerogative powers: they are revoked by the operation of the Act itself' (*Miller* (n 1), [219]). Nevertheless, this must be read in context: Lord Reed envisages the 'operation of the Act' permitting a *prerogative* power to be exercised, rather than creating a *statutory* right. But it is not, then, the Act that is revoking the rights—it is the actions of the executive (pursuant to prerogative powers), which, even on the ambulatory thesis, Parliament has not authored or expressly created, only implicitly permitted or envisaged. For Lord Reed's conclusion to follow (that the executive can so act), he has to use the ambulatory thesis in the context of arguing for a positive statutory authority. But he does not.

rights would, in fact, be removed if the purported power were to be used. This naturally involves a construction of the relevant domestic legislation (or common law) to see how it might be affected by the substantive action proposed (however authorised). But this is a materially different interpretive exercise from both the ambulatory thesis's function and the exclusion control's, *De Keyser's*, sort of statutory construction, searching for an express or replied *restriction* of a *pre-existing* executive power.[101]

A core component of the ambulatory thesis, namely parliamentary indifference about the existence of those particular rights or membership of an international agreement, thereby falls aside as simply immaterial to the extent that it concerns the purported creation or expansion of a prerogative power. Once a domestic law or right has been created, the conditionality, *simpliciter*, of any such law or right cannot by itself achieve such an expansion of prerogative power. If Parliament had intended that indifference or ambivalence to have been seized upon *by the executive*, rather than, in the ordinary course, Parliament itself amending or repealing its own legislation, then it would have created a *new statutory* power positively *enabling* the executive to do so.[102] This makes sense from a normative perspective (even if one were to somehow overcome the prior hurdle of the conceptual differences in origin of prerogative and statutory powers): Parliament is not, especially through silence, to be presumed as legislating in spite of the principles of the separation of powers, Parliamentary supremacy or dualism. Parliament is, though, taken to legislate knowing the law, including the inherent delimitations of the prerogative. As Professor Wade said in his 1980 Hamlyn lectures:[103]

> If the government wishes to take new powers, it is fundamental to our constitution that it should seek them from Parliament, and that they should be conferred by Parliament,

---

[101] In repeatedly searching for a *restriction* of the foreign relations treaty prerogative (and not finding one) the minority judgments in *Miller* (n 1) are, with respect, plagued by a conflation of the relevant interpretive exercise for an extent case (like *Miller* (n 1)) and an exclusion case (like *De Keyser's* (n 4)). For example, Lord Reed found that, in his view, there was no evidence in the ECA 'that Parliament intended to depart from the fundamental principle that powers relating to the UK's participation in treaty arrangements are exercisable by the Crown' (*Miller* (n 1), [203]) because the existence of other statutes that expressly limited the prerogative tended 'to support the conclusion that no such restriction was intended to arise by implication' in the ECA (ibid, [213]). See also ibid, [160], [177], [194] and [197].

[102] I concede that Parliament may, theoretically at least, achieve this by necessary implication (though perhaps not for constitutional statutes). However, that would still lead to a statutory, as opposed to a prerogative, power. As explained above, neither John Finnis, nor Mark Elliott or any of the minority judges in *Miller* (n 1) contends for such a statutory power. The ambulatory thesis always proves too little if it concerns the prerogative power, because a statute cannot create, or expand the inherent extent of, a prerogative power. Once domestic law is shown to have been changed, or domestic rights lost, that is the end of the matter. The ambulatory thesis alone is likely to prove too little, even for the creation of an implied statutory power: it has to go beyond demonstrating that Parliament is indifferent (whether expressly or by implication) about its own laws/rights, but additionally has to demonstrate that Parliament intended the executive be the one to alter its (Parliament's) laws/rights. This second element is unlikely to be easily 'read into' any provision, even of a Type 1 ambulatory nature, for similar reasons given in the main text plus the principles of legality (*Miller* (n 1), [112]) and constitutional statutes. See *Miller* (n 1), [108].

[103] Wade (n 7), 56.

if at all, under the due forms of law, ie by statute. The powers are then defined and the courts can protect the citizen in case of their abuse. To attempt to govern without Parliament by abuse of miscellaneous powers, in the manner that the Stuart kings did by abuse of the royal prerogative, is a complete repudiation of primary constitutional principle. The Stuart kings at least had the excuse that the legislation they wanted was difficult to obtain, something which no government can plead under our present party system.

The ambulatory thesis, however, depends upon the recognition of a type of statute which gives effect to international obligations as passive conduits or channels for obligations to enter the legal system, and those statutes not being subject to these normal rules of statutory construction. The normal rules mean that when a Treaty which is capable of having direct effect in domestic law has that direct effect switched on by domestic law, it is not possible without express wording for Parliament's intention to be construed in a manner which suggests that Parliament envisaged that the Treaty or a right which it, Parliament, granted (on an assumption the international obligations continued to exist) could be removed.

In any event, it cannot, for the reasons given, readily be presumed that Parliament envisaged the Treaty or conditional statutory right being removed *by the executive*. (I stress that this is in addition to the prior hurdle of the conceptual differences in origin of prerogative and statutory powers somehow being overcome.) The problems of the opposite rule of statutory construction on which the ambulatory thesis depends are not over-stated or hypothetical. The thesis is expressly claimed by Elliott and Lord Reed to go beyond requiring any analysis dependent on the actual words of the statute. For example, Lord Reed states that the rights in the European Parliamentary Elections Act 2002 'are obviously conditional on the UK's continued membership of the EU'.[104] Yet this Act has no equivalent of section 2(1) of the ECA. How are the judiciary to determine such conditionality or any parliamentary intent for an ambulatory nature—and, crucially, an ambulatory nature which specifically envisages executive as opposed to parliamentary action? As Lord Reid once stated, the judiciary 'often say that we are looking for the intention of Parliament, but that is not quite accurate. We are seeking the meaning of the words which Parliament used. We are not seeking what Parliament meant but the true meaning of what they said.'[105] Yet the ambulatory thesis would require judges essentially to second-guess Parliament on the basis of silence.

iii. *The Ambiguity of the Ambulatory Thesis: Applying Extent Control*

The ambulatory thesis is itself open to interpretation. On a less charitable interpretation, the thesis does not simply function to demonstrate that no (domestic) laws/rights are, in practice, affected, but instead attempts to go further by *accepting* that, in practice, domestic law is changed and domestic rights would be lost by a hypothetical exercise of the power, but that, in circumstances where its conditions

---

[104] *Miller* (n 1), [221].
[105] *Black-Clawson International Ltd v Papierwerke Waldholf-Aschaffenburg AG* [1975] AC 591, 613.

are satisfied, Parliament has (whether expressly or by necessary implication) permitted or has allowed for this to happen and so the prerogative can be used. At times Lord Reed's usage of the ambulatory thesis suggests that he has this in mind. He says, for example, '[w]ithdrawal under Article 50 alters the application of the 1972 Act, but is not inconsistent with it'.[106] This less charitable application of the thesis suffers from the core fallacy explained in section IV.B.ii; an Act cannot purport to remove the inherent delimitations of a prerogative power, and cannot purport to restrict what never was. If this is how proponents wish to use the thesis, it can only be used to argue for a *statutory* authorisation. There is no pre-existing prerogative of the extent required; searching for any restriction is illusory.

On a more charitable interpretation, the ambulatory thesis simply serves to deny that triggering Article 50 (or any other proposed executive act) would, in practice, affect any domestic laws or rights. On this view, the function of the ambulatory thesis is not to create or expand a prerogative power, but instead to argue that the inherent delimitations on the extent of the foreign relations treaty prerogative are not engaged.[107] As such, the foreign relations treaty prerogative remains exercisable because the effects in the domestic sphere would not be borne out. To succeed, this proposition ultimately depends on two factors: first, that *domestic* laws/rights would not be engaged; and, second, that these domestic laws/rights would not be *affected*. It does not succeed on either.

a. Domestic

It is indisputable that the ECA itself is a matter of domestic law. It therefore necessarily passes the first hurdle. As for the laws (Treaty articles, regulations, directives, jurisprudence of the Court of Justice of the European Union (CJEU) and general principles) and the rights created thereunder, Elliott suggests that this 'EU law is not domestic law in any normal or ultimate sense. Rather it forms a distinct body of law that *has effect* in domestic law, in the sense of being enforceable in national legal proceedings'.[108] In similar vein, Lord Reed states that the ECA 'did not create statutory rights in the same sense as other statutes, but gave legal effect in the UK to a body of law'.[109] This distinction between what might be termed direct domestic law and indirect domestic law is novel and rightly rejected by the majority in *Miller*.

These rights were not simply created by the foreign affairs prerogative. It is trite law, due to the dualist nature of the UK constitution, that

> as a matter of constitutional law of the United Kingdom, the Royal Prerogative while it embraces the making of treaties, does not extend to altering the law or conferring rights upon individuals or depriving individuals of rights which they enjoy in domestic law

---

[106] *Miller* (n 1), [204].
[107] Elliott (n 2), 271.
[108] ibid (original emphasis).
[109] *Miller* (n 1), [216].

without the intervention of Parliament ... So far as individuals are concerned [a treaty] is res inter alios acta from which they cannot derive rights and by which they cannot be deprived of rights or subjected to obligations and it is outside the purview of the court not only because it is made in the conduct of foreign relations which are the prerogative of the Crown but also because as a source of rights and obligations it is irrelevant.[110]

As such, by their very nature, the laws and rights must have been transformed into domestic law, and depend for their validity and exercise in domestic law on a domestic norm, namely the ECA. Each time an individual relies upon such a law or right, he or she is effectively relying on the ECA. Such rights are exercised and enjoyed on the domestic plane precisely because Parliament intended such (in full knowledge of the doctrines of direct effect and supremacy, which were already developed by 1972) when Parliament enacted the ECA bringing the rights into domestic law. Without such an Act (which was necessary for the UK to become a full member of the EU and for EU law to become part of UK's law) such rights would not be enjoyed by UK citizens. If this is not clear from the ECA alone then the European Union Act 2011 puts it beyond doubt. Section 18 of that Act provides that EU law, defined as 'the rights, powers, liabilities, obligations, restrictions, remedies and procedures referred to in section 2(1) of the [ECA]', is 'recognised and available in law in the UK' by virtue of the ECA. Thus, through the 2011 Act, Parliament has preserved the consequent 'availability' in UK law of the rights, remedies and procedures (etc) conferred by EU institutions. From a domestic actor's perspective, it was Parliament which created the rights and authorised EU law's place in the domestic constitution. From the domestic perspective, Parliament not only endorsed EU law as domestic law, but also authorised it.

The 'basic flaw' of the allegation that the rights and laws are not domestic is, therefore, to suggest that EU institutions rather than Parliament were the real source of UK law obligations such that they cannot be domestic.[111] It is tempting to criticise the majority for inconsistency in the use of the word 'source'—in one place suggesting that the EU is the source of the laws and rights, but at another point suggesting that the one source is Parliament via the ECA. It surely cannot be both at once? This criticism is misguided, however. The Court is using the word 'source' in two different senses: first, 'source' meaning derivation (the point of origin); and, second, 'source' meaning authorisation (the point of warrant).[112] In the first sense, the laws and rights are derived from the international sphere— EU institutions. In the second sense, the very authority for treating this originally external law as now domestic is the authority derived from the ECA itself. The latter (domestic) norm is what transforms the external into the internal.

Treating them as domestic laws and rights also makes sense from a normative perspective. Section 2(1) of the ECA is an entirely legitimate legislative drafting

---

[110] *JH Rayner (Mincing Lane) Ltd v Department of Trade and Industry* [1990] 2 AC 418, 500.

[111] T Poole, 'Devotion to Legalism: On the Brexit Case' (2017) 80 *MLR* 685, 701. See also Poole (n 28).

[112] Poole, 'Devotion to Legalism' (n 111), 702.

technique for incorporating international rights into domestic law without having to expressly copy out *verbatim* such rights in the statute itself: the ECA is more than a mere 'conduit'—it is an active and an express endorsement of such rights. The technique is a pragmatic one to save domestic energy every time the law varies. Further, as Paul Craig has put it, it may be 'entirely fortuitous whether Parliament chooses to create rights in a free-standing UK statute, or whether it embodies them through adherence to an international treaty, which is given effect in the UK through a statute'.[113] This point can be pushed further. Under the Reed/Elliott view, directives which had been implemented in domestic secondary legislation would count as domestic law, whereas regulations (higher in the EU hierarchy of norms) would not. There is 'no basis for concluding that Parliament has any greater attachment' to the former rather than the latter.[114] The Reed/Elliott view would be formalistic in the extreme without justification.[115]

The Reed/Elliott argument puts form over substance in another way. From the citizens' perspective, they are relying on the laws/rights as their own, directly, in their own courts, against their own state's institutions. In every practical sense, they are domestically enjoyed and enforced rights. Where the rights are 'enjoyed' is indeed the determinative and materially-relevant factor rather than, as the Reed/Elliott view depends upon, looking at who penned the laws/rights (ie the EU institutions and Member States on the international plane). As Lord Oliver stated in the *Tin Council case*, 'the Royal prerogative ... does not extend to altering the law or conferring rights upon individuals or *depriving individuals of rights which they enjoy in domestic law without the intervention of Parliament*'.[116] It is undeniable that the relevant laws and rights are 'enjoyed' in domestic law (even if one were to accept that the EU institutions and Member States, rather than Parliament, are the authors of them). In looking only at the authorship, rather than application, of the rights, the minority and critical academic commentators fall into error.

This explains why, even prior to *Miller*, treating such laws and rights as domestic law and rights was considered orthodoxy. For example, in *Julian Sundberg Jensen v Corporation of the Trinity House of Deptford*, Lord Denning MR stated that 'That Article of Community law [Article 7 of the Treaty of Rome] *is incorporated into our law*',[117] and Kerr LJ said that '[t]here can be no doubt, of course, that rights and obligations arising from the Treaty, as well as from regulations and from decisions of the European Court of Justice, *form part of the corpus juris of the member states*'.[118] More recently, Lord Mance, in *Pham v Secretary of State for the Home Department*,

---

[113] Craig (n 54), 59.

[114] ibid.

[115] See also AL Young, '*R (Miller) v The Secretary of State for Exiting the European Union* [2016] EWHC 2786 (Admin): Constitutional Adjudication—Reality over Legality?' *UKCLA Blog* (9 November 2016), available at https://ukconstitutionallaw.org.

[116] *The Tin Council case* (n 30), 500 (emphasis added) (cited with approval in *Miller* (n 1), [56]).

[117] *Julian Sundberg Jensen v Corporation of the Trinity House of Deptford* [1982] 2 CMLR 218, [3] (emphasis added).

[118] ibid, [39] (emphasis added).

stated that 'we must view the United Kingdom as independent, Parliament as sovereign and European Law *as part of domestic law* because Parliament has so willed'.[119] The laws (Treaty articles, regulations, directives, CJEU jurisprudence and general principles) and the rights created thereunder accordingly also pass the hurdle of being domestic norms, as well as the ECA itself.

b. Affected

Further, both the ECA and, separately, the laws and rights (etc) flowing through it would by default, indeed possibly definitely, be affected in consequence of triggering Article 50.[120]

It is indisputable that the rights contained in the European Treaty, regulations, directives, CJEU jurisprudence and EU general principles are affected. They are lost. It is no answer to claim that Parliament 'retains full competence to legislate to protect rights before withdrawal occurs'.[121] First, there are many non-replicable rights that depend on co-operation from other states and institutions, which it is not within Parliament's sole competence to re-enact.[122] Second, Parliament cannot be pre-empted by the executive or effectively forced to act in order to re-enact rights that are lost. In any event, this argument does not work conceptually—the old rights are lost, so the prerogative cannot extend to such a situation in the first place; this is not solved by claiming that new rights can be granted thereafter.

Separately, the ECA itself is affected. As the Divisional Court held in *Miller*, the provisions of the ECA 'would be stripped of any practical effect'[123] and would 'inevitably be deprived of any practical application'.[124] The whole raison d'être of the Act is undone. Its provisions, not limited to section 2(1), are effectively stripped of all meaning and application. A citizen cannot rely on any of the provisions. For all intents and purposes, the Act is repealed.[125] A corollary of the

---

[119] *Pham v Secretary of State for the Home Department* [2015] UKSC 19, [2015] 1 WLR 1591, [80] (emphasis added).

[120] Depending on whether Article 50 is held, as a matter of EU law, to be unilaterally irrevocable or not. The answer to this question was irrelevant for the purposes of answering the relevant UK law question in *Miller* (n 1). It was enough that the default effect of Article 50 could lead, without anything more, to domestic laws and/or rights being affected. Parliament cannot be pre-empted or forced to act in order to save its statutes on account of an executive act. Separately, a question of competence to trigger a process cannot be answered by the courts once it has already been actioned and/or had (irreversible) effects. The core reasoning in the majority's judgment therefore does not depend upon the Government's concessions that, as a matter of law, its view is that Article 50 is unilaterally irrevocable, or that, as a matter of fact, the Government's policy is to not attempt to unilaterally revoke the notice.

[121] *Miller* (n 1), [219] (Lord Reed).

[122] Furthermore, it cannot be claimed that these sorts of rights are currently not domestic rights: first, they depended on authorisation by Parliament for their existence, and second, they are (pre-withdrawal) exercised and enforced in domestic law as the UK Parliament cannot legislate, and the UK executive branches cannot act to frustrate the exercise of these rights.

[123] [2016] EWHC 2768 (Admin); [2017] 1 All E.R. 158 at [51].

[124] ibid, at [52].

[125] Sir Stephen Sedley, 'The Judges' Verdicts' (30 Jan. 2017), available at: https://www.lrb.co.uk/2017/01/30/stephen-sedley/the-judges-verdicts.

fact that the ECA is a constitutional statute—which means that it 'conditions the legal relationship between citizen and the State in some general, overarching manner'[126]—is, as Sir John Laws has stated in his contribution in this book, that once its application is affected, this 'of necessity ... alters the general law of the land in some fundamental respect'.[127] As such, domestic law is altered, with the result that the prerogative cannot be used.

It is no answer to the particular charge that domestic law, in the form of the ECA, is affected to claim that, on account of the ambulatory thesis, the ECA is not truly affected because it has to be interpreted as conditional on EU membership, such that it envisages itself as having no application due to actions by the executive. This would be tautologous. It is tantamount to claiming that domestic law is not actually affected because it envisages itself to be affected. The simple point in response is that *it would be affected*. The attempted utilisation of the ambulatory thesis as a defence collapses the charitable interpretation of the ambulatory thesis straight back into the less charitable interpretation. This follows because the very reason why domestic laws/rights are said not to be affected is because Parliament has, *ex ante*, sanctioned or allowed that to be done (and done so by the executive). This immediately suffers from key elements of the core fallacy, namely: assuming that a prerogative power of the relevant extent exists in the first place; assuming that a statute can create or expand the inherent nature and scope of a prerogative power (by removing an inherent delimitation hardwired into the initial concept); and claiming that the proper exercise is looking for restrictions on the prerogative in the (allegedly affected) statute rather than looking for positive statutory authority. As stated in section IV.B.ii, not only is this a conceptual nonsense, but it also depends upon taking a normative leap of faith—that Parliament intended its rights not only to be conditional, but also contingent upon the *executive* affecting them. As such, the ambulatory thesis cannot properly be used defensively to claim that no laws are affected, without logically suffering from the core fallacy.

Further, Lawton LJ's enquiry in *Laker* as to 'the reality, if not the form' of whether a particular exercise of prerogative power would remove rights from citizens by emptying them of effective content, even if preserving their theoretical existence,[128] exposes the flaw in the argument that any supposed prerogative power to withdraw from the EU would not conflict with the ECA because it would continue to exist, but without any content on which to 'bite'. As we have seen, it is where the rights are enjoyed that makes them domestic. It is therefore unreal to suggest that an Act that has been turned into a mere zombie Act, without meaning, has not been affected because it continues formally to exist. If this distinction were valid, it would also undermine the Bill of Rights and frustration lines of cases

---

[126] *Thoburn v. Sunderland City Council* [2002] EWHC 195, [2003] QB 151 at [62].
[127] See ch 9, section VIII.
[128] *Laker* (n 59), 728A–B.

explored in section II. It is incumbent on the critics to describe how *Fitzgerald*,[129] *Laker*[130] and *Fire Brigade Union*[131] are also incorrectly decided.

C. Summary

Lord Bingham stated that if an asserted prerogative power is to be found in law then it will be found in our books. For the purposes of triggering Article 50, it is not. Far from a myopic focus on the exploration of whether the ECA excluded any prerogative, the majority's judgment in *Miller* reveals the full panoply of control when assessing purported prerogatives: what I have called the 'four E's'. The extent category of control was crucial; the *Miller* case never was about statutory exclusion.[132] The truth is that the foreign relations prerogative has never, and can never be, extended to changing domestic law or rights. This consequence would be a logically possible, indeed possibly definite, effect of triggering Article 50. As such, there never was any sufficient prerogative in the first place. As Helen Mountfield QC put it in her oral submissions to the Supreme Court, the Government's (and indeed the minority's and critical academics') approaches 'are the equivalent to arguing that because none of the attempts to catch the Loch Ness monster succeeded, the Loch Ness monster still roams free'.

Elliott baldly criticises the majority in *Miller* on the basis that their judgment 'lacks support in authority, imports into the law a novel and highly imprecise criterion by which prerogative power is delimited and rests upon normative constitutional foundations that are unarticulated and arguably absent'.[133] The same criticism can be levelled at the ambulatory thesis. Elliott gives us two options for assessing this thesis: to congratulate it on account of its 'logical punctiliousness', or castigate it 'for adopting a narrowly technical perspective'.[134] I do neither. It is impressionistic and illogical; it is unprincipled and unprecedented. For the

---

[129] *Fitzgerald* (n 44).

[130] *Laker* (n 59).

[131] *Fire Brigade Union* (n 60).

[132] And yet eminent academics continue to criticise the Supreme Court's judgment on the mistaken assumption that it purported to hold (wrongly in their view) that the ECA *excluded* a prerogative. The Court did no such thing. See, eg, D Feldman, 'Pulling a trigger or starting a journey? Brexit in the Supreme Court' (2017) 76 *CLJ* 217, 221–22: 'The Act says nothing about withdrawing from the EU ... yet the majority read it as prohibiting, by necessary implication, the use of the prerogative to give notice under Article 50 ... it thereby excluded the prerogative ... treating the Act as impliedly supplanting the prerogative ... None of these can make up for the absence of any express provision excluding the royal prerogative; the majority effectively stood on its head the important constitutional rule that only clear statutory provisions can displace a prerogative power ... We should beware of courts, magically producing statutory prohibitions where no such prohibition appears on the face of the Act, particularly in areas of constitutional sensitivity.'

[133] Elliott (n 2), 258.

[134] ibid, 284.

ambulatory thesis to be successful even on its own terms, it has to demonstrate both that no domestic laws/rights are in question and that these would not be affected. It cannot do either.

V. Conclusion

The *Miller* case demystifies the limits of prerogative powers and re-clarifies the proper framework for when a court reviews such powers. The majority judgment achieves this by bringing to the fore that which hitherto has been shrouded by a preoccupation with one case, *De Keyser's*, focused, as it was, on merely one category of limiting prerogative powers, exclusion by statute, to the detriment of the full analytical framework. In particular, *Miller* reminds us of the need to conduct Lord Bingham's 'historical enquiry' into the very existence and extent of any purported prerogative power in the first place. This enquiry comes prior to any questions concerning Parliament's intent to restrict, or exclude, any such executive power of the nature and scope as is found to exist. In doing so, the Court has followed a long trend in UK constitutional history, dating from at least the seventeenth century, of delimiting and limiting such ill-defined powers derived from the Crown. Whilst the immediate impact of the judgment may have been small—the European Union (Notification of Withdrawal) Act 2017 was quickly passed, without amendments, giving the Prime Minister the bare authority to notify the UK's intention to leave the EU—the case has important implications for the UK's contemporary constitutional settlement: just as, as we have seen, the London County Council was in no better position than James II,[135] it transpires that neither is any modern-day Prime Minister. The only surprise is that some continue to find this result (and reasoning) surprising. Perhaps, as one academic has framed it, the Cavalier versus Roundhead battle continues to be waged in unexpected ways.[136]

---

[135] *The King v The London County Council* (n 42), 228–29.
[136] Robert Craig in discussions at conferences at the LSE and Durham University (2016–17).

3

Miller and the Prerogative

ANNE TWOMEY

The *Miller* case[1] is difficult to disentangle from the highly charged political circumstances that spawned it. The fierce debate amongst legal academics that materialised in blog-posts, papers and articles during the legal proceedings seemed to be unusually influenced by views both as to the preferred outcome and the merits of the advocates for the different outcomes. This chapter takes an outsider's perspective on the case, where neither the politics nor the personalities have any influence.

From an Australian point of view, the key interest in the case is its analysis of the prerogative and its relevance to the power to enter into and withdraw from treaties. Australia has the same dualist system as the United Kingdom (UK) when it comes to the ratification and implementation of treaties, and the executive in Australia has inherited the same prerogative powers from the UK, subject to abrogation by Australian legislation. The relationship between the prerogative, the common law and statute is also the same as in the UK.

This chapter addresses the manner in which the prerogative was characterised and limited by the Supreme Court in *Miller*, both in general and with respect to treaties. It considers whether the Court has gone too far in imposing limitations on the prerogative, or whether the judgment really turns upon a constitutional understanding that goes beyond the question of the legal bounds of the prerogative. It concludes with a consideration of whether there is value in retaining prerogative powers, or whether all such powers should be put on a statutory basis.

I. *Miller* and Limits on the Prerogative

In the public and academic debate about whether the prerogative could be used by the British Government to notify withdrawal from the European Union (EU),

---

[1] *R (Miller) v Secretary of State for Exiting the European Union* [2017] UKSC 5, [2017] 2 WLR 583.

numerous propositions were made concerning the limits on prerogative power. This chapter will focus on two of the key propositions,[2] being:

(a) that the prerogative cannot alter statute or common law,[3] or affect the rights and duties of persons;[4] and

(b) that the prerogative with respect to treaties operates wholly on the international plane and cannot affect domestic law or the rights of individuals without parliamentary sanction.[5]

Before giving consideration to these limitations, it is necessary first to distinguish the different types of prerogative power and narrow the discussion to the type of prerogative at issue.

A. The Different Types of Prerogative Power

The prerogative powers are those powers historically held by the Sovereign that have not been abrogated over time by statute. In *Miller*, following Dicey,[6] the majority described the prerogative as encompassing 'the residue of powers which remain vested in the Crown'.[7] The prerogative powers originally held by the Sovereign were not just executive in nature[8] but also included legislative and judicial powers. That 'residue of powers which remain vested in the Crown' is not necessarily, therefore, confined to executive power.

Remaining judicial prerogatives were recognised and regularised by the Judicial Committee Acts of 1833 and 1844, with only vestigial traces remaining.[9] The more significant exercise of the prerogative, however, was in the executive and legislative fields. Distinguishing the difference between executive and legislative exercises of the prerogative can prove difficult. For example, is the prerogative power to assent to, or withhold assent from, bills passed by the Houses of Parliament a power of an executive or a legislative nature?

---

[2] Note the other important issues, which are not addressed here, concerning when the prerogative is abrogated, whether the prerogative can revive after abrogation and whether the prerogative can be used in a manner that 'frustrates' the application of legislation.

[3] See *Miller* (n 1), [50].

[4] *R (Miller) v Secretary of State for Exiting the European Union* [2016] EWHC 2768 (Admin), [2017] 1 All ER 158, [33].

[5] *Miller* (n 1), [86].

[6] AV Dicey, *Introduction to the Study of the Law of the Constitution*, 10th edn (London, Macmillan, 1959) 424–25. Compare Blackstone, who confined the prerogative to those powers unique to the Crown, excluding the capacities held in common with other legal persons: Sir William Blackstone, *Commentaries on the Laws of England*, vol 1 (1st edn facsimile, 1765) 232.

[7] *Miller* (n 1), [47] (Lord Neuberger, with whom Lady Hale and Lords Mance, Kerr, Clarke, Wilson, Sumption and Hodge agreed).

[8] ibid, [41].

[9] *De Morgan v Director-General of Social Welfare* [1998] AC 275, 285.

In the UK, the prerogative of royal assent is not exercised on ministerial advice,[10] despite assumptions to the contrary. A pertinent illustration of the confusion regarding the status of royal assent concerns the efforts of Alan McWhirter in 1972 to prevent the UK from entering into the European Community. After he failed in his legal challenge to the executive acts involved in the signing of the Treaty of Accession to the Treaty of Rome in 1972,[11] he petitioned the British Government, praying that the Queen refuse assent to the European Communities Bill 1972 because signing it would breach her coronation oath. The initial draft response from the Prime Minister's Office said that it is an established constitutional convention that royal assent is not refused to bills that have been passed by both Houses and 'which Ministers advise should receive assent'. This was corrected by the Lord Chancellor's Office, on the ground that ministerial advice is not tendered in relation to the grant of royal assent.[12] Instead, McWhirter was advised that it is a constitutional convention and custom that assent is not withheld from bills which have been passed by both Houses of Parliament.[13] It may therefore be contended that the Queen, in giving royal assent, is acting on the advice of the two Houses, as a constituent part of Parliament, as described by the enacting words to British statutes.[14]

In contrast, the Queen does act upon ministerial advice when giving assent to reserved bills from her realms or colonies, usually acting 'in Council'.[15] Bills of the Scottish Parliament are given assent by the Queen pursuant to Letters Patent, after the bill is submitted to her by the Presiding Officer of the Scottish Parliament.[16] In all cases the prerogative act of granting or withholding assent to bills has the effect of making law or preventing the making of a law. Whether it should be classified as a prerogative of an executive or a legislative nature remains a matter for debate, but if it were classified as an executive prerogative then it would undermine any proposition that the prerogative cannot be exercised in the UK to make or alter the law.

Most power of a legislative nature that is exercised by the executive finds its source in statute and is an exercise of delegated legislative power. Orders in Council,

---

[10] Royal assent is given by the Queen by signing Letters Patent prepared by the Clerk of the Crown. This is not done in Council and no ministerial advice is given. See G Wheeler, 'Royal Assent in the British Constitution' (2016) 132 *LQR* 495, 500.

[11] *McWhirter v Attorney-General* [1972] CMLR 882.

[12] Letter by Mr de Winton, Law Officers Dept, to RT Armstrong, 10 Downing St, 12 September 1972: The National Archives of the UK ('TNA') PREM 15/1183.

[13] Prime Minister's Office, No 10 Downing St, draft letter to Mr McWhirter, 21 September 1972: TNA PREM 15/1183.

[14] The enacting words provide: 'Be it enacted by the Queen's most Excellent Majesty, by and with the advice and consent of the Lords Spiritual and Temporal, and Commons, in this present Parliament assembled, and by the authority of the same, as follows:'. Note the observation that 'legislation enacted by the Crown with the consent of both Houses of Parliament is supreme': *Miller* (n 4), [20].

[15] See, eg, *Rutledge v Victoria* (2013) 251 CLR 457. The same is true in relation to royal assent to bills from the Channel Islands and the Isle of Man: TNA HO 284/89.

[16] Scotland Act 1998, s 32 and s 38. For an example of the Letters Patent, see *The Gazette*, Issue No 7969, 4 August 2017, 566.

made by the Sovereign upon ministerial advice, may have a legislative effect in terms of 'making' law, but they are usually authorised and limited by statute.[17] An Order in Council cannot, ordinarily, alter primary legislation, unless the authorising statute, by way of the inclusion of a Henry VIII clause, so authorises. The Order in Council must be confined in its operation within the scope of the statutory authorisation, or else be held to be *ultra vires*.

Alternatively, Orders in Council may be made in the exercise of prerogative power. Other instruments, such as Letters Patent, may also be made in the exercise of prerogative power. These instruments have legal effects and may impose obligations and duties. In some cases, most notably in relation to the government of colonies, they clearly have legislative effect.[18] Constitutions of both colonies and realms have been made by way of Order in Council.[19] It therefore overreaches to state, as the majority did in *Miller*, that the 'legislative power of the Crown is today exercisable only through Parliament'.[20] As was shown in the *Bancoult* litigation,[21] the Crown continues to exercise legislative power through the making of Orders in Council in relation to British overseas territories, some of which find their source in the prerogative.[22] Lord Bingham observed that as 'an exercise of legislative power by the executive without the authority of Parliament, the royal prerogative to legislate by order in council is indeed an anachronistic survival'.[23] But survive it has.

The majority in *Miller* might more accurately have asserted that the legislative power of the Crown is today only exercisable with respect to the UK by Parliament or as authorised by it. Even then, there are aspects of Orders in Council and Letters Patent made under the prerogative within the UK that appear to be legislative in nature, at least to the extent that they create legal obligations, duties or rights, as discussed in section I.B. When it comes to the prerogative, the borderline between exercises of legislative and executive power is greyer than is commonly recognised.

---

[17] *Miller* (n 1), [46].

[18] In relation to conquered and ceded colonies, the Crown had plenary power to legislate for the colony until a constitution was granted to it. In relation to settled colonies, the settlers brought the common law with them, and the power of the Crown to legislate was confined to providing it with a representative legislature: *Kielley v Carson* (1842) 4 Moo PCCC 63, 84–85; *Phillips v Eyre* (1870) LR 6 QB 1; *Sammut v Strickland* [1938] AC 678; and *Sabally and N'Jie v Attorney-General* [1965] 1 QB 273.

[19] See, with respect to Australia, the Constitution of Queensland, which was first conferred by an Order in Council issued by Queen Victoria on 6 June 1859. See also the discussion by Finnis of the Independence Constitution of the Bahamas, made by the Bahamas Independence Order 1973, SI 1973/1080, under both statute and prerogative powers: J Finnis, 'Brexit and the Balance of Our Constitution', *Judicial Power Project*, 2 December 2016, p 8, available at https://judicialpowerproject.org.uk/john-finnis-brexit-and-the-balance-of-our-constitution/.

[20] *Miller* (n 1), [43].

[21] *R (Bancoult) v Secretary of State for Foreign and Commonwealth Affairs (No 2)* [2007] EWCA Civ 498, [2008] QB 365; and *R (Bancoult) v Secretary of State for Foreign and Commonwealth Affairs (No 2)* [2008] UKHL 6, [2009] 1 AC 453.

[22] Note that the British Settlements Act 1887 provides a legislative source of power with respect to certain settled colonies, but the prerogative is still used to legislate with respect to others.

[23] *R (Bancoult) v Secretary of State for Foreign and Commonwealth Affairs (No 2)* [2008] UKHL 6, [2009] 1 AC 453, [69] (Lord Bingham, dissenting).

B. The Prerogative Cannot Alter Statute or Common Law or Affect the Legal Rights and Duties of Persons

In *Miller*, the majority stated that if 'a prerogative would result in a change in domestic law, the act can only lawfully be carried out with the sanction of primary legislation enacted by the Queen in Parliament'.[24] It has long been recognised that the executive prerogative[25] cannot override statutes.[26] This is due to the application, in the UK, of the doctrine of parliamentary sovereignty. As a consequence, the prerogative cannot be used to suspend laws or dispense with the application of laws.[27] The exercise of the prerogative must therefore be compatible with legislation.[28]

The position becomes more complex when it comes to the common law. Although the prerogative preceded the existence of the common law, its existence is recognised by the common law and its extent is determined by the common law.[29] While there are many assertions that the prerogative cannot 'change any part of the common law',[30] they need to be read with a close understanding of the way in which the prerogative may operate.

As Wade observed, the 'prerogative consists of *legal* power—that is to say, the ability to alter people's rights, duties or status under the laws of this country which the courts of this country enforce'.[31] His test for a genuine prerogative power is one that is unique to the Crown and produces legal effects at common law.[32] While not all executive powers that are usually categorised as prerogative would fall within Wade's narrower test,[33] it is clear that many prerogative powers, if arguably not all, do have the capacity to affect the application of the law, including rights granted by law.

This does not always mean that the exercise of such powers will conflict with existing laws. The prerogative may create legal rights and obligations that supplement existing laws and are not inconsistent with them. In some cases, however, it is undeniable that the exercise of a prerogative power may have the effect of

---

[24] *Miller* (n 1), [122].

[25] From here on, this chapter will refer to the prerogative in its executive nature, excluding the judicial and legislative prerogatives from the discussion.

[26] *Case of Proclamations* (1610) 12 Co Rep 74; 77 ER 1352.

[27] Bill of Rights 1688. See also *Port of Portland Pty Ltd v Victoria* (2010) 242 CLR 348, [9]–[13] (French CJ, Gummow, Hayne, Heydon, Crennan, Kiefel and Bell JJ).

[28] *Miller* (n 1), [45].

[29] *Halsbury's Laws of England*, 4th edn (Reissue) vol 8(2) (1996) para 368; and S Payne, 'The Royal Prerogative' in M Sunkin and S Payne (eds), *The Nature of the Crown* (Oxford, Oxford University Press, 1999) 78–79 and 106–07.

[30] *Case of Proclamations* (n 26), 75; 1353: 'The King cannot change any part of the common law, nor create any offence by his proclamation, which was not an offence before, without Parliament'. See also *Bancoult* (n 23), [44] (Lord Hoffmann); *Miller* (n 4), [33]; *Miller* (n 1), [50].

[31] HWR Wade, *Constitutional Fundamentals* (London, Stevens & Sons, 1980) 46.

[32] HWR Wade, 'Procedure and Prerogative in Public Law' (1985) 101 *LQR* 180, 193.

[33] For criticism of the test as unduly narrow, see BV Harris, 'Replacement of the Royal Prerogative in New Zealand' (2009) 23 *New Zealand Universities Law Review* 285, 291–92.

altering legal rights or the manner in which laws apply. As Justice Gageler of the High Court of Australia has observed, an 'act done in the execution of a preroga- tive executive power is an act which is capable of interfering with legal rights of others'.[34]

To this extent it could be said that the prerogative does change the common law by altering its application in particular circumstances or in relation to particular people. However, the better view is that such an exercise of the prerogative does not involve the executive in 'changing' the common law,[35] for the prerogative itself forms part of the common law. Rather, it is a case of the common law accom- modating the exercise of prerogative power and adjusting conflicting rights and interests.[36] A court may, therefore, interpret an exercise of prerogative power as being incapable of affecting fundamental common law rights,[37] even though it may reduce or remove other common law rights of an individual.

A benign illustration of the effect of the prerogative on legal rights and duties is the appointment of a person as a judge, a Minister of the Crown or a royal commissioner. For example, Letters Patent that appoint a person to hold a royal commission ordinarily impose obligations upon that person to inquire and report. Letters Patent that appoint a judge may require the judge to reside within the jurisdiction, to execute the judicial office except when leave of absence is granted and not to engage in any other form of employment. More signifi- cantly, the conferral of the status of judge, Minister or royal commissioner on a person will result in that person's being the subject of duties imposed by statute or the common law, as well as the beneficiary of rights and powers. In such a case the prerogative affects the rights and duties of individuals but does not change the existing law.

A less benign example is the exercise of the prerogative to declare war, which has many serious legal effects upon the rights and duties of persons who by virtue of that act become 'enemy aliens'. Their property can be confiscated,[38] they may be interned[39] and they may lose their rights to sue in courts unless they are present

---

[34] *Plaintiff M68/2015 v Minister for Immigration and Border Protection* (2016) 257 CLR 42, [135] (Gageler J). See also L Zines, 'The inherent executive power of the Commonwealth' (2005) 16 *PLR* 279, 280; and J Stellios, *Zines's The High Court and the Constitution*, 6th edn, (Sydney, Federation Press, 2015) 374–75.

[35] *Miller* (n 1), [52].

[36] See, eg, the accommodation of the prerogative powers of the Crown and common law rights by the House of Lords in *Council of Civil Service Unions v Minister for the Civil Service* [1985] AC 374.

[37] *Campbell v Hall* (1774) 20 St Tr 239, 323. Note that while this case applied to the legislative form of the prerogative, there is no reason why it would not also apply to the executive form of the prerogative.

[38] *Porter v Freudenberg* [1915] 1 KB 857, 869–70.

[39] *R v Superintendent of Vine Street Police Station, ex parte Liebmann* [1916] 1 KB 268; *ex parte Weber* [1916] 1 AC 421; *R v Bottrill, ex parte Kuechenmeister* [1947] 1 KB 41. Note that the Aliens Restriction Act 1914 (UK) included an express preservation of the prerogative, and it was the prerogative, rather than the statute, that was initially relied upon to intern Germans and Austrians during World War I. See further P McDermott, 'Internment During the Great War—A Challenge to the Rule of Law' (2005) 28 *University of New South Wales Law Journal* 330.

in the country by permission of the Crown. Blackstone stated that 'alien-enemies have no rights, no privileges, unless by the king's special favour, during the time of war'.[40] Prerogatives also exist concerning the regulation of trade with the enemy, the requisitioning of British ships in times of urgent national necessity and the power to appropriate the property of citizens of neutral states within the realm during war when necessary.[41]

Another form of prerogative that significantly affects a person's common law rights, including his or her liberty, is the prerogative of mercy. In the UK, where it appears that a miscarriage of justice has occurred, a convicted person may be granted a free pardon or a conditional pardon. A free pardon releases the person from the effect of the sentence, entitling him or her to be released from prison. A conditional pardon substitutes a different type of sentence, such as life imprisonment in substitution for the death penalty.[42] The abolition of the death penalty in Britain, the expansion of rights of appeal and other statutory remedies have largely displaced the need for the exercise of this prerogative, but it remains an option where no statutory remedy is available.[43]

Other prerogatives that have the potential to affect the rights and duties of people include the prerogative to maintain the peace,[44] the grant and revocation of passports,[45] powers concerning civil servants,[46] such as those imposing security vetting, the employment of 'non-alien' citizens of Commonwealth countries and the freedom of speech of civil servants in relation to political or electoral matters, and prerogative powers with respect to the guardianship of infants and those with certain mental disorders.[47] Some of these prerogatives have been abrogated or regulated by legislation because of their significant impact upon the rights of people, but that simply shows that the prerogative has been, and in some cases can still be, exercised in a manner that affects the legal rights and duties of persons.

---

[40] Sir William Blackstone, *Commentaries on the Laws of England*, vol 1 (1st edn facsimile, 1765) 361. See also *Porter v Freudenberg* [1915] 1 KB 857, 869.

[41] UK, The Governance of Britain—Review of the Executive Royal Prerogative Powers: Final Report, October 2009, Annexure, 32.

[42] UK, House of Commons, Public Administration Select Committee, 'Taming the Prerogative': Strengthening Ministerial Accountability to Parliament, HC 422, March 2004, p 7; The Governance of Britain—Review of the Executive Royal Prerogative Powers: Final Report (n 41), 15–18.

[43] The Governance of Britain—Review of the Executive Royal Prerogative Powers: Final Report (n 41), 16.

[44] *R v Secretary of State for the Home Department; ex parte Northumbria Police Authority* [1989] QB 26; 'Taming the Prerogative' (n 42), 6; UK, The Governance of Britain—Review of the Executive Royal Prerogative Powers: Final Report (n 41), 26–27.

[45] Note the non-statutory rules that ministers routinely applied in exercising the prerogative to refuse a passport to persons: 'Taming the Prerogative' (n 42), Appendix 1, 28.

[46] See the list of such powers in The Governance of Britain—Review of the Executive Royal Prerogative Powers: Final Report (n 41), Annexure, 31.

[47] ibid, Annexure, 34.

The majority in *Miller* accepted that the 'fact that the exercise of prerogative powers cannot change the domestic law' does not mean that their exercise cannot 'affect the legal rights or duties of others' where this is 'inherent in the prerogative power'.[48] Their Lordships referred to the power of the Crown to alter the terms of service of civil servants and its power to destroy property in wartime in the interests of national defence. They concluded that while an 'exercise of the prerogative power in such cases may affect individual rights, the important point is that it does not change the law, because the law has always authorised the exercise of the power'.[49] By this, they presumably meant that the prerogative forms part of the law, rather than amounting to a change to it.

Their Lordships also accepted that exercises of the prerogative may change the facts to which the law applies, such as the status of persons, with the consequence that the law applies differently to them. They concluded that 'in such cases the exercise has not created or changed the law, merely the extent of its application'.[50]

The proposition that the prerogative cannot alter statute or common law or affect the rights and duties of persons is thus not an accurate one. It is clear from *Miller* that the Supreme Court continues to accept that an exercise of the prerogative may affect the rights and duties of people, and affect the application of the common law. The common law recognises the existence of the prerogative and the legitimacy of its exercise, including its effect upon the legal rights and interests of persons, which may have the consequence of diminishing the application of a person's common law rights. Whether this can be described as changing the common law, or whether it is better described as the common law recognising and accommodating the prerogative, is a matter of language rather than substance. It is nonetheless clear that while the common law may be affected by exercises of the prerogative, the prerogative cannot alter statute.

II. Treaties and the Prerogative

The UK and Australia both have dualist systems when it comes to the relationship between international law and domestic law. While the executive may sign and ratify treaties, they are not self-executing. Any rights and obligations within the treaty do not have force as part of domestic law unless given effect by statute.[51] This does not mean, however, that the prerogative act of entering into a treaty cannot have any legal effects within the nation concerned.

---

[48] *Miller* (n 1), [52].
[49] ibid.
[50] ibid, [53].
[51] Note Wade's argument that the power to enter into treaties is not a true prerogative because treaties cannot alter the law of the land: Wade (n 32), 193–94.

First, as a matter of statutory interpretation, there is a presumption recognised both in the UK[52] and Australia[53] that Parliament intends to comply with the nation's international obligations, and that laws should therefore be construed consistently with international obligations, where such a construction is permissible. Lord Diplock described the position as follows:

> If the terms of the legislation are clear and unambiguous, they must be given effect to, whether or not they carry out Her Majesty's treaty obligations, for the sovereign power of the Queen in Parliament extends to breaking treaties … But if the terms of the legislation are not clear but are reasonably capable of more than one meaning, the treaty itself becomes relevant, for there is a prima facie presumption that Parliament does not intend to act in breach of international law, including therein specific treaty obligations; and if one of the meanings which can reasonably be ascribed to the legislation is consonant with the treaty obligations and another or others are not, the meaning which is consonant is to be preferred.[54]

Second, international treaty obligations may influence the development of the common law by the courts,[55] particularly when it comes to the declaration of fundamental rights.[56] This may have a flow-on effect to the application of the principle of legality, to the extent that words of general application in a statute are not to be interpreted in a way that would override fundamental rights unless such an intention is expressed with irresistible clearness. As Lord Hoffmann observed, in 'the absence of express language or necessary implication to the contrary, the courts … presume that even the most general words were intended to be subject to the basic rights of the individual'.[57]

---

[52] *Salomon v Commissioners of Customs and Excise* [1967] 2 QB 116, 143; *Corocraft Ltd v Pan American Airways Inc* [1969] 1 QB 616, 653 (Lord Denning MR); *R v Secretary of State for the Home Department, ex parte Brind* [1991] 1 AC 696, 747–48 (Lord Bridge). This presumption, of course, cannot overcome express words in a statute to the contrary: *Collco Dealings Ltd v Inland Revenue Commissioners* [1962] AC 1, 18–19 (Viscount Simonds). See further FAR Bennion, *Bennion on Statutory Interpretation*, 5th edn (London, LexisNexis, 2008) 818–19.

[53] The High Court of Australia has accepted 'the proposition that courts should, in a case of ambiguity, favour a construction of a Commonwealth statute which accords with the obligations of Australia under an international treaty': *Chu Kheng Lim v Minister for Immigration* (1992) 176 CLR 1, 38. See also *Minister for Immigration and Ethnic Affairs v Teoh* (1995) 183 CLR 273, 286. See also, with respect to New Zealand, *New Zealand Airline Pilots' Association Inc v Attorney-General* [1997] 3 NZLR 269, 289 (Keith J).

[54] *Saloman* (n 52), 143 (Diplock LJ).

[55] *Derbyshire Council Council v Times Newspapers Ltd* [1992] 1 QB 770, 812 (Balcombe LJ); 819 (Ralph Gibson LJ); 830 (Butler-Sloss LJ). See also to the same effect Lord Bingham of Cornhill, UK HL Deb 3 July 1996, vol 573, col 1466.

[56] *Minister for Immigration and Ethnic Affairs v Teoh* (1995) 183 CLR 273, 288; *Mabo v Queensland (No 2)* (1992) 175 CLR 1, 42 (Brennan J). See also, with respect to New Zealand, *Takamore v Clarke* [2012] 1 NZLR 573, [240]–[242].

[57] *R v Secretary of State for the Home Department, ex parte Simms* [2000] 2 AC 115, 131 (Lord Hoffmann).

Third, in both the UK[58] and Australia,[59] the executive's ratification of a treaty may give rise to a legitimate expectation that the executive will comply with its treaty obligations and that its Ministers and officials will do so when making administrative decisions. At the very least, it may guide the exercise of administrative discretion, although decision makers are not under an obligation to exercise their discretionary powers in a manner that complies with unincorporated treaty obligations.[60]

Fourth, ratification of a treaty may give rights at international law to citizens within the ratifying country. For example, ratification of the First Optional Protocol to the International Covenant on Civil and Political Rights gives rise to a right on the part of citizens to make complaints to the UN Human Rights Committee about breaches of rights under the Covenant. This right arises through the prerogative act of ratification, without the need for any implementation at domestic law.

Fifth, ratification of a treaty may confer or alter a status that gives rise to immediate legal consequences without any alteration of domestic law. For example, where a treaty recognises a foreign government, this may give rights to that government with respect to property held by its predecessor government within the country,[61] or to other benefits such as immunity from suit. Ratification of 'a peace treaty will, without legislation, change the status of enemy aliens in [domestic] courts'.[62] The determination of land and maritime boundaries by treaty may also affect the validity of acts done within or without those boundaries.[63]

Lastly, where existing legislation gives effect to treaty obligations of a particular class, as they exist from time to time, the ratification of a treaty which contains obligations of that class will have the effect of triggering the application of the legislation, giving effect to those obligations, without the need for further legislative action unless the relevant statute so provides. Equally, if those treaty obligations cease to exist at a particular time then the legislation would no longer give effect to them, even though the legislation itself has not been altered.

---

[58] *R v Secretary of State for the Home Department, ex parte Ahmed* [1998] INLR 570, 583 (Lord Woolf MR); *R v Uxbridge Magistrates' Court, ex parte Adimi* [2001] QB 667, 686 (Simon Brown LJ). Note, however, that when Parliament has addressed the extent to which the treaty obligations are to be given effect, that 'determination having been made, it is the duty of the courts to give effect to it' and a legitimate expectation to the contrary cannot arise: *R v Asfaw (United Nations High Commissioner for Refugees intervening)* [2008] UKHL 31, [2008] 1 AC 1061, [30] (Lord Bingham) and [69] (Lord Hope).

[59] *Minister for Immigration and Ethnic Affairs v Teoh* (1995) 183 CLR 273, 291. But see the limitation of this principle in *Minister for Immigration and Multicultural Affairs, ex parte Lam* (2003) 214 CLR 1 and the Court's retreat from the doctrine of legitimate expectation in *Minister for Immigration and Border Protection v WZARH* (2015) 256 CLR 326.

[60] *R (Hurst) v London Northern District Coroner* [2007] UKHL 13, [2007] 2 AC 189, [56] (Lord Brown); *R v Secretary of State for the Home Department, ex parte Brind* [1991] 1 AC 696, 748 (Lord Bridge).

[61] *Bank of Ethiopia v National Bank of Egypt and Liguori* [1937] 1 Ch 513.

[62] *Lam* (n 59), 33 (McHugh and Gummow JJ), referring to *Porter v Freudenberg* [1915] 1 KB 857, 869–70.

[63] *Post Office v Estuary Radio Ltd* [1968] 2 QB 740; *Miller* (n 1), [53]. See further M Leeming, 'Federal Treaty Jurisdiction' (1999) 10 *Public Law Review* 173, 175.

For example, in Australia, the Australian Human Rights Commission Act 1986 (Cth) confers power on the Commission to inquire into acts or practices that are inconsistent with human rights recognised in certain international instruments, including treaties and declarations, and to seek to effect a settlement of the matter by conciliation. It only applies, however, to human rights contained in those international instruments to the extent that they apply to Australia.[64] Withdrawal from any of those international instruments would mean that they ceased to be human rights for the purposes of the Act. Addition of other international instruments may occur by way of a declaration made by the relevant Minister, in accordance with section 47 of the Act.

Similar examples have arisen in the UK with respect to matters such as extradition and double taxation, as noted by Finnis,[65] and most notably with respect to the implementation of EU treaties.[66] The critical question is the extent to which Parliament chooses to take control over how the application of the statute is triggered or negated. Parliament may choose to tie the application of its legislation to the mere fact that the treaty is operative with respect to the country, leaving this as a matter for the exercise of the prerogative in relation to the ratification and denunciation of treaties. Alternatively, it may choose to add further controls. These may include the delegation of legislative power to the executive to activate the application of the legislation to a treaty by way of an instrument that may be disallowed by either House of Parliament,[67] or which must receive the prior approval of a House by way of a resolution.[68] Parliament may also require the enactment of legislation to add or remove treaties to which the statute gives effect, or even to ratify a particular class of treaty, due to the effect of ratification on existing legislation.[69]

This is ultimately a matter for Parliament to decide in enacting its legislation. In *Miller*, the majority assumed that even though Parliament had taken express action to constrain the ratification of treaties without parliamentary authorisation and took no action to constrain withdrawal from treaties without parliamentary authorisation (despite contemplation of withdrawal evidenced by referenda in 1975 and 2016), there was still an unexpressed parliamentary intention that such a limitation should apply.[70] Lord Reed, on the other hand, took the view that Parliament is 'perfectly capable of making clear its intention to restrict the exercise of the prerogative when it wishes to do so', but in this case had not done so.[71]

---

[64] Australian Human Rights Commission Act 1986 (Cth), s 3(4).

[65] Finnis (n 19), 15–19.

[66] European Communities Act 1972 (UK), s 2.

[67] For example, this is how extradition treaties between Australia and other nations are given effect under the Extradition Act 1988 (Cth).

[68] Taxation (International and Other Provisions) Act 2010 (UK), s 5(2). See also *Miller* (n 1), [98].

[69] European Union (Amendment) Act 2008, s 5; and European Union Act 2011, s 2 (and note the additional referendum requirement in cases specified in s 4).

[70] *Miller* (n 1), [87] and [111].

[71] ibid, [205] and [212].

Apart from this dispute about the intention of Parliament, the majority also suggested that because the treaties, through the application of section 2 of the European Communities Act 1972, are a 'source of domestic law' and a 'source of domestic legal rights', the 'Royal prerogative to make and unmake treaties, which operates on the international plane, cannot be exercised in relation to the EU Treaties, at least in the absence of domestic sanction in appropriate statutory form'.[72] If this were to be taken as meaning that whenever a treaty is implemented by statute the executive cannot exercise a prerogative power to withdraw from the treaty without parliamentary authorisation, it would be a very controversial finding which is inconsistent with past practice, at least in relation to Australia, as noted in section III. The preferable view, however, is that this proposition must be regarded as confined to the special constitutional status of EU law as 'an independent and overriding source of domestic law',[73] as recognised by the majority of the Supreme Court, and that it is not a principle of general application.

III. Treaty-making Reform and Increasing Parliamentary Accountability

In the UK, Parliament has acted to oversee the ratification of treaties by giving legal effect to the Ponsonby Rule. Section 20 of the Constitutional Reform and Governance Act 2010 (UK) provides that, with some exceptions, a treaty is not to be ratified unless a copy of it has been laid before Parliament for a period of 21 sitting days and during that period neither House has resolved that it should not be ratified.[74] If the House of Lords alone votes against the ratification of the treaty, the Government may still proceed with its ratification, but the House of Commons may effectively block ratification through a protracted process of resolutions and government responses.[75] Similar reforms regarding the tabling of treaties in Parliament have taken place in New Zealand[76] and Canada,[77] although in

---

[72] ibid, [86].

[73] ibid, [65].

[74] Note that there are procedures for a Minister to override the resolution of a House in particular circumstances. Sections 22 and 23 provide that s 20 does not apply in exceptional cases or to certain categories of treaties, such as double taxation treaties and EU treaties, which are dealt with by separate legislative provisions.

[75] For a more detailed discussion, see A Lang, 'Parliament's Role in Ratifying Treaties', House of Commons Library, Briefing Paper, 17 February 2017, 10–16.

[76] In New Zealand, treaties and national interest analyses are tabled in accordance with Standing Order 397 and referred to the Foreign Affairs, Defence and Trade Committee of the House of Representatives. Any recommendations by the Committee are considered by the Government and a response is given within 60 days of the report: New Zealand, *International Treaty Making* (August 2017), 50–51, available at https://www.mfat.govt.nz/assets/Treaties/International-Treaty-Making-Guide-2017.pdf.

[77] The Canadian system was reformed in 2008. The Government committed to the tabling of treaties, accompanied by an explanatory memorandum, at least 21 sitting days before ratification. Exceptions apply in the case of urgency. The House of Commons may debate treaties and pass a motion

each case the executive retains the power to decide whether or not to proceed with ratification.

In Australia, the treaty-making system was the subject of a comprehensive review by a Senate Committee in 1995. As a consequence, a number of major changes were implemented. The Committee considered whether the prerogative power to ratify treaties should and could be controlled by Parliament. This raised issues concerning the application of the constitutional doctrine of the separation of powers in Australia. A former Solicitor-General, Sir Maurice Byers, contended that Parliament could regulate the manner in which the executive exercised its prerogative to enter into treaties, but that it could not take that power away from the executive or make its exercise conditional upon the prior approval of Parliament, as this would breach the constitutional separation of powers.[78]

Other constitutional experts, such as Professor George Winterton, disagreed, arguing that Parliament can always abrogate or control the exercise of the prerogative through the enactment of legislation.[79] Professor Enid Campbell considered that while Parliament could abrogate the prerogative or make its authorisation a condition precedent to the ratification of treaties, it was possible that the High Court would hold that Parliament could not invest itself or either of its Houses with the executive power to ratify treaties.[80] Henry Burmester, from the Commonwealth Attorney-General's Department, provided legal advice to the Committee that Parliament could not itself assume the executive power to conclude treaties but could enact legislation to regulate the exercise of the prerogative by the executive, including the requirement of parliamentary authorisation prior to ratification.[81]

The Committee noted that its other recommendations might, once implemented, be sufficient to avert the need for parliamentary approval of treaties. It therefore recommended that the issue be inquired into at a future time.[82] The Committee's other recommendations were largely implemented by the Commonwealth in a major reform package in 1996. They included parliamentary involvement in treaty action through a dedicated parliamentary committee, the Joint Standing Committee on Treaties. It reviews the case for ratifying treaties before the Government takes action to do so. As part of that process the Government

---

recommending actions, but it remains a matter for the executive to decide whether to enter into the treaty: Canada, 'Policy on Tabling of Treaties in Parliament', available at http://www.treaty-accord. gc.ca/procedures.aspx; and Canada, Library of Parliament, *Canada's Approach to the Treaty-Making Process* (Background Paper, November 2012) 3.

[78] Australia, Senate Legal and Constitutional References Committee, *Trick or Treaty? Commonwealth Power to Make and Implement Treaties*, November 1995, 275.

[79] ibid, 275–76.

[80] ibid, 276.

[81] ibid, 278.

[82] ibid, 299.

committed to tabling a 'national interest analysis' with respect to each treaty, which sets out the advantages and disadvantages of ratifying the treaty. It includes 'discussion of the foreseeable economic, environmental, social and cultural effects of the treaty action; the obligations imposed by the treaty; its direct financial costs to Australia; how the treaty will be implemented domestically; what consultation has occurred in relation to the treaty action and whether the treaty provides for withdrawal or denunciation'.[83]

The Joint Standing Committee on Treaties also considers the withdrawal from treaties, and a national interest analysis is tabled in relation to any act of denunciation of a treaty.[84] Even when the treaty proposed to be denounced had been given effect by legislation, denunciation still occurred by way of prerogative act without the need for legislative authorisation of the denunciation,[85] although legislation was enacted to give effect to a new legislative scheme to replace the one that had implemented the denounced treaty.[86]

In 2012, a Treaties Ratification Bill 2012 was introduced in the Commonwealth Parliament. It had one substantive provision, which stated that 'The Governor-General must not ratify a treaty unless both Houses of the Parliament have, by resolution, approved the ratification.' The Private Member who introduced the Bill argued that treaties have a direct and serious impact upon people, such as costing them their jobs, and that they should only be entered into after a proper debate in Parliament.[87] The Bill was not passed. The Joint Standing Committee on Treaties again considered the issue of the extent to which Parliament could control or assume the exercise of the prerogative with respect to treaties. While doubts remained about whether Parliament itself could exercise the power of ratifying a treaty, the Committee accepted advice that Parliament could legislate to require parliamentary approval prior to the ratification of treaties by the executive.[88]

The Committee identified fundamental political problems in the requirement that treaties be approved by both Houses before ratification. It noted evidence that the Government rarely has control over the Upper House, and that such a proposal would take control of a significant part of Australia's foreign policy out

---

[83] Australia, Department of Foreign Affairs and Trade, 'Treaty making process', available at http://dfat.gov.au/international-relations/treaties/treaty-making-process/Pages/treaty-making-process.aspx#constitution.

[84] See, eg, Australia, Joint Standing Committee on Treaties, 'Australia's Denunciation of the Convention Relating to International Exhibitions and Protocol of Signature', *Report 155*, August 2015, ch 2.

[85] Australia, Joint Standing Committee on Treaties, 'Denunciation of the Convention on Damage Caused by Foreign Aircraft to Third Parties on the Surface', *Report 30*, April 2000, ch 5.

[86] See the Damage by Aircraft Act 1999 (Cth), which replaced the Civil Aviation (Damage to Aircraft) Act 1958 (Cth).

[87] Australia, HR Deb 13 February 2012, pp 801–02 (Mr Katter).

[88] Australia, Joint Standing Committee on Treaties, 'Inquiry into the Treaties Ratification Bill 2012, *Report 128*, August 2012, 18.

of the hands of the executive and place it in the hands of whoever held the balance of power in the Senate. This would potentially leave the Government hamstrung in its ability to conduct a consistent and effective foreign policy and undermine its position in negotiating treaties.[89] A similar point was made by Lord Reed in *Miller*, where he referred to Blackstone's observation that the power to make treaties is 'wisely placed in a single hand ... for the sake of unanimity, strength and despatch', and noted that the value of unanimity, strength and dispatch is as evident in the twenty-first century as in the eighteenth.[90]

Lastly, the Committee appeared to consider that the democratic deficit in relation to treaties was adequately addressed by the scrutiny of treaties, prior to their ratification, through the parliamentary committee system, and that the formal approval of each House of Parliament was unnecessary.[91] It recommended that the Bill not be passed due to the practical and political difficulties it would pose. A subsequent inquiry by a Senate Committee also recommended against a statutory requirement of parliamentary approval of treaty action,[92] but did advocate greater involvement of Parliament, particularly during the negotiation stage of treaties.[93]

One significant difference between Australia and the UK is that the ratification of a treaty by Australia can have a direct constitutional effect due to the federal system. The Commonwealth Parliament may only legislate with respect to a limited number of subjects set out in the Commonwealth Constitution. One of those powers is the power in section 51(xxix) of the Constitution to make laws with respect to external affairs. The High Court has held that section 51(xxix) confers power on the Commonwealth Parliament to enact laws that implement *bona fide* treaties to which Australia is a party, even though the subject matter of the law would not otherwise be supported by a Commonwealth head of legislative power.[94]

This leads to a particularly interesting issue in the light of *Miller*. If the Commonwealth Parliament has enacted a law that implements obligations under a treaty to which Australia is a party and the Commonwealth has no head of power to support the law other than the external affairs power, then if the Commonwealth were to withdraw from that treaty, the law giving effect to it would cease to be a valid law. The Commonwealth's prerogative act of withdrawal from the treaty would have the effect of terminating the validity of a law enacted by Parliament.

---

[89] ibid, 21–22. Note that the Constitutional Commission in 1988 had rejected a similar proposal for the same reason: Constitutional Commission, *Final Report of the Constitutional Commission* (Canberra, AGPS, 1988) vol 2, 745.

[90] *Miller* (n 1), [160] (Lord Reed).

[91] Australia, Joint Standing Committee on Treaties (n 88), 15.

[92] Australia, Senate, Foreign Affairs, Defence and Trade References Committee, *Blind agreement: reforming Australia's treaty-making process*, June 2015, 27–28.

[93] ibid, 71–76.

[94] *Commonwealth v Tasmania* (1983) 158 CLR 1.

This would be the case not only when the statute gave effect to treaty obligations as they existed from time to time, but also when the statute gave substantive and enduring rights that were not ambulatory in nature.

If the reasoning in *Miller* turns upon the proposition that a prerogative act cannot cause the termination of rights granted under a statute and cannot alter the law by terminating the validity of a statute, then if it were to be followed in Australia it could have significant consequences. It would mean that the executive would not have the capacity to withdraw from a treaty without parliamentary authorisation when any statute that implemented the treaty found its sole source of legislative power in the implementation of a treaty under section 51(xxix) of the Constitution. This is a surprising notion which has never seriously been contemplated in Australia before. As the denunciation of or withdrawal from treaties is a relatively rare event, the issue has not been tested before the Australian courts, but it is doubtful that they would take a similar approach to that in *Miller*, given that the executive has long had a recognised capacity to expand Commonwealth legislative power through the prerogative act of the ratification of treaties, and that the contraction of that power is likely to be treated in the same fashion.

As noted above, when the Commonwealth denounced the *Convention on Damage Caused by Foreign Aircraft to Third Parties on the Surface*, which had been given effect by the Civil Aviation (Damage to Aircraft) Act 1958 (Cth),[95] it enacted the Damage by Aircraft Act 1999 (Cth) to implement a new set of standards, but did not legislate to authorise the denunciation.[96] As the Damage by Aircraft Act 1999 (Cth) could not rely on the implementation of a treaty under section 51(xxix) of the Constitution as its constitutional source of power, it instead relied upon a patchwork of other heads of powers, including those with respect to overseas and interstate trade and commerce, corporations, Australia's territories and designated Commonwealth places, such as airports.[97] The prerogative act of denouncing the Convention would have had the effect of rendering invalid Part 2 of the Civil Aviation (Damage to Aircraft) Act 1958 (Cth), but Parliament legislated to repeal and replace the entirety of the Act with new legislation, just as the Westminster Parliament will no doubt do through its Great Repeal legislation. No question arose in Australia as to whether the executive was constitutionally impeded from exercising its prerogative power to denounce the Convention in this case.

---

[95] Section 8 stated that the 'provisions of the Convention have the force of law in Australia': Civil Aviation (Damage to Aircraft) Act 1958 (Cth). Part 2 of the Act relied solely on the implementation of the Convention for its constitutional support. Part 3, which dealt with 'other damage', relied on a patchwork of other constitutional powers.

[96] Commencement of the Act was qualified by the requirement that it could only happen after denunciation of the treaty took effect: Damage by Aircraft Act 1999 (Cth), s 2.

[97] Damage by Aircraft Act 1999 (Cth), s 9.

IV. *Miller*—A Constitutional, Rather Than a Legal, Outcome

The critical difference between the Australian example and that arising in *Miller* is the much greater significance of withdrawal from the EU. In *Miller*, the judgment seemed to turn neither on a finding that the prerogative cannot be used to diminish legal rights or affect the application of existing laws, nor on a finding that the executive cannot withdraw from a treaty, which has been implemented by legislation, without statutory authorisation. The key determinative factor in *Miller* was the constitutional effect of withdrawal, as opposed to the ordinary application of legal rules concerning the prerogative and treaties.

The majority regarded withdrawal as amounting to 'a unilateral action' that 'effects a fundamental change in the constitutional arrangements of the United Kingdom'.[98] Their Lordships concluded:

> A complete withdrawal represents a change which is different not just in degree but in kind from the abrogation of particular rights, duties or rules derived from EU law. It will constitute as significant a constitutional change as that which occurred when EU law was first incorporated in domestic law by the 1972 Act ... It would be inconsistent with long-standing and fundamental principle for such a far-reaching change to the UK constitutional arrangements to be brought about by ministerial decision or ministerial action alone.[99]

This makes it clear that the majority were relying on their view of 'fundamental principle' rather than legal requirements. Their Lordships confirmed this when they stated:

> We cannot accept that a major change to UK constitutional arrangements can be achieved by a ministers [*sic*] alone; it must be effected in the only way that the UK constitution recognises, namely by Parliamentary legislation. This conclusion appears to us to follow from the ordinary application of basic concepts of constitutional law to the present issue.[100]

The outcome of the case therefore turned on a political understanding of the nature of the constitution of the UK and how major change should be effected. It was not a strictly legal issue but one that is constitutional in the broader sense of the term.[101] It would therefore be possible to confine *Miller* to the singular and

---

[98] *Miller* (n 1), [78].

[99] ibid, [81].

[100] ibid, [82]. See also the reference at [100] to the 'constitutional propriety of prior Parliamentary sanction for the process'.

[101] In Australia, what is 'constitutional' is what is legally valid under an entrenched written constitution. In the UK, the notion of what is 'constitutional' is much broader, incorporating convention, custom, principle and political understandings of the nature of the state.

exceptional nature of the method of implementing EU law in the UK and with-drawal from it. It ought not, therefore, necessarily affect the extent of the Crown's prerogative powers in other circumstances, although whether its effect will be thus confined remains to be seen.

V. The Value in Retaining the Prerogative

In the UK the prerogative is often looked upon as 'anachronistic',[102] a 'relic of a past age',[103] undemocratic[104] and in need of taming.[105] It has been argued that the prerogative has been used 'as a smoke-screen by ministers to obfuscate the use of power for which they are insufficiently accountable'.[106] Concern about the lack of accountability of the exercise of prerogative power in the UK was reflected in a series of reports culminating in a Green Paper[107] and a White Paper.[108] In the former it was stated:

> The Government believes that in general the prerogative powers should be put onto a statutory basis and brought under stronger parliamentary scrutiny and control. This will ensure that government is more clearly subject to the mandate of the people's representatives.[109]

Yet the prerogative is almost always[110] exercised by, or on the advice of, repre-sentatives of the people, being Ministers who sit in Parliament and are responsible to it.[111] Moreover, Parliament can act at any time to abrogate the prerogative or control it.

From an outsider's point of view, the argument about whether notification of withdrawal from the EU would proceed under the prerogative or with parliamen-tary approval seemed to be artificial and overblown, as at any time before or after the referendum Parliament could have legislated to remove this prerogative from

---

[102] *Bancoult* (n 23), [69] (Lord Bingham), although in reference to the legislative prerogative, rather than the executive prerogative. Compare the observation by the majority in *Miller* that the prerogative is not 'anomalous or anachronistic': *Miller* (n 1), [49].

[103] *Burmah Oil Company (Burma Trading) Ltd v The Lord Advocate* [1965] AC 75, 115 (Lord Reid).

[104] See, eg, the statement by Jeremy Corbyn that as 'a democrat, I object to all Orders in Council': UK, HC Deb 23 April 2009, vol 491, col 165WH.

[105] 'Taming the Prerogative' (n 42).

[106] J Straw, 'Abolish the Royal Prerogative' in A Barnett (ed), *Power and the Throne: The Monarchy Debate* (London, Vintage, 1994) 125, 129.

[107] UK, Ministry of Justice, *The Governance of Britain*, Cm 7170, July 2007.

[108] UK, Ministry of Justice, *The Governance of Britain—Constitutional Renewal*, Cm 7342, March 2008.

[109] *The Governance of Britain*, Cm 7170 (n 107), 17–18.

[110] In some rare cases the Queen may exercise personal prerogatives without advice. See further A Twomey, *The Veiled Sceptre: Reserve Powers of Heads of State in Westminster Systems* (Cambridge, Cambridge University Press, 2018).

[111] Note, however, the criticism that such accountability usually occurs after the event: 'Taming the Prerogative' (n 42), 8.

Ministers if it had objected to their proposed course of action.[112] It is hard to see how there is a democratic deficit in the exercise of the prerogative if it is exercised by Ministers who remain responsible to, and retain the confidence of, the House of Commons, and if Parliament chooses not to act to constrain a well-forecasted exercise of the prerogative.[113] This is reinforced by the facts that (i) withdrawal from the EU had been supported by a majority of the people in a referendum, and (ii) once the Supreme Court held that parliamentary authorisation was required, such authorisation was readily given.

There are, nonetheless, advantages in replacing or regulating the exercise of some prerogative powers with statutes. One of the major difficulties with prerogative powers is uncertainty as to their existence and scope. As Brazier has noted, 'Government should not have imprecise powers'.[114] Prerogative powers are, by definition, residual powers that find their source in historical exercises of royal power.[115] There are difficulties in determining whether certain prerogatives still exist and, if so, their extent. This is done by the courts, drawing upon history and precedent. Nonetheless, in many cases there is no existing or recent judicial authority concerning an asserted prerogative power, and the historical record of its existence and use is at best inadequate.[116]

While many exercises of the prerogative are now regarded as being subject to judicial review,[117] there is difficulty in exercising such a review where there is uncertainty as to the full extent of the prerogative power. If a prerogative is replaced by the delegation of power to the executive by statute, the exercise of this power is limited by the terms of the statutory delegation. This provides greater certainty and permits more effective judicial review, as the exercise of a delegated statutory power can be readily challenged if it is *ultra vires*. As Evans has noted, 'the exercise of powers under statute is susceptible to more effective channels of judicial review than the exercise of prerogative powers'.[118]

---

[112] There would, however, have been procedural difficulties in a Private Member's Bill on the subject coming to a vote, and doing so within a reasonable time. This is due to Government control over the business of the House.

[113] Note, in contrast, the contention in *Miller* that ministerial exercise of the prerogative pre-empts parliamentary action: *Miller* (n 1), [92]. But in this case it also reflected the subsequent parliamentary action. The position might have been different if an equivalent situation had arisen in Australia, because the democratically elected Senate, which is usually not controlled by the Government, could have legitimately blocked any such legislation. Such an argument concerning mandates and democratic deficits is more difficult to run in relation to an appointed Upper House, the House of Lords, especially in the face of a referendum vote by the people and the passage of a bill by the House of Commons.

[114] 'Taming the Prerogative' (n 42), Appendix 1, Paper by Rodney Brazier, 24.

[115] Dicey (n 6), 424–25.

[116] See The Governance of Britain—Review of the Executive Royal Prerogative Powers: Final Report (n 41), 7.

[117] Most are reviewable, but some are non-justiciable. See further *Council of Civil Service Unions v Minister for the Civil Service* [1985] AC 374, 418 (Lord Roskill); *R (Bancoult) v Secretary of State for Foreign and Commonwealth Affairs (No 2)* [2007] EWCA Civ 498, [2008] QB 365, 399 (Sedley LJ); and *Bancoult* (n 23).

[118] S Evans, 'The Rule of Law, Constitutionalism and the MV Tampa' (2002) 13 *Public Law Review* 94, 99.

This is particularly significant where the exercise of a prerogative has the potential to intimately affect the rights of individuals, such as the prerogative concerning the establishment and operation of the Civil Service. Placing the Civil Service on a statutory footing has increased the opportunity for judicial review in relation to the employment contracts of civil servants.[119] The Employment Appeals Tribunal has held that section 10 of the Constitutional Reform and Governance Act 2010 (UK) now 'occupies the ground leaving no residual power or discretion' to appoint persons to the Civil Service.[120]

Some prerogative powers, such as the archaic power to 'impress men into the Royal Navy'[121] or the controversial power to exclude or prevent aliens from entering the country without permission,[122] have such direct and serious effects upon the human rights of individuals that they ought to be abrogated by legislation and, where appropriate, replaced by statutory powers that have been the subject of parliamentary debate and scrutiny.

There are other prerogatives, however, that are inherently political in nature and need to be undertaken in a decisive and unreviewable manner. Codification of all prerogative powers, giving them a statutory basis, would not be wise.[123] Even the majority in *Miller* conceded that some prerogative powers, such as those involved in 'the conduct of diplomacy and war, are by their very nature at least normally best reserved to ministers just as much in modern times as in the past'.[124] Some discernment therefore needs to be exercised in identifying those prerogatives that require a statutory basis and regulation and those best left to executive discretion. If Parliament were to legislate to authorise the executive to enter into treaties, or the Queen to appoint or dismiss the Prime Minister, then this would most likely make justiciable the question of whether or not the exercise of the power was within power, which would be inappropriate and potentially damaging to the conduct of foreign policy or the stability of government.

In some countries, for example, the prerogative to appoint and remove the Prime Minister has been controlled by legislation, which provides that the head of state shall appoint as chief minister the member of the Lower House of Parliament best able to command the confidence of a majority of the members of that House.[125]

---

[119] *Secretary of State for Justice v Betts* UKEAT/0284/16/DA. See also G Bartlett and M Everett, 'The Royal Prerogative' UK House of Commons Library Briefing Paper, 17 August 2017, 13, referring to legal proceedings in the Employment Appeals Tribunal in April 2017.

[120] *Secretary of State for Justice v Betts* UKEAT/0284/16/DA, [44].

[121] *The Governance of Britain*, Cm 7170 (n 107), 23; and The Governance of Britain—Review of the Executive Royal Prerogative Powers: Final Report (n 41), 34.

[122] See *Ruddock v Vadarlis* [2001] 110 FCR 491, [197] (French J, Beaumont J agreeing), where it was held by a majority of the Federal Court of Australia that absent statutory abrogation there was an executive power to bar entry by a vessel to an Australian port and to restrain a person or boat from proceeding into Australia or to compel it to leave. Note, however, the strong dissent by Black CJ, arguing at [29] that 'it is, at best, doubtful that the asserted prerogative continues to exist at common law'.

[123] See the discussion of codification in UK, House of Commons, Political and Constitutional Reform Committee, *Role and Powers of the Prime Minister* (HC June 2014, 351, 10–12).

[124] *Miller* (n 1), [49].

[125] See, eg, the Constitutions of Barbados (s 65), Jamaica (s 70), Malta (art 80) and Mauritius (s 59).

Others have done away with the prerogative of appointment altogether, replacing it with a vote by Parliament.[126] Some countries also have prescriptive provisions concerning when the Prime Minister may be or shall be dismissed from office.[127] This can lead to destabilising litigation about who is validly Prime Minister,[128] with the result swinging from one outcome to another as the case is appealed over months or years to higher courts,[129] or with two persons purporting to fulfil the function of Prime Minister at the same time.[130] When it comes to the appointment and dismissal of the head of government, the flexibility of convention and accountability through political processes, such as votes in Parliament or at elections, are preferable to prescriptive legislative regulation and judicial review.

The same is true in relation to the declaration of war and the deployment of troops. In 2016, the then UK Secretary of State for Defence, Michael Fallon, recognised the development of a convention that before troops were committed to conflict situations, the House of Commons should have an opportunity to debate the matter, except where there was an emergency and such action would not be appropriate. He noted that in observing the convention, it was important to ensure that the Armed Forces could act quickly and decisively, and that the security of their operations was not compromised. He concluded by noting that the Government had decided that it would not codify the convention in law or by resolution of the House because of the need to protect the security and interests of the UK in unpredictable circumstances, and 'to avoid such decisions becoming subject to legal action'.[131]

There is also the risk that a statutory power may not be sufficiently flexible to deal with the circumstances of an emergency. In the UK, there is statutory support for the exercise of emergency powers in the Civil Contingencies Act 2004 (UK).

---

[126] See, eg, the Constitutions of the Solomon Islands (s 33), Tuvalu (s 63) and Vanuatu (art 41).

[127] See, eg, the Constitutions of Papua New Guinea (s 142), Singapore (art 26) and the Solomon Islands (s 34).

[128] See, eg, *Stephen Kalong Ningkan v Tun Abang Haji Openg & Tawi Sli* [1966] 2 MLJ 187 regarding the dismissal and restoration of the chief minister of Sarawak, Malaysia, and the complex litigation in Vanuatu concerning who validly held office as Prime Minister: *Kilman v Speaker of Parliament of the Republic of Vanuatu* [2011] VUCA 15; *Natapei v Korman* [2011] VUSC 72; and *Kilman v Natapei* [2012] 1 LRC 726.

[129] See, eg, the challenge to the dismissal of the Premier of Western Nigeria in 1962. The Federal Supreme Court held that he had been invalidly dismissed (*Akintola v Aderemi and Adegbenro* [1962] 1 All NLR 442). He was later restored to office and won votes of confidence in the legislature. Then, just over a year after his 'invalid' dismissal occurred, the Privy Council held that he had in fact been validly dismissed (*Adegbenro v Akintola and Aderemi* [1963] AC 614), leading to the enactment of a constitutional amendment, which applied with retrospective effect to invalidate his original dismissal.

[130] See, eg, the litigation concerning the vacation of the office of Sir Michael Somare as Prime Minister of Papua New Guinea and the resulting crisis, in which the courts recognised Somare as the Prime Minister and the Parliament recognised Peter O'Neill as the Prime Minister: *Supreme Court Reference No 3 of 2011: Reference by the East Sepik Provincial Executive* [2011] PGSC 41; and *Supreme Court References No 1 and No 2 of 2012: Special References by Allan Marat and the National Parliament* [2012] PGSC 20.

[131] 'Armed Forces Update', Written statement, HCWS678, 18 April 2016.

It has been argued that the existence of this legislative framework does not mean that the prerogative to deal with emergencies has been abrogated and that it may still operate outside that framework. The Ministry of Justice, in its review of prerogative powers, observed that enacting a statutory power to replace the prerogative power to deal with emergencies 'could result in either an undesirably broad statutory power or one that is insufficiently flexible'.[132] Moreover, if action needed to be taken immediately, such as dealing with a terrorist or hostage incident, and it was not possible to make the necessary regulations under the Act in time, the prerogative might still need to be employed.[133] It has the advantage of speed of execution, as well as flexibility to deal with any crisis. In 2009, the British Government took the view that as there is 'no higher duty on a Government than that to guarantee the safety and security of its citizens', the prerogative to deal with emergencies should be retained.[134]

VI. Conclusion

While the Supreme Court in *Miller* dealt with broad issues concerning the interaction of the prerogative with statute and its potential effect on rights, the outcome turned on the unique issue of the constitutional status of the integration of EU law into UK domestic law—a constitutional status that is unlikely to be replicated in the future. The Court did not otherwise limit the application of the prerogative, although the impression that it did so abounds. The case also added to the public impression that the prerogative is an 'ancient secretive' power[135] that lacks democratic legitimacy and must be tamed by Parliament. There remains, however, a legitimate role for the prerogative, including in the ratification of and withdrawal from treaties.

---

[132] The Governance of Britain—Review of the Executive Royal Prerogative Powers: Final Report (n 41), 27–28.

[133] ibid, 20.

[134] ibid, 21.

[135] T Endicott, 'Parliament and the Prerogative: From the *Case of Proclamations* to *Miller*', *Judicial Power Project*, 1 December 2016, quoting Gina Miller, available at http://judicialpowerproject.org.uk/wp-content/uploads/2016/12/Endicott-2016-Parliament-and-the-Prerogative.pdf.

4

Miller, Treaty Making and the Rights of Subjects

EIRIK BJORGE

The argument of the present chapter is that the ratio of *Miller*[1] is an affirmation of the principle that the prerogative—whether the treaty-making aspect of it or any other—cannot be relied on to affect or infringe the legal rights of individuals. The international law aspect of *Miller* concerns, in the first instance, the relationship between treaties and UK law, and therefore also the power to make and unmake treaties, as well as the attendant effect or otherwise in domestic law of this treaty making and unmaking. It is accepted by all that the treaty-making power rests in the Crown, and that, when ministers negotiate and sign a treaty, they do so exercising the prerogative of the Crown.[2] *Miller* demarcates the constitutional bounds of this power of the Crown as regards the power of the executive to unmake treaties. The limits of that power were a matter of some academic contestation until the Supreme Court handed down its judgment. Indeed, both before and after the Supreme Court's judgment in *Miller*, some commentators argued along the lines that 'the claim that the prerogative cannot be used to deprive people of rights, either absolutely or conditionally, is untenable as a matter of law',[3] and that one might have expected that the Supreme Court would have concluded that 'the prerogative could, unless limited by statute, be used to restrict or remove' the rights of individuals.[4]

As *Miller* makes clear, however, the claim that is untenable is rather the claim that the foreign affairs prerogative *could* be used to deprive individuals of legal rights, which was a view put forward both before and after the judgment by other commentators.[5]

---

[1] *R (on the application of Miller) v Secretary of State for Exiting the European Union* [2017] UKSC 5, [2017] 2 WLR 583.

[2] *Blackburn v Attorney-General* [1971] 1 WLR 1037, 1040; M Elliott, 'The Supreme Court's Judgment in *Miller*: In Search of Constitutional Principle' (2017) 76 *CLJ* 257, 260.

[3] D Feldman, 'Brexit, the Royal prerogative, and Parliamentary sovereignty', *UKCLA Blog* (8 November 2016), available at https:/ukconstitutionallaw.org/.

[4] D Feldman, 'Pulling a Trigger or Starting a Journey? Brexit in the Supreme Court' (2017) 76 *CLJ* 217, 220.

[5] See, eg, C McLachlan, 'The Foreign Affairs Treaty Prerogative and the Law of the Land', *UKCLA Blog* (14 November 2016), available at https:/ukconstitutionallaw.org/; C McLachlan, 'The Foreign Relations Power in the Supreme Court' (2018) 134 *LQR* (forthcoming).

The proposition that the prerogative can be used to deprive people of rights, whether absolutely or conditionally, was not supported by any of the Justices in the case: '[i]t garnered no support at all in the Supreme Court'.[6] For, instead of acceding to such a line of argument, the Justices in the minority took their stand on the conditional way in which the European Communities Act 1972 ('ECA') operated to incorporate European Union (EU) law into UK law 'from time to time'.

Miller affirms the positive function of dualism by confirming that, within the separation of powers, only Parliament can take away legal rights; the underlying principle operates with a view to 'protecting the individual from executive power, which is its real justification'.[7] The protection of the rights of individuals is thus at the heart of the underlying reasoning. The fact that the EU rights brought into UK law through the ECA could vary from time to time, and that this would cease when the UK withdrew from the EU, meant that withdrawal, with its attendant impact on rights, could not be effected through the prerogative without parliamentary authorisation.[8] The central role played by the rights of individuals is evident from the following passage in the judgment:

> While the consequential loss of a source of law is a fundamental legal change which justifies the conclusion that prerogative powers cannot be invoked to withdraw from the EU Treaties, the Divisional Court was also right to hold that changes in domestic rights acquired through that source as summarised in para 70 above, represent another, albeit related, ground for justifying that conclusion. Indeed, the consequences of withdrawal go further than affecting rights acquired pursuant to section 2 of the 1972 Act ... More centrally, ..., section 2 of that Act envisages domestic law, and therefore rights of UK citizens, changing as EU law varies, but it does not envisage those rights changing as a result of ministers unilaterally deciding that the United Kingdom should withdraw from the EU Treaties.[9]

In relation to the particular question of the relationship between domestic and international law, *Miller* speaks with two tongues, in so far as it could be thought to say one thing by way of obiter dicta in the introductory passages of the judgment, and another in its ratio. It is well known that 'the only part of a previous case which is binding is the *ratio decidenci*'.[10] A question as important as whether there are circumstances in which unincorporated treaty obligations can be part of English law is not likely to be decided by a side-wind: it will be decided in a case where that determination is necessary for the outcome of the case, until which time it cannot be taken to have been definitively settled.

---

[6] McLachlan (n 5).

[7] ibid, referring to *R (SG) v Secretary of State for Work and Pensions* [2015] UKSC 16, [2015] 1 WLR 1449, [255] (Lord Kerr) and *R v McKerr* [2004] UKHL 12, [2004] 1 WLR 807, [52] (Lord Steyn).

[8] P Craig, '*Miller*, Structural Constitutional Review and the Limits of Prerogative Power' [2017] *PL* 48.

[9] *Miller* (n 1), [83].

[10] R Cross and JW Harris, *Precedent in English Law*, 4th edn (Oxford, Oxford University Press, 1991) 39. See also Sir W Holdsworth, *Essays in Law and History* (Oxford, Clarendon Press, 1946) 158; *Close v Steel Company of Wales Ltd* [1962] AC 367, 388–89 (Lord Denning); F Pollock, 'Introduction' in J Drake and others (eds), *The Progress of Continental Law in the Nineteenth Century* (Boston, MA, Little, Brown & Co, 1918) xliv; *Quinn v Leathem* [1901] AC 495, 506 (Earl of Halsbury LC).

I. Frontispiece

Under the heading 'The Royal prerogative and Treaties', the majority of the Supreme Court in *Miller* set out in a number of important obiter statements what the Justices took to be the backdrop to the questions that fell to be settled in the case before the Court. It would be wrong to see these statements as bereft of judicial weight simply because of their obiter nature: but it would also be wrong to see them as in some way being the last word on the many questions on which they touch but which the judgment did not definitively settle, as they were not questions on which the factual matrix of the case required the Supreme Court to adjudicate. These paragraphs are, as one jurist once observed in relation to a similarly impressive set of prefatory remarks in a landmark judgment in another field of law, a feat of doctrinal exposition, and thus an impressive and fitting 'frontispiece'[11] to the actual holding in the judgment.

The result is a number of propositions that are pitched at a relatively high level of generality. They are clarifying and useful statements of the law as far as they go. But, owing to their nature, they do not definitively settle the questions on which they touch and therefore, to an even higher degree than the parts of the judgment that definitively settle the questions that were actually at bar, lend themselves to several different readings.

The first such proposition is the first part of the paragraphs dealing with the Royal prerogative and treaties, where the majority cite with approbation the first edition of what would become known as Wade and Forsyth on *Administrative Law*, to the effect that

> the residual prerogative is now confined to such matters as summoning and dissolving Parliament, declaring war and peace, regulating the armed forces in some respects, governing certain colonial territories, making treaties (though as such they cannot affect the rights of subjects), and conferring honours. The one drastic internal power of an administrative kind is the power to intern enemy aliens in time of war.[12]

For the purposes of the Royal prerogative and treaties, the germane part of the passage is that, by operation of the Royal prerogative, 'making treaties (though as such they cannot affect the rights of subjects)' remains one of the activities entrusted to the executive. It is worth noting that the passage cited by the Supreme Court was introduced by the words, 'In the seventeenth century the Crown lost most of its *powers of oppressing the subject*':[13] the broader framework of the development of reining in prerogative powers over time is one that operates to protect the subject

---

[11] F de Visscher, 'L'arbitrage de l'Île de Palmas' (1929) 10 *Revue du droit international et de législation comparée* 735, 738.

[12] HWR Wade, *Administrative Law* (Oxford, Oxford University Press, 1961) 13; *Miller* (n 1), [47] and [48] (emphasis added).

[13] Wade (n 12), 13 (emphasis added).

vis-à-vis the Crown. Given that the statements pertaining to the Royal prerogative and treaty making are prefatory only, it is not surprising that the Supreme Court did not go into any detail as to why it is that Wade added that treaties 'as such ... cannot affect the rights of subjects'.

The majority went on to observe that, consistently with the passage quoted from Wade, 'it is a fundamental principle of the UK constitution that, unless primary legislation permits it, the Royal prerogative does not enable ministers to change statute law or common law',[14] adding that Lord Hoffmann observed in *Bancoult* that 'since the 17th century the prerogative has not empowered the Crown to change English common or statute law'.[15]

The majority then observed that the 'most significant area in which ministers exercise the Royal prerogative is the conduct of the United Kingdom's foreign affairs. This includes diplomatic relations, the deployment of armed forces abroad, and, particularly in point for present purposes, the making of treaties'.[16] It pointed out that the case law on the power to terminate or withdraw from treaties was scant 'but, as a matter of both logic and practical necessity, it must be part of the treaty-making prerogative'.[17] The majority also cited Lord Templeman's words in *Tin Council*, according to which '[t]he Government may negotiate, conclude, construe, observe, breach, repudiate or terminate a treaty'.[18]

The Supreme Court was clear that, as a matter of both logical and practical necessity, the power to make treaties is mirrored by the power to unmake them, such that the power to terminate a treaty is a part of the treaty-making prerogative. The reason the prerogative could not be used to *unmake* the EU Treaties was a simple and two-tined line of reasoning: first, the triggering would perforce mean that 'rights enjoyed by UK residents granted through EU law will be affected';[19] second, the executive did not have the right, whether on the basis solely of the prerogative or on the basis of the ECA, 'to remove an important source of domestic law and important domestic rights'.[20]

Wade's reference to how treaties could not 'as such' be allowed to 'affect the rights of subjects' is beginning to make sense against this background. It was mentioned above that the reference was prefaced by words to the effect that in the seventeenth century the executive 'lost most of its powers of oppressing the subject';[21] later in the book Wade explains, in connection with *Walker v Baird*,[22] that

---

[14] *Miller* (n 1), [50].

[15] ibid; *R (Bancoult) v Secretary of State for Foreign and Commonwealth Affairs (No 2)* [2008] UKHL 61, [2009] 1 AC 453, [44].

[16] *Miller* (n 1), [54].

[17] ibid.

[18] ibid; *JH Rayner (Mincing Lane) Ltd v Department of Trade and Industry* [1990] 2 AC 418, 476 ('*Tin Council*').

[19] *Miller* (n 1), [69].

[20] *Miller* (n 1), [87].

[21] Wade (n 12), 13.

[22] *Walker v Baird* [1892] AC 491 (PC).

'The enforcement of treaties, so far as it affects the rights of persons within the jurisdiction, must be authorized by Act of Parliament.'[23]

Entirely in keeping with the rights-orientated approach that writers such as Wade had already taken more than half a century earlier, the majority's judgment in *Miller* is shot through with statements to the effect that the reason the executive could not act as it was proposing to was that it did not possess the power to affect the rights of subjects. The triggering of Article 50 of the Treaty on European Union would, amongst other things, mean that '*rights* enjoyed by UK residents granted through EU law will be *affected*'.[24] Another reason prerogative powers could not be invoked to withdraw from the EU Treaties was that 'the consequences of withdrawal go further than *affecting rights* acquired pursuant to section 2 of the 1972 Act';[25] 'section 2 of that Act envisages domestic law, and therefore the rights of UK citizens, changing as EU law varies, but it does not envisage *those rights changing* as a result of ministers unilaterally deciding that the United Kingdom should withdraw from the EU Treaties'.[26]

The majority of the Supreme Court spoke of how there are circumstances 'where the exercise of prerogative powers can affect domestic legal rights'; but 'they plainly do not apply in the present case'.[27] These were the categories of case where it would be inherent in the prerogative power that its exercise would 'affect the legal rights or duties of others'. The first category concerns circumstances in which the Crown uses its prerogative power to alter the terms of service of its servants,[28] so as in certain cases to remove rights, or to destroy property in wartime.[29] The majority explained that while 'the exercise of the prerogative power in such cases may affect individual rights, the important thing is that it does not change the law, because the law has always authorised the exercise of power'.[30] The second category comprised cases where the effect of an exercise of prerogative powers 'is to change the facts to which the law applies',[31] such as declaring war, with the effect that actions which were previously lawful become treasonable,[32] or to extend UK territorial waters, with the effect that broadcasts from ships which had previously been lawful become unlawful.[33] The majority concluded that the executive did not have the power to 'remove an important source of domestic law and important domestic rights'.[34]

---

[23] Wade (n 12), 229.
[24] *Miller* (n 1), [69] (emphases added).
[25] ibid, [83] (emphasis added).
[26] ibid (emphasis added).
[27] ibid, [84].
[28] ibid, [52]; *Council of Civil Service Unions v Minister for the Civil Service* [1985] AC 378.
[29] *Miller* (n 1), [53]; *Burmah Oil Co (Burma Trading) Ltd v Lord Advocate* [1965] AC 75.
[30] *Miller* (n 1), [52].
[31] ibid, [53].
[32] ibid; *Joyce v Director of Public Prosecutions* [1946] AC 347.
[33] *Miller* (n 1), [53]; *Post Office v Estuary Radio Ltd* [1968] 2 QB 740.
[34] *Miller* (n 1), [87].

It is difficult in this regard to improve on the analysis of *Miller* given by McLachlan, which referred to *Miller* as in no way heralding a novel approach to the reception of international law, the Supreme Court's judgment being 'a striking affirmation of the positive function of dualism in conforming the supreme law-making power of Parliament within the separation of powers and doing so for the purpose of protecting the individual from executive power, which is its real justification'.[35]

In fact the protection of the individual from executive power runs like a thread through the whole field of law at issue, whether one looks to cases about the relationship between the prerogative and legislation, or cases about the incorporation of general international law and the executive's role therein. It is clear from the ratio of authorities as diverse as *De Keyser's*[36] and *Jones (Margaret)*.[37] In both cases the liberty of the individual and individual rights were held up as the main preoccupation making constitutionally impossible the executive action at issue. What was being upheld in the first instance was not the protection of branches of government against each other but the individual vis-à-vis executive power. Thus Lord Parmoor in *De Keyser's* said, in connection with the prerogative power to take a subject's property in time of war:

> The constitutional principle is that when the power of the Executive to interfere with *the property or liberty of subjects* has been placed under Parliamentary control, and directly regulated by statute, the Executive no longer derives its authority from the Royal Prerogative of the Crown but from Parliament, and that in exercising such authority the Executive is bound to observe *the restrictions which Parliament has imposed in favour of the subject*.[38]

Similarly this seems to have been the main thrust of the following point made by Sir Frank Berman, cited and relied on by Lord Bingham in *Jones (Margaret)*,[39] in connection with the question of whether customary international law is capable of creating a crime directly triable in a national court, a question which was

> inevitably tied up with the attitude taken towards the possibility of the creation of new offences under common law. Inasmuch as the reception of customary international law into English law takes place under common law, and inasmuch as the development of new customary international law remains very much the consequence of international behaviour by the Executive, in which neither the Legislature nor the Courts, nor any other branch of the constitution, need have played any part, it would be odd if the Executive could, by means of that kind, acting in concert with other States, amend or modify specifically the *criminal* law, with all the consequences that flow for the liberty of the individual and rights of personal property.[40]

---

[35] McLachlan (n 5).
[36] *Attorney-General v De Keyser's Royal Hotel* [1920] AC 508 ('*De Keyser's*').
[37] *R v Jones (Margaret)* [2006] UKHL 16, [2007] 1 AC 136.
[38] *De Keyser's* (n 36), 575 (Lord Parmoor).
[39] *Jones (Margaret)* (n 37), [23].
[40] F Berman, 'Jurisdiction: The State' in P Capps, M Evans and S Konstantinidis (eds), *Asserting Jurisdiction* (Oxford, Hart Publishing, 2003) 11.

By parity of reasoning, the power to *make* treaties—which the Supreme Court explained was 'as a matter of both logic and practical necessity' the pendant of the treaty-unmaking power[41]—is similarly conditioned. It is similarly conditioned in both the permissive and the restrictive senses.

That explains the reason—left somewhat hanging in the air in the majority judgment's doctrinal frontispiece in *Miller*—why Wade in 1961 added in relation to the treaties that the executive is entitled to make them under the prerogative, although '*as such* they cannot affect the rights of subjects'.[42]

For a treaty that is in fact incorporated through legislation—or a treaty in respect of which an act has been passed in order to enable effect to be given to certain of the treaty's provisions—can indeed 'affect the rights of subjects'. To give one example, that is the case with the United Nations Charter, where the provisions of Article 41[43] have been given effect in UK law through the passage of the United Nations Act 1946. Article 41 is the provision of the Charter under which individuals, such as the claimant in *Ahmed v Her Majesty's Treasury*,[44] may, by operation of Security Council Resolutions, end up having their assets frozen and having their rights affected in other ways too.[45] The reason that incorporated treaties can so affect private rights is that Parliament has given its assent, and only Parliament is competent to do so.

Against this background, there is reason to question the majority's general proposition in *Miller* according to which, 'although they are binding on the United Kingdom in international law, treaties are not part of UK law and give rise to no legal rights or obligations in domestic law'.[46] Viewed historically, the test as to whether or not an unincorporated treaty obligation, as such, could have effect in domestic law was whether the treaty obligation effected a change of domestic law that infringed the existing legal rights of the subject.

It is necessary in this regard to go back to the judgment that is by common acclamation the *fons et origo* of the law governing the relationship between English

---

[41] *Miller* (n 1), [54].

[42] Wade (n 12), 13 (emphasis added); *Miller* (n 1), [47] and [48].

[43] Article 41 provides: 'The Security Council may decide what measures not involving the use of armed force are to be employed to give effect to its decisions, and it may call upon the Members of the United Nations to apply such measures. These may include complete or partial interruption of economic relations and of rail, sea, air, postal, telegraphic, radio, and other means of communications, and the severance of diplomatic relations.' On introducing the United Nations Bill at its Second Reading in the House of Lords, the Lord Chancellor, Lord Jowitt, said this of the Bill: 'As its title indicates, it is an Act to enable effect to be given to certain provisions of the Charter of the United Nations. An examination has been made of all the provisions of the Articles of the Charter leading to the conclusion that there is only one Article, namely Article 41, which requires immediate legislation in order to put His Majesty's Government in a position to fulfil their obligations as a member of the United Nations.' HL Deb 12 February 1946, vol 139, col 374.

[44] *Ahmed v Her Majesty's Treasury* [2010] UKSC 2; [2010] 2 AC 534.

[45] See E Bjorge, 'Common Law Rights: Balancing Domestic and International Exigencies' (2016) 75 *CLJ* 220, 235–37.

[46] *Miller* (n 1), [55].

law and international treaties—the judgment in *The Parlement Belge*,[47] where
on the facts of the case the question of unincorporated treaties was squarely at
issue before the court. The judgment was cited in the proceeding but, probably
as the question to be decided did not depend upon it, which is part and parcel of
the argument made in this chapter, was not referred to, let alone relied upon, by
the Court in its judgment. *The Parlement Belge* is generally considered to be the
authority from which the rule on English law and unincorporated treaties flows.[48]
The case was decided by Sir Robert Phillimore, perhaps the most distinguished
authority on international law in the English judiciary of his day.[49] In addition to
what the judgment said about treaties, it also developed certain aspects of the law
of state immunity; these latter aspects were overturned on appeal,[50] in a judgment
where the Court of Appeal expressed no opinion upon Sir Robert Phillimore's
judgment on the treaty point. As Lord McNair put it in 1928, the judgment at
first instance 'has since been regarded as the authoritative statement' of the relationship between international treaties and English law.[51] Thus the Privy Council observed in *John Junior Higgs* that 'unincorporated treaties cannot change the
law of the land'; '[t]hey have no effect upon the rights and duties of citizens in
common or statute law: see the classic judgment of Sir Robert Phillimore in *The
Parlement Belge*'.[52]

The statement of the law in the introductory parts of *Miller* is too bald to give
a convincing representation of the correct position. *The Parlement Belge* and contemporary (as well as both earlier and later) constitutional and judicial authorities
recognise that there are in fact situations in which the courts may give effect to
obligations contained in unincorporated treaties. These authorities follow a pattern that is based on a discernible and attractive rule—the rule, it will be argued,
that animated *Miller*—'protecting the individual from executive power'[53] by
making sure that only Parliament can take away the legal rights of the individual.

---

[47] *The Parlement Belge* (1879) 4 PD 129.

[48] See, eg, HWR Wade and CF Forsyth, *Administrative Law*, 11th edn (Oxford, Oxford University Press, 2014) 289; R Jennings and A Watts (eds), *Oppenheim's International Law* (Harlow, Longman, 1992) 58–59; G Marston, 'Unincorporated Treaties and Colonial Law' (1990) 20 *Hong Kong Law Journal* 178; F Vallat, *International Law and the Practitioner* (Manchester, Manchester University Press, 1966) 7–8; W Holdsworth, *A History of English Law*, vol XIV (London, Methuen & Co, 1964) 73; WR Anson, *Law and Custom of the Constitution*, vol II (Oxford, Oxford University Press, 1911) 109–10.

[49] See, eg, Lord McNair, 'The Debt of International Law in Britain to The Civil Law and the Civilians' (1953) 39 *Transactions of the Grotius Society* 183, 198. Phillimore's *Commentaries upon International Law* (London, Butterworths, 1854–61) ran to three editions.

[50] *The Parlement Belge* (1880) PD 197.

[51] Lord McNair, 'When Do British Treaties Involve Legislation?' (1928) 9 *BYIL* 59, 60–61. See also ECS Wade, 'Act of State in English Law: Its Relations with International Law' (1934) 15 *BYIL* 98, 98; G Marston, 'Unincorporated Treaties and Colonial Law' (1990) 20 *Hong Kong Law Journal* 178, 178–80; P Sales and J Clement, 'International Law in Domestic Courts: The Developing Framework' (2008) 124 *LQR* 388, 395 fn 27.

[52] *John Junior Higgs v Minister of National Security* [2000] 2 AC 228 (PC), 241 (Lord Hoffmann).

[53] McLachlan (n 5).

II. The Orthodoxy as Recently Questioned

As explained, there is reason to question the Supreme Court's general proposition that, 'although they are binding on the United Kingdom in international law, treaties are not part of UK law and give rise to no legal rights or obligations in domestic law'.[54] As Craig has observed, it remains an open question whether the courts will countenance any exceptions to the general position set out in *Miller*:[55]

> The answer will depend, explicitly or implicitly, on the policy underpinning the dualist perspective. Insofar as that is taken to be the protection of parliamentary sovereignty, it would lend force to the conclusion that there should be no exceptions, this being predicated on the assumption that it is for Parliament to decide on domestic law, including the rights and obligations of individual. Insofar as the rationale is taken to be protective of executive abuse, there is more room for some limited exceptions whereby unincorporated treaty obligations might have effect in national law, provided that rights of the subject are not infringed.[56]

The traditional view that the rationale is taken to be protective of executive abuse is once again gaining ground. Craig observed that recent judicial statements have questioned the generality of the orthodoxy, pointing to Lord Steyn in *McKerr*,[57] Lord Kerr in *JS*[58] and Lady Hale in *Nzolamseo*.[59] I have myself argued for this position elsewhere.[60] Lastly, McLachlan has argued, with reference to Lord Kerr's judgment in *JS*, that 'the rationale for the dualist theory [is] a form of protection of the citizen from abuses by the executive'.[61]

Sales and Clement have delivered a sustained and powerful critique of the proposition that the core of the rule at issue is protecting the individual from executive power,[62] arguing that it is incorrect to say that the underlying principle on which the general rule is based is to guard against 'abuses by the executive to the detriment of citizens'.[63] In their view the true rationale is that 'the Crown cannot change domestic law by the exercise of its powers under the prerogative, which is a rule reflecting and supporting the sovereignty of Parliament and its primacy as the domestic law-making institution in our constitution'.[64]

---

[54] *Miller* (n 1), [55].
[55] P Craig, 'Engagement and Disengagement with International Institutions: The UK Perspective' in C Bradley (ed), *The Oxford Handbook on Foreign Relations Law* (Oxford, Oxford University Press, forthcoming).
[56] ibid.
[57] *McKerr* [2004] UKHL 12, [2004] 1 WLR 807, [52].
[58] *R (JS) v Secretary of State for Work and Pensions* [2015] UKSC 16, [2015] 1 WLR 1449, [254].
[59] *Nzolameso v City of Westminster* [2015] UKSC 22, [2015] WLR 165, [29].
[60] E Bjorge, 'Can Unincorporated Treaty Obligations Be Part of English Law?' [2017] *PL* 571.
[61] McLachlan (n 5).
[62] Sales and Clement (n 51), 398–400.
[63] *McKerr* (n 57), [50] (Lord Steyn).
[64] Sales and Clement (n 51), 399.

III. Historical Antecedents

As already discussed, the judgment by Sir Robert Phillimore in *The Parlement Belge*[65] is taken to be the source and origin of how English law views the question of whether an unincorporated treaty obligation is or is not domestically operative.[66] It concerned a collision at sea between a Belgian mail packet and the vessel of a British subject. The Crown had, based on the unincorporated Belgium–Great Britain Postal Convention, entered into in 1876,[67] purported to confer immunity on the Belgian vessel, thus effectively depriving the British subject of the right to bring proceedings against the vessel for damage sustained in the collision. Sir Robert Phillimore determined in the judgment that there could in principle exist treaties which operated domestically without the confirmation of the legislature. There was 'a class of treaties the provisions of which were inoperative without the confirmation of the legislature; *while there were others which operated without such confirmation*'.[68] Pausing there, that statement is noteworthy in so far as it plainly goes against the grain of the idea that no unincorporated treaty obligation can be part of domestic law. Phillimore went on to observe that one example in this regard was

> the Declaration of Paris in 1856, by which the Crown in the exercise of its prerogative deprived this country of belligerent rights, which very high authorities in the state and in the law had considered to be of vital importance to it. But this declaration did not affect the private rights of the subject; and *the question before me is whether this treaty does affect private rights, and therefore required the sanction of the legislature.* ... If the Crown had power without the authority of parliament by this treaty to order that the *Parlement Belge* should be entitled to all the privileges of a ship of war, then the warrant, which is prayed for against her as wrong-doer on account of the collision, cannot issue, and the right of the subject, but for this order unquestionable, to recover damages for the injuries done to him by her is extinguished.[69]

The test for whether the court could base its judgment on the treaty provisions at issue was not whether or not the treaty had been incorporated: it was whether the treaty affected or extinguished the private rights of the subject. Given that the British–Belgian Postal Convention in *The Parlement Belge* would deprive the British subject of his rights, by taking away his right to sue the Belgian mail packet following the collision, the treaty must be inoperative without the confirmation of the legislature. According to *The Parlement Belge*, then, the pertinent question is not simply whether or not the treaty had been incorporated; it was 'whether this treaty does affect private rights, and therefore required the sanction of the legislature'.[70]

---

[65] *The Parlement Belge* (n 47).
[66] For example, *John Junior Higgs* (n 52), 241 (Lord Hoffmann).
[67] 17 February 1876, 160 CTS 99.
[68] *The Parlement Belge* (n 47), 150 (emphasis added).
[69] ibid (emphasis added).
[70] ibid.

Several examples could be given which combine to bear out that that was in principle the correct test to be applied—four will be given here. These instances go back as far as to the first year of the new constitutional dispensation ushered in by the Glorious Revolution, and continue up to and beyond the period when *The Parlement Belge* was decided. As will be shown, when cases emerged, in the period after *The Parlement Belge*, in which the principle laid down in that case was put to the test, the judges were prepared to give individuals rights on the basis of unincorporated treaty provisions.

In Holdsworth's words:

> Sir Robert Phillimore refused to allow that the Crown could, by a treaty with the King of the Belgians, which was not sanctioned by Parliament, give the *Parlement Belge* a status of a public ship, *because the effect of such a treaty was to deprive his subjects of rights against the ship which they would otherwise have had.*[71]

Numerous other examples could be given, which shed light on what Wade would have meant in the passage cited by the Supreme Court where he said that treaties 'as such cannot affect the rights of subjects'.[72] As mentioned, four will be given here.[73]

First, the analysis of *The Parlement Belge* set out above finds support in an opinion by, amongst others, the Chief Justices of the King's Bench (Sir John Holt) and Common Pleas (Sir Henry Pollexfen), and the Judge of the High Court of Admiralty (Sir Charles Hedges), in response to a question regarding English goods in foreign prize referred to it by the Crown in 1689,[74] hot on the heels of the Glorious Revolution. The title of the report was *Opinion of the judges as to the power of the crown to affect by treaty the right of English subjects to arrest and claim their goods in prizes brought to England by a foreign captor,* and it held that it was

> not consistent with the laws of England to make it an article of treaty with another Kingdome or state that in case prizes be taken by the privateers of the one Kingdome or state, and brought into the ports of the other, they shall in all cases be judged by the respective Admiraltys of that Kingdom or state to which the privateers belong, and shall be permitted to go thether from out of those ports for that purpose. For if any ship or goods be taken by a forreign privateer, and brought into any port of this kingdome, and such ship or goods shall be here claimed by your Majesty's subjects as belonging to them, they have a *right by law* to have a warrant out of your Majesty's court of Admiralty to arrest the same, in order to try their claimes; and *no article in any treaty can exclude them from such their right.*[75]

---

[71] W Holdsworth, 'Treaty-making Power of the Crown' (1942) 58 *LQR* 175, 182 (emphasis added).

[72] Wade (n 12), 13; *Miller* (n 1), [47]–[48].

[73] Reference should also be made to the important judgments in *Porter v Freudenberg* [1915] 1 KB 857; *Imperial Japanese Government v P & O Steam Navigation Company* [1895] AC 644, both of which are dealt with in detail in Bjorge (n 60), 580–85.

[74] RG Marsden (ed), *Documents Relating to Law and Custom of the Sea*, vol II (London, Navy Records Society, 1916) 124.

[75] ibid, 125–26 (original spelling kept; emphases added).

By way of background, in authorities pre-dating the Glorious Revolution, it had been held that an unincorporated treaty could indeed apply as the law of the land even though it detrimentally altered the rights of English subjects.[76] After 1688 that was no longer possible, and the 1689 opinion of the Chief Justices is early and clear proof that English constitutional law, after the Glorious Revolution, did not accept as operative unincorporated treaties that deprived the subject of existing legal rights. But this authority falls short of proving the *negative*, in the sense that it does not show that, had the treaty provisions *not* excluded the individuals in question from their right but instead strengthened their rights or created new rights for them, then the treaty obligations would have been operative. For that, the second exemplar, it is necessary to spool a few decades forward, to the opinion that the House of Lords treated as a source of domestic law in *Nissan*.

In 1728, Attorney-General Sir Philip Yorke and Solicitor-General Sir Charles Talbot[77] had been asked to advise on the legality of a provision in His Majesty's general instructions to his several governors in America, which contained a reference to Articles 5 and 6 of the unincorporated Anglo–French Treaty of Peace for a Neutrality in America,[78] according to which

> the subjects, inhabitants, &c of each kingdom are prohibited to trade and fish, in all places possessed, or which shall be possessed, by them, or either of them, in America; and that if any ships shall be found trading contrary to the said treaty, upon due proof, the said ships shall be confiscated; but in case the subjects of either king shall be forced, by stress or weather, enemies, or other necessity, into the ports of the other, in America, they shall be treated with humanity and kindness, and may provide themselves with victuals, and other things necessary for their sustenance, and reparation of their ships, at reasonable rates, provided they do not break bulk, nor carry any goods out of their ships, exposing them to sale, nor receive any merchandize on board, under penalty of confiscation of ship and goods.

In spite of the injunctions of the treaty—'provided they do not ... carry any goods out of their ships, exposing them to sale'—trade had been carried on between the British and French settlements in America, 'on pretence that there is no law in force against such trade'.[79] In the view of Yorke and Talbot, this pretence was incorrect: their advice to the commissioners for trade and plantations was that

> you signify to our subjects, under your government, the purport and intent of the abovesaid two articles, and that you take particular care that the same be punctually observed and put in execution, and that no illegal trade be carried on between the British and French subjects in the settlements.[80]

---

[76] See, eg, the 1665 judgment by Sir Leoline Jenkins, sitting in the Admiralty Court, determining that certain goods of Englishmen ought to be restored to their English owners, but only 'if the league between England and Portugal did not hinder' such restoral: Marsden (n 74), 59–61; W Wynne, *Life of Leoline Jenkins*, vol II (London, 1724) 732–33.

[77] G Chalmers (ed), *Opinions of Eminent Lawyers*, vol II (London, C Goodrich & Co, 1858) 339.

[78] 16 November 1686, 18 CTS 83.

[79] Chalmers (ed) (n 77), 340.

[80] ibid, 340–41.

In other words, Yorke and Talbot took Articles 5 and 6 to have overridden the law of the land in the colonies in question. But they went on to say that it was not the intent of the treaty to provide that either Britain or France 'should seize and confiscate the ships or goods of their own subjects, for contravening the said articles'.[81] Had that been the case, such an intention 'could not have had its effect with respect to his majesty's subjects, unless the said articles had been confirmed either by the act of Parliament of Great Britain, or by acts of assembly, within the respective plantations'.[82] That is significant. What Yorke and Talbot's opinion shows is that whereas the provisions that were thought not to affect the rights of His Majesty's subjects were held to be operative without incorporation, those concerning seizure and confiscation of the ships and goods of British subjects could not be operative. The latter—and only the latter—would have required legislation.

Third, in connection with collisions between English and foreign ships in the 1860s to 1880s there is ample constitutional practice bearing out the reading made above of Phillimore's judgment in *The Parlement Belge*.[83] In respect of a collision in the English Channel of the Jersey vessel *Antagonist* and the Belgian mail packet *Rubis*, the owners of the former obtained a warrant from the Admiralty Court to arrest the latter. Belgium, through its Minister in London, observed that the vessel enjoyed immunity by reason of the 1844 Anglo–Belgian Postal Convention.[84] On 12 April 1861 the Foreign Office was advised by the Attorney-General, Sir Richard Bethell, that

> [t]he words of the Treaty are so large that they must have been understood as containing an engagement that a vessel 'freighted' that is, taken up, by the Belgian Government for the postal service should be free from every Civil process when in an English harbour. *But unless there is an Act of Parliament expressly authorizing this Government to enter into such a stipulation, it would have no effect on the rights of individuals.*[85]

Furthermore, in a letter to the Spanish Minister in London of 20 July 1887 (and in similar letters to the Belgian,[86] German[87] and Italian[88] representatives in London from the same period), the Foreign Secretary, the Marquess of Salisbury, made reference to the judgment of Sir Robert Phillimore in *The Parlement Belge* and went on to say that 'The Courts held that it was not competent to the Crown, without the authority of Parliament, to clothe these subsidized vessels with the immunities of foreign ships of war, so as to *deprive British subjects of their right to proceed against them for the enforcement of their legal rights.*'[89]

---

[81] ibid, 342.
[82] ibid.
[83] See generally Marston (n 51).
[84] 1844, 19 CTS 345.
[85] Foreign Office Confidential Print No 1123 (FO 881/1123) 62 (emphasis added).
[86] Foreign Office Confidential Print No 5475 (FO 881/1123) 43 (1 November 1886).
[87] Foreign Office Confidential Print No 5475 (FO 881/1123) 24–25 (26 April 1886).
[88] Foreign Office Confidential Print No 5475 (FO 881/1123) 34–35 (29 November 1887).
[89] Foreign Office Confidential Print No 5475 (FO 881/1123) 22 (emphasis added).

Fourth, the reading made above of *The Parlement Belge* is reinforced by the language adopted by the Judicial Board of the Privy Council in *Walker v Baird*.[90] There, a lobster factory on the coast of Newfoundland was shut down by a government officer charged with the enforcement of a British–French treaty regulating lobster fisheries,[91] and the owner brought an action against the Crown. The Attorney-General assumed in argument that the mere allegation that the acts were done in pursuance of a treaty took the matter out of the cognisance of the court. He argued that as the Crown had unfettered powers to enter into a treaty designed to put an end to or prevent war, there was incidental to that power also a right on the part of the Crown to make any orders and carry out any acts necessary to implement such a treaty, even if the acts would encroach on the legal rights of private persons. Lord Herschell LC, delivering judgment, did not share this view. He observed that the Crown could not sanction an invasion by its officers of the rights of private individuals whenever it was necessary in order to compel obedience to the terms of the treaty; this was a question of whether 'interference with private rights can be authorized otherwise than by the Legislature'.[92] *Walker v Baird* therefore seems to be valuable Privy Council authority for the proposition that the real question that needs asking in connection with an unincorporated treaty obligation is whether or not it interferes with private rights. As Lord Reid held in *Nissan*:

> It is sometimes said, or at least suggested, that an act of the executive obtains some additional protection if it is done in execution or furtherance of some treaty. I do not see why that should be so. ... There is no doubt that it is within the prerogative right of the Crown to make treaties and no subject, whether within or outside the realm, can object on the ground that the making of the treaty has caused him loss. ... *But it would be quite another matter if the Crown infringed his ordinary legal rights and founded on its obligations under a treaty as a defence.* That was made clear by the decision in *Walker v Baird*.[93]

Similarly, Lawton LJ in *Laker Airways* observed, in connection with the treaty-making powers of the Crown, that 'the Secretary of State cannot use the Crown's powers in this sphere in such a way as to take away the rights of citizens: see *Walker v Baird*'.[94]

Thus the protection of the rights of the citizen seems to have been at the heart of the rule applied in the constitutional practice referred to from the period from the 1680s up until the 1880s, in *The Parlement Belge* and up until *Walker v Baird*. It was only later, however, that the test set out in *The Parlement Belge* and the other authorities analysed was actually put to the test in court cases that showed that the judges were actually prepared to treat certain unincorporated treaty obligations as being a part of the law of the land.

---

[90] *Walker v Baird* (n 22), 496–97 (Lord Herschell LC).
[91] It is not clear from the judgment exactly what was the treaty in question.
[92] *Walker v Baird* (n 22), 497.
[93] *Attorney-General v Nissan* [1970] AC 179, 211 (Lord Reid) (emphasis added).
[94] *Laker Airways Ltd v Department of Trade* [1977] QB 643, 728 (Lawton LJ).

IV. The Separation of Powers

Tin Council was handed down in 1989, three centuries after the beginnings of a new constitutional order was heralded in 1689. The principle on which the case is taken to be authority is one which has a long back-story. We should, putting the point at its lowest, be open to the possibility that the hinterland of constitutional authority, which lies between 1689 and 1989, can complement our understanding of the treaty-making power of the Crown and whether unincorporated treaty obligations can in some cases be operative domestically. Academic argument must, as Craig recently observed in the context of historical perspectives on questions of public law, be grounded in some knowledge of what came before the here and now: '[i]nsofar as this knowledge is exiguous it thereby diminishes the value of academic judgement'.[95]

In that regard the discussion has shown that authorities such as the 1728 Opinion of Attorney-General Sir Philip Yorke and Solicitor-General Sir Charles Talbot held that an unincorporated treaty could regulate certain aspects of life in British settlements in America. Crucially, however, it could not direct the seizure and confiscation of the property of British subjects, as that, and only that, would necessitate legislation incorporating the treaty obligations.[96] There are high judicial authorities for the proposition that an unincorporated treaty can be operative so long as it does not deprive British citizens of rights they otherwise would have had.

Dicey understood this. He was alive to the importance of judgments such as *The Parlement Belge* and *Walker v Baird*, to which he explicitly referred in his *Law of the Constitution*, observing that it was 'open to question whether the treaty-making power of the executive might not in some cases override the law of the land'.[97] It is significant that perhaps the strongest and most authoritative proponent of parliamentary sovereignty should have taken this position.

More generally the thrust of the authorities makes it possible to question statements such as Sales and Clement's averment that the true rationale for the rule governing the operation in domestic law of unincorporated treaties 'is that the Crown cannot change domestic law by the exercise of its powers under the prerogative'.[98] The authorities are instead on all fours with what Lord Steyn held in *McKerr*, that is, that the underlying principle on which the general rule is based is to guard against 'abuses by the executive to the detriment of citizens'.[99]

---

[95] P Craig, 'Proportionality and Judicial Review: A UK Historical Perspective' in S Vogenauer and S Weatherill (eds), *General Principles of Law* (Oxford, Hart Publishing, 2017) 145, 145.

[96] Chalmers (ed) (n 7), 340–42.

[97] AV Dicey, *Introduction to the Study of the Law of the Constitution*, 8th edn (London, Macmillan & Co, 1915) 460–61.

[98] Sales and Clement (n 51), 399.

[99] *McKerr* (n 57), [50].

A broader question of constitutional law arises, however. The question of whether a treaty can be part of English law unless and until it has been incorporated into the law by legislation has rightly been conceived of as having a bearing on what the Supreme Court in *Moohan* called 'the fundamental separation of powers in our constitution'.[100]

The principle of the separation of powers can no doubt be defined in different ways, and may be thought to be a difficult concept.[101] Emanations of it is increasingly relied on directly by the courts, especially in what is becoming known as structural constitutional review, the demarcation of the respective ambit of legislative and executive power.[102] If we try to operationalise it for the present purposes, it can be pointed out that there is strong authority to suggest that the principle has at its core the protection of individual liberty and individual rights. 'If', observed Sir William Holdsworth in his *History of English Law*, 'a lawyer, a statesman, or a political philosopher of the eighteenth century had been asked what was, in his opinion, the most distinctive feature of the British constitution, he would have replied that its most distinctive feature was the separation of powers of the different organs of government'.[103] Throughout the eighteenth century the fact that the powers of the state were divided between separate organs of government, which checked and balanced one another, 'was regarded by men of all parties, by peers as well as commoners, and by statement as well as by publicists, as its most salient characteristic'.[104] The protection of the rights of the individual was at the core of the principle of separation of powers already in the eighteenth century. Blackstone in 1765 observed that fundamental rights were secured through the operation, first, of the 'constitution, powers, and privileges of parliament'; second, of '[t]he limitation of the king's prerogative by bounds so certain and notorious, that it is impossible he should exceed them without the consent of the people'; and, third, [s]ince the law is in England the supreme arbiter of every man's life, liberty, and property, courts of justice must at all times be open to the subject, and the law be duly administred therein'.[105] Of the two first limbs, the powers of Parliament and those of the Crown, he observed:

> The former of these keeps the legislative power in due health and vigour, so as to make it improbable that laws should be enacted destructive of general liberty: the latter is a guard upon executive power, by restraining it from acting either beyond or in contradiction to the laws, that are framed and established by the other.[106]

---

[100] *Moohan v The Lord Advocate* [2014] UKSC 67, [2014] WLR 544, [29] (Lord Hodge).

[101] For example, R Masterman and S Wheatle, 'Unpacking Separation of Powers: Judicial Independence, Sovereignty and Conceptual Flexibility in the United Kingdom Constitution' [2017] *PL* 469; N Barber, 'Self-Defence for Institutions' (2013) 72 *CLJ* 558; E Barendt, 'Separation of Powers and Constitutional Government' [1995] *PL* 599.

[102] Craig (n 8), 48.

[103] W Holdsworth, *A History of English Law*, vol X (Methuen & Co 1938) 713.

[104] ibid, 715.

[105] W Blackstone, *Commentaries on the Laws of England*, Book I (Oxford, Clarendon Press, 1765) 136–37.

[106] ibid, 137.

Blackstone said specifically of the Crown that 'one of the principal bulwarks of civil liberty, or (in other words) of the British constitution, was the limitation of the king's prerogative by bounds so certain and notorious that it is impossible he should ever exceed them'.[107] Blackstone was not alone among prominent British commentators to form the view that the core of the principle of the separation of powers was the protection of individual liberty: Sir Philip Yorke,[108] Paley[109] and Hume[110] took the same view. Holdsworth in fact concluded that, in the view of the eighteenth-century writers, the separation of powers was the 'main guarantee for the preservation of liberty', indeed the 'most essential safeguard of constitutional liberty'.[111]

As a matter of English constitutional law the courts are right to have stressed the principle of the separation of powers, as they began to do in the post-war period.[112] In this connection the focus has, as Craig has pointed out, 'shifted towards the direct protection of the individual'.[113] As Lord Mustill classically observed in *ex parte Fire Brigades Union*, the application of the principle of the separation of powers operates to avoid a situation in which 'the citizen would be left without protection against a misuse of executive powers'.[114] The principle, Lord Mance pointed out in *Khoyratty*, operates 'as a primary protection of individual liberty'.[115] That seems to accord with the approach taken by the authorities analysed in this essay.

The courts have, in keeping with the core of the principle of the separation of powers, acted on the rule according to which the executive cannot override the common law if, to use the language of Lord Reid in *Nissan*,[116] that change of the law infringed ordinary legal rights of citizens. It has been seen that unincorporated treaty obligations have been allowed in certain circumstances to override domestic law, as even Dicey countenanced.[117] The constitutional long stop has been whether the treaty obligation at issue infringed the citizen's existing legal rights. As the Privy Council expressed it more recently in *Thomas v Baptiste*, the test is whether the treaty obligations would 'deprive the subject of existing legal rights'.[118]

---

[107] ibid, 230.

[108] PC Yorke, *The Life and Correspondence of Phillip Yorke, Earl of Hardwicke*, vol III (Cambridge, Cambridge University Press, 1913) 15.

[109] W Paley, *The Principles of Moral and Political Philosophy*, 2nd edn (1786) 478.

[110] D Hume, *Essays, Moral, Political, and Literary* (London, 1777, reprinted 1987) 41.

[111] W Holdsworth, *A History of English Law*, vol X (London, Methuen & Co, 1938) 715–16.

[112] For example, *Attorney-General for Australia v The Queen* [1957] AC 288 (PC), 315 (Viscount Simonds); *Hinds v The Queen* [1977] AC 195 (PC); *Duport Steels Ltd v Sirs* [1980] 1 WLR 142, 157 (Lord Diplock).

[113] P Craig, 'Prerogative, Precedent and Power' in C Forsyth and I Hare (eds), *The Golden Metwand and the Crooked Cord* (Oxford, Clarendon Press, 1998) 66.

[114] *R v Secretary of State for the Home Department, ex parte Fire Brigades Union* [1995] 2 AC 513, 567 (Lord Mustill).

[115] *The State v Khoyratty* [2006] UKPC 13, [2007] 1 AC 80, [36] (Lord Mance).

[116] *Attorney-General v Nissan* (n 93), 211 (Lord Reid).

[117] Dicey (n 97), 460–61.

[118] *Thomas v Baptiste* [2000] 2 AC 1 (PC), 23 (Lord Millett).

Had such a deprivation been in issue in the cases analysed in this chapter, the courts would no doubt have taken the view that the principle of the separation of powers was breached. The conclusion would, in that situation, have had to have been the same as in *The Parlement Belge*. There Sir Robert Phillimore concluded that the treaty obligations in question were such that they would extinguish existing legal rights of the citizen: for an English court to rely on them would then be 'without precedent, and in principle contrary to the laws of the constitution'.[119]

V. Conclusion

The courts have allowed treaty rights to override the common law in certain situations where the general rules set out in *Miller* would, were they entirely valid and a definitive statement of the law, not have allowed such an application. But this has been done only on narrow grounds. The question the courts should ask in each case is this: Does the obligation effect a change of the law that infringes the existing legal rights of the subject? If it does not then the court can hold that the treaty right may, to use Dicey's phrase, 'override the law of the land'.[120] That is what lies behind the proposition, put forward by Wade in 1961, and cited with approbation by the Supreme Court in *Miller*, to the effect that treaties *as such* cannot affect the rights of subject[121]—so far as it affects the rights of individuals, the enforcement of treaties must be authorised by Act of Parliament.[122]

---

[119] *The Parlement Belge* (n 47), 154.
[120] Dicey (n 97), 460–61.
[121] Wade (n 12), 13; *Miller* (n 1), [47] and [48] (emphasis added).
[122] Wade (n 12), 229.

5

Miller, EU Law and the UK

PAUL CRAIG

This book attests to the importance of the *Miller* decision[1] on United Kingdom (UK) law, particularly, although not exclusively, constitutional law. This chapter considers the impact of *Miller* on the relationship between UK and European Union (EU) law. In keeping with the theme of the book, the ensuing discussion places *Miller* in the broader context of the case law and legislation that have shaped that relationship.

The analysis begins in section I with the relationship between UK and EU law pre-Brexit. The conceptual architecture of EU law is examined through consideration of its foundational precepts. This is a condition precedent to the discussion of the conceptual architecture of EU law in the UK prior to Brexit. The conceptual frame through which EU law was accommodated in the UK was legislative and common law pragmatism, coupled with statutory and judicial reserve grounded on normative principle. This admixture is evident in case law and legislation prior to *Miller*, and it underpins the Supreme Court's reasoning. *Miller* represents continuity with the status quo ante in this respect, not a novel reconceptualisation of EU law within the UK legal order.

The focus in section II of the chapter shifts to the relationship between EU and UK law in the period between the triggering of Article 50 of the Treaty on European Union (TEU) and exit from the EU. There is discussion of the political and legal forces that shape the withdrawal negotiations. The UK remains fully bound by EU law pending exit, with the rights and obligations of membership, subject to qualifications laid down in the Lisbon Treaty. The corollary is that the Court of Justice of the European Union (CJEU) retains its status as the ultimate authority on issues of EU law that are central to the withdrawal agreement, and subsequent agreement on trade and related matters. Thus, if issues require legal resolution, it would be for the CJEU to make the ultimate determination on matters such as revocability of the Article 50 withdrawal notice; the UK's legal liability in relation to the costs of exit, with or without a withdrawal agreement; and the compatibility with the Lisbon Treaty of any transitional deal struck between the EU and the UK.

---

[1] *R (Miller) v Secretary of State for Exiting the European Union* [2017] UKSC 5.

Section III of the chapter concerns the relation between UK and EU law post-Brexit. The discussion begins with *Miller* and explains the ways in which the decision determined essential elements of the conceptual frame for that relation in a post-Brexit world. The remainder of this section explores the degree of control that the UK will exercise over the connection between the two legal orders when we leave the EU. It might be thought that this is a non-issue, in the sense that the UK will have unfettered choice in this respect in a post-Brexit world. This is mistaken. The legal and political reality is that the control and choice wielded by the UK concerning the future relationship between UK and EU law ranges on a spectrum. It has maximal, albeit not absolute, control in so far as it is for the UK to decide on the terms of the European Union (Withdrawal) Bill 2017, including the extent to which it allows EU law and CJEU decisions to have any weight post-exit. It has only partial control over the relationship between UK and EU law in important areas where the UK wishes to be recognised as having equivalent regulatory standards to those in the EU. The UK has no control over that relationship in so far as EU regulatory provisions will continue to apply to any UK firm trading in the EU post-Brexit; while it would in theory be possible for the UK to enact separate regulatory standards the double regulatory burden thereby imposed on UK industry renders this highly unlikely.

I. Pre-Brexit

A. Conceptual Architecture of EU Law: Foundational Precepts

There is a conceptual legal architecture in all legal systems, and the EU is no exception in this respect. The fact that the architecture may be contestable, descriptively or normatively, is also commonplace. It is tempting to say that it 'goes with the territory', if one is allowed this somewhat inelegant pun. It is, nonetheless, important to sketch the EU architecture, since this is a condition precedent to the section that follows, dealing with the conceptual framework of EU law within the UK legal order. The underlying precepts may be characterised as follows.

There is a foundational hierarchy of norms, with the Lisbon Treaty at the apex, coupled with the Charter of Rights, which is deemed to have the same status as the TEU and the Treaty on the Functioning of the European Union (TFEU). General principles of law feature next in the hierarchy, a status warranted by the fact that they can both function as interpretive tools in relation to any EU legal norm, including the Treaty itself, and also be the grounds for invalidation of any such norm, apart from the Treaty or the Charter. It is this feature that places them above legislative acts, followed by the twin progeny of the Lisbon Treaty, delegated acts and implementing acts, introduced in the name of simplification, an objective belied by the reality of their operation.

There are, in addition, foundational principles read into the Treaty by the then European Court of Justice (ECJ), which shaped the very nature of the EU, and that is so irrespective of how much, or little, weight one accords to the transformation by law thesis. Direct effect and supremacy are most significant in this respect. Direct effect complemented public enforcement of EU law by the Commission through what is now Article 258 TFEU, with private enforcement at the behest of individuals via national courts. The limitations of public enforcement were alleviated by the advent of the private action, which in addition transformed the Rome Treaty from a compact between states to the new legal order in which individuals, subject to certain conditions, were recipients of rights derived from the Treaty and EU legislation. The supremacy of EU law gave added bite to direct effect, more especially because the ECJ made clear that both direct effect and supremacy could be pleaded before national courts, which had the power and the duty, for cases that came within their subject matter jurisdiction, to give effect to these EU precepts. National courts thus became Community courts of general jurisdiction, a crucial element in the effective implementation of EU law.[2]

There were, moreover, from the outset foundational substantive dimensions to EU law, which have changed over time and remain contestable to this day. The Rome Treaty was born from the ashes of earlier failed attempts at more far-reaching integration in the form of the European Political Community and the European Defence Community. The architects of European integration learned from this setback. They built on the success of the European Coal and Steel Community, making economic integration the cornerstone of the more far-reaching integration that became the Rome Treaty. It has remained central to the European project. The balance between the economic and the social has, however, been contested. The change in appellation from the European Economic Community to the European Community (EC) was formal recognition that the Community could no longer be thought of in purely economic terms. The proximate connectedness between economic ordering and social consequence was the substantive manifestation of the same theme. It was further fuelled by Treaty change, whereby Member States accorded the EC with new heads of competence over social policy broadly conceived. The balance between the economic and the social was cast into sharp relief by the financial crisis that hit when the new millennium was but a decade old. The shockwaves from the crisis continue to reverberate in the EU, and the challenges have been exacerbated by the migration crisis, consequent on displacement from the Middle East and Africa, and the rule-of-law crisis, flowing from illiberal policies adopted by Poland, Hungary and Romania.

---

[2] Case 26/62 *NV Algemene Transport—en Expeditie Onderneming van Gend en Loos v Nederlandse Administratie der Belastingen* [1963] ECR 1; Cases 28–30/62 *Da Costa en Schaake NV v Nederlandse Berlastingadministratie* [1963] ECR 31; Case 6/64 *Costa v ENEL* [1964] ECR 585; Case 106/77 *Amministrazione delle Finanze dello Stato v Simmenthal SpA* [1978] ECR 629.

B. Conceptual Architecture of EU Law in the UK: Foundational Precepts

The focus now shifts to the conceptual architecture of EU law in the UK pre-Brexit. The *Miller* decision has important things to say in this respect, as will be seen in section I.B.iii. It is, nonetheless, important to place that decision in its legal context, for it is only by doing so that its significance can be appreciated. The conceptual frame through which EU law was accommodated in the UK was legislative and common law pragmatism, coupled with statutory and judicial reserve grounded on normative principle. These components of this conceptual architecture will be examined in turn.

i. Legislative and Judicial Pragmatism

It is fitting to begin with the pragmatism that was apparent in the legislature and the courts. The European Communities Act 1972 ('ECA') was the enactment through which EU law entered the UK legal order. It was an elegant piece of legislation, which has stood the test of time, notwithstanding the ambiguities surrounding section 2(4). It attested to the dualism that underpins the relationship between Treaties and statute in the UK, with parliamentary incorporation being the sine qua non for the application of Treaty norms in order to protect parliamentary sovereignty.[3] Strict application of this dualist precept could require separate incorporation of each legislative-type provision that emanated from the international organisation. This would, however, have been inconsistent with the dictates of Community law, which stipulated that regulations were directly applicable in national legal orders,[4] such that when enacted by the Community, they were law throughout the Member States without the need for national incorporation.

This concept of direct applicability was driven by essentially practical considerations, the concern being that if separate national adoption were required for each regulation then there would inevitably be very uneven implementation across the Member States, with serious negative implications for the equality of application of such legislation and its efficacy. The UK legislative response was equally pragmatic, and embodied in the ECA 1972, section 2(2). It preserved the core of dualism, but signified legislative acceptance in advance that regulations duly enacted by the Community would be given effect in the UK without the need for adoption or transformation of each regulation in a separate piece of national legislation.

---

[3] *JH Rayner (Mincing Lane Ltd) v Department of Trade and Industry* [1990] 2 AC 418; *Thomas v Baptiste* [2000] 2 AC 1, 23; *The Parlement Belge* (1879) 4 PD 129; *R v Home Secretary, ex parte Brind* [1991] 1 AC 696; *John Junior Higgs v Minister of National Security* [2000] 2 AC 228, 241; *Miller* (n 1), [55]; *Belhaj v Straw* [2017] 2 WLR 456, [123]; *R v Lyons* [2003] 1 AC 976, 995; P Sales and J Clement, 'International Law in Domestic Courts: The Developing Framework' (2008) 124 *LQR* 388.

[4] Article 289 TFEU.

The same pragmatism underpins the judicial response to the UK's accession to the EU. It was assumed during the accession debates that Community membership would be deeply problematic for the UK, given the primacy accorded to the sovereignty of Parliament, and the consequential difficulty of accepting the supremacy of EC law.[5] The reality proved to the contrary. The judicial approach was doubly pragmatic. It was manifest in the technique of avoidance, which meant that if a case could be resolved without having to confront the sovereignty issue then this would be the preferred judicial choice. Thus it was that the courts managed, for the first 20 years of UK membership, to resolve disputes largely through recourse to principles of interpretation.[6]

The pragmatism was evident once again when the House of Lords had to confront the issue in *Factortame*.[7] Lord Bridge's famous dictum is predicated on the need to make the legal sovereignty principle cohere with the political reality of accession to the Community. This is readily apparent from the beginning of the dictum, where his Lordship emphasised that if there had been loss of sovereignty attendant on Community membership, this was consequent on the legislative choice to join the EC, a choice that was made fully cognisant of the ECJ's jurisprudence on supremacy. We knew what we were signing up to, and this contractarian reasoning was used in tandem with the functionalist argument, to the effect that such supremacy was always inherent in the nature of the Community project, since otherwise Member States could take the benefits of membership without having to accept the burdens, thereby preventing the creation of a level economic playing field.

Lord Bridge deftly used these arguments as the normative foundation for interpreting the ECA 1972 to mean that any rule of national law found to be in conflict with any directly enforceable rule of Community law would be overridden. Whether this conclusion was sustainable on a strict reading of the principle of parliamentary sovereignty may be contestable.[8] Lord Bridge's reasoning nonetheless provided a practical accommodation between UK constitutional principle and the reality of Community membership, which stood the test of time. There might well have been issues as to what would occur if Parliament, while remaining in the Community, sought expressly to disavow an enacted Community measure. The courts would, however, in accord with common law pragmatism, deal with this if and when the issue arose. The 'bridge' would be crossed at that time, and not before.

Common law pragmatism in relation to Community membership was evident not only in the context of sovereignty, but also in relation to direct effect

---

[5] D Nicol, *EC Membership and the Judicialization of British Politics* (Oxford, Oxford University Press, 2001).

[6] *Litster v Forth Dry Dock Co Ltd* [1990] 1 AC 546; *Pickstone v Freemans* [1989] AC 66; *Webb v EMO* [1993] 1 WLR 49.

[7] *Factortame Ltd v Secretary of State for Transport (No 2)* [1991] 1 AC 603.

[8] Sir W Wade, 'Sovereignty—Revolution or Evolution?' (1996) 112 *LQR* 568.

and indirect effect. Courts in the UK accepted with equanimity the direct effect of Community law, and created fewer problems in this respect than did other Member States.[9] They regarded EC law as part of national law, and duly applied it when pleaded before them. It became commonplace and unremarkable for there to be multiple pleadings in the same case, some of which raised points of national law, others of which relied on EC law. The courts took indirect effect, and the principle of interpretation embodied therein, seriously, and were willing on occasion to modify their previous interpretation of a domestic statute to accommodate a subsequent ruling by the ECJ.[10]

ii. Legislative and Judicial Reservation

While legislative and judicial pragmatism constituted the general approach to accommodation of Community law, it was tempered by reservations that were expressive of normative limits. These were evident in legislation and in case law.

In legislative terms, it is arguable that the entirety of the European Union Act 2011 should be regarded as a reservation, using that word in the sense adumbrated in section I.B.i. The Act not only embodied limits as to the reception of Treaty amendment in the UK, but also placed constraints on the procedure for acceptance of some other EU measures into the national legal order. The creation of multiple 'locks' was David Cameron's first major concession to the Eurosceptic wing of the Conservative Party;[11] we are living with the consequences of the last such concession, which was the promise to hold a referendum on EU membership. The 2011 Act also contained what became known as the 'sovereignty clause'.[12] Section 18 provides as follows:

> Directly applicable or directly effective EU law (that is, the rights, powers, liabilities, obligations, restrictions, remedies and procedures referred to in section 2(1) of the European Communities Act 1972) falls to be recognised and available in law in the United Kingdom only by virtue of that Act or where it is required to be recognised and available in law by virtue of any other Act.

It is clear from the Explanatory Notes that a major concern driving section 18 was parliamentary sovereignty.[13] The legal reality is, however, that section 18 is concerned with 'sovereignty as dualism'. It embodies in statutory form the common law concept of dualism. Viewed from this perspective, there was nothing novel about section 18. The ECA 1972, and in particular section 2(1), was the gateway

---

[9] P Craig, 'Report on the United Kingdom' in A-M Slaughter, A Stone Sweet and J Weiler (eds), *The European Courts and National Courts, Doctrine and Jurisprudence* (Oxford, Hart Publishing, 1998) ch 7.

[10] *Webb* (n 6).

[11] P Craig, 'The European Union Act 2011: Locks, Limits and Legality' (2011) 48 *CML Rev* 1881.

[12] House of Commons, European Scrutiny Committee, The EU Bill and Parliamentary Sovereignty (HC 633-I, 7 December 2010); House of Lords Select Committee on the Constitution's Thirteenth Report of Session 2010–11: European Union Bill (HL 121, 2011), [52]–[63].

[13] European Union Act 2011, Explanatory Notes, [120].

for EU law to become part of UK law. There was nothing that undermined sovereignty in the sense of dualism. There was nothing in the EU case law that attacked the idea of dualism as the basis of the relationship between the UK and the EU. Nor did the principle of directly applicable EU law offend sovereignty as dualism. In so far as rules of EU law can have effect without the foundation of a particular statute, this is because the EU Treaty and case law thereunder affirmed that this was so. The UK agreed to this regime when joining the EEC, and accommodated it via section 2(2) of the ECA 1972.

Section 18 was never concerned with 'sovereignty as primacy'. It tells us nothing about the relation between EU law and national law in the event of a clash between the two. Indeed the Explanatory Notes stated that section 18 was not intended to affect the primacy of EU law.[14] The UK courts in *Factortame*[15] and the *EOC* case[16] accepted that EU law can in general have primacy over national law in the event of a clash.

There were, however, clearly fears concerning the possible 'entrenchment' of EU law independent of UK statute. Thus the Explanatory Notes stated that section 18 would 'counter arguments that EU law constitutes a new higher autonomous legal order derived from the EU Treaties or international law and principles which has become an integral part of the UK's legal system independent of statute'.[17] This concern was fuelled by argument of counsel in the *Thoburn* case[18] that, 'in effect, the law of the EU includes the entrenchment of its own supremacy as an autonomous legal order, and the prohibition of its abrogation by the Member States'.[19] This argument was rejected by Laws J in *Thoburn*, who held that the constitutional foundation for acceptance of EU law in the UK was based on UK constitutional principle. The ECJ has not, moreover, made such a claim.

While the general judicial approach was pragmatic in the sense articulated in section I.B.i, the courts also tempered this with reservations cast in normative terms. These came to the fore in the *HS2* case,[20] which articulated interpretive and substantive limits to the reach of EU law in the UK.

The interpretive dimension was evident in the Supreme Court's affirmation that CJEU judgments should be read, whenever possible, so as to avoid conflict with national law, more especially where that conflict could be serious. This interpretive precept was used when considering whether EU law should be construed so as to require a national court to undertake an in-depth review of the quality of the legislative process that was regarded as problematic from the perspective of UK constitutional law. Lord Reed held that it was unlikely that the CJEU intended

---

[14] ibid, [123]–[124].
[15] *Factortame* (n 7).
[16] *R v Secretary of State for Employment, ex parte Equal Opportunities Commission* [1995] 1 AC 1.
[17] European Union Act 2011, Explanatory Notes, [120].
[18] *Thoburn v Sunderland City Council* [2003] QB 151.
[19] European Union Act 2011, Explanatory Notes, [121].
[20] *R (on the application of HS2 Action Alliance Ltd) v Secretary of State for Transport* [2014] UKSC 3.

to require national courts to exercise a supervisory jurisdiction over the internal proceedings of national legislatures for which the claimants contended, and that a CJEU decision 'should not be read by a national court in a way that places in question the identity of the national constitutional order'.[21] This was echoed by Lord Neuberger and Lord Mance, who held that it would be inconsistent with the principle of mutual trust that underpinned the EU, that the Council of Ministers should have envisaged the close scrutiny of the operation of parliamentary democracy contended for by the claimants in reliance on statements made by two Advocates General.[22]

There were two substantive limits to the reception of EU law in the UK. The Supreme Court reaffirmed *Thoburn*,[23] and held that the supremacy of EU law did not flow per se from the CJEU's jurisprudence, but from its acceptance in and through the ECA 1972. The corollary was that any conflict between the 1972 Act and another constitutional principle would be resolved by UK courts as a matter of UK constitutional law, even where the reason for the conflict flowed from EU law.[24] The Supreme Court also held that while the UK had no written constitution, there were a number of constitutional statutes and common law principles of a constitutional nature, 'of which Parliament when it enacted the European Communities Act 1972 did not either contemplate or authorise the abrogation'.[25] While the UK Parliament might expressly amend or repeal such legislation, it could not be assumed that it could be impliedly repealed on the ground that it was inconsistent with some later norm derived from EU law.

iii. Miller, *Pragmatism and Normative Reservation*

The combination of pragmatism and normative reservation that characterised previous case law is evident in the way in which EU law was dealt with in *Miller*.

The pragmatic and realist strain is readily apparent in the majority's conceptualisation of EU law within the UK legal order. While the ECA 1972 was the formal basis for EU law in the UK, the substantive reality was that 'where EU law applies in the United Kingdom, it is the EU institutions which are the relevant source of that law',[26] since they made the rules that the ECA then incorporated into UK law. Thus so long as the ECA 1972 remained in force, the EU Treaties, EU legislation and the rulings of the CJEU were 'direct sources of UK law',[27] and constituted 'an independent and overriding source of domestic law'.[28]

---

[21] ibid, [111].
[22] ibid, [202].
[23] *Thoburn* (n 18).
[24] *HS2* (n 20), [79].
[25] ibid, [207].
[26] *Miller* (n 1), [61].
[27] ibid.
[28] ibid, [65].

While there has been debate as to how to conceptualise rights that owe their origin to the EU, the better view is that they should be regarded as both EU rights and UK statutory rights. The rationale for regarding directly effective rights as EU rights is simple and compelling. The EU is the source of these rights, which can alter from time to time; they do not require specific statutory foundation over and beyond the ECA 1972; and thus it is meaningful to conceptualise the ECA 1972 as the conduit for these rights in UK law.

There is nonetheless a formal and a substantive rationale for also regarding these as UK statutory rights. The formal rationale is that without the ECA 1972, there would be no basis for EU rights in UK law. The language of conduit underplays the importance of the ECA 1972, which is the condition precedent for application of any EU law in the UK, a point reaffirmed by the European Union Act 2011, section 18.

The substantive rationale for regarding the rights also as UK statutory rights is equally important. Membership of the EU meant that Parliament accepted the rights that emanated from EU law. The fact that EU rights can alter from time to time is no reason to deny that Parliament accepted those rights in the form that they currently exist. There is, moreover, no basis for concluding that Parliament has any greater attachment to EU rights that emanate from directives, which must then be transformed into UK law, than regulations, which are directly applicable, thereby obviating the need for such transformation. This is more especially so, given that the EU will often have discretion as to whether to proceed via regulations or directives, and given also that a regulatory scheme may be constructed from an admixture of regulations and directives.

The normative dimension of *Miller* built on the conception of constitutional statutes articulated in *HS2*, where the Supreme Court held that this category included the ECA 1972.[29] The reasoning in *Miller* was a natural corollary of that in *HS2*.[30] A statute worthy of the denomination 'constitutional' should not be rendered devoid of effect through recourse to the prerogative. Thus, while the triggering of Article 50 TEU would not in itself repeal the ECA 1972, withdrawal would deprive it of substance, since we would no longer be party to the EU. The majority in *Miller* believed that this consequence should not ensue without parliamentary authorisation; or to put the same point in a different way, recourse to the prerogative could only be countenanced if the executive could show specific authority for this course of action, thereby ensuring, in accord with the principle of legality, that Parliament had thought through the consequences of its action.

The requirement that triggering exit via prerogative power was dependent on proof of specific statutory authorisation coheres with the reasoning in *HS2* and is sound in terms of normative principle. If statutes of such importance should

---

[29] *HS2* (n 20), [207].
[30] This reasoning is taken from P Craig, '*Miller*, Structural Constitutional Review and the Limits of Prerogative Power' [2017] PL (Brexit Special Extra Issue) 48.

not generally be susceptible to implied repeal, in order thereby to safeguard the sovereign Parliament, then it follows a fortiori that they should not be capable of being deprived of effect by the executive, without specific authorisation from the sovereign Parliament.[31] If that had been the intent it was, in accord with the principle of legality,[32] incumbent on Parliament to have made this clear, and thus pay the political cost of the choice. There was, said the majority, no evidence that the ECA 1972 was intended to clothe the executive with that far-reaching choice.[33]

II. Brexit, Betwixt and Between

The discussion thus far has been concerned with the relationship between UK and EU law pre-Brexit, and the way in which *Miller* related to this. The focus now turns to that relationship in the period after the referendum and prior to exit. This was the interregnum, the end point of which marked the change of legal orders consequent upon the UK's formal exit from the EU, with or without a withdrawal agreement. There was much drama during this period, which unfolded on an almost daily basis.[34] The political manoeuvres were complex, within the UK and within the Conservative Party.

The political gaming between the EU and the UK was pronounced, as the two sides stuck to the negotiating strategies that would best serve their respective interests. The UK was wedded to parallelism of negotiations concerning withdrawal and future trade relations, since it was concerned that business interests would become increasingly nervous the longer the negotiations continued with no discourse on trade. The EU rejected parallelism from the outset, insisting on a phased approach whereby discussion on trade would only occur when sufficient progress had been made on withdrawal, cognisant that this would thereby increase the pressure on the UK to agree key issues concerning withdrawal, such as the exit payment, and the rights of EU citizens living in the UK and vice versa.

The summer of 2017 saw increased output from the Department for Exiting the EU, as it published a series of position papers, some of which concerned withdrawal issues, many of which were directed towards future trade.[35] The hope was that it would thereby convince the EU that sufficient progress had been made on withdrawal to warrant the inception of talks on future trade. As summer turned to autumn, the UK's hopes in this respect were diminished. The EU regarded many of the papers on trade issues as unsatisfactory, and it reaffirmed that trade discussions

---

[31] *Miller* (n 1), [86], [87], [108].
[32] *R v Secretary of State for the Home Department, ex parte Simms* [2000] 2 AC 115, 131.
[33] *Miller* (n 1), [87]–[88].
[34] P Craig, 'Brexit, A Drama: The Interregnum' [2017] *Yearbook of European Law* 1.
[35] Available at https://www.gov.uk/government/collections/article-50-and-negotiations-with-the-eu.

would not begin until sufficient progress had been made on withdrawal, in particular the payment that the UK would have to make when it left the EU.

The UK's position papers, and those that emanated from the EU, revealed the complexity of the legal issues that would have to be resolved concerning withdrawal, and relating to future trade. A legal glance at these documents confirms that academic and practising lawyers will be very busy in a post-Brexit world, as will be exemplified in the discussion in the section that follows.

The preceding complexity should not, however, be allowed to mask the nature of the legal relationship between the UK and the EU during the interregnum period. The simple and fundamental point is that the UK remained fully bound by EU law. This included the obligations as well as the rights of membership, and also included the jurisdiction of the EU courts. The CJEU remained the ultimate repository of legal interpretation of any issue concerning Treaty interpretation that related to Brexit during this period. Whether a case reached the CJEU might in some instances be fortuitous; it might in other instances be demanded by the very provisions of the Lisbon Treaty. It depended on the nature of the legal dispute.

The salient point to emphasise for present purposes is that the CJEU's interpretive prerogative covered all key legal issues surrounding the exit negotiations, including, to name but three, revocability, liability for the exit bill and the legality of any transitional agreement. The legal determination of such issues turned on the interpretation of provisions of the Lisbon Treaty, coupled with more general principles of law that shape the nature of the EU legal order. There has been much discussion of the legal pros and cons of revocability, but less on the other two issues, both of which are important.

Consider, by way of example, the UK's monetary liability when leaving the EU. The size of the bill raised complex issues that were contestable.[36] The House of Lords' Select Committee came, however, to more definitive conclusions concerning legal liability to pay in the event that no withdrawal agreement was reached, concluding that in such an eventuality there would be no enforceable legal obligation. There was division of opinion between those who gave legal advice on this issue, with the more senior witnesses[37] concluding that there was such liability, but the Committee's conclusions followed closely the views of its legal adviser who took the contrary view.[38] The detailed reasoning is not of immediate concern, and has been examined elsewhere.[39]

The apposite point for present purposes is that the Committee's view turned on the meaning of the phrase in Article 50 TEU that the 'Treaties shall cease to

---

[36] M Tutty, 'The Potential €60 Billion Cost to the UK of Exiting the EU', Institute of International and European Affairs, available at https://www.iiea.com/publication/the-potential-60-billion-cost-to-the-uk-of-exiting-the-eu/, contains a short and useful guide. The House of Lords, European Union Committee, *Brexit and the EU Budget* (HL 125, 2017) provides a valuable, more detailed guide.

[37] Professor Takis Tridimas and Rhodri Morgan QC.

[38] *Brexit and the EU Budget* (n 36) at Appendix 3.

[39] Craig (n 34).

apply to the State in question', from which the Committee concluded that there was no provision 'for ensuring that EU legal obligations on the withdrawing State persist after the Treaties cease to apply'.[40] Current and future legal obligations of a financial nature could not, therefore, be enforced against the UK in the absence of a withdrawal agreement.[41] Any recourse against the UK would have to be by EU Member States, seeking to use an international court.

There are, however, considerable difficulties with this argument.[42] The legal meaning of Article 50 is for the CJEU. The key legal issue is the meaning of the phrase 'the Treaties shall cease to apply to the State in question' two years after the notice of withdrawal. The preceding phrase carries no implication that legal obligations incurred prior to cessation should be unenforceable, and it is very unlikely that it would be thus interpreted by the CJEU. That is not the natural meaning of the words as adjudged by either linguistic text, or normative policy. In textual terms, the phrase clearly speaks to the future, it says nothing as to the discontinuation of obligations already incurred in the past. In normative terms, there is no basis for assuming that future cessation should mean that obligations already imposed, including those that might last beyond exit, should be dispensed with. This does not cohere with the text, nor with any purposive interpretation of the wording.[43]

III. Post-Brexit

The remainder of this chapter considers the relationship between UK and EU law in a post-Brexit world. The discussion begins with the contribution from *Miller* as to the relationship between UK and EU law after the UK exits the EU. The subsequent analysis focuses on the extent to which EU law may still impact on the UK after Brexit, and the degree of control that the UK has in this respect. There are, as will be seen, three different scenarios, the first of which covers situations where the UK has maximum control, the second in which it has partial control and the third where it has no control.

A. Miller: The Conceptual Frame

The *Miller* decision was, as seen in section I, the concluding legal chapter of the relationship between the UK and the EU pre-Brexit. It also articulated the conceptual frame for the relationship post-Brexit, although there were perforce

---

[40] *Brexit and the EU Budget* (n 36), [133].
[41] ibid.
[42] For related arguments to those set out below, see ibid, [128]–[131].
[43] The judicial venue in which such an obligation could be enforced is discussed in Craig (n 34).

dimensions of that relationship that were not addressed, because they were not relevant to the decision in the instant case. The Supreme Court's decision was, nonetheless, predicated on two related constitutional propositions that are important for future interaction between UK and EU law.

The first was the reaffirmation of dualist constitutional orthodoxy and its application to treaty termination, as well as treaty accession. The Supreme Court acknowledged that there was little case law on the power to terminate or withdraw from treaties, but held that 'as a matter of both logic and practical necessity, it must be part of the treaty-making prerogative',[44] which was in accord with previous authority.[45] The corollary was that dualist precepts must be equally applicable to termination: the treaty terminating UK membership of the EU would bind the UK and take effect in international law, but it would not per se give rise to legal rights and obligations in UK law.[46] The exercise of the prerogative power to unmake a treaty could not therefore alter UK domestic law.[47]

The second point followed inexorably from the first, which was that future legal relations between the UK and the EU were predicated on repeal of the ECA 1972. This was accepted by the Government, which had set out plans for what was termed a Great Repeal Bill, later renamed the European Union (Withdrawal) Bill 2017. The Government sought to argue that this legislation would be enacted prior to the end of the two-year period stipulated under Article 50 TEU, and therefore that this was the medium through which parliamentary assent to exit from the EU could be secured.[48] The Supreme Court rejected this argument: a court must proceed on the law as it stood at the time; ministerial intention to change the law was irrelevant in this respect;[49] the precise content of any such future legislation was uncertain; and even if EU law were retained, it would have a different status post-Brexit than hitherto.[50]

B. Maximum Control: The European Union (Withdrawal) Bill 2017

The future legal relations between UK and EU law will be determined to a considerable extent by the terms of the European Union (Withdrawal) Bill 2017. This is not the place for detailed exegesis on this legislation and the problems attendant thereon. That can be found elsewhere.[51] The present objective is to consider the

---

[44] *Miller* (n 1), [54].
[45] *Rayner* (n 3), 476.
[46] *Miller* (n 1), [55].
[47] ibid, [56].
[48] ibid, [34].
[49] ibid, [35].
[50] ibid, [70], [80].
[51] P Craig, 'The European Union (Withdrawal) Act 2018: Substance, Process and Accountability', forthcoming.

framework of the legislation, and the choices made therein as to the impact of EU law in the UK in a post-Brexit world. The Bill duly begins in clause 1 by complying with constitutional necessity and repealing the ECA 1972, this taking effect on exit day.

The legislative strategy embodied in the Bill is to bring the great majority of EU law into UK law, and then decide whether to keep, amend or repeal it. Different types of EU law are retained in the UK legal order through clauses 2–4. Clause 2 preserves EU-derived domestic legislation enacted in UK law to fulfil Treaty obligations, normally flowing from directives. The requisite UK legislation commonly took the form of a statutory instrument enacted pursuant to section 2(2) of the ECA 1972, and such legislation had to be saved since it would have otherwise have been deemed repealed as a consequence of repeal of the ECA 1972. Clause 3 of the European Union (Withdrawal) Bill deals with what is termed 'direct EU legislation', which forms part of domestic law on or after exit day. The principal, although not sole, target of this section is the incorporation into domestic law of directly applicable regulations, which had, prior to exit, taken effect in the UK legal order without the need for transposition into domestic law. Clause 4 of the 2017 Bill is, in effect, designed to preserve directly effective rights that had hitherto taken effect in the UK through section 2(1) of the ECA 1972, which continue after exit day to be recognised in UK law.

Clause 5 qualifies the foregoing sections, by making clear that the supremacy of EU law does not apply to any enactment or rule of law passed or made after exit day, although it does continue to apply so far as relevant to the interpretation, disapplication or quashing of any enactment or rule of law passed or made before exit day. The Charter of Fundamental Rights is not brought into UK law, but this does not affect the retention in UK law of any fundamental rights or principles that exist irrespective of the Charter. This saving for general principles of law is, nonetheless, severely qualified by schedule 1, paragraph 3, which provides that such principles give rise to no cause of action in domestic law post-Brexit, and that it is not open to a court or public authority to disapply or quash any enactment, or any other rule of law, or quash any conduct, or otherwise decide that it is unlawful, because it is incompatible with any of the general principles of EU law.

Clause 6(1) is concerned with the status of rulings by the EU courts after the UK has exited from the EU. It provides, not surprisingly, that CJEU judgments are not binding on the UK, nor can there be a reference to the CJEU, post-Brexit. However, clause 6(2) states that while a national court is not obliged to have regard to anything done by the CJEU, another EU entity or the EU after Brexit, it may do so if it considers this to be appropriate. Moreover, clause 6(3) mandates that a question concerning the validity, meaning or effect of retained EU law is to be decided, so far as that law is unmodified on or after exit day and so far as they are relevant to it, in accordance with any retained case law and any retained general principles of EU law, subject to the limits of EU competence. In deciding whether to depart from such EU case law, the Supreme Court and High Court of Justiciary must apply the same test as they would use when deciding whether to depart from their own case law.

While clauses 2–6 are primarily directed towards bringing the corpus of EU law into national law, clause 7 of the Bill is directed towards dealing with deficiencies that arise as the result of withdrawal, which must be addressed prior to exit in order that the law makes sense on that date. There may, for example, be regulatory provisions brought into UK law through clause 3 that contain reporting obligations to the Commission or an EU agency; this may equally be true in relation to an EU directive that has been converted into UK law through a statutory instrument enacted pursuant to section 2(2) of the ECA 1972. In either eventuality the law will need to be changed, since such obligations make no sense in a post-Brexit world. There will, more dramatically, need to be significant repeal of many of the directly effective provisions of EU law brought into UK law through clause 4 of the Bill. Brexiteers will not be pleased to learn that we have exited the EU but that directly effective free movement rights have been retained in a post-Brexit world. Clause 7 of the Bill is, therefore, designed to enable expeditious change prior to exit of those parts of EU law that no longer make sense post-Brexit, while allowing time thereafter for Parliament to decide which parts of EU legislation to retain for the longer term, which to amend and which to repeal.

There are detailed, complex and controversial provisions of the Bill that deal with the application of the preceding schema to the devolved regions. The controversy stems from the fact, noted by Michael Russell, MSP, the Scottish Minister responsible for Scottish input to Brexit plans, that the competence restrictions imposed by the Bill were asymmetrical, since the Bill lifted from the UK Government and Parliament the requirement to comply with EU law, but did the opposite for the devolved legislatures by imposing a new set of strict restrictions. In reserved areas currently subject to EU law, the UK Parliament regains the ability to legislate without restriction; in devolved areas, the Scottish Parliament will only be able to do so if the UK Government grants permission by Order in Council. The result of those asymmetrical competence restrictions will be to leave the ultimate decisions on UK-wide frameworks on matters that are otherwise devolved to the UK Government and Parliament.[52]

This is, as stated above, not the place for a detailed exegesis on the provisions of the Bill, which may well be amended in certain respects in its passage through Parliament. The object is rather to reflect on the post-exit relationship between UK and EU law in the light of the Bill. The UK Parliament exercises maximum choice in this respect, although that is not so for the devolved legislatures. Whatsoever the terms of the Bill, and the statute that follows, they embody the considered will of Parliament. It is Parliament's choice to bring the great majority of the EU

---

[52] https://news.gov.scot/news/eu-bill-doesnt-reflect-reality-of-devolution; https://news.gov.scot/news/eu-withdrawal-bill.

acquis communautaire into UK law; it is Parliament's choice as to how this should be dealt with, with the necessary changes pre-Brexit, followed by more considered reflection thereafter; and it is Parliament's choice to embrace a method for pre-exit amendment that places strain on parliamentary oversight, and accords very considerable power to the executive. While the choice that Parliament exercises is maximal, it is not absolute. It is constrained in four ways.

First, there was, in regulatory terms, little choice but to enact legislation of this kind. A great many areas are subject to EU regulation, ranging from financial services to product safety, from pharmaceuticals to insurance, and from the environment to air and sea transport. If this body of EU legislation were abandoned at the date of exit there would be multiple regulatory black holes. There was no domestic legislation that would magically revive when the UK left the EU, and there could not simply be an absence of rules in such areas, hence the need to bring in the body of EU law prior to exit.

Second, in regulatory terms the reality is that there will continue to be considerable substantive commonality between UK and EU law in the post-Brexit years. This is in part because it will take time to decide whether we wish to retain the same substantive rules post-Brexit; it is in part because widespread change would generate uncertainty for business and consumers alike; and it is in part because the UK was perfectly happy with much of this regulatory legislation.

Third, in judicial terms, the choices that Parliament made in the Bill as to the temporal and substantive scope of authority to accord to rulings of the CJEU and General Court (GC) were also constrained. To be sure, some provisions were simply the logical consequence of exit, such as the principle in clause 6(1) to the effect that UK courts were not bound by CJEU rulings after leaving the EU. Other provisions, such as clause 6(3), whereby retained EU law was to be interpreted in the light of retained EU case law, were, however, necessary in order to carry through the underlying legislative principle that the EU *acquis communautaire* would be incorporated into UK law. This had to include the case law interpreting the relevant regulations, since if it did not the UK would only be incorporating part of that *acquis*. By way of contrast, clause 6(2) reveals the triumph of pragmatism over ideology. Thus while some fervent Brexiteers might have barred national courts from having any regard to CJEU decisions post-Brexit, this would have been problematic given that so much UK regulatory legislation would be EU progeny. This is the rationale for according national courts discretion to take account of CJEU decisions when they interpret what may be the self-same national provisions, if they feel that it will aid in their interpretation.

The fourth constraint on Parliament's choice as to the post-Brexit relationship between UK and EU law as expressed through the European Union (Withdrawal) Bill is the very terms of the withdrawal agreement concluded under Article 50 TEU, and the terms of the subsequent agreement on trade and future relations, assuming that there is one. These agreements will, in accord with the best dualist tradition, bind as treaties and will have no domestic effect until incorporated into domestic law. The precise form of their incorporation, or transformation, will depend on their content. The provisions thereof will limit national choice as to the relationship between UK and EU law in a post-Brexit world. They may do so in a plethora of ways. Consider the following by way of example: a transition agreement will constrain UK legislative options; the rights of EU citizens in the UK may be legally connected to EU legislation, case law and adjudication after exit; and any deal forged concerning security cooperation may be based in part on EU law and/or CJEU jurisdiction. Decisions made pursuant to the 2017 Bill will have to cohere with the terms of the withdrawal and trade agreements.

C. Partial Control: Tracking and Equivalence

The European Union (Withdrawal) Bill 2017 will be the principal instrument that shapes the future relationship between UK and EU law. It will not be the only one. The exit process will entail legislation that deals in greater detail with matters such as customs, immigration and the like, since the complex regulatory schema in these areas cannot be dealt with merely through the Withdrawal Bill. There will, in addition, be separate legislation in areas where the UK wishes to track closely the relevant provisions of EU law. It is this legislation that is of interest here, since it sheds light on the relation between UK and EU law in a post-Brexit world. The reality is that such legislation exemplifies partial control over our legal future, where national freedom of choice is more constrained than in the previous section. This can be explicated through the example of the exchange and protection of personal data, which was the subject matter of a government 'future partnership' paper prepared for the negotiations concerning withdrawal.[53]

The principal objective of the paper was to minimise disruption in data flow in a post-Brexit world. Data are big business, with the Commission estimating that the EU data economy was estimated to be worth €272 billion in 2015. Data flow is relevant to all trade in goods and services, and the UK is a significant player in this regard, since it has the largest Internet economy as a percentage of GDP of all the G20 countries. Sharing personal data is also essential in the fight against serious crime and terrorism.

The EU legal framework was embodied in the EU Data Protection Directive 1995, which was recently updated by the General Data Protection Regulation (GDPR),[54] combined with a separate Data Protection Directive (DPD) relating

---

[53] Department for Exiting the European Union, *The Exchange and Protection of Personal Data*, 24 August 2017, available at https://www.gov.uk/government/collections/article-50-and-negotiations-with-the-eu.

[54] Regulation (EU) 2016/679 of the European Parliament and of the Council of 27 April 2016 on the protection of natural persons with regard to the processing of personal data and on the free movement of such data, and repealing Directive 95/46/EC (General Data Protection Regulation) [2016] OJ L119/1.

to personal data and law enforcement. The GDPR applies to processing of personal data that takes place in third countries outside the European Economic Area (EEA), if it is related to the offering of goods or services to individuals in the EEA, or monitoring their behaviour. It follows that UK businesses and public authorities will still have to comply with GDPR criteria post-Brexit.

The significance of data for trade and security, combined with the jurisdictional reach of the GDPR, shaped the UK Government's response: there would be a new UK Data Protection Act, which would ensure that 'the UK's framework is aligned with the updated EU legal framework at the date of withdrawal'.[55] This was, said the Government, essential to ensure that there was a continuing free flow of data between the UK and the EU, and certainty as to the future regulatory schema.[56] The UK Government hoped that the quid pro quo would be that the EU would recognise the UK law as 'adequate', which would obviate the need for separate checks on each occasion when data were transferred, and that the UK Information Commissioner would 'be fully involved in future EU regulatory dialogue'.[57]

Data exchange is but one of many areas where the UK will seek to ensure that there is a close equivalence between UK and EU law in a post-Brexit world. It can be accepted that the UK is in partial control of its own legal and political destiny, since it is for the UK to make the initial determination to seek regulatory equivalence. The UK has signalled that it wishes to do so in the context of data exchange and protection. The UK's freedom for legislative manoeuvre will be closely circumscribed in this, and any other, area where it seeks regulatory equivalence.

This is so in relation to the initial legislative schema that will operate in the UK post-Brexit. The UK legislation will effectively mirror that in the EU, as is made clear in the UK Government's paper discussed above. This is in part for practical commercial reasons already touched on, since UK legislation that reflects that in the EU will lower business transaction costs and increase commercial certainty. It is, however, in large part because the UK's chances of being accorded equivalency or adequacy status will be greater if its legislation is very closely akin to that of the EU.

The circumscription of national legislative choice, with the consequence that the UK exercises only partial control over this regulatory area, will also continue in the future, since there will be pressure on the UK to track subsequent EU legal developments. Regulation is dynamic, not static. The change may result from legislative amendment, judicial interpretation or an admixture of the two. There is no formal legal obligation forcing the UK to keep pace with such developments. However, the commercial and legal reasons, adumbrated above, will remain relevant in the years post-Brexit. Thus, to the extent that the two systems diverge,

---

[55] *The Exchange and Protection of Personal Data* (n 53), [16].
[56] ibid, [22], [28].
[57] ibid, [26], [44].

business will face higher transaction costs, plus uncertainty, and there will be increased risk that the EU will review its determination that the UK has an equivalent or adequate regime in this area.

D. No Control: EU Regulatory Obligations and UK Business

The referendum campaign was marked by claim and counter-claims, with each side contesting the 'facts' advanced by the other. An oft-repeated claim by the Brexit camp is that a vote to leave would enhance our sovereignty, such that the UK would be able to make its own autonomous choices about matters currently decided by Brussels. This sovereignty argument has always concealed far more than it revealed.

It is certainly true in theory that the UK post-Brexit can choose the regulatory standards that it wishes to govern different industries. It is, however, also true that in a post-Brexit world, any individual or company seeking to do business in the EU will continue to be bound to comply with EU rules if they wish to sell goods or services into the EU. The company might decide that it does not wish to be thus bound, and hence pursues sales elsewhere, but that choice is equally open to it now. If, to the contrary, it does wish to trade, it must comply with the EU rules, and that is so whether it is selling cars, washing machines, financial services or insurance. The real difference in a post-Brexit world is that the UK will have no seat at the table, and hence no voice, when the relevant regulations are being drafted.

This will perforce influence UK legislative choices after we leave the EU. To be sure, it would be possible for the UK to set different regulatory standards from those in the EU, but if it does so it will thereby impose extra regulatory costs on UK industry that exports significantly to the EU. Such firms will have to comply with the national regulatory obligations to satisfy UK law, and then modify their products to meet with the corresponding EU rules. This double regulatory burden would be particularly problematic for a Conservative Party traditionally committed to cutting red tape, and there would be significant lobbying from industry against such double burdens.

The EU regulatory obligations will bind UK firms trading therein judicially as well as legislatively. Failure to comply with the EU rules will lead to judicial sanction either at national level, or before the GC or CJEU depending on the nature of the case. Thus, if non-compliance with EU standards leads to loss or harm, this will be legally actionable before the national courts of the relevant Member State. The case will be resolved at that level, unless the national court feels the need to make a reference to the CJEU under Article 267 TFEU because the meaning of the relevant EU obligation is unclear. Prior to Brexit, the rulings of such courts would be recognised and enforced by UK courts pursuant to the EU rules on recognition of foreign judgments. It is unclear what will happen in this respect when we leave the EU.[58] It is, however, likely that any future regime would include some arrangements for recognition of such judgments, including those from the CJEU and GC, where they pertain to legal issues concerning UK firms trading in the EU. This may well not be to the liking of Brexiteers who have strong anti-CJEU sentiments, but it is likely to be the reality nonetheless.

There is, moreover, another constraint on sovereign choice and a further dimension to the loss of voice post-exit. Even if an individual or a company does not trade in the EU, the UK's sovereignty over economic and regulatory issues is nonetheless significantly circumscribed. This is because a great many standards that regulate safety and the like are set at the global level, through transnational or international regulatory organisations. These standards are binding factually and legally in the UK, and this will not change in a post-Brexit world. What will change is that the UK will, once again, have little or no voice in the framing of these rules. The principal players in this regard are the EU and the USA, and while we currently have influence through the former, this will cease when we leave the EU. The point being made here is equally relevant in relation to the new breed of trade deals, such as the Transatlantic Trade and Investment Partnership (TTIP) being negotiated between the EU and the USA. There are valid concerns about the content of such deals. The reality is that the UK will have little influence in this regard if we leave the EU, but we will be very significantly affected by the rules if the agreement is finalised.

IV. Conclusion

The relationship between UK and EU law has been of interest since the UK acceded to the Community, and it will remain so in the years after Brexit becomes a legal reality. The legislative and judicial pragmatism, coupled with normative statutory and judicial reservation, which shaped UK–EU legal relations for over 40 years, reflects, not surprisingly, deeper historical strains in the modus operandi of the UK Parliament and courts. *Miller* continued this tradition, with respect both to the pragmatic and normative dimensions of the interaction between UK and EU law.

The relationship between the legal orders post-Brexit remains to be seen, but the UK will not have unfettered choice in this respect. The degree of control that it exercises will be maximal, partial or zero, using those terms in the manner set out in this chapter. The perceptive reader will, moreover, have recognised what

---

[58] A Briggs, 'Secession from the European Union and Private International Law: The Cloud with a Silver Lining', Combar Lecture, 24 January 2017; J Hill, 'Brexit and Private International Law', available at http://legalresearch.blogs.bris.ac.uk/2016/07/brexit-and-private-international-law/; M Requejo, 'Brexit and private international law, over and over', available at https://lawofnationsblog.com/2017/03/27/brexit-private-international-law/.

is in effect a feedback loop between the discourse concerning maximal and zero control. It is both paradoxical and powerful: since UK firms trading in the EU will remain subject to EU regulatory standards, and since a UK government is unlikely to wish to impose double regulatory burdens on its own firms, this will therefore circumscribe choices made pursuant to the European Union (Withdrawal) Bill 2017 as to whether to retain, amend or repeal the EU legislation that has been brought into the UK. It would indeed be interesting to 'run a book' and take odds on the degree of regulatory divergence between the UK and EU five or 10 years out from Brexit, in order to determine just how far we have exercised our rediscovered sovereign autonomy so beloved of Brexiteers. It is indeed unsurprising that there is increased talk of 'regulatory alignment' the closer that we get to the beginning of formal talks on trade.

6

Of Power Cables and Bridges: Individual Rights and Retrospectivity in *Miller* and Beyond

DAVID HOWARTH

In the Divisional Court's judgment in *Miller* the fate of individuals' legal rights in the event of the United Kingdom's (UK's) leaving the European Union (EU) loomed large.[1] The Supreme Court shifted the focus to other aspects of the case, specifically to EU law as a 'source of law'.[2] Nevertheless, the consequences of the decision for individual rights remain important, in particular since Parliament moved, in the form of the European Union (Notice of Withdrawal) Act 2017, to grant the Prime Minister a statutory power to do the very thing the Court had denied could be done by prerogative. The larger question of exactly how individual rights under EU law became enforceable in UK domestic law remains important, not just for historical or analytical reasons but also for the future relationship between the UK and the EU. The concerns of the 27 remaining Member States of the EU ('the EU-27') about the rights of their citizens resident in the UK after the UK leaves the EU have been central to the negotiations between the UK and the rest of the EU, and threaten to remain a point of dissension for decades to come. Similarly, how some but not all EU-derived rights and obligations might survive Brexit, either permanently or just for a transitional period, is likely to become an issue if any kind of withdrawal agreement is to be implemented. And if the UK eventually remains in the EU, or rejoins it, understanding the precise mechanism

---

[1] *R (Miller) v Secretary of State for Exiting the European Union* [2016] EWHC 2768 (Admin), [2017] 1 All ER 158, [57]–[66]. The court considered individual rights divided, perhaps eccentrically, into three categories: (i) those that could be reproduced in domestic legislation; (ii) rights against other Member States; and (iii) rights that could not be replicated in domestic law (mainly rights against the EU itself).

[2] *R (Miller) v Secretary of State for Exiting the European Union* [2017] UKSC 5, [2017] 2 WLR 583, [61]–[68]. The Supreme Court adds by way of a brief afterthought that 'the Divisional Court was also right to hold that changes in domestic rights … represent another, albeit related, ground for justifying that conclusion' (at [83]), in the process shifting attention from category (iii) rights, thought decisive by the Divisional Court, to category (i) rights.

through which EU law digs its way into domestic law will re-appear as an issue of both theoretical and practical importance.

The thesis of this chapter, put simply, is that the judges in *Miller*, largely inadvertently, took a wrong turn on the road to understanding how the relationship between EU law and UK law has worked—wrong both because it is textually difficult to justify and because it would take UK law along a road lined with unacceptable forms of retrospectivity. If the problems of the future are to be solved, it would be better to turn back and take a different route.

I. The Power Cable or the Bridge?

Any account of how EU law has created individual rights in UK domestic law has to start with the adherence of the UK to a dualist view of the relationship between international law in general and UK law. Dualism means that the international and domestic legal orders operate separately.[3] A change in international law applicable to the UK has no effect in domestic law unless domestic law says so. That usually means that even fully ratified treaties have no effect in domestic law unless Parliament passes a statute giving the treaty domestic effect.[4] As the Supreme Court explained in *Miller*, the purpose of dualism is not to protect the executive's power to make treaties from Parliament but the exact opposite: to protect Parliament's exclusive right to exercise or to control the power to legislate.[5]

The problem the UK authorities faced in 1972 was that EU law is predicated not on dualism but on monism, at least internally within the EU. The European Court of Justice (ECJ) had already decided *Costa v ENEL*,[6] laying down the doctrine of the primacy of European law, and *Van Gend en Loos v Nederlandse Administratie der Belastingen*,[7] establishing, significantly in a case arising out a monist legal system, the doctrine of direct effect. The solution was section 2 of the European Communities Act 1972 ('ECA'), which in effect created an island of monism in the UK's sea of dualism. That monism, or at least an imitation of monism, is created by the combination of section 2(1) and section 2(4). The former says:

> All such rights, powers, liabilities, obligations and restrictions from time to time created or arising by or under the Treaties, and all such remedies and procedures from time to

---

[3] The terms 'dualism' and 'monism' are not used in an entirely consistent way in the literature. The usage here reflects that in, eg, G de Búrca and O Gerstenberg, 'The Denationalization of Constitutional Law' (2005) 47 *Harvard International Law Journal* 243; and G de Búrca, 'The European Court of Justice and the International Legal Order after *Kadi*' (2010) 51 *Harvard International Law Journal* 1.

[4] See, eg, P Sales and J Clement, 'International Law in Domestic Courts: the Developing Framework' (2008) 124 *LQR* 388.

[5] *Miller* (n 2), [57].

[6] *Costa v ENEL* [1964] ECR 585. See also *Internationale Handelsgesellschaft* [1970] ECR 1125.

[7] *Van Gend en Loos v Nederlandse Administratie der Belastingen* [1963] ECR 1.

time provided for by or under the Treaties, as in accordance with the Treaties are without further enactment to be given legal effect or used in the United Kingdom shall be recognised and available in law, and be enforced, allowed and followed accordingly.

The key words creating a monist space inside UK law are 'are without further enactment to be give legal effect'. Section 2(4) reinforces not only the primacy of European law but also its direct effect by providing that 'any enactment passed or to be passed, other than one contained in this part of this Act, shall be construed and have effect subject to the foregoing provisions of this section'. Section 2(2), in contrast, retained the forms of dualism. It established a power for the Crown or Ministers to enact secondary legislation for the purpose of implementing the UK's 'Community obligations' (later 'EU obligations') under the treaties.

The contrast between the Community or EU 'rights' dealt with by section 2(1) and the Community or EU 'obligations' dealt with by section 2(2) is fundamental. The rights referred to in section 2(1) are those of individuals, who are entitled to benefit from them as individuals. The obligations referred to in section 2(2) are those of the UK as a state subject to international law arising under the treaties. The Act preceded the further complications of *Van Duyn v Home Office*[8] and the vertical effect of directives and the *Francovich* rights of individuals against Member States who fail to fulfil their obligations under the treaties, but the distinction between the monist and dualist aspects of section 2 remained tolerably clear: individual rights, including rights against the UK Government when it failed to fulfil its obligations, were given force by the monist section 2(1). Section 2(2) remained a dualist power under which the UK Government could fulfil those obligations.

While the UK's membership of the EU remained unquestioned, no need arose to ask precisely how section 2(1) worked and, in particular, how it was possible to combine dualism and monism in the same system. According to the purest form of monism, international law and domestic law form part of a single hierarchy of norms, with international law placed higher than domestic law. International law's superiority is not only static, in the sense that international law takes precedence over domestic law if the two clash, but also dynamic, in the sense that international law authorises domestic law, and so, if interpreted correctly, the two ultimately cannot clash.[9] On this view, domestic law that is contrary to international law is simply not law in the first place, and its continued apparent existence is merely a function of procedural defects in domestic law.[10] The problem with this form of monism as an explanation of section 2, however, is that section 2(2) shows that Parliament intended to maintain dualism for any matter to which section 2(1) did not apply. The UK was not submitting to the position that its entire legal order arose out of international law. It was conceding only that some parts of

---

[8] *Van Duyn v Home Office* [1974] ECR 1337.
[9] See JG Starke, 'Monism and Dualism in the Theory of International Law' (1936) 17 *BYBIL* 66 and H Kelsen, *Pure Theory of Law* (M Knight, trans) (Berkeley, CA, University of California Press, 1967) 328–31.
[10] Kelsen (n 9).

international law created individual rights that could not be contradicted even by subsequent domestic law. The situation is further complicated by the ECJ's adoption of a dualist position for the law of the EU itself, a stance that cannot be maintained alongside a claim that the domestic law of the Member States derives its authority from international law in a single hierarchy of norms.[11]

These puzzles might have remained in the realms of high theory had the UK electorate not voted to leave the EU. With the events leading to *Miller*, the issue of how section 2 worked became live. Withdrawal from the treaties using Article 50 of the Treaty of European Union (TEU) is first and foremost an action taken in international law. After two years, unless the contrary is agreed, and reserving the question of unilateral revocation, the treaties (the TEU and the Treaty on the Functioning of the European Union) no longer apply to the Member State. From a thorough-going dualist point of view that would mean that the UK would no longer be subject to a duty in international law to bring its law into line with future changes to EU law and, presumably, to any duty in international law to maintain its law in a state compliant with EU law as it stood before withdrawal. But, from the same dualist point of view, nothing at all would happen in domestic law. The difficulty, however, was the ECA had abandoned pure dualism, at least for the period of its own validity. The question arose of what happens on exit to individual rights imported into domestic law through the monist, or quasi-monist, section 2(1)? The answer depends on the effect of the treaties' no longer applying to the UK on the legal force within the UK of those individual rights.

At least two possibilities exist for explaining the legal force of EU law in UK domestic law through section 2(1). In one theory, that legal force comes from the EU Treaties themselves. Section 2(1) facilitates that legal force's being felt in the UK but does not itself supply any force. In the other theory, the legal force of EU law in UK domestic law is entirely domestic, the domestic effect being brought about by section 2(1) itself as a piece of UK legislation. The former might be called a 'power cable' theory. The legal force of EU rights and obligations in the UK is powered by EU law, as if a power cable carried electricity across the Channel from Brussels. The latter is a 'bridge' theory, that the ECA provided a bridge over which rights and obligations are carried from Brussels, but on arrival they are plugged in to the UK legal system, rather as, for example, clauses in individual contracts of employment can create a 'bridge' to bring into legal effect provisions in collective agreements that are not in themselves otherwise legally enforceable.[12]

The crucial difference between the two theories is what happens to existing EU rights if the treaties no longer apply to the UK. The effect of the treaties' no longer applying to the UK under the power cable theory is that the legal force powering the relevant individual rights is at that point turned off, and as a consequence all of the rights simply disappear. They go out like lights. In contrast, under the bridge

---

[11] de Búrca, 'The European Court of Justice and the International Legal Order after *Kadi*' (n 3).
[12] S Deakin and D Morris, *Labour Law*, 6th edn (Oxford, Hart Publishing, 2016) paras 4.27–4.32.

theory, the effect of the treaties' no longer applying is that no new rights are sent across the bridge, but the rights previously sent, having been plugged into the UK system, remain on and fully functional.

The power cable theory is the more monist of the two. It locates the primary authority for the relevant rights in international law and treats the domestic statute as merely a procedure that enables the system as a whole to operate as a single hierarchy of norms. What matters for domestic law is whether international law, in the form of the treaties, continues to require that the relevant individual rights exist in a specific place, namely the UK. If it does, they exist. If not, not. The bridge theory in contrast is still fundamentally dualist. The ultimate source of legal authority lies in the domestic legal system, which opens itself up to rules flowing from another legal system as long as the UK remains part of that system but does not cede domestic authority to it.

The first port of call is the text of section 2 itself. One can just about read it as supporting the power cable theory. The only EU rights, according to this reading, that 'are to be given legal effect' are those 'arising by or under the treaties' at the time we consider the question of their enforceability. As a result, after the treaties no longer apply to the UK, no EU rights exist regardless of when they came into being. The bridge reading, in contrast, is that references to rights 'arising' or being 'created' under the treaties 'from time to time' show that the section contemplates not a state of affairs but a series of events. On this view, the question is not whether the treaties still apply at the time an issue comes before a court, but whether the treaties applied at the time the rights were created or arose. The bridge theory requires less to be read into the section and accounts for more of its words, in particular 'created' and 'from time to time', than the power cable reading.

Moreover, the bridge theory, and not the power cable theory, seems more consonant with section 18 of the European Union Act 2011, which provided:

> Directly applicable or directly effective EU law (that is, the rights, powers, liabilities, obligations, restrictions, remedies and procedures referred to in section 2(1) of the European Communities Act 1972) falls to be recognised and available in law in the United Kingdom only by virtue of that Act or where it is required to be recognised and available in law by virtue of any other Act.

The difficult word for the power cable theory is 'only'. In the power cable view, the ECA might have had some role in facilitating the recognition of EU law within the UK, but it does not do so alone. The force of EU law comes from the EU Treaties, not exclusively from UK domestic law. In contrast, under the bridge view, one can say without any qualification that directly effective EU law is recognised and available in UK law 'only by virtue' of domestic legislation.[13]

---

[13] Section 18 of the 2011 Act was passed to cut off any development, including 'common law' development of the idea that EU law could restrict UK parliamentary legislative supremacy by forbidding or making ineffective any repeal or amendment of the ECA. See William Hague (then Foreign Secretary), HC Deb 7 December 2010, vol 520, col 204.

II. The Retrospective Consequences of the Power Cable Theory

A purely textual approach, however, ignores what both Parliament and the courts have come to call the background of constitutional principle.[14] In particular, one needs to consider the consequences of the two competing interpretations for the principle of non-retrospectivity.

A. Non-retrospectivity

Parliamentary legislative supremacy means that retrospective legislation is not impossible in the UK. No equivalent exists to the rule in the US Constitution that the States may not make ex post facto laws or any law 'impairing the obligation of contracts'.[15] Indeed, some very useful and not at all obnoxious ex post facto laws have been passed, for example confirming the validity of cases decided by magistrates who might accidentally have been appointed contrary to the Act of Settlement.[16] Sometimes, a degree of retrospectivity is necessary to prevent a greater injustice, for which reason purely procedural retrospective changes are often not interpreted harshly.[17] Nevertheless, retrospectivity is usually deprecated by judges and by commentators.[18] Lon Fuller, who himself accepted that some forms of retrospectivity were not inimical to legality and could even promote it, averred that in general such laws were a 'monstrosity'.[19]

Retrospective laws are not only unfair, as in the case of retrospective criminal offences,[20] but also, and more importantly, they undermine legal certainty and thus social stability.[21] The threat to certainty and stability comes both in the

---

[14] Constitutional Reform Act 2005, s 1 (the 'constitutional principle of the rule of law'); judicial examples include *Miller* in the Divisional Court (n 1), [82]–[94] and in the Supreme Court (n 2), [39]; *R (Wheeler) v Office of the Prime Minister* [2008] EWHC 1409 (Admin); *Thoburn v Sunderland City Council* [2002] EWHC 195 (Admin), [2003] QB 151.

[15] US Constitution, Article 1, s 10, cl 1.

[16] Courts Act 2003, s 42. For an explanation, see C Leslie, HC Deb 1 July 2003, vol 408, col 115. For 'curative' retrospectivity in general, see L Fuller, *The Morality of Law*, 2nd edn (New Haven, CT, Yale University Press, 1969) 74 and 240.

[17] *Alam v Secretary of State for the Home Department* [2012] EWCA Civ 960; *L'Office Cherifien des Phosphates v Yamashita-Shinnihon Steamship Co Ltd, The Boucraa* [1994] 1 AC 486; *Phillips v Eyre* (1870) LR 6 QB 1. For the 'procedural exception', see *Bennion on Statutory Interpretation*, available at http://lexisweb.co.uk/guides/sources/bennion-on-statutory-interpretation?contentonly=true, s 98.

[18] See *Bennion on Statutory Interpretation* (n 17), s 97.

[19] See Fuller (n 16), 53.

[20] See the European Convention on Human Rights (ECHR), Article 7, reflecting the general principle *nulla poena sine lege*. Retrospectivity in civil law is not necessarily a breach of the Convention, but it can violate Article 6: *Zielinski v France* (1999) 31 EHRR 19.

[21] See, eg, D Feldman, 'Commencement, transition and retrospective legislation' (1992) 108 LQR 212.

specific field in which the retrospective statute applies and, in addition and more dangerously, beyond that field and affecting the whole of the law, by suggesting to citizens the possibility that they cannot rely on any existing legal structure. Admittedly, no one has a right to expect the law to remain completely unchanged. One cannot complain merely because one has made choices in the past in anticipation of choosing a future option which a change in the law has now eliminated or made less attractive. That would be to freeze the law and to eliminate democratic change. But one can complain if the law purports to reverse the legally enforceable consequences of past decisions.

Retrospectivity and retroactivity are sometimes regarded as different things, with the former being considered much less of a problem than the latter. On this view retrospectivity is 'looking back' from now to take into account events that occurred before the law came into force, but only to do so for future decisions. In contrast, 'retroactivity' is law that 'operates backwards', changing the law as it applied at the time of a past transaction or act.[22] For similar reasons, Fuller thought that new taxation of actions or states of affairs that occurred or subsisted before the tax came into force were not a threat to legality because the liability to pay the tax would be itself purely prospective.[23] The difficulty with this point of view, however, is that although 'retrospective' laws might be less unfair than 'retroactive' ones, they are just as much a threat to legal certainty and social stability. Imposing new burdens on past decisions about which one can now do nothing creates just as much anxiety about the reliability of the legal and social structure within which we have to live as declaring the effect of past decisions to be void. Indeed, the latter can be seen as merely a special case of the former.

As a consequence, unless a clear contrary intention appears, UK judges generally interpret statutes so that retrospectivity is avoided.[24] Even when the contrary intention does appear, judges are capable of finding other reasons for interpreting retrospective provisions away, or declaring them incompatible with the right to a fair trial because they interfere with active litigation.[25] Although UK judges

---

[22] See, eg, E Driedger, 'Statutes: Retroactive Retrospective Reflections' (1978) 56 *Canadian Bar Review* 264, 268–69.

[23] Fuller (n 16), 59–61. Other commentators on tax law, however, would place retrospective taxation in the obnoxious category. See generally H Gribnau, *Legal certainty: a matter of principle*, Tilburg Law School Legal Studies Research Paper Series 12/2014; and M Pauwels, 'Retroactive and retrospective tax legislation: a principle-based approach; a theory of priority principles of transitional law and the method of the catalogue of circumstances' in H Gribnau and M Pauwels (eds), *Retroactivity of Tax Legislation* (Amsterdam, EATLP/IBFD, 2013) 95–116.

[24] See, eg, Lindley LJ in *Lauri v Renad* [1892] 3 Ch 402, 421: 'It is a fundamental rule of English law that no statute shall be construed so as to have a retrospective operation unless its language is such as plainly to require such a construction; and the same rule involves another and subordinate rule to the effect that a statute is not to be construed so as to have a greater retrospective operation than its language renders necessary.' See further *Bennion on Statutory Interpretation* (n 17), s 97.

[25] *R (Reilly) v Secretary of State for Work and Pensions (No 2)* [2016] EWCA Civ 413, [2017] QB 657, following *Zielinski v France* (1999) 31 EHRR 19 and distinguishing *National & Provincial Building Society v United Kingdom* [1997] STC 1466, 25 EHRR 127 and *Tarbuk v Croatia* CE:ECHR:2012:1211 JUD003136010.

cannot deny the possibility of retrospective legislation, because of the doctrine of parliamentary legislative supremacy, they can alleviate the social consequences of that possibility by reducing the probability of its application, and by incentivising both Government and Parliament to declare their intentions more openly, thus giving more time for public and media debate about the consequences of retrospectivity.

B. Turning Off the Power and Retrospectivity

If the power cable theory is correct, at the conclusion of the Article 50 process all the individual rights created under the EU Treaties cease to have legal force in the UK. Since under the power cable theory no independent domestic basis for these rights would exist, the effect of withdrawal is that the law is then as if the rights had never existed.

This effect is clearest for rights that came into force through section 2(1). If the power cable view is correct, the effect of withdrawal is that, because the Treaties do not apply to the UK, no EU rights arising out of the Treaties, regardless of when they arose and what the legal situation was then, are now enforceable in the UK. The plug will have been pulled on all of them, and no back-up source of power can switch them back on again without further domestic legislation (which is, of course, the intention behind the European Union (Withdrawal) Bill 2017–19).

The retrospective effect of the power cable theory on section 2(1) rights is the heart of the matter. But even the position of some rights created under section 2(2) might be affected. That is because section 2(2)(b) specifically creates a power to make provision 'for the purpose of dealing with matters arising out of or related to any such obligation or rights or the coming into force, or the operation from time to time, of subsection (1) above'. Regulations resting solely on section 2(2)(b) would arguably lack a legal basis after the Treaties no longer apply to the UK, since no 'such obligation or rights' would exist. One argument against that interpretation is that section 2(2)(b) refers to rights 'coming into force' or to 'the operation from time to time' of section 2(1), suggesting that what matters is the law as it stood at the time the regulation was made. But the problem with that argument from the point of view of the power cable theory is that it would suggest in turn a similar interpretation of 'from time to time' as it occurs in section 2(1) itself, an interpretation incompatible with the power cable theory itself.

Even if the loss of rights applies only to section 2(1) rights, the effect is dramatic. Withdrawal deprives of legal effect all EU rights going back to 1973. Moreover, we are not talking about retrospectivity that falls into any of the categories of unobjectionable retrospectivity. It is not merely procedural and it is not curative of an accidental lacuna in authority or jurisdiction. It is also at least prima facie an interference not only in hopes for the future, but also in currently existing rights.

One possible argument for saying that the effect of withdrawal is not retrospective under the power cable view is to say that it applies only prospectively to future attempts to rely on EU rights. The claim would be that it leaves alone, for example, the results of previous cases that applied those rights. Those cases are *res judicata* and cannot be reopened. But even if that is so, the problem with this view is that the vast majority of applications of rights are never *judicata*, and even those that are only bind the parties to the judgment. They are relied on every day in transactions between private parties and between private parties and the state. Doubtless many, if not most, of these parties will be happy to let sleeping dogs lie, and in many of the cases in which one of the parties wants to disturb the dogs, limitation periods will have run and the lack of legal justification for the resulting position cannot be disturbed. But in some cases, the position will be different.

For example, if before withdrawal the UK has violated EU law by failing to implement a directive correctly or in time, the rights of UK citizens to enforce their rights vertically against the UK Government, including their rights to damages under *Francovich*, will disappear on withdrawal. That will be the removal of an existing right, not just the removal of a hope of taking up a practical option previously open. It might be that no damages under *Francovich* would have payable in respect of the period after withdrawal, on the ground that in that period no loss has occurred, but the loss with respect to the period before withdrawal incontrovertibly becomes uncompensatable.[26]

The point does not apply only to rights against the UK Government. It also applies to horizontally enforceable rights. In *Benkharbouche v Embassy of the Republic of Sudan*,[27] the courts disapplied the State Immunity Act 1978 in so far as it barred embassy service staff from enforcing their EU-based employment rights in the UK. The case itself is *res judicata* as between the parties, but as between other members of staff of other embassies it is not. The power cable view implies that embassy staff would no longer have a right for the 1978 Act to be disapplied and so will have lost their employment rights.[28]

C. Is Turning the Power Off 'Repeal'?

One possible way out for the power cable view is to treat withdrawal from the EU and the consequent loss of legal force for EU rights as a form of 'repeal'.

---

[26] Note that the European Union (Withdrawal) Bill 2017–19, as passed at second reading in the Commons, explicitly excluded any saving for *Francovich* rights (sch 1, para 4) and so the retrospective effect would survive the enactment of the Bill.

[27] Case C-300/11 *Benkharbouche v Embassy of the Republic of Sudan*, 4 June 2013 (Grand Chamber); [2015] EWCA Civ 33, affirmed [2017] UKSC 62.

[28] The position would presumably also not be saved by the European Union (Withdrawal) Bill 2017–19, were it enacted in the form passed at second reading, because the disapplication of the ECA (as opposed to the declaration of incompatibility under the Human Rights Act) was based on the provisions of the Charter of Fundamental Rights. Rights arising under the Charter are excluded from preservation by cl 5(4) of the Bill.

If withdrawal could be treated as 'repeal', one might argue that the provisions of the Interpretation Act 1978 apply, in particular section 16(1), which provides:

16. General savings

(1)   Without prejudice to section 15, where an Act repeals an enactment, the repeal does not, unless the contrary intention appears,—

    …

    (b)   affect the previous operation of the enactment repealed or anything duly done or suffered under that enactment;

    (c)   affect any right, privilege, obligation or liability acquired, accrued or incurred under that enactment …

If section 16(1) were to apply, nothing done under the law as it stood before withdrawal would be undone and no rights enjoyed before withdrawal would be extinguished. The question, however, is whether it applies. The obvious difficulty is that section 16(1) applies only 'where an Act repeals an enactment'.

The first problem is that although the Interpretation Act helpfully includes within 'enactment' all forms of 'subordinate legislation',[29] and says that '"subordinate legislation" means Orders in Council, orders, rules, regulations, schemes, warrants, byelaws and other instruments made or to be made under any Act',[30] it is not clear whether, at least under the power cable theory, this definition covers EU rights brought into domestic force by section 2(1) of the ECA. That is because in *Miller*, the majority in the Supreme Court declared that EU law was not 'delegated legislation',[31] but rather that section 2(1) had transferred law-making power to the EU. The issue is whether EU rights are nevertheless covered by section 16(1) of the Interpretation Act because they derive from instruments 'made under' an Act of Parliament, namely the ECA. The problem is that those rights, according to the power cable theory (and the *Miller* majority) derive directly from the EU treaty: *EU* regulations, as opposed to domestic regulations, are, on the basis of the theory, not 'made under' the ECA. The appropriate words for covering the legal position as proposed by the power cable theory would have been 'brought into force through', not 'made under'.

The other obstacle standing in the way of bringing withdrawal from the EU within the Interpretation Act is that section 16 requires an 'Act' that 'repeals' the enactment. The obstacle has two hurdles. It has to be 'an Act', that is to say an Act of Parliament, and the Act has to 'repeal'. The power cable theory has trouble with both hurdles. First, according to the power cable theory, the loss of legal effect comes about from an event in international law, namely the treaties' no longer applying to the UK, rather from an Act of Parliament. Secondly, the loss of legal force comes about not from a 'repeal' but by operation of law, namely by the application of the power cable theory.

---

[29]   Interpretation Act 1978, s 23(2).
[30]   ibid, s 21.
[31]   *Miller* (n 2), [68].

To meet these objections, proponents of the power cable theory might argue that there are two possibly relevant Acts: the ECA 1972 and the European Union (Notification of Withdrawal) Act 2017. The problem with the former is that *Miller* holds that neither it nor its successors gives a power to Ministers to issue an Article 50 notice. If it gives no power to withdraw in the first place, it cannot count as repealing anything. That leaves only the 2017 Act.

The 2017 Act, which was Parliament's response to the *Miller* judgment, is very short. Its operative words are, in full:

1. Power to notify withdrawal from the EU

(1) The Prime Minister may notify, under Article 50(2) of the Treaty on European Union, the United Kingdom's intention to withdraw from the EU.

(2) This section has effect despite any provision made by or under the European Communities Act 1972 or any other enactment.

It will be noticed immediately that the Act does not mention repeal of any sort. All it does is give the Prime Minister authority to take a step in international law, namely, to issue a notice of intention to withdraw under Article 50(2) TEU. That was the step the Supreme Court said in *Miller* no Minister had power, either prerogative or statutory, to take. The Act takes no position on what the domestic consequences of that step might be, or what the legal nature of the process might be that brings about those consequences. The argument for nevertheless treating the 2017 Act as a repeal Act is that Parliament would have known, from the reasoning of the majority in *Miller*, that one of the successful arguments deployed against the Secretary of State was that the foreign affairs prerogative could not be used to alter domestic law. That means that Parliament would have known that one consequence of granting the Prime Minister a statutory power to do what she could not do by prerogative was that rights might be taken away. That means that the instrument taking away those rights is, ultimately, some might argue, an Act of Parliament.

But does that mean that the 2017 Act 'repeals' anything? This is where the argument becomes more difficult. On occasion judges have declared that 'ceasing to have effect' means the same thing as 'repeal',[32] but that was in the context of a 'double repeal', where a statute had said both. More generally, where a statute turns off the effect of an instrument, either through its own terms or by giving a power to a Minister to turn it off, revocation or repeal of the instrument is treated as a separate operation. In the Statutory Instruments Act 1946, for example, if a House of Parliament passes a motion annulling an order made under the negative procedure, no further proceedings can be taken under the order but the process of revoking the order itself is separate, for which purpose the Act creates a ministerial power.[33] A ministerial power to order that part of the General Rate Act 1967

---

[32] *R v West London Stipendiary Magistrate, ex parte Simeon* [1983] 1 AC 234.
[33] Statutory Instruments Act 1946, s 5(1).

should cease to have effect was accompanied by a power to bring it back into effect, and so was not accompanied by a power to repeal.[34] In the case of EU rights, the issue is even clearer, because the Prime Minister has no power to make EU rights disappear in EU law. All she has is a power to turn them off for the purposes of domestic law. They would not have ceased to exist in the meantime. They only became inapplicable in the UK.

Another possibility is that the statutory power under the 2017 Act itself can be interpreted as restricting the effects of withdrawal in domestic law. The problem with that interpretation is that the power to send an Article 50 notice and the effect of that notice are different things. The former is not conditional on the latter. Parliament would have been surprised to learn that the Prime Minister was only being given a power to end the application of the Treaty if the effect of ending the Treaty was exclusively prospective. The intention of Parliament was to give the Prime Minister the power to send the notice regardless of its broader effects. A variation on that theme would be to interpret the 2017 Act as giving not a conditional but a limited power, so that it only applies to prospective rights. But that interpretation gives rise to another problem. How can we explain the existence of the unaffected rights? Are they now powered by domestic law? If so, how, under the power cable theory, did that happen? Or are they still powered by EU law? But if that is the case, how is EU law still operative after the Treaties no longer apply? And if Parliament really did want to annul these rights retrospectively, how could it do that, given that they are powered by a different legal order?

One remaining possibility is that the 2017 Act could be treated as a repealing Act but one not subject to the Interpretation Act. That seems a strained interpretation, but even if it were correct, it would leave much retrospectivity in place, since the effect of repeal at common law, and the reason for Parliament's intervention through the Interpretation Act 1889,[35] was that the common law treated the situation as if the Act had never existed, removing even vested rights and leaving unaffected only matters 'past and closed'.[36]

D. The 2017 Act and International Law

We are left with the situation that the power cable theory, despite its popularity, leads to retrospectivity of an obnoxious kind. If we adopt it we have to conclude, for example, that Parliament in the 2017 Act granted the Prime Minister a power the effect of using which would be to extinguish vested rights, including

---

[34] See, eg, Local Government, Planning and Land Act 1980, s 41, discussed in *Bennion on Statutory Interpretation* (n 17), s 30.2.

[35] See s 38. As Bennion (*Bennion on Statutory Interpretation* (n 17)) says (at s 89), 'the common law doctrine [was] that at repeal the "floodlight" is switched off, plunging everything illuminated by it into immediate darkness'.

[36] *Surtees v Ellison* (1829) 109 ER 278, 9 B & C 750; see also *Eton College v Minister of Agriculture, Fisheries and Food* [1964] Ch 274. One last throw of the dice would be to argue that the common law has 'developed' since 1889 and is now the same as the Interpretation Act.

Francovich rights and employment rights under EU regulations. One response to that situation would be to accept it and to treat it as a consequence of Brexit. The Prime Minister has exercised the power, and that will lead to retrospective effects unless Parliament legislates otherwise (which in the case of *Francovich* rights and Charter rights it has been invited by the Government to refuse to do).[37]

Another reaction, however, is to look for other ways of avoiding the conclusion that the Prime Minister was given a power retrospectively to destroy rights. One such is to claim that the TEU itself envisages that vested rights cannot be destroyed by the use of Article 50, so that despite the Treaties' no longer applying to the UK, they continue to power old rights. Such an interpretation of Article 50 TEU might follow, for example, from Article 70 of the Vienna Convention on the Law of Treaties ('VCLT'), which says:

1. Unless the treaty otherwise provides or the parties otherwise agree, the termination of a treaty under its provisions or in accordance with the present Convention:
   (a) releases the parties from any obligation further to perform the treaty;
   (b) does not affect any right, obligation or legal situation of the parties created through the execution of the treaty prior to its termination.[38]

The difficulty with this interpretation is that Article 70 VCLT in terms applies only to international legal rights and obligations, not to domestic ones. It applies to the rights and obligations '*of the parties*', which in international law are states, not individuals.[39] International law does have a separate doctrine of acquired rights, protecting the domestic rights of individuals acquired under a treaty, but its scope is disputed and would probably not protect anything near the full range of EU rights.[40] In particular, it is difficult to see how international law could protect the rights of British citizens in the UK.

In any case, even to the extent that acquired rights might be protected, the problem would remain that any obligation to protect them is an obligation of the UK in international law, and so, in a dualist system, has no automatic consequences in domestic law. If the power cable theory is a doctrine of domestic law, it takes precedence over those obligations.[41] Moreover, where Parliament does intend that the UK breach its international obligations, the courts are obligated to follow Parliament's lead. Of course, an undoubted doctrine exists in UK domestic law that domestic law should be interpreted as far possible so that it does not place the UK

---

[37] See European Union (Withdrawal) Bill 2017–19 as introduced in the Commons, sch 1, para 4 and cl 5(4).

[38] Article 70 probably reflects customary international law, so the inconvenience that two EU members, France and Romania, have not ratified the VCLT is of no account in this instance. See, eg, S Wittich, 'Consequences of Invalidity, Termination or Suspension of the Operation of a Treaty' in O Dörr and K Schmalenbach, *Vienna Convention on the Law of Treaties: A Commentary* (Heidelberg, Springer, 2011) 1201.

[39] Wittich (n 38), 1206.

[40] ibid, 1206. See also S Douglas-Scott, 'What Happens to "Acquired Rights" in the Event of a Brexit?', *UKCLA Blog* (16 May 2016), available at https://ukconstitutionallaw.org/.

[41] *Bennion on Statutory Interpretation* (n 17), s 270; *Collco Dealings Ltd v IRC* [1962] AC 1; *R v Secretary of State for the Home Department, ex parte Brind* [1991] 1 AC 696; Sales and Clement (n 4).

in violation of its international obligations.[42] But that doctrine arguably implies abandoning the power cable theory altogether, since the UK's international obligations would have included granting the rights required by EU law when the UK was subject to the treaties, and so retrospectively removing those rights means that the UK would be in a position of violating its obligations as they stood at the time.

   The underlying problem with looking for international legal reasons for restricting the retrospective effect of the power cable theory is similar to that with trying to interpret the power granted by the 2017 Act as a power to 'repeal' EU rights. It is the difficulty of combining any degree of monism with the doctrine of parliamentary legislative supremacy. Dualism is designed to protect Parliament's legislative power, but the relationship goes both ways. Parliamentary legislative supremacy also protects dualism by making monism impossible to implement in full.[43]

E. Non-retrospectivity and the Bridge Theory

In contrast, the bridge theory of the relationship between EU law and UK domestic law entails no retrospectivity. The bridging provision in domestic law, like a bridging term in a contract, carries the rules formed by the external process into the internal system, but it is the internal system that gives those rules force. Domestic law gives legal force to the bridge, and thus domestic law gives legal force to the rights and obligations carried over the bridge. As a consequence, even if the external process is brought to an end, anything already carried over the bridge continues in force. To continue with the analogy with contracts of employment, once a term of a collective agreement has been incorporated into an individual contract of employment through a bridge in the individual contract of employment, the termination of the collective agreement does not itself affect the continued validity of the incorporated term.[44] As a result the bridge theory produces no retrospective effects if the EU Treaties no longer apply to the UK.

III. The Adoption of the Power Cable Theory in *Miller*

The bridge theory seems superior to the power cable theory in its fit with the text of section 2(1), the requirements of section 18 of the 2011 Act and in avoiding retrospectivity. In *Miller*, however, the Divisional Court seems to have assumed

---

[42] *Bennion on Statutory Interpretation* (n 17), s 270; *Saad v Secretary of State for the Home Department* [2001] EWCA Civ 2008, [2002] Imm AR 471, [15], [16].

[43] Kelsen (n 9), 333, thought that it was theoretically possible for monism to accept the supremacy of domestic law, but most commentators aver that monism entails the supremacy of international law.

[44] *Robertson v British Gas Corporation* [1983] ICR 351, 356 (Ackner LJ), 358 (Kerr LJ); and *Gibbons v Associated British Ports* [1985] IRLR 376. See *Chitty on Contracts*, available at https://legalresearch. westlaw.co.uk/books/chitty-contracts/, 40-051.

the truth of the power cable theory: 'It is common ground that if the UK withdraws from the Treaties pursuant to a notice given under article 50 EU, there will no longer be any enforceable EU rights.'[45] The Supreme Court went further. It expressly adopts the view that EU rights are powered by the EU Treaties:

> In one sense, of course, it can be said that the 1972 Act is the source of EU law, in that, without that Act, EU law would have no domestic status. But in a more fundamental sense and, we consider, a more realistic sense, where EU law applies in the United Kingdom, it is the EU institutions which are the relevant source of that law.[46]

It is worth noting, however, how these courts came to these conclusions. In the Divisional Court, as the phrase '[i]t is common ground' makes clear, the parties agreed, and so did not debate the view that withdrawal from the Treaties in international law entailed the complete loss of legal force of all EU-derived rights in domestic law. The applicants had an obvious reason to adopt that view. Their case would have been undermined if the effect of withdrawal on the international plane was that only future EU rights and obligations were cut off but not existing ones. It is less clear why the Government accepted it. In a better-known example in *Miller* of the Government's adopting a position contrary to one that might have helped its case, the issue of the unilateral revocability of an Article 50 TEU notice, one can immediately discern a political motive. The Government wanted to give no comfort to those who hoped that Brexit might be overthrown. But in the power cable example, the motive is less obvious.

For one thing, the power cable theory leaves one wondering why, if all directly effective rights come to an end in domestic law simply because of the Article 50 process, it is necessary to repeal the ECA itself. Repeal would seem only to undermine the validity of all the secondary legislation passed under section 2(2) (because of the doctrine that repeal of a parent Act entails repeal of all the secondary legislation made under it),[47] thus creating a problem the European Union (Withdrawal) Bill has to solve that would otherwise not exist. Since repeal of the ECA has a great symbolic value for those who support Brexit, one would have thought that the bridge theory would have better suited the Government's political requirements.

Perhaps the answer is that the Government simply wanted to maximise the increased scope of ministerial power that would flow from winning the case. It positively wanted to win recognition for a power to destroy existing domestic rights, and its desire for that outcome overrode the risk that pursuing it reduced the Government's chances of winning the case in the first place.

In the Supreme Court another factor came into play: judicial entrepreneurialism. Central to the majority's reasoning is the 'source of law' theory, relegating the

---

[45] *Miller* (n 1), [51]. See also ibid, [14].

[46] *Miller* (n 2), [61].

[47] *Watson v Winch* [1916] 1 KB 688; *R (Chaudhary) v Bristol Crown Court* [2015] EWHC 723 (Admin), [2016] 1 WLR 631. See further *Bennion on Statutory Interpretation* (n 17), s 70.

Divisional Court's emphasis on the fate of rights to a secondary role.[48] But the phrase 'source of law' occurs nowhere in the written cases of the parties and interveners. Related expressions (for example 'sources of rights and obligations') occur but in the submissions of the applicants, where they are arguing *against* the Government's position that it had a power to change or remove EU rights because their origin was *not* in a UK statute.[49] Just as oddly, the metaphor used by the majority in relation to how the 'source of law' was connected to the UK domestic system, namely a 'conduit', comes out of the Government's arguments, not the applicants' arguments, but was then deployed against the Government.[50] The phrase 'source of law' makes its first appearance in the case when raised in oral argument by one of the judges, Lord Hodge,[51] before being taken up enthusiastically by Lords Sumption,[52] Kerr[53] and Carnwath,[54] and only then being adopted, opportunistically, by counsel for the main applicant.[55] When the 'source of law' theory was put (by Lord Mance) to counsel for the Government, on the last day of oral argument, counsel could only reply, somewhat feebly, that the ECA did not in terms transfer law-making power to the EU and that the theory was just another way of talking about rights and obligations.[56]

The majority does, nevertheless, make two oblique references to the problem of retrospectivity, even though counsel neither offered nor were asked to offer any observations on the problem. In the first reference, the majority says:

> Other rights, arising under EU Regulations or directly under the EU Treaties, will cease to have effect upon withdrawal (save in relation to rights and liabilities already accrued).[57]

In the second, it says:

> Upon the United Kingdom's withdrawal from the European Union, EU law will cease to be a source of domestic law for the future (even if the Great Repeal Bill provides that

---

[48] The reasons for the switch of emphasis are not explored openly. One possibility is that the Divisional Court's reasoning on what it called 'category ii' rights was shaky—it is not clear why the prerogative should not be used to alter UK citizens' rights against foreign governments—and on 'category iii' rights was conspicuously absent. That left only category (i) rights, the trouble with which was that even the Divisional Court refused to rely on them because of the argument that they themselves could be changed at any time through the legislative processes of the EU and so could not be treated as immune from a form of prerogative action.

[49] See the documents listed at https://www.supremecourt.uk/news/article-50-brexit-appeal.html.

[50] See Printed Case of the Appellant, available at https://www.gov.uk/government/uploads/system/uploads/attachment_data/file/570778/Supreme_Court_Printed_Case_of_the_Secretary_of_State_for_Exiting_the_European_Union.PDF, at, eg, [7], [8], [11], [46], [78] and [86].

[51] Transcript of the Second Day of Oral Argument, available at https://www.supremecourt.uk/news/article-50-brexit-appeal.html, p 55 line 6.

[52] ibid, p 144 line 25.

[53] ibid, p 145 line 17.

[54] ibid, p 172 line 24.

[55] ibid, p 178 line 24 and p 187 line 4.

[56] Transcript of the Fourth Day of Oral Argument, available at https://www.supremecourt.uk/docs/draft-transcript-thursday-161208.pdf, p 160 line 22, p 162 lines 3–10, p 177 lines 2–18.

[57] *Miller* (n 2), [70].

some legal rules derived from it should remain in force or continue to apply to accrued rights and liabilities).[58]

One can immediately see an inconsistency. In the first passage the majority assumes that withdrawal will not have an effect on 'rights and liabilities already accrued', but in the second passage it assumes that the 'Great Repeal Bill' (the Government's pre-publication nickname for the European Union (Withdrawal) Bill) would have to include provision to save accrued rights and liabilities. As it happens, since the effects of turning off the power cable are not the same as a repeal, and in particular as a repeal under section 16 of the Interpretation Act, the latter view is the better one. But the inconsistency itself illustrates the point that the Court does not seem to have fully turned its mind to the problems of adopting the power cable theory. None of the arguments against the power cable theory or in favour of the bridge theory were put to the judges in *Miller*.

In broader discussions of the case, in seminars and lectures, some oblique discussions did take place, but they were dominated and distracted by the ultimately misleading issue of whether section 2(1) was 'ambulatory'.[59] Section 2(1) is undoubtedly 'ambulatory' in the sense that it authorises and legitimates a frequently changing corpus of EU rights and obligations, just as assets covered by a floating charge or terms incorporated into a contract by reference can constantly change. But the issue is not whether the content can change but *how* it changes, and what happens when, in this game of legal musical chairs, the music is turned off. Floating charges crystallise on the assets held by the debtor at the relevant time. Terms incorporated by reference also crystallise for the purposes of litigation at the point of breach. In neither case do the claimant's rights disappear retrospectively just because the precise content is different from what it was when it was first created.

One argument for the power cable view and implicitly against the bridge view occasionally materialised, but it is less than convincing. The argument was that rejecting the power cable view would entail the UK's remaining subject to new EU law even after the Treaties no longer applied, an arrangement so politically unlikely that it is difficult to imagine its being envisaged in 1972 as the intended result of a UK withdrawal from the Treaties in international law. It is true that, first, the EU would continue to exist and make law if the Treaties no longer applied to the UK, and that, second, it would be technically possible for the UK to continue to incorporate that law even if it were no longer a member, just as individual contracts of employment can incorporate terms from a collective agreement even if neither employee nor employer is a party to the collective agreement. But that is not how the bridge theory works. The bridge view accepts that the EU will continue to legislate for its members, but it asserts that if the UK ceases to be a member, the bridge closes.

---

[58] ibid, [80].

[59] See, eg, J Finnis, 'Brexit and the Balance of Our Constitution', *Judicial Power Project*, 2 December 2016, available at http://judicialpowerproject.org.uk/wp-content/uploads/2016/12/Finnis-2016-Brexit-and-the-Balance-of-Our-Constitution3.pdf.

As a result, it would be unwise to take the issue as settled by *Miller* and the debates surrounding it. If the UK were again to take on obligations in international law similar to those imposed by the EU Treaties, one should not assume that the starting point for analysing the relationship between domestic and international law would or should be the power cable theory. Even if the Brexit process were to be reversed and the ECA either saved or revived, it would still be worth suggesting that the point was not fully argued in *Miller*. Admittedly it is difficult to deny that the source of law argument was crucial to the result of the case, and that adopting the bridge view would have resulted not only in the failure of that line of reasoning but also of the majority's secondary line that withdrawal would result in the loss of individual rights. But a way does exist to preserve the result of *Miller* using the bridge theory and so to avoid having to argue that *Miller* was wrongly decided (although some might want to do that anyway). The argument would be a purified version of the *Miller* majority's constitutional change argument, the argument that cutting off a 'source of law' was too 'fundamental' a constitutional change to be achievable without the authority of statute.[60] The argument consistent with the bridge theory would be that cutting off even purely future EU rights was too great a constitutional change to bring about by prerogative action. The argument would be that cutting off the supply of rights crossing the bridge requires statutory authority even though the effect is only prospective.

The argument for the *Miller* result's using the bridge theory would be reinforced by the statutory basis of the bridge itself, a point that perhaps distinguishes it from the majority's use in *Miller* itself of a somewhat indistinct and uncalibrated argument from 'constitutional scale'.[61] The argument would be that Parliament, in creating the bridge, had assumed that rights and obligations would be crossing it, so that halting all traffic over the bridge was an action that only Parliament could take. It would amount to applying *Secretary of State for the Home Department, ex parte Fire Brigades Union* ('*ex parte FBU*'), in which the House of Lords held that Ministers could not use their powers to empty legislation of its content.[62] In the words of Lord Browne-Wilkinson:

> It is for Parliament, not the executive, to repeal legislation. The constitutional history of this country is the history of the prerogative powers of the Crown being made subject to the overriding powers of the democratically elected legislature as the sovereign body.[63]

One of the dissenters in *Miller* heavily criticised the decision in *ex parte FBU* as an inappropriate intrusion by the courts into the relationship between government and parliament, and attempted to restrict its effect by claiming that it turned on a narrow point about a duty to keep the possibility of issuing a commencement

---

[60] *Miller* (n 2), [78]–[82].
[61] M Elliott, 'The Supreme Court's Judgment in *Miller*: In Search of Constitutional Principle' (2017) 76 *CLJ* 257.
[62] *Secretary of State for the Home Department, ex parte Fire Brigades Union* [1995] 2 AC 513.
[63] ibid, 552.

order under review.[64] The contrary argument is that Lord Browne-Wilkinson's remark applies more aptly in *Miller* than it did in *ex parte FBU* itself. Where a statutory scheme has not been commenced, as in *ex parte FBU*, one might plausibly take into account the fact that the parent statute gave to a Minister the power not just to commence it, but also not to commence it. Parliament knows that when it gives a Minister an unqualified commencement power it risks the legislation never coming into effect.[65] But where a statutory scheme has been in full force for more than 40 years, in use virtually every working day in that time, with no ministerial power appearing on the face of the Act to repeal it, a court might be forgiven for thinking that the scheme should not be defeated by another, non-parliamentary route. That is the constitutional argument of *Miller*, shorn of its reliance on 'sources of law', 'conduits', 'constitutional scale' and the power cable theory.

IV. The Inconsistent Assumptions of the European Union (Withdrawal) Bill

Another possible source of support for the power cable theory comes in the form of the Government's argument for aspects of the European Union (Withdrawal) Bill 2017–19. In the White Paper preceding the Bill, for example, the Government said:

> [S]ome types of EU law (such as EU regulations) are directly applicable in the UK's legal system. This means they have effect here without the need to pass specific UK implementing legislation. They will therefore cease to have effect in the UK once we have left the EU …[66]

But the situation is not as straightforward as it might seem. The Bill as presented to Parliament in 2017 had two quite different aims. One, covered by clause 1, is completely to repeal the ECA. The other, covered by the rest of the Bill, is to retain in domestic law, as far as is practicable, the substance of EU rights and obligations as they stand at the date of exit. The problem is explaining why both of those provisions are needed at the same time on the same theory. The bulk of the Bill—the creation and regulation of 'retained EU law' out of existing statutes, secondary legislation, and directly effective EU rights and obligations—does indeed seem to assume that the power cable view is correct. It takes for granted the view that on the day of exit, all directly effective EU law, including vested rights, will lapse and so need to be rescued and preserved. But the complete repeal of the ECA assumes, on the contrary, that the power cable view is not correct, since if the power cable view were correct, withdrawal on the international level itself would have all the

---

[64] See *Miller* (n 2), [250]–[255] (Lord Carnwath).

[65] See, eg, the debate initiated by Lord Norton of Louth, HL Deb (GC) 7 November 2013, vol 749, cols 146–56.

[66] *Legislating for the United Kingdom's withdrawal from the European Union* (Cm 9446), 13.

desired effects of extricating UK domestic law from EU law. Indeed, one might also wonder what the point of repeal of the ECA might be if the bridge view is correct, since under the bridge view UK domestic law is unaffected by future EU legislation and past EU legislation is left undisturbed. Clause 1 of the Bill seems rather to assume that unless the ECA is repealed, EU law will continue to be incorporated into UK domestic law, a view inconsistent with both the power cable and bridge views.

In fact, on closer inspection, the Government is careful in the White Paper to claim neither that the repeal of the ECA is necessary for Brexit to happen, nor that withdrawal alone removes EU rights and obligations. On the first point it says that

> it is important to repeal the ECA to ensure there is maximum clarity as to the law that applies in the UK, and to reflect the fact that following the UK's exit from the EU it will be UK law, not EU law, that is supreme.

The Government's argument works slightly better in reverse order. It would be confusing, it is claiming, to leave in place those parts of the ECA, section 2(4) for example, that give supremacy to the EU legal order when 'in fact' that supremacy would already have ended (which is true, note, under both power cable and bridge theories). But rather than just excise the confusing and otiose sections, the cause of clarity would be best served by repealing the whole Act.

Deciding to repeal the whole Act (presumably for political and symbolic reasons in addition to the technical reasons offered in the White Paper) itself raises doubts about the continued domestic validity of existing EU law. Indeed, the White Paper adds to the phrase 'They will therefore cease to have effect in the UK once we have left the EU' the words 'and repealed the ECA'. It is the combination of withdrawal and repeal that gives rise to the Government's anxiety about the continued validity of EU rights, not just withdrawal by itself. That is true not only of the secondary legislation passed under section 2(2), which falls automatically on repeal of its parent legislation,[67] but also of directly effective rules given effect by section 2(1).

The Bill does not, therefore, lend any support to the power cable theory. It is merely covering several possible theories of the relationship between EU law and UK law, and trying both to extricate the UK from the EU legal order and to preserve EU substantive law whichever theory turns out to be correct.

V. Some Implications and Lessons for the Future

The Supreme Court in *Miller* managed to decide the case without considering the implications of how it was deciding it for an important constitutional and legal principle, namely, the principle that retrospectivity should be discouraged.

---

[67] *Watson v Winch* [1916] 1 KB 688; *R (Chaudhary) v Bristol Crown Court* [2015] EWHC 723 (Admin), [2016] 1 WLR 631. See further *Bennion on Statutory Interpretation* (n 17), s 70.

It also managed to decide the case without thinking about the full range of options for how domestic individual rights might arise out of EU law. As a consequence, it failed to notice some less-than-complex textual objections to what it was doing, for example the effect of section 18 of the European Union Act 2011 and what section 2(1) of the ECA actually says. But the implications go further.

First, a broader point, but one worth noting: lawyers tend to interpret statutes as if they take consistent points of view, but it is apparent that the European Union (Withdrawal) Bill has no consistent point of view. It takes one theoretical perspective for one purpose and another (or another two) for other purposes. That approach is driven partly by political imperatives, in particular that the Government promised its pro-Brexit supporters that it would repeal the ECA, and that is what it then had to propose, regardless of whether doing so had any legal point and of whether repeal itself creates problems that would not otherwise arise. But it is also driven by a lack of confidence inside government in the stability of the judges' views about fundamental matters such as the mechanics of dualism. Legislation of this type is essentially an exercise in fire prevention. It is trying to anticipate the different types of fire the courts might light. One should not therefore interpret it as encouraging or approving of any of those types of fire.

Second, and also a broad point, the process courts use to decide cases has some obvious flaws as a method of resolving constitutional issues. That courts are bad at producing good solutions to 'polycentric' disputes is a thought with a long and distinguished history.[68] The story of *Miller* and the power cable theory shows how that criticism of courts works at its most simple and basic. Even the most important constitutional cases can produce situations in which the parties before the court do not represent the full range of options the court should be considering. Indeed, the parties might collude in suppressing options. The lack of any real debate about the possible unilateral revocability of an Article 50 notice is another example of the same phenomenon in *Miller* itself. We need judges to resolve disputes, but their solutions should not be taken as the best possible advice as to how best to organise the state.

Lack of time, or perhaps more precisely caving in to a politically determined timetable,[69] might have played a part. If so, a further implication is that we should return to an older tradition of taking less seriously judicial decisions arrived at in a hurry. It is not just courts that should take adequate time for consideration.

---

[68] L Fuller and K Winston, 'The Forms and Limits of Adjudication' (1978) 92 *Harvard Law Review* 353 (first circulated privately by Fuller in 1957); JWF Allison, 'Fuller's Analysis of Polycentric Disputes and the Limits of Adjudication' (1994) 53 *CLJ* 367; though see also J King, 'The Pervasiveness of Polycentricity' [2008] *PL* 101.

[69] The Prime Minister had announced that she wanted to issue the Article 50 notice 'before the end of March' (see http://www.bbc.co.uk/news/uk-politics-37532364), presumably because she was anxious to avoid any possibility of holding elections in the UK for the European Parliament, which would otherwise be due in early June 2019, and which might have acted as a substitute for a second referendum on Brexit.

For if a case is to be taken very seriously, counsel and academics too need time to work through all the options. The more important the case, the longer it should take. That is not perhaps a very congenial suggestion for an age of instant news and comment restricted to 280 characters, but greater rapidity of communication has not meant that lawyers and judges (or indeed anyone else) have become any cleverer than they used to be.

Third, and of more immediate interest, the adoption of the power cable theory in *Miller* has implications for other legal aspects of the Brexit process. If the power cable theory is correct, one can only conclude that Parliament was happy to grant the Prime Minister, through the 2017 Act, a statutory power retrospectively to empty another Act of Parliament, the ECA, of all of its effective content. The extent of the legislative powers granted to Ministers in the European Union (Withdrawal) Bill caused concern,[70] but the almost equally extensive powers granted by the 2017 Act seem to have been accepted with equanimity. The danger is that future governments will say that the 2017 Act shows that Parliament is capable of granting Ministers extensive powers retrospectively to eliminate legislation.

Perhaps more significantly, questions arise about the interpretation of the European Union (Withdrawal) Bill. For example, the Bill as drafted said 'There is no right in domestic law on or after exit day to damages in accordance with the rule in *Francovich*.'[71] The question might arise whether *Francovich* rights are enforceable if the alleged breach occurred before exit day. Clause 4 of the Bill says that rights arising out of section 2(1) of the ECA 'continue on and after exit day to be recognised and available in domestic law'. One might think that, as a consequence, *Francovich* actions arising out of pre-exit breaches would 'continue', and thus the bar on *Francovich* actions 'on or after' exit day would not apply. But the power cable theory provides a route to coming to the opposite conclusion. If all section 2(1) rights are turned off by leaving the EU in international law, the words 'continue on and after' in clause 4 could be read as referring to new rights created at the point exit happens, rights to which the bar on *Francovich* actions would apply. Under the power cable theory, the EU rights destroyed by leaving the EU are not the same as those 'continued' under the Bill because they come from different sources. The point is reinforced by the possibility, not fully removed by amendments in committee in the Commons, that 'exit day' in UK law might be different from the day the UK leaves the EU in international law.[72] In contrast, under the bridge theory,

---

[70] For example, House of Lords Select Committee on the Constitution, *European Union (Withdrawal) Bill: interim report* (TSO, 2017).

[71] European Union (Withdrawal) Bill (as passed at Second Reading in the House of Commons), sch 1, para 4.

[72] The Bill originally left the determination of 'exit day' in UK law to the Secretary of State. At committee stage in the Commons, that changed. Exit day became fixed as 29 March 2019, but the Secretary of State was given a power, but not a duty, to change the day to ensure coincidence of domestic and international exit days. If the Secretary of State omits to exercise that power, it is still possible for domestic and international law to prescribe different exit days.

no such difficulty arises, since the relevant rights are powered and continue to be powered by domestic law through exit day.[73]

In addition, if the withdrawal negotiations result in an agreement for a 'transitional' or 'implementation' phase, in which the UK leaves the EU but the Treaties continue to apply for many but not all purposes, including the application of new EU law arising during the transition period, questions will arise about precisely how that agreement can be put into operation on the UK side. The power cable view gives rise to a difficulty: if the UK is no longer a member of the EU, how can the Treaties power any of the content of UK domestic law? And perhaps worse from a political point of view, how can the power cable be turned back on again so that it powers only some EU rights and obligations but not all? If the legal force of EU rights comes from the Treaties, how can one pick and choose which ones work? There might need to be a completely new treaty enforcing not EU law but the law of that treaty, a situation which would raise yet more difficulties about the role and powers of the Court of Justice of the European Union (CJEU).[74] In contrast, under the bridge view, since the motive force comes from UK law, the UK Parliament can control which EU rights and obligations receive legal force and which not during the transition period.[75]

Beyond any transition period, if the UK reverts to dualist purity, the difficulties of the power cable theory might begin to fade away. As long as any regulatory alignment is achieved by a process akin to section 2(2) of the ECA rather than section 2(1), separating international obligations from the domestic action taken to comply with them, law making would become entirely domestic. That appears to be the position for dualist EEA members such as Norway and Iceland (although Liechtenstein appears to be monist),[76] so that even membership of the internal market would not require a return to the previous position.

At one stage, negotiations around continuing individual rights of EU citizens in the UK looked as if they might lead to an exception, but the Joint Report between the UK and the Commission of December 2017 seems to envisage an entirely static system in which the UK courts are permitted, but not required, to refer questions

---

[73] Similar problems might arise out of the exclusion of the Charter of Fundamental Rights. Clause 5(4) is worded slightly differently from sch 1, para 4, saying 'The Charter of Fundamental Rights is not part of domestic law on or after exit', but a possibly even stronger argument might be constructed: all rights arising out of the Charter before exit day are destroyed on exit by the operation of international law and no new rights are created by cl 4.

[74] For a non-technical summary, see R Hogarth, *Dispute Resolution after Brexit* (London, Institute for Government, 2017).

[75] Or at least UK Ministers can do this, if the European Union (Withdrawal) Bill is passed with all of its Henry VIII powers intact on the issue of implementing the withdrawal agreement. An amendment making those powers conditional on Parliament's passing a statute approving the withdrawal agreement leaves the powers intact but gives Parliament control over the purposes for which they can be used.

[76] C Baudenbacher, 'If Not EEA State Liability, Then What: Reflections Ten Years after the EFTA Court's *Sveinbjornsdottir* Ruling' (2009) 10 *Chicago Journal of International Law* 333, 353.

of interpretation of EU law to the ECJ for a limited period.[77] The Joint Report does say that EU citizens must be able to enforce their rights under the Withdrawal Agreement 'directly', which implies a return to quasi-monism, and that their rights must prevail even over subsequent legislation, implying a recreation of part of section 2(4) of the ECA,[78] but the Report does not seem to presage any kind of dynamic law-making process.[79]

Nevertheless, in theory the old difficulties could recur if a future UK Government wanted to remove the protection of EU citizens' rights that might arise out of the Withdrawal Agreement. If the power cable theory is correct, the only thing standing between the Government and a retrospective destruction of EU citizens' rights through denunciation of the Withdrawal Agreement would be a second *Miller* case, in which arguments of 'constitutional scale' would have far less purchase and the fact that the treaty had no dynamic aspect would eliminate any 'source of law' argument.

Ultimately, even under the bridge theory, if Parliament wanted to remove individual rights retrospectively, it could legislate for retrospectivity expressly and unequivocally. That fact is an aspect of the characteristically British combination of parliamentary legislative supremacy and dualism, a combination that stands in the way of any UK Government's giving cast-iron guarantees about the future content of UK law. That combination has not in the past been fatal for the UK's credibility in international affairs, although it appears to have become a problem in the negotiations between the UK and the EU-27,[80] and so the search to find ways around the problem is probably in vain. The power cable theory might nevertheless seem to some to on the EU-27 side to be a possible solution, because it places the motive force for a set of rights outside the UK system. But in the end, the combination of dualism and, if necessary, parliamentary supremacy will defeat it. All that adopting the power cable theory can ultimately achieve is to make destroying rights retrospectively just a little easier.

---

[77] Negotiators of the European Union and the United Kingdom Government, *Joint report from the negotiators of the European Union and the United Kingdom Government on progress during phase 1 of negotiations under Article 50 TEU on the United Kingdom's orderly withdrawal from the European Union* (Commission of the EU 27, Brussels, 2017).

[78] ibid, paras 35–36.

[79] ibid, para 9 (at least if interpreted in conjunction with items 1 and 2 of the accompanying Joint Technical Note).

[80] See C McCrudden, 'An Early Deal-Breaker? EU Citizens' Rights in the UK after Brexit, and the future role of the European Court of Justice', *UKCLA Blog* (27 June 2017), available at http://ukconstitutionallaw.org/.

7

Constitutional Change and Territorial Consent: The *Miller* Case and the Sewel Convention

AILEEN McHARG

I. Brexit and the Territorial Constitution

The United Kingdom (UK) that voted in 1975 on whether to remain in what was then the European Economic Community was a unitary state with a single legislature and single source of sovereign authority. Direct rule had recently been restored in Northern Ireland, and its devolved Parliament abolished;[1] devolution to Scotland and Wales was under discussion, but no firm proposals were yet being considered. The referendum vote was counted on a territorial basis, and there was concern about the political implications of a territorially-divided result, particularly in the context of rising Scottish nationalism. But it would have been difficult to argue that territorial difference—which in the event never materialised—was *constitutionally* relevant.

By the time of the 2016 referendum on European Union (EU) membership, by contrast, the territorial dimension of withdrawing from the EU was significantly complicated by the existence of devolved legislatures in Scotland, Wales and Northern Ireland. For one thing, devolution raised practical implications for the process of withdrawal given the way in which EU decision-making competences cut across the division between UK and devolved competences, and obligations to comply with EU law and shared responsibility for its implementation were written into the devolution statutes. Brexit would necessarily, therefore, require amendment of the devolution legislation and cooperation between the UK and devolved governments in adjusting laws and policies currently governed by EU law.

---

[1] Northern Ireland Constitution Act 1973.

More importantly, territorial divisions on EU membership were much more pronounced in 2016. Whereas England and Wales both voted, narrowly, to Leave the EU,[2] Scotland and Northern Ireland voted more emphatically to Remain,[3] although England's much larger population (boosted by higher turnouts in England and Wales)[4] ensured a slim UK-wide majority for Leave.[5] It is, moreover, clear that these territorial divergences were themselves exacerbated by devolution. This is true, first, in the sense that the existence of devolved institutions provided a platform for the articulation and amplification of political difference; the preoccupations of the devolved political systems were different from those of the UK political system, and in no case (even in Wales) was Euro-scepticism a significant feature of debate. Euro-scepticism—and the associated rise of the UK Independence Party—was therefore a predominantly *English* phenomenon. But, second, devolution—and the perceived advantages that this gave to the devolved nations—was also one of the constitutional discontents fuelling the rise in English nationalism with which the desire for Brexit was clearly associated.[6]

Further, by 2016, territorial difference on the question of EU membership clearly had taken on a constitutional significance. In Northern Ireland, this was due to the role of EU membership in facilitating the cross-border cooperation within the island of Ireland on which the 1998 Good Friday Agreement was based. In Scotland, where the best way to ensure Scotland's continued membership of the EU had been a key issue in the 2014 independence referendum, the Scottish National Party (SNP) had clearly stated in its 2016 Holyrood election manifesto that it would regard Scotland being taken out of the EU against the will of Scottish voters as amounting to 'a significant and material change in the circumstances that prevailed in 2014', sufficient to justify a second independence referendum.[7] And even in Wales, the Welsh Government regards Brexit as unbalancing the devolution settlement in such a way as to strengthen the case for fundamental reform of the territorial constitution.[8]

In anticipation of a territorially-divided result, the SNP (with the support of Plaid Cymru) made the case during debates on the European Union Referendum Bill for the adoption of a principle of parallel consent: in other words, for Leave to win the referendum, it would need to secure a majority of votes across the UK *and*

---

[2] By 53.4% and 52.5%, respectively.

[3] By 62% and 55.8%, respectively.

[4] Turnout was 73% in England and 71.7% in Wales, but 67.2% in Scotland and just 62.7% in Northern Ireland.

[5] 51.9%.

[6] See generally A Henderson et al, 'How Brexit was Made in England' (2017) 19 *British Journal of Politics and International Relations* 631.

[7] Scottish National Party, *The Next Steps to a Better Scotland* (2016), 23.

[8] See, eg, Carwyn Jones, *Our Future Union—a Perspective from Wales*, speech to the Institute for Government, 15 October 2014; Welsh Government and Plaid Cymru, *Securing Wales' Future: Transition from the European Union to a New Relationship with Europe* (2017).

in each of the constituent parts of the UK. The analogy was drawn with federal countries like the United States of America, in which constitutional amendment would require consent at both State and federal level.[9] However, this argument was rejected by both Conservative and Labour MPs on the basis that relations with the EU were reserved to the UK level, and therefore the decision to withdraw was one for the UK as a whole. Indeed, one Labour MP rejected the federal analogy, arguing that since Brexit was a matter of international relations rather than constitutional amendment, there would be no veto for States in the USA.[10]

However, the 'reconstitutionalisation' of the withdrawal decision in *R (Miller) v Secretary of State for Exiting the European Union*[11]—that is, the rejection of the characterisation of the decision to notify the UK's intention to withdraw from the UK under Article 50 of the Treaty on European Union as being purely a matter of foreign affairs, which could validly be made under the prerogative—created an opportunity to revive the argument for devolved consent, this time via the Sewel Convention. If, so the argument went, withdrawal from the EU was a decision requiring statutory authorisation because of its necessary implications for legislation giving effect to EU membership, then it followed that it also had implications for the devolution statutes, which similarly operated on the assumption of continuing EU membership. That being so, legislation authorising withdrawal would require the consent of the devolved legislatures, because it would be legislation regarding devolved matters within the meaning of the Sewel Convention.

The argument was first raised in the Northern Irish High Court ('HCNI') in the *McCord* case, in which the court held that legislation was not required to trigger Article 50, but that even if it had been, it would not attract the operation of the Sewel Convention, at least in the Northern Irish context.[12] Devolution points were also raised in argument in the Divisional Court proceedings in *Miller*, but the court did not find it necessary to address them.[13] When the case reached the Supreme Court, however, the devolution dimension took on far greater importance—both because of the joining of the Northern Irish appeals and devolution references with the *Miller* proceedings, and because of the decision by the Scottish and Welsh Governments to intervene in the case. At least as far as the Scottish Government was concerned, this was a decision taken reluctantly, and as much for defensive reasons—to challenge the very narrow reading of the Sewel Convention adopted by the HCNI—as for offensive ones—to gain leverage with which to persuade the

---

[9] See Alex Salmond MP and Tasmina Ahmed-Sheik MP, HC Deb 16 June 2015, vol 596, cols 189, 190 and 231.

[10] Kevin Brennan MP, ibid, col 190. See also Chris Philp MP, ibid, col 189; Dominic Grieve MP, ibid, col 189; Pat McFadden MP, ibid, col 206; David Lidington MP, ibid, col 231.

[11] *R (Miller) v Secretary of State for Exiting the European Union* [2017] UKSC 5, [2017] 2 WLR 583.

[12] *McCord and Agnew* [2016] NIQB 85.

[13] *R (Miller) v Secretary of State for Exiting the European Union* [2016] EWHC 2768 (Admin), [2017] 1 All ER 158, [102].

UK Government to accept the devolved governments' views regarding the form and domestic implications of Brexit.[14]

Ultimately, the argument for devolved consent was unsuccessful. The Supreme Court unanimously refused to decide the issue, holding that as a matter of convention rather than law, the Sewel Convention did not give rise to legally enforceable obligations, nor could the courts give rulings on its operation or scope. Moreover, according to the Court, the statutory 'recognition' of the Convention by section 2 of the Scotland Act 2016 (inserting a new section 28(8) into the Scotland Act 1998) had not rendered it any more justiciable. In disposing of the issue in this way, the Court articulated a very narrow conception of its constitutional role, and a very traditional understanding of the territorial constitution, in which the pluralist and decentralised accounts of the location of constitutional authority articulated by or on behalf of the devolved institutions[15] operate only as political understandings in the shadow of the Westminster Parliament's legal omnipotence.

The effect was to hand a de facto victory to the UK Government, which simply maintained the position it had argued before the Supreme Court that the resulting European Union (Notification of Withdrawal) Act 2017 did not require devolved consent. Notification of withdrawal under Article 50 was duly given without securing the agreement of the devolved governments as to the UK's negotiating position, nor making any concessions to them regarding the domestic implications of Brexit. Nevertheless, the issue of devolved consent to the process of withdrawing from the EU has only been postponed rather than resolved by *Miller*. The UK Government has conceded that the European Union (Withdrawal) Bill 2017–19, before Parliament at the time of writing, *does* in certain respects engage the Sewel Convention,[16] and the devolved governments in Edinburgh and Cardiff are so far insisting that they will not recommend consent unless substantial changes are made.[17]

In the remainder of this chapter, I explore in more detail—and primarily from a Scottish perspective—the territorial dimension to the *Miller* decision. I discuss, first, the plausibility of the argument that the Sewel Convention required devolved consent to the EU (Notification of Withdrawal) Act. Second, I examine the Supreme Court's reasoning about the justiciability of conventions and

---

[14] See Scottish Government, *Scotland's Place in Europe* (December 2016); Welsh Government, *Securing Wales' Future* (n 8).

[15] See the written submissions of the Lord Advocate, Counsel General for Wales, and the *Agnew* claimants, available at https://www.supremecourt.uk/news/article-50-brexit-appeal.html.

[16] See Explanatory Notes to the European Union (Withdrawal) Bill, 29–20 and Annex A.

[17] Scottish Government, Legislative Consent Memorandum: European Union (Withdrawal) Bill, LCM-S5-10, Session 5 (2017), available at http://www.parliament.scot/S5ChamberOffice/SPLCM-S05-10-2017.pdf; Welsh Government, Legislative Consent Memorandum: European Union (Withdrawal) Bill (2017), available at http://www.assembly.wales/laid%20documents/lcm-ld11177/lcm-ld11177-e.pdf.

of section 28(8) of the Scotland Act 1998. Lastly, I consider the implications of *Miller* for the future of the territorial constitution and of the Sewel Convention as a technique for managing territorial relations.

II. The Sewel Convention and Constitutional Change

A. The Evolution of the Sewel Convention

The Sewel Convention, as it has developed since 1999, has become a central mechanism for the management of territorial relations within the UK; in particular for regulating the interface between reserved and devolved legislative competences. It performs two important functions. The first is a defensive one. It provides the devolved legislatures with a reassurance, in the face of the continuing assertion of Westminster's legislative omnipotence, that their primary *political* authority in relation to devolved matters will be respected through the requirement that Westminster will normally gain the consent of the relevant devolved legislature before legislating with regard to devolved matters. Secondly—and arguably more importantly in practice, at least in the early years of devolution[18]—it performs a facilitative function. In other words, it enables cooperation between the UK and devolved governments over the achievement of their policy goals, either where a UK-wide approach is considered desirable notwithstanding devolution, or where competence constraints might inhibit the effective realisation of devolved policy aims. The Convention thus addresses two key weaknesses in the UK's formal arrangements for territorial governance: the lack of legal *entrenchment* of the powers of the devolved legislatures; and the weakness of mechanisms for *shared rule*. In so doing, it shifts the UK's territorial constitution *in practice* from a system of devolution within a unitary state towards a more federal model, thus underlining its constitutional significance.

The Sewel Convention is somewhat unusual in that it originated in an explicit statement of intent by the Scottish Office Minister, Lord Sewel, during parliamentary debate on the Scotland Bill 1998. Discussing the use of what was to become section 28(7) of the Scotland Act 1998, which states that the power of the UK Parliament to make laws for Scotland is unaffected by the establishment of the Scottish Parliament, Lord Sewel went on to say, '[h]owever, as happened in Northern Ireland earlier in the century, we would expect a convention to be established that Westminster would not normally legislate with regard to devolved matters in Scotland without the consent of the Scottish Parliament'.[19] This expectation was

---

[18] See A Page and A Batey, 'Scotland's Other Parliament: Westminster Legislation about Devolved Matters in Scotland Since Devolution' [2002] *PL* 501.

[19] HL Deb 21 July 1998, vol 592, col 791.

subsequently reflected in, and amplified by, the Memorandum of Understanding agreed between the UK and devolved governments and various Devolution Guidance Notes (DGNs), first published in December 1999. Devolution Guidance Note 10 (on *Post-Devolution Primary Legislation Affecting Scotland*)[20] provides that the consent of the Scottish Parliament is normally required for legislation that 'contains provisions applying to Scotland and which are for devolved purposes' *or* 'which alter the legislative competence of the Parliament or the executive competence of the Scottish Ministers'. Trench refers to these two categories as the *policy arm* and *constitutional arm* of the Convention, respectively.[21] According to DGN 10, consent is *not*, however, required for legislation affecting Scotland that is for reserved purposes but which makes 'incidental or consequential changes to Scots law on non-reserved matters', even though it recognises that such effects might in some cases be significant.[22] Nevertheless, the distinction between legislation for reserved and devolved purposes is not watertight. Varying the scope of devolved legislative or executive competence is itself a reserved matter yet attracts the requirement of consent. Giving evidence to the Scottish Parliament's Procedures Committee in 2005, Lord Sewel argued that the inclusion of such legislation within the scope of the Convention went beyond its original purpose and 'results in real confusion'.[23]

McCorkindale notes that the practice of seeking devolved consent in Scotland has also evolved in other ways since 1999,[24] including the development of a much more formal procedure for seeking consent and scrutinising legislative consent memorandums,[25] and the granting of conditional consent.[26] There is also a range of obligations on the UK Government, for instance, concerning when and how consent will be sought to government Bills, and an expectation that it will oppose Private Members' Bills where devolved consent has not been granted.[27]

The evolving nature of legislative consent has created some uncertainty as to which elements are properly regarded as part of the Convention (and therefore constitutionally binding) and which are mere practice. In giving effect to the Smith Commission's recommendation that the Convention should be put on a statutory footing,[28] the UK Government chose to employ the precise words used by

---

[20] Available at https://www.gov.uk/government/publications/devolution-guidance-notes.

[21] A Trench, 'Brexit, Article 50 and Devolved Legislative Consent', *Devolution Matters Blog* (23 November 2016), available at https://devolutionmatters.wordpress.com/.

[22] Department for Constitutional Affairs, DGN10 (2005), paras 4 and 7.

[23] Submission by Lord Sewel, Scottish Parliament Procedures Committee, *The Sewel Convention*, 7th Report 2005, SP Paper 428 (Session 2), Annex C, paras 9–10.

[24] C McCorkindale, 'Echo Chamber: The 2015 General Election at Holyrood—A Word on Sewel', *Scottish Constitutional Futures Forum Blog* (13 May 2015), available at https://www.scottishconstitutionalfutures.org/.

[25] See *Standing Orders of the Scottish Parliament* (5th edn, 5th rev, May 2017) ch 9B.

[26] For example, to what became the Scotland Act 2012, S3M-8813, SP OR, 10 March 2011.

[27] DGN 10 (n 20).

[28] *Report of the Smith Commission for Further Devolution of Powers to the Scottish Parliament* (2014).

Lord Sewel in 1998. Resisting attempts to amend the provision to make it clear that the statutory provision covered *both* the policy arm and the constitutional arm of the Sewel Convention, the Advocate-General for Scotland, Lord Keen of Elie QC, sought to distinguish the Convention *per se*, which he claimed was limited to Lord Sewel's original statement, from the broader practice that had grown up around legislative consent as detailed in DGN 10[29]—a claim he repeated during oral argument before the Supreme Court in *Miller*.[30] Indeed, the importance of resisting this attempt to narrow the scope of the Convention was one reason why the Scottish Government felt it necessary to intervene in the Supreme Court proceedings.

Seeking to distinguish the Convention from the practice of the Convention was, however, misconceived. As I have argued elsewhere, the obligatory quality of a convention cannot be established by mere declaration, but rather is constituted through the practice of constitutional actors.[31] While Lord Sewel's statement may be understood as an *attempt to create* a constitutional rule regarding the seeking of devolved consent, it is not determinative of the scope of that rule. Rather it depends, as in Jennings' celebrated formulation, upon a combination of constitutional practice, the attitudes of the relevant constitutional actors towards that practice and the existence of sound constitutional reasons for regarding the practice as obligatory.[32] Thus, in the *McCord* case, it was the absence of 'consistent practice and usage', under either the Government of Ireland Act 1920 or under the Northern Ireland Act 1998, which led Maguire J to reject the broader understanding of the Convention as encompassing the constitutional arm as well as the policy arm.[33] In relation to Scotland, however, the Lord Advocate presented copious evidence of legislative consent motions being sought and granted in relation *both* to Bills legislating for devolved purposes *and* Bills altering legislative or executive competence.[34] In both cases, moreover, there is evidence that a refusal or grant of only qualified consent has been respected.[35]

Nevertheless, some uncertainty continues to surround the scope of the Sewel Convention as it applies to the Scottish Parliament. One issue concerns how far the Convention extends to *legislation on reserved matters* that also has implications

---

[29] HL Deb 24 February 2016, vol 769, cols 305–06.

[30] Transcript, day 4 (8 December 2016) 135–36, available at https://www.supremecourt.uk/news/article-50-brexit-appeal.html.

[31] A McHarg, 'Reforming the United Kingdom Constitution: Law, Convention, Soft Law' (2008) 71 *MLR* 853, 857–61.

[32] I Jennings, *The Law and the Constitution*, 5th edn (London, University of London Press, 1959) 136.

[33] *McCord and Agnew* (n 12), [119].

[34] See the written submissions of the Lord Advocate (n 15), Annex 1. The practice in Wales is more complex, but also supports the wider understanding of the Convention—see A Trench, 'Legislative Consent in Wales', *Devolution Matters Blog* (28 October 2015), available at https://devolutionmatters.wordpress.com/.

[35] For example, in relation to the Welfare Reform Act 2012 and the Scotland Act 2012.

for devolved matters. A number of controversies have arisen in recent years concerning Bills that would clearly be outwith Holyrood's legislative competence but nonetheless have effects on devolved matters which might be regarded as more than merely incidental.[36] Conversely, debate has also arisen over whether some Bills affecting the scope of devolved competence (such as a Bill repealing or reforming the Human Rights Act 1998) might have too minimal an effect to engage the requirement of legislative consent.[37]

The second area of uncertainty relates to the existence of *exceptions* to the Convention. The wording consistently adopted both by Lord Sewel and in subsequent formulations is that consent is *normally* required for legislation with regard to devolved matters, a proviso that must be understood in normative rather than purely descriptive terms. Since the only significant examples of the UK Parliament legislating with regard to devolved matters *without* devolved consent[38] relate to the wholly exceptional circumstances of Northern Ireland—in situations in which devolved government has actually or effectively broken down—it is unclear for what reasons it might be legitimate either to dispense with the requirement to seek consent, or to ignore a refusal of consent.

Both of these areas of uncertainty were implicated in the application of the Sewel Convention to legislation authorising withdrawal from the EU.

B. The Sewel Convention and EU Withdrawal

In assessing whether the EU (Notification of Withdrawal) Act 2017 should have been subject to devolved consent, two issues therefore require to be addressed. First, was it legislation 'with regard to devolved matters'? Secondly, if so, was this nevertheless a situation in which the requirement of devolved consent could justifiably be dispensed with?

The argument in *Miller* was mainly addressed to the first issue. The Lord Advocate, the Counsel General for Wales and the *Agnew* claimants in the Northern

---

[36] For example, in relation to the Trade Union Act 2016, see A Trench, 'Legislative Consent for the Trade Union Bill', *Devolution Matters Blog* (17 October 2015), available at https://devolutionmatters. wordpress.com/; in relation to the Immigration Act 2016, see T Mullen and S Craig, 'The Immigration Bill, Reserved Matters and the Sewel Convention', *Scottish Constitutional Futures Forum Blog* (15 April 2016), available at https://www.scottishconstitutionalfutures.org/; I Jamieson, 'Interpretation of the Sewel Convention, the Purpose Test and the Immigration Bill', *Scottish Constitutional Futures Forum Blog* (7 May 2017), ibid; T Mullen and S Craig, 'The Immigration Act 2016, Reserved Matters and the Sewel Convention: A Reply', *Scottish Constitutional Futures Forum Blog* (28 May 2016), ibid.

[37] See I Jamieson, 'The Repeal of the Human Rights Act and the Sewel Convention in Scotland', *Scottish Constitutional Futures Forum Blog* (12 June 2015), available at https://www. scottishconstitutionalfutures.org/; M Elliott, 'The Scottish Parliament, the Sewel Convention and Repeal of the Human Rights Act: a Postscript', *Public Law for Everyone Blog* (28 September 2015), available at https://publiclawforeveryone.com/.

[38] There has been at least one inadvertent breach of the Convention—see R Edwards, 'Scottish Councils Robbed of Powers to Deal with Litter—By Westminster', *Sunday Herald* (20 March 2016).

Ireland reference all agreed with the *Miller* claimants that legislation was required in order to trigger Article 50. However, they claimed that the impact of EU withdrawal on the devolution statutes—like the European Communities Act 1972 ('ECA'), also regarded as constitutional statutes[39]—provided an independent reason why notification of withdrawal could not be given under the foreign affairs prerogative. That being so, they argued, an Article 50 Bill would engage the Sewel Convention both in its policy arm—because it would interfere with legislation in devolved policy areas which relied upon EU law—and, more importantly, in its constitutional arm, by interfering with key provisions in the devolution statutes requiring the devolved governments and legislatures to implement and comply with EU law.

The UK Government's response[40] was to insist upon its characterisation of the decision to withdraw from the EU as a matter of foreign affairs, and upon the ambulatory nature of the relationship between domestic statutes and EU law. Thus, since international relations, including relations with the EU, are matters reserved to the UK level, and since the devolution statutes assumed, but did not require, continuing EU membership, they did not, it argued, have the effect of ousting the foreign affairs prerogative. Indeed, according to the UK Government, the EU law provisions in the devolution statutes were mere 'belt and braces' provisions—included to ensure that the UK remained in compliance with its EU law obligations, but strictly speaking unnecessary—the removal of which would not render the devolution legislation unworkable. Thus, even if legislation was required to trigger Article 50, the Sewel Convention would not be engaged because the reservation of relations with the EU meant that it would not be legislation 'with regard to a devolved matter'.

The UK Government's attempt to downplay the significance of the embedding of EU law into the devolution statutes is unconvincing. In the first place, although *relations with* the EU may be reserved, observing and implementing EU law is not. It was recognised from the outset of devolution that this made EU law effectively an area of *shared power* in which the devolved governments were active participants in the formulation of UK policy on EU matters in devolved areas,[41] and where there was dual UK and devolved responsibility for implementation and compliance with EU law.[42] The inclusion of specific implementation and

---

[39] *Thoburn v Sunderland City Council* [2001] EWHC Admin 195, [2003] QB 151; *H v Lord Advocate* [2012] UKSC 24, [2013] 1 AC 413.

[40] See Supplementary Supreme Court Printed Case of the Secretary of State for Exiting the European Union, available at https://www.supremecourt.uk/news/article-50-brexit-appeal.html.

[41] Indeed, Harrington identifies a more general sharing of the UK Government's treaty-making powers with sub-national authorities—see J Harrington, 'Scrutiny and Approval: the Role for Westminster-Style Parliaments in Treaty-Making' (2006) 55 *ICLQ* 121, 148–51.

[42] See Scottish Office, *Scotland's Parliament* (Cm 3658, 1997) ch 5; Concordat on Coordination of EU Policy Issues, in the *Memorandum of Understanding and Supplementary Agreements Between the United Kingdom Government, the Scottish Ministers, the Welsh Ministers, and the Northern Ireland Executive Committee* (2013).

compliance obligations in the devolution statutes, although from one perspective strictly unnecessary, therefore has had real consequences for the ways in which EU law has been implemented and enforced in the devolved territories. More generally, the removal of the EU tier of governmental decision making will necessarily have major implications for policymaking in devolved areas, and for the balance of power between the UK and devolved levels.

That said, what *precisely* the implications of Brexit will be for the devolution settlements—and indeed its implications for the status of EU law in the domestic legal systems more generally—is not a straightforward issue, as subsequent debates over the EU (Withdrawal) Bill have demonstrated. Nevertheless, having accepted the *Miller* claimants' arguments about the inevitable domestic effects of triggering Article 50, thereby collapsing the distinction between action on the international and domestic planes, it was difficult for the Supreme Court majority to resist the logic that the devolution statutes would also be affected:

> As already explained, it is normally impermissible for statutory rights to be removed by the exercise of prerogative powers in the international sphere. It would accordingly be incongruous if constraints imposed on the legislative competence of the devolved administrations by specific statutory provisions were to be removed, thereby enlarging that competence, other than by statute. A related incongruity arises by virtue of the fact that observance and implementation of EU obligations are a transferred matter and therefore the responsibility of the devolved administration in Northern Ireland. The removal of a responsibility imposed by Parliament by ministerial use of prerogative powers might also be considered a constitutional anomaly.[43]

But even if the devolution statutes were necessarily affected by the triggering of Article 50, the argument that withdrawal legislation would then engage the Sewel Convention faced the further problem that—as the UK Government pointed out and the Supreme Court acknowledged—devolved consent had *not* previously been sought for other legislation affecting the EU, including the European Communities (Amendment) Act 2002, the European Parliamentary Election Act 2002, the European Union Amendment Act 2008, the European Union Act 2011 and the European Union Referendum Act 2015.[44]

If conventions are founded in practice, is the absence of a direct precedent fatal to the argument that a conventional obligation arises? Not necessarily. In any system of rule making based on precedent, situations are unlikely to recur exactly. A judgment therefore has to be made about whether the current situation is materially the same as or materially different from those in which the rule has (or has not) previously been applied. For instance, the Lord Advocate pointed to a precedent where consent had been sought for a UK Bill affecting foreign affairs, but which nevertheless touched upon reserved matters.[45] Conversely, the issues

---

[43] *Miller* (n 11), [132].
[44] Supplementary Printed Case (n 40), para 36.
[45] See the written submissions (n 15), para 77, citing the International Organisations Bill.

raised by previous EU-related legislation might have been materially different—for instance, it is hard to see how the EU Referendum Act could by itself be said to have affected devolved matters. Alternatively, a previous failure to seek consent might simply have been an oversight, or may be an indication that the Convention has since evolved, or that a relevant exception to the Convention applied.

To assist in making sense of ambiguous practice, regard must be had the constitutional purpose(s) that the Convention may be said to serve or the constitutional values that it protects. Elliott argues that the constitutional value served by Sewel is respect for devolved autonomy.[46] In its original, policy arm, it serves that value in a fairly direct way—by preserving the sphere of devolved competence against Westminster encroachment. As regards the constitutional arm of the Convention, Elliott argues it again reflects the value of respect for devolved autonomy, 'but in broader, more diffuse terms':

> While it is relatively easy to see why the Convention should require consent before any *reduction* in devolved authority ... the position is more complex in respect of UK legislation *extending* devolved authority. At first glance ... it is difficult to see what the constitutional rationale might be for requiring consent to more devolution. However, the argument, presumably, is that the devolved institutions should be masters—or at least participants in the shaping—of their own destiny, and that it would contravene the spirit of devolution and the constitutional value of respect for devolved autonomy to foist upon devolved institutions unwanted powers (or, for that matter, to confer powers in a way or subject to conditions that were unpalatable to the relevant devolved body).

In fact, it is often argued that the requirement of devolved consent to changes in executive or legislative competences derives from the fact that the devolution statutes themselves contain mechanisms for adjusting the allocation of competences by Order in Council, which require the consent of both the UK and devolved legislatures.[47] The Sewel Convention thus prevents this procedure being bypassed through the use of primary rather than secondary legislation. But in a more fundamental sense it may be seen to reflect an important general principle underpinning devolution, which is that powers are devolved to particular territories only with their consent.[48] In practice, the contemporary history of devolution is not one of a top-down transfer of power from Westminster to the devolved territories, but rather of bottom-up demand for increased autonomy to which Westminster has given effect. Accordingly, the constitutional arm of the Sewel Convention secures the *sharing* of political and legal authority in relation to the determination of the scope of devolved autonomy. Indeed, as already noted, this idea of power sharing—of cooperation in the fulfilment of political aspirations—is as important to an understanding of the operation of the Sewel Convention in general as is its role in preserving the boundary between reserved and devolved competences.

---

[46] Elliott (n 37).

[47] Scotland Act 1998, s 30; Northern Ireland Act 1998, s 4(2); Government of Wales Act 2006, s 109.

[48] See A Tomkins, 'Scotland's Choice, Britain's Future' (2014) 130 *LQR* 215, 228.

As regards the demand for devolved consent in relation to withdrawal from the EU (as also for the demand for consent to a putative human rights reform Bill), then, whether this is regarded as falling within the scope of the principles underpinning the Convention depends on which of these constitutional rationales—autonomy or power-sharing—is emphasised. If the focus is on devolved autonomy then the devolved governments might be accused of seeking to extend the consent requirement into new constitutional territory. What is novel about these situations is that they involve a demand for devolved consent not in relation to the *direct* amendment of the devolution legislation, but rather in relation to *UK-wide* legislation that forms part of the broader constitutional context in which the devolution arrangements are situated. Alternatively, however, this can be seen as a natural extension of a principle of constitutional power-sharing which the Convention *already* embodies, understanding the devolution statutes not as discrete sub-national constitutions of purely local significance, but rather as conditioned by and conditioning the UK constitution as a whole.

But even if the argument can be made in principle that the Convention was engaged by Article 50 legislation, the question still needs to be addressed whether this was a situation in which an exception could legitimately have been made. After all, withdrawing from the EU is anything but 'normal'. In their submissions to the Supreme Court, neither the claimants and interveners nor the UK Government addressed what 'normally' means within the terms of the Sewel Convention; all parties accepted that it must be determined politically rather than judicially.[49] Nevertheless, political decisions as to when it is appropriate to depart from convention ought also to be guided by considerations of constitutional propriety.

Extrapolating from experience in relation to Northern Ireland, and from what little discussion there has been of this issue, two classes of cases can be suggested in which devolved consent in relation to UK legislation on devolved matters might legitimately be disregarded. The first are cases of necessity. Thus, for example, the enactment by the UK Parliament in November 2017 of a Budget Act for Northern Ireland[50] can be regarded as justified by necessity in the circumstances of ongoing failure to form a government in Northern Ireland following the Assembly elections in March 2017. Similarly, it was suggested during debate on the Scotland Bill 1998 that, were the Scottish Parliament to refuse to legislate in conformity with international obligations, the UK Parliament would be justified in legislating for it[51]—such action being necessary to avoid breaching international law.

---

[49] See also Lady Hale, 'The United Kingdom Constitution on the Move', *The Canadian Institute for Advanced Legal Studies' Cambridge Lectures 2017* (7 July 2017) 8, available at https://www.supremecourt.uk/docs/speech-170707.pdf.

[50] Northern Ireland Budget Act 2017.

[51] Dominic Grieve MP, HC Deb 13 January 1998, vol 305, col 151.

The second class of cases, identified by Calvert[52] and evidenced by the resumption of direct rule in Northern Ireland in 1972 in circumstances of civil unrest provoked by perceived systematic discrimination against the Catholic minority, is where the devolved legislature can be regarded as having abused the power entrusted to it. Again, it was suggested during debates on the Scotland Bill that if the Scottish Parliament proposed to budget outwith its means, the UK Parliament would be justified in legislating to remedy the situation.[53]

Can either of these exceptions be said to apply to the EU (Notification of Withdrawal) Act? Clearly, the majority of MPs and peers considered themselves constitutionally bound to give effect to the referendum result and, in so far as a requirement of devolved consent might have prevented that, it might therefore be said to have been *necessary* to disregard the Sewel Convention. However, this argument is problematic given that the constitutional authority of the referendum itself is disputed—both generally and specifically in relation to Scotland and Northern Ireland. Certainly, the constitutional recognition of the Sewel Convention is stronger than that of any equivalent putative convention that referendum results should be respected. Alternatively, it might be argued that the devolved governments were *abusing their power* by seeking to do indirectly via the Sewel Convention what they had failed to do directly in the EU Referendum Act, namely, to secure a principle of parallel consent to Brexit. But again, this argument is problematic: first, in that, as a general proposition, the Sewel Convention acts to modify the strict letter of the law; second, because devolution itself operates as a protective mechanism in light of the permanent minority status of the devolved nations in the UK Parliament; and, third, because an express reason given for rejecting the principle of parallel consent was that the referendum was only advisory.[54]

In both respects, then, the application of the Sewel Convention to the EU (Notification of Withdrawal) Act took us into highly uncertain constitutional territory. Here we see both the advantages and disadvantages of constitutional regulation through conventions. On the one hand, their inherent flexibility allows them to evolve and adapt to new situations and to accommodate new constitutional claims. On the other hand, such evolution depends upon consensus amongst the relevant constitutional actors as to what obligations they impose. Absent such consensus, there is no mechanism—unlike for legal rules—for the authoritative resolution of disputes about the meaning of conventions, and this is most problematic precisely in circumstances such as Brexit, where the constitutional stakes are high and the likelihood of achieving consensus is correspondingly low.

---

[52] H Calvert, *Constitutional Law in Northern Ireland: A Study in Regional Government* (1968), 91–92.
[53] Lord Sewel, HL Deb 30 July 1998, vol 592, col 1704.
[54] David Lidington MP, HC Deb 16 June 2015, vol 597, col 231.

III. The Justiciability of the Sewel Convention

In the end, this key distinction between legal and conventional rules was determinative of the way in which the Supreme Court handled the issue of devolved
consent. Notwithstanding the passage quoted in section II.B, the Court ultimately
considered it unnecessary to reach a definitive view on whether the devolution
statutes imposed an independent requirement for legislation to authorise the triggering of Article 50.[55] This was because the consequences of such a finding—the
implications for the application of the Sewel Convention—were, in the Court's
view, non-justiciable. Citing the decisions of the Supreme Court of Canada in
Re Resolution to Amend the Constitution (Patriation Reference)[56] and of the Privy
Council in *Madzimbamuto v Lardner-Burke*,[57] the Court considered it inherent in
the nature of conventions that they are not legally enforceable. While this does not
necessarily render them legally irrelevant, the Court nevertheless considered that
the role of judges in relation to conventions was a very narrow one:

> Judges … are neither the parents nor the guardians of political conventions; they are
> merely observers. As such, they can recognise the operation of a political convention
> in the context of deciding a legal question (as in the Crossman diaries case—Attorney
> General v Jonathan Cape Ltd [1976] 1 QB 752), but they cannot give legal rulings on its
> operation or scope, because those matters are determined within the political world. As
> Professor Colin Munro has stated, 'the validity of conventions cannot be the subject of
> proceedings in a court of law'—(1975) 91 LQR 218, 228.[58]

Nor in the Court's view, did the statutory recognition of the Sewel Convention
change its juridical status. In inserting section 28(8) into the Scotland Act 1998
(and enacting a similar provision in the Wales Act 2017),

> the UK Parliament is not seeking to convert the Sewel Convention into a rule which can
> be interpreted, let alone enforced, by the courts; rather, it is recognising the convention
> for what it is, namely a political convention, and is effectively declaring that it is a perma-
> nent feature of the relevant devolution settlement.[59]

All three elements of the Court's decision—the necessity of resolving the issue
of devolved consent; the role of the courts in the interpretation of conventions;
and the effect of statutory recognition—were more contestable than its relatively
cursory treatment of them acknowledged.

---

[55] *Miller* (n 11), [132].
[56] *Re Resolution to Amend the Constitution (Patriation Reference)* [1981] 1 SCR 753.
[57] *Madzimbamuto v Lardner-Burke* [1969] 1 AC 645.
[58] *Miller* (n 11), [146].
[59] ibid, [148].

A. Was the Sewel Convention Relevant to the Legal Question Before the Court?

Conventions may be relevant to the resolution of legal issues in various ways, both direct and indirect. Directly, a legal rule may refer to a convention—for instance, statutory references to the conventional institutions of the Cabinet and the Prime Minister—such that the operation of the legal rule cannot be understood without also understanding the relevant convention. Alternatively, the application of a legal rule may depend upon the existence or scope of a convention. In the *Jonathan Cape* case,[60] for example, the existence of a conventional obligation of Cabinet confidentiality established the factual nexus of confidentiality, plus the public interest justification, for holding that the unauthorised publication of ministerial memoirs amounted prima facie to the common law tort of breach of confidence. Similarly, in *Evans v Information Commissioner*,[61] whether the Government was justified, on public interest grounds, in refusing to release Prince Charles's correspondence with Ministers under the Freedom of Information Act 2000 depended upon whether or not the Government was correct to claim that the correspondence fell within the scope of the education convention.

Indirectly, the background presence of a conventional rule may act as a source of constitutional principle affecting the development or application of legal rules.[62] For instance, in *Carltona Ltd v Commissioner of Works*,[63] the conventional relationship between Ministers and civil servants was the justification for holding that the non-delegation doctrine does not apply in circumstances where decisions are made by civil servants on behalf of Ministers. More generally, the convention of ministerial responsibility to Parliament provides support for judicial deference to Ministers on questions of particular political sensitivity.

In *Miller*, arguments of both a direct and an indirect nature were made for the relevance of the Sewel Convention to the resolution of the legal issues before the Supreme Court. The Lord Advocate and the *Agnew* appellants argued that it was directly relevant to the question of the UK's 'constitutional requirements' for a decision to withdraw from the EU under Article 50.[64] This was undoubtedly a legal question on which the domestic courts could legitimately rule (Article 50 having been incorporated into domestic law by the European Union (Amendment) Act 2008); and there was no reason why, they argued, 'constitutional requirements' should be regarded as being limited to legal rules. More indirectly, the Counsel

---

[60] *Attorney-General v Jonathan Cape Ltd and Others* [1976] 1 QB 752.
[61] *Evans v Information Commissioner* [2012] UKUT 313 (AAC).
[62] See generally, M Elliott, 'Parliamentary Sovereignty and the New Constitutional Order: Legislative Freedom, Political Reality and Convention' (2002) 25 *Legal Studies* 341.
[63] *Carltona Ltd v Commissioner of Works* [1943] 2 All ER 560.
[64] Lord Advocate's written case (n 15), paras 8, 85; *Agnew* (n 15), [123]–[125].

General for Wales argued that the scope of the prerogative should be interpreted in the light of background constitutional principles, including the Sewel Convention, and should therefore not be given a meaning which would allow Ministers (in effect) to amend the devolution statutes without devolved consent.[65] For its part, the UK Government argued that the Convention was *not* relevant to the issues before the Court. The issue was the proper use of the prerogative, not the enactment of legislation; accordingly, any question of the application of the Sewel Convention was moot.[66]

The Supreme Court did not address these arguments directly. However, given the generally advisory nature of the decision in *Miller*—there was no actual use of the prerogative under review by the Court either—the UK Government's argument about mootness seems unpersuasive. On the other hand, the Counsel General's argument also seems weak, in so far as the arguments about the impact on the devolution statutes simply reinforced the more general arguments for holding that there was no prerogative power to trigger Article 50, rather than raising distinct legal issues. As Elliott has put it, 'the resolution of the legal question ("Was legislation needed?") bore on the question whether the convention was engaged, but the latter did not bear upon the former'.[67]

As regards the argument that the Sewel Convention was one of the 'constitutional requirements' referred to in Article 50, Grant describes this as also being 'clearly flawed'.[68] But it is not obvious that this is the case. Admittedly, the Supreme Court did not present the issue as one of interpretation of Article 50. As described in the majority judgment,

> [t]he question before this Court concerns the steps which are required as a matter of UK domestic law before the process of leaving the European Union can be initiated. *The particular issue* is whether a formal notice of withdrawal can lawfully be given by ministers without prior legislation passed in both Houses of Parliament and assented to by HM The Queen.[69]

However, the Court appears to have deliberately chosen to narrow the issues in this way so as to avoid engaging with the wider requirements of withdrawal, such as the constitutional (rather than legal) authority of the referendum (referred to in *Shindler* as *one of* the requirements of a decision to withdraw from the EU)[70] and the role of the devolved legislatures. That the case was actually concerned with the constitutional validity of the decision to leave the EU, rather than purely with

---

[65] Counsel General's written case (n 15), paras 19–21.

[66] 'Supplementary Supreme Court Printed Case (n 40), para 3.

[67] M Elliott, 'The Supreme Court's Judgment in *Miller*: In Search of Constitutional Principle' (2017) 76 *CLJ* 257, 277.

[68] J Grant, 'Prerogative, Parliament and Creative Constitutional Adjudication: Reflections on *Miller*' (2017) 28 *King's Law Journal* 35, 57.

[69] *Miller* (n 11), [2] (emphasis added).

[70] *Shindler v Chancellor of the Duchy of Lancaster* [2016] EWCA Civ 469, [2017] QB 226.

the legal validity of a withdrawal *notification*, is made clear by the absurdity of subsequent arguments that, notwithstanding that Parliament has now authorised the making of a valid withdrawal notification as required by *Miller*, the constitutional requirements for a decision to leave the EU have still not been met.[71] This being so, there is no obvious justification for limiting the meaning of the 'constitutional requirements' referred to in Article 50 to legal rules, especially in view of the Supreme Court's acknowledgement of the fundamentally important role that conventions play in the UK constitution.[72]

B. The Role of the Courts in Relation to Conventions

If it is plausible to argue that the Sewel Convention *was* relevant to the resolution of the legal issues before the Supreme Court, was it nevertheless correct to say that courts are only permitted to *recognise* the existence of conventions and not to give rulings on their operation or scope? In fact, the Supreme Court again seems to have adopted an excessively narrow view of the appropriate judicial role in relation to conventions. There are several cases, both in the UK and elsewhere, in which courts have gone further and given rulings on the meaning of disputed conventional rules, hearing evidence and argument to enable them to do so.[73] Indeed, in the *McCord* case, the HCNI was prepared to rule on the scope of the Sewel Convention, even though it considered that no issue of the application of the Convention arose on the facts of the case. As others have pointed out,[74] the Supreme Court was not bound to follow the precedents of lower UK or foreign courts. Nevertheless, it gave no reasons for adopting a narrower view of the permissible judicial role in relation to conventions, nor even acknowledged that it was doing so.

If courts are permitted to recognise conventions, it is, of course, inevitable that they will have to take a view on the meaning of those conventions. There is, nevertheless, a distinction between this unavoidable process of interpretation and being willing to settle *disputes about* the correct interpretation of conventions. There might well be a concern that a declaratory role for judges in relation to the

---

[71] See, eg, the so-called 'Three Knights Opinion', which argues that Parliamentary approval of the terms of withdrawal is also required (D Edward et al, *In the Matter of Article 50 of the Treaty on European Union* (10 February 2017, available at https://www.bindmans.com/uploads/files/documents/Final_Article_50_Opinion_10.2.17.pdf); or Sir Louis Blom-Cooper's bizarre argument that 'The "constitutional requirements" [referred to in Article 50] must surely take account of the general election of 8 June.' ('The Referendum of 23 June 2017: Voting on Europe' [2017] *PL (Brexit Special Issue)* 1, 8).

[72] *Miller* (n 11), [151].

[73] For example, *Jonathan Cape* (n 60); *Evans* (n 61); *Patriation Reference* (n 56). See generally, F Ahmed, R Albert and A Perry, 'Judging Constitutional Conventions' (2017), available at https://ssrn.com/abstract=3043190.

[74] Elliott (n 67), 276; T Mullen, 'The Brexit Case and Constitutional Conventions' (2017) 21 *Edinburgh Law Review* 442, 446.

meaning of disputed conventions would be tantamount to enforcement because of the resulting moral pressure to comply with a judicial ruling,[75] and hence would collapse the distinction between judicially-enforceable laws and politically-enforceable conventions. This would be particularly problematic in cases where conventions modify the operation of legal rules because, as the Supreme Court of Canada noted in the *Patriation Reference*, 'the courts are bound to enforce the legal rules'.[76] There was thus a specific concern in *Miller* that for the Supreme Court to rule on the meaning of the Sewel Convention would lead it to question proceedings in Parliament, contrary to Article 9 of the Bill of Rights.[77]

A number of responses can be made to these concerns. In the first place, it is not clear that judicial enforcement, or the lack thereof, *is* the key distinction between laws and conventions.[78] On the one hand, some legal rules are non-justiciable, or non-legally enforceable; on the other hand, some soft law rules are legally enforceable, and subject to interpretation by the courts.[79] Moreover, some conventional rules operate to *supplement* rather than to modify legal rules, and therefore no issue of conflict with judges' duty to uphold the law arises.

Of course, that is not the case for all conventions, including the Sewel Convention. Moreover, there might be greater concern, given the political importance and sensitivity of some conventions (again including the Sewel Convention) about the appropriateness of judicial enforcement than there is in relation to other forms of soft law. However, here one might question the premise that judicial declaration of the meaning of a convention is tantamount to enforcement. As a general proposition, in other contexts the distinction between judicial declaration and judicial enforcement *is* regarded as constitutionally significant. The power of courts to issue declarations of incompatibility under section 4 of the Human Rights Act 1998, but not to invalidate legislation, is one example; the Crown's immunity from coercive remedies under section 21 of the Crown Proceedings Act 1948 is another. Moreover, the *effect* of any judicial ruling as to the meaning of a convention will depend both on how far the court is prepared to go in clarifying its meaning and upon the context in which the ruling is given. In *Miller*, for example, the Lord Advocate accepted that the meaning of the word 'normally' in the Sewel Convention was non-justiciable, but argued that the Supreme Court could properly rule on the meaning of 'with regard to devolved matters'.[80] Thus, even if the Court had held that the Convention did in principle apply to withdrawal legislation, it would

---

[75] Ahmed et al (n 73), 30.

[76] *Patriation Reference* (n 56), 880–81.

[77] *Miller* (n 11), [145].

[78] See generally J Jaconnelli, 'Do Constitutional Conventions Bind?' (2005) 64 *CLJ* 149; N Barber, *The Constitutional State* (Oxford, Oxford University Press, 2010) ch 10.

[79] See A McHarg, 'Administrative Discretion, Administrative Rule-Making and Judicial Review' (2017) *Current Legal Problems* 267, 279–81 and 284–85.

[80] Oral transcript, day 3 (7 December 2016) 163, available at https://www.supremecourt.uk/news/article-50-brexit-appeal.html.

If that was the purpose of section 28(8) then it is essentially a meaningless one. In the absence of an independent means of adjudication or enforcement, the Convention is no more secure than it was previously. As Elliott puts it:

> If the Sewel Convention continues to be nothing more than a convention, then its normative source lies outside any legislation, and it remains a product of political consensus. If that consensus develops (or breaks down) then the convention will evolve (or disintegrate).[89]

In fact, the precise effect of statutory recognition was a matter of considerable controversy during the enactment of the Scotland Act 2016.[90] The *UK Government*, certainly, was clear that it did not intend the Convention to become justiciable. According to the Advocate-General for Scotland during the House of Lords Third Reading Debate,

> we are not seeking, and nor are we able, to impose a restriction on Parliamentary sovereignty, … This clause is clearly intended to indicate that the discretion of Parliament to legislate for devolved matters will continue exactly as before and that it is not intended to subject that discretion to judicial control. I would add that the words 'it is recognised' … also reflect the continued sovereignty of the UK Parliament and that it is for Parliament to determine when a circumstance may be considered not normal. This is not a matter that the courts could meaningfully engage with.[91]

Others, however, were less convinced. For instance, Lord Hope of Craighead objected that

> [w]ith all due respect to the Minister, he cannot get away with simply declaring that the 'issue' is not justiciable … there is a crucial difference between the position of Parliament legislating—and Ministers declaring what words mean when they legislate—and the position of the courts. The courts will assert their right to interpret the legislation according to the meaning of the words as they judge them to be … the courts cannot close their door to arguments.[92]

Clearly, not every statutory provision is intended to create legal effects.[93] Nevertheless, the usual starting point is a presumption that legislation *is* intended to change the law,[94] which presumption needs to be convincingly rebutted.

---

[89] Elliott (n 67), 279.

[90] See House of Commons Political and Constitutional Reform Committee, *Constitutional Implications of the Government's Draft Scotland Clauses* (9th Report, 2014–15, HC 1022), ch 2; House of Lords Constitution Committee, *Scotland Bill* (6th Report, 2015–16, HL Paper 59), paras 37–41.

[91] HL Deb 21 March 2016, vol 769, cols 2070–71.

[92] HL Deb 24 February 2016, vol 769, col 308. And see also Lord Hope, HL Deb 21 March 2016, vol 769, col 2075; Lord Lang of Monkton, HL Deb 24 November 2015, vol 767, cols 603–04 and HL Deb 24 February 2016, vol 769, col 281; Lord McCluskey, HL Deb 24 February 2016, vol 769, col 289 and HL Deb 21 March 2016, vol 769, cols 2071–72.

[93] See D Feldman, 'Legislation Which Bears No Law' (2016) 37 *Statute Law Review* 212.

[94] Cf *R (SL) v Westminster City Council* [2013] UKSC 27, per Lord Carnwath, [46]–[48]. See also K Campbell, 'The "Scotland Clauses" and Parliamentary Sovereignty' (2015) *Juridical Review* 259; C Crummey and E Velasco, 'Statutorily Entrenched Conventions: Conceptual Confusion or Sound Constitutional Development', paper presented at *ICON-S British and Irish Chapter Inaugural Conference*, Trinity College Dublin, September 2017 (paper on file with the author).

Arguably, the Supreme Court did not do enough to discharge this burden of proof. As regards the *language* of section 28(8), it is not self-evidently incapable of having legal effect. As the Lord Advocate argued with reference to other statutory contexts, the phrase 'it is recognised' 'doesn't point to any particular conclusion as to its juridical effect'.[95] Similarly, the inclusion of the word 'normally', while undoubtedly vague, does not necessarily render the provision incapable of legal effect—any more so than, for example, the use of the phrase 'necessary in a democratic society' in the European Convention on Human Rights.

As regards the *content* of section 28(8), the Supreme Court did not explain what it was about its content that suggested it was not intended to have legal effect, but presumably again it was the fact that it appears to limit Parliament's competence to legislate for Scotland. In other words, it seems to be in conflict with the principle of parliamentary sovereignty. This, however, is a problem of the *enforceability* of section 28(8), rather than its justiciability: it is not clear why it should also deprive the provision of the status of a legal rule. As judges have been willing to do in other contexts, the Supreme Court could have found a way to give the provision some meaningful legal effect, whilst also respecting Parliament's sovereign right to ignore it. For instance, both the *Agnew* appellants and the Counsel General for Wales placed emphasis on the duty on *UK Ministers to seek* devolved consent in circumstances in which the Convention applies, rather than on the obligation of the UK Parliament to respect any refusal of consent.[96] Drawing an explicit analogy with the principle of legality,[97] the *Agnew* appellants argued that

> if the Westminster Parliament wishes to legislate on EU withdrawal in the teeth of opposition from a devolved legislature (should that be the outcome of a request for an LCM [Legislative Consent Motion]), it should squarely confront what it is doing and accept the political cost.[98]

Moreover, the Court could have resisted any suggestion of breaching Article 9 of the Bill of Rights[99] by insisting—as the House of Lords did in the *Jackson* case—that '[t]he proper interpretation of a statute is a matter for the courts, not Parliament'.[100]

In a decision premised on the claim that the Supreme Court majority were merely upholding constitutional orthodoxy by defending Parliament's legislative supremacy against executive encroachment, it was perhaps impolitic to suggest that its sovereignty might in fact be constrained by a requirement of devolved consent. But the contrast between the majority's willingness to find meaning in

---

[95] Oral transcript, day 4 (8 December 2016), 9–10, available at https://www.supremecourt.uk/news/article-50-brexit-appeal.html.

[96] *Agnew* (n 15), [127]–[129]; Counsel General (n 15), paras 82–83.

[97] *R v Secretary of State for the Home Department, ex parte Simms* [2000] 2 AC 115, [131] (Lord Hoffman).

[98] *Agnew* (n 15), [141].

[99] See, eg, Grant (n 68), 58.

[100] *R (Jackson) v Attorney-General* [2006] 1 AC 262, [51].

the ECA 1972 going well beyond the words actually used on the question whether the prerogative power to withdraw from the EU had been ousted by Parliament, while simultaneously denying legal effect to section 28(8), is striking.[101] The retreat from creativity into formalism in relation to the devolution issues[102] suggests that the Court simply did not regard them as important—or at least not sufficiently important to risk compromising its fragile legitimacy.[103]

IV. The Implications of *Miller* for the Territorial Constitution

Although they were unsuccessful in their claim that devolved consent was required to begin the process of withdrawing from the EU, it is too simplistic to present *Miller* as a straightforward loss for the devolved governments. They were, after all, no worse off than if the UK Government had maintained its position that Article 50 could lawfully be triggered under the prerogative. Moreover, given the novelty of the constitutional claim that the devolved parties were advancing, there was no guarantee, even if the Supreme Court had been willing to rule on the meaning of the Sewel Convention, that it would have found that devolved consent was required. At the very least, the Court's refusal to intervene avoided the risk of another unhelpfully narrow statement of the Convention of the kind made by the HCNI in *McCord*. Thus, if the devolved governments failed in their offensive campaign, they at least succeeded in their defensive one: preserving their position on the need for devolved consent to the domestic implications of Brexit. Accordingly, as noted earlier, the UK Government has not sought to dispute that Sewel *does* apply to the EU (Withdrawal) Bill, even where this engages the constitutional rather than the policy arm of the Convention (and notwithstanding that, as currently drafted, the change to devolved competences is largely one of form rather than substance). This has given the devolved governments a means by which to force the UK Government—albeit belatedly—to negotiate over the terms of the legislation.[104]

However, the *Miller* decision has undoubtedly done some damage to territorial relations within the UK. In the first place, in refusing to give legal effect

---

[101] Cf K Ewing, 'Brexit and Parliamentary Sovereignty' (2017) 80 *MLR* 711, 722–23.

[102] P Daly, '*Miller*: Legal and Political Faultlines' [2017] *PL (Brexit Special Issue)* 73.

[103] Cf JEK Murkens, 'Mixed Messages in Bottles: the European Union, Devolution, and the Future of the Constitution' (2017) 80 *MLR* 685, 686, 690–91; C McCrudden and D Halberstam, 'Northern Ireland's Supreme Court Brexit Problem (and the UK's too)', *UKCLA Blog* (21 November 2017), available at https://ukconstitutionallaw.org/.

[104] See Joint Ministerial Committee (European Negotiations) Communiqué, 16 October 2017, available at https://www.gov.uk/government/uploads/system/uploads/attachment_data/file/652285/Joint_Ministerial_Committee_communique.pdf.

to the statutory recognition of the Sewel Convention, the Supreme Court has undermined a central element of the post-independence referendum attempt to strengthen the devolution settlement in Scotland (and subsequently also in Wales). Although the provisions may still have some legal relevance in supporting a presumption that Parliament does not intend to legislate in regard to devolved matters without consent,[105] and although they may never have been intended to provide more than symbolic reassurance, for the Supreme Court to have so casually dismissed them simply confirms a key anxiety in the UK's minority nations about their lack of constitutional security, which cannot be resolved without root-and-branch constitutional reform, if at all.[106]

Second, the decision may also have done some damage to the Sewel Convention *as a convention*. Page claims that the Convention 'remains no less politically binding than before',[107] but *Miller* has arguably weakened it in several different ways. The ability of conventions to constrain constitutional behaviour depends upon a combination of two factors: the sense of obligation felt by those actors subject to the convention to follow it; and the likelihood of political sanctions if the convention is breached. As regards the sense of obligation, although the Supreme Court was careful to emphasise the importance of constitutional conventions notwithstanding their lack of legal enforceability, the contrast in the decision between strong protection for legal rules and the absence of equivalent protection for conventional rules does tend to undermine the significance of the latter.[108] More specifically, the hardening of political attitudes engendered by the litigation may well have made it *less* likely that the UK Government would accept the expansive claim to constitutional power-sharing being made in the name of the Sewel Convention. Thus, despite initially committing to the 'full engagement' of the devolved governments in establishing the UK's negotiating position on Brexit,[109] this commitment waned over time in favour of a reassertion of the decisiveness of the UK-wide Brexit vote and of the UK Government's right to determine its meaning.

The *Miller* decision may also have contributed to a weakening of the political risks associated with ignoring the Sewel Convention, at least as regards Scotland. Having been denied a voice in the decision to leave the EU, Scotland's First Minister Nicola Sturgeon invoked the option that had been 'on the table' since the EU referendum of Scotland's exit from the Union. Two weeks before the Prime Minister formally triggered Article 50, Sturgeon acted—precipitously as it

---

[105] See R Ekins, 'Legislative Freedom in the United Kingdom' (2017) 133 *LQR* 582, 583.

[106] See A McHarg, 'The Future of the United Kingdom's Territorial Constitution: Can the Union Survive?' (2016), available at https://papers.ssrn.com/sol3/papers.cfm?abstract_id=2771614.

[107] A Page, 'Brexit, The Repatriation of Competences and the Future of the Union' (2017) 1 *Juridical Review* 38, 41.

[108] Cf Lord Wilson of Dinton, 'The Robustness of Conventions in a Time of Modernisation and Change' [2004] *PL* 407; House of Commons Political and Constitutional Reform Committee, *A New Magna Carta* (2nd Report 2014–15, HC 463), 385–86.

[109] See David Cameron's resignation speech on 24 July 2016, available at http://www.telegraph.co.uk/news/2016/06/24/david-cameron-announces-his-resignation---full-statement/.

turned out—on her threat to call a second independence referendum. With this threat apparently neutralised by the result of the unexpected General Election of 8 June 2017, in which the SNP lost both seats and votes following a campaign in which opposition to a second independence referendum had been a key issue in Scotland, the UK Government's unitarist approach to Brexit seems to have been further emboldened. Thus, when the EU (Withdrawal) Bill was published in July 2017, far from enhancing the powers of the devolved legislatures, it allocated all policy competences returning from the EU to the UK Parliament, leaving it to UK Ministers unilaterally to decide if and when powers were to be devolved. At the time of writing it is unclear whether agreement will be reached on a different approach, or what will happen if it is not.

The third problem is the damage that *Miller* may have done to the perception of the Supreme Court as a neutral arbiter in future disputes in which the status of devolution, or the conflicting authority of UK and devolved institutions, is at stake. Certainly, it may be argued that such disputes are best kept out of the courts anyway. In *Miller*, the constitutional merits of requiring devolved consent were far from clear-cut, and could have produced significant anomalies given the variations in constitutional practice and statutory recognition as between the various devolved territories. If the litigation had never occurred, a more satisfactory political solution might have been found. But successful reliance on convention and political agreement requires a high degree of constitutional trust; where such trust is weak or absent, actors will naturally look for an independent referee. *Miller* is symptomatic of the stronger expectation in recent years that UK courts will become involved in resolving high-profile constitutional disputes, and of judges' greater willingness to do so. But it also illustrates the difficulties of negotiating the judicial role in a complex constitutional order which is (still) only partially regulated by law. In choosing to cast themselves as defenders of the rule of law, rather than as guardians of the constitution, there is a danger that that role becomes a partial one, in both senses of the word.

8

Sovereignty, Consent and Constitutions: The Northern Ireland References

GORDON ANTHONY*

I. Introduction

The starting point for this chapter is a rudimentary proposition about sovereignty: that it is a concept with 'legal' and 'political' dimensions, and that, in democratic systems at least, the former is legitimated by the latter.[1] Prior to the Supreme Court's ruling in *Miller* and the references in *Agnew* and *McCord*,[2] it had become widely accepted that the United Kingdom's (UK's) dominant, Diceyan narrative of sovereignty had been complicated by European Union (EU) membership and devolution.[3] In terms of EU membership, this was of course a result of competing claims to ultimate legal authority, where the common law had accommodated EU law's primacy doctrine through its recognition of 'constitutional statutes'.[4]

* My thanks are due to a number of people who commented upon earlier drafts of this chapter: Brice Dickson, Chris McCrudden (with whom I also worked as Junior Counsel for Mr Agnew and others in the Reference from Northern Ireland); John Morison; David Phinnemore; and Lisa Whitten. My thanks are also due to the editors, Alison Young, Mark Elliott and Jack Williams, and to Dagmar Schiek, who was the Principal Investigator on the European Commission-funded project, *Tensions at the Fringes of the European Union* (part of the research for this chapter was conducted under that project). The responsibility for any errors and/or omissions is mine.

[1] Literature on the point is voluminous. For key themes, see D Grimm, *Sovereignty: The Origin and Future of a Political and Legal Concept* (New York, Columbia Studies in Political Thought/Political History, 2015; trans B Cooper).

[2] *R (Miller) v Secretary of State for Exiting the European Union; In re McCord; In re Agnew* [2017] UKSC 5, [2017] 2 WLR 583.

[3] For Diceyan sovereignty, see R Weill, 'Dicey was not Diceyan' (2003) 62 *CLJ* 474. On the challenges of EU membership and devolution, see M Elliott, 'The Principle of Parliamentary Sovereignty in Legal, Constitutional, and Political Perspective' in J Jowell, D Oliver and C O'Cinneide (eds), *The Changing Constitution*, 8th edn (Oxford, Oxford University Press, 2015) ch 2.

[4] *Thoburn v Sunderland City Council* [2002] EWHC 195 (Admin), [2003] QB 151, 187–89.

However, the challenge of devolution was different in so far as it raised questions about the position of sub-state, democratic institutions and their nationally defined electorates. While the case law did not formally reject the sovereignty of the Westminster Parliament—the devolution legislation includes express provisions about its final authority[5]—it did make mention of 'divided sovereignty' and the democratic importance of the devolved legislatures.[6] That importance was to be underscored by later statutory recognition of the permanence of the Scottish and Welsh institutions and of a legislative consent convention that was argued, in *Miller/Agnew/McCord*, to apply to (what became) the European Union (Notification of Withdrawal) Act 2017.[7] It was an argument that was rejected in short order: having found that only the Westminster Parliament could authorise notification under Article 50 of the Treaty on European Union (TEU), the Supreme Court held its legal authority to do so was unconstrained by the convention.

For Northern Ireland—where 55.8% of the the electorate voted in favour of 'remain' at the time of the EU referendum—this return to unfettered legal sovereignty raises complex questions about the outworkings of its 'constitution'. Its constitution, for these purposes, is the Northern Ireland Act 1998, which was given the epithet by Lord Bingham in *Robinson* when he said that the Act should be interpreted 'generously and purposively, bearing in mind the values which the constitutional provisions are intended to embody'.[8] The corresponding values are found in the Belfast (or Good Friday) Agreement of 1998, which was endorsed by parallel referendums in Northern Ireland and Ireland, and which includes a value, or principle, of 'consent'.[9] The fundamental purpose of that principle is to accommodate competing ethno-national aspirations in Northern Ireland by recognising (i) that Northern Ireland is a part of the UK but that (ii) it will form a part of a United Ireland should that become the expressed wish of the majority of its electorate and that in Ireland.[10] At one level, the principle retains a direct link to UK legal sovereignty, in that a majority preference for retaining the status quo lends authority to the Northern Ireland Assembly and, by extension, the Westminster Parliament—something that perhaps explains periods of 'direct rule' at times of

---

[5] Northern Ireland Act 1998, s 5(6); Scotland Act 1998, s 28(7); Government of Wales Act 2006, s 107(5).

[6] For divided sovereignty, see *Jackson v Attorney-General* [2005] UKHL 56, [2006] 1 AC 262, [102] (Lord Steyn). On the devolved legislatures, see *AXA General Insurance Ltd v HM Advocate* [2011] UKSC 46, [2012] 1 AC 868, [46] (Lord Hope) and [146] (Lord Reed). See also *Re Recovery of Medical Costs for Asbestos Diseases (Wales) Bill* [2015] UKSC 3, [2015] AC 1016, [118]–[120] (Lord Thomas).

[7] Scotland Act 2016, ss 1–2; Wales Act 2017, ss 1–2.

[8] *Robinson v Secretary of State for Northern Ireland* [2002] UKHL 32, [2002] NI 390, [11]. See also Lord Hoffmann's comments, ibid, [25].

[9] On the Agreement, see C Harvey (ed), *Human Rights, Equality and Democratic Renewal in Northern Ireland* (Oxford, Hart Publishing, 2001). On consent, see R MacGinty et al, 'Consenting Adults: The Principle of Consent and Northern Ireland's Constitutional Futures' (2001) 36 *Government and Opposition* 472.

[10] Belfast Agreement, Annex (British–Irish Agreement), 'Constitutional Issues'; Northern Ireland Act 1998, s 1; and Irish Constitution of 1937, Article 3.

political instability.[11] However, the difficulty with such an approach is that it does not fully contextualise the principle or its contingent nature within the Belfast Agreement. In short, the acceptance of Northern Ireland's 'either/or' constitutional status under the Agreement depends upon related values of mutual recognition and political equality, as well as commitments about rights and the development of North/South and East–West institutional relationships.[12] Viewed in this way, the consent principle thus becomes less about majoritarian preferences and much more about legal and political guarantees that can transcend either of Northern Ireland's constitutional statuses. It is a principle that arguably also becomes relevant to the legislative consent convention—if devolution is synonymous with democratic renewal, then it would follow that the consent of Northern Ireland's institutions should be required for any Westminster legislation that would touch upon their competences.[13]

The differences between these two approaches have been brought into sharp focus by Brexit. Certainly, the UK-wide vote to leave the EU has presented challenges that are specific to Northern Ireland and which go beyond those facing Scotland and Wales. This is a well-rehearsed point about North/South cooperation under the Belfast Agreement, which did not specify EU membership as a condition precedent for devolution but took it as an assumed—and ongoing—reality. However, when the Supreme Court was presented with arguments about EU membership and the Northern Ireland constitution in *Miller/Agnew/McCord*, it side-stepped them by adopting a Diceyan analysis that, in effect, subsumed each of the devolution questions that had been referred to it. This inevitably diminished the significance of devolution not just in Northern Ireland but also in Scotland and Wales, where political concerns about a concentration of power at Westminster came to characterise early debates about, among other things, clause 11 of the European Union (Withdrawal) Bill.[14] While such concerns were not articulated in quite the same terms in Northern Ireland—local political difficulties had led to the de facto suspension of its institutions in early 2017—a number of possible 'constitutional futures' were identified in debates in advance of the EU–UK's Phase 1 agreement of 8 December 2017 (which contained a heading titled, 'Ireland and Northern Ireland').[15] Of those futures, one was UK-centric, in the sense that

---

[11] Northern Ireland Act 2000 (repealed by para 1 of Sch 4 to the Northern Ireland (St Andrews Agreement) Act 2006); and D Birrell, *Direct Rule and the Governance of Northern Ireland* (Manchester, Manchester University Press, 2009).

[12] On which see B O'Leary, 'The Nature of the Agreement' (1999) 22 *Fordham International Law Journal* 1628.

[13] C McCrudden and D Halberstam, 'Miller and Northern Ireland: A Critical Constitutional Response' (2017) 8 *UK Supreme Court Yearbook* 1, 11–12.

[14] See M Elliott, 'A "Blatant Power Grab"? The Scottish Government on the EU (Withdrawal) Bill', available at https://publiclawforeveryone.com/2017/08/10/a-blatant-power-grab-the-scottish-government-on-the-eu-withdrawal-bill/.

[15] 'Joint report from the negotiators of the European Union and the United Kingdom Government on progress during phase 1 of negotiations under Article 50 TEU on the United Kingdom's

it focused upon federalism for the UK under the organising principles of a written constitutional text.[16] However, another favoured a more innovative approach to Northern Ireland's post-Brexit relationships, by suggesting that it might become a member of the European Economic Area whilst remaining a part of the UK.[17] A further option was much more immediately concerned with the Irish dimension to the Belfast Agreement and, in particular, the prospect of Irish unification in accordance with the consent principle.[18]

This chapter traces the implications of Brexit through *Miller/Agnew/McCord* and into these constitutional futures. Its central point is that each of the futures may conceivably be realised in some form or another in what might be called 'cause and effect' circumstances. Certainly, on the face of the Phase 1 agreement of 8 December 2017, there is now a shared EU–UK commitment to avoid regulatory barriers between Ireland and Northern Ireland and between Northern Ireland and the rest of the UK, irrespective of whether there is any final EU–UK agreement within the terms of Article 50 TEU.[19] While it is unclear quite what such arrangments would look like in practice—they may potentially require the UK 'to maintain full alignment with those rules of the Internal Market and Customs Union which, now or in the future, support North-South cooperation, the all-island economy and the protection of the [Belfast Agreement]'—they have been expressly linked to each of the Belfast Agreement's underlying values and principles, including that of consent.[20] However, to the extent that this has been justified in terms of safeguarding the Northern Ireland 'peace process', it has already given rise to political statements about comparative disadvantage in the other devolved territories in the UK, as well as in London.[21] This is thus where the first 'cause and effect' might be noticed, as an even more pronounced asymmetry within devolution as regards Northern Ireland might intensify debates about the merit of adopting a federal model for the UK. While this rather assumes that the Scottish electorate would wish to remain within the UK for the foreseeable future—a state of affairs that is far from guaranteed[22]—a written constitutional text could expressly acknowledge the 'plurinational' bases of relationships within

---

orderly withdrawal from the European Union', available at https://ec.europa.eu/commission/sites/beta-political/files/joint_report.pdf.

[16] G Brown, 'Brexit is an opportunity to make a federal United Kingdom', *Financial Times* (28 March 2017), available at https://www.ft.com/content/c4658ba8-130a-11e7-b0c1-37e417ee6c76.

[17] See B Doherty, J Temple Lang, C McCrudden, L McGowan, D Phinnemore and D Schiek, *Northern Ireland and Brexit: The European Economic Area Option* (2017), available at http://pure.qub.ac.uk/portal/en/publications/northern-ireland-and-brexit-the-european-economic-area-option(a97451c1-63f7-4b3c-8bc0-2394c7c7e61f).html.

[18] See, eg, the position paper, *Uniting Ireland and Its People in Peace and Prosperity* (2017), available at https://senatormarkdaly.org/2017/04/24/uniting-ireland-and-its-people-in-peace-prosperity/.

[19] Joint report, Phase 1 (n 15), esp paras 49–50.

[20] ibid, para 44. The quotation is at para 49.

[21] 'Alignment question at heart of Britain's Brexit dilemma', *Financial Times* (4 December 2017), available at https://www.ft.com/content/d1659034-d900-11e7-a039-c64b1c09b482.

[22] On which matter see Aileen McHarg's contribution, in ch 7 of this volume.

and between the federation's component parts.[23] In normative terms, this is something that might allow the UK constitution to move towards a fuller conception of 'divided' sovereignty, where it could entrench majority voting requirements on questions that would include Northern Ireland's constitutional status. The next 'cause and effect' might then occur were this formulation of the consent principle to operate in favour of Irish unification—in that instance, Northern Ireland's experience with federalism and divided sovereignty might well mean that any new, all-Ireland constitution would also wish to incorporate such values.

The chapter begins by examining more closely the features of the Northern Ireland constitution that gave rise to the devolution questions that were referred to the Supreme Court in *Agnew* and *McCord*. It then considers the Supreme Court's approach to those questions, where it uses Anthony King's well-known imagery of 'power-hoarding' to criticise the ruling and the UK constitution's centralising tendencies.[24] The final section of the chapter analyses aspects of the European Union (Withdrawal) Bill and how the Phase 1 agreement might potentially shape Northern Ireland's futures; while the conclusion returns to the nature of the Belfast Agreement's consent principle and some of Brexit's complicating effects.

II. The (Pre-Brexit) Northern Ireland Constitution: Some Fundamentals

The first point that might be made about the Northern Ireland constitution is that it has never really been analysable in terms of devolution alone.[25] Although the Northern Ireland Act 1998 was enacted in tandem with legislation for Scotland and Wales, the Belfast Agreement had implications for the Irish Constitution of 1937, and also included a British–Irish Agreement on, amongst other things, the creation of a North/South Ministerial Council (NSMC) and a British–Irish Council (BIC).[26] In reality, this meant that devolution was to occur only after parallel referendums had taken place on both sides of the Irish border, at which time the UK and Irish Governments were required to take steps to implement the Belfast Agreement in full. Of course, the conditions for devolution were also— and more immediately—made possible by the 'peace process' in Northern Ireland

---

[23] On plurinationalism, see S Tierney, *Constitutional Law and National Pluralism* (Oxford, Oxford University Press, 2005), esp chs 1–4.

[24] On which see A King, *Does the United Kingdom still have a constitution?* (London, Sweet & Maxwell, 2001) 9–10; and A King, *The British Constitution* (Oxford, Oxford University Press, 2007) 50.

[25] See C Campbell, F Ni Aolain and C Harvey, 'The frontiers of legal analysis: reframing the transition in Northern Ireland' (2003) 66 *MLR* 317. On earlier experiments, see B Hafield, *The Constitution of Northern Ireland* (Belfast, SLS Publishing, 1989).

[26] Annex: *Agreement between the Government of the United Kingdom of Great Britain and Northern Ireland the Government of Ireland*, Article 2.

and a number of political compromises that had facilitated a 'constitutional transition'.[27] This is where the consent principle came to intersect with the range of values that were alluded to in the introduction and which included equality, power-sharing and a commitment to the protection of rights.[28] Such values were to characterise the Belfast Agreement as 'consociational' in nature,[29] and they coincided with equal entitlement to British and/or Irish citizenship for those born in Northern Ireland.[30] Relevant, too, were European influences—the (soon to be incorporated) European Convention on Human Rights (ECHR), and Irish and UK membership of the EU.[31]

The Northern Ireland Act 1998 subsequently performed a dual function in that it (i) gave legal effect to many of the values in the Belfast Agreement whilst (ii) devolving power to Northern Ireland as an integral part of the UK. The Act has since been amended on a number of occasions, but it retains the following original features—confirmation that Northern Ireland is a part of the UK and 'shall not cease to be so without the consent of a majority' of its people;[32] confirmation that the UK Government will facilitate a united Ireland should that be 'the wish expressed by a majority' in Northern Ireland;[33] confirmation that devolution 'does not affect the power of the [UK] Parliament ... to make laws for Northern Ireland';[34] devolution of legislative competence according to a three-way distinction between 'transferred', 'reserved' and 'excepted' matters;[35] constraints on legislative and executive power based upon the ECHR and EU law (including the Charter on Fundamental Rights);[36] a prohibition on discrimination on grounds of religious belief or political opinion;[37] compulsory power-sharing within the Northern Ireland Executive;[38] and the imposition of 'section 75' equality duties on government departments and other public bodies in Northern Ireland.[39] Of course, it has already been noted that government within this framework has not

---

[27] On which idea see C Bell, 'Constitutional transitions: the peculiarities of the British Constitution and the politics of comparison' [2014] *PL* 446, esp 448–56.

[28] *Agreement reached in the multi-party negotiations*, esp parts 3 and 6.

[29] O'Leary (n 12), 1631–41.

[30] *Agreement reached in the multi-party negotiations*, 'Constitutional Issues', para 1(vi) and *Annex: Agreement between the Government of the United Kingdom of Great Britain and Northern Ireland the Government of Ireland*, Article 1(vi).

[31] For context, see E Meehan, 'Europe and the Europeanisation of the Irish question' in M Cox, A Guelke and F Stephen (eds), *A Farewell to Arms? Beyond the Good Friday Agreement*, 2nd edn (Manchester, Manchester University Press, 2006) ch 22.

[32] Northern Ireland Act 1998, s 1(1).

[33] ibid, s 1(2).

[34] ibid, s 5(6).

[35] ibid, ss 4–8 and Schs 2–3.

[36] ibid, s 6(2)(c)–(d); s 7(1)(a)–(b); s 24(1)(a)–(b), (e); and, eg, *Re JR65's Application* [2016] NICA 20.

[37] ibid, s 6(2)(e); s 24(1)(c)–(d).

[38] ibid, ss 16A–21C. But see also Assembly and Executive Reform (Assembly Opposition) Act (Northern Ireland) 2016.

[39] ibid, s 75 and Sch 9.

always functioned as was intended, and *Robinson's* description of the Act as a 'constitution' carried with it a comment about the 'staccato' nature of devolution to the time of that case.[40] However, there have also been some sustained periods when the institutions have worked effectively, and in which Northern Ireland's experience with devolution has operated along similar lines to Scotland and Wales. The most relevant example for present purposes is the legislative consent convention ('Sewel Convention') that was in issue in *Miller/Agnew/McCord*: while the Convention does not have a statutory basis in Northern Ireland, it works on the shared assumption that the UK Parliament will 'not normally legislate with regard to devolved matters without the agreement of the [Northern Ireland Assembly]'.[41]

The corresponding relationship that the devolved institutions have with the NSMC—formally a creature of international law—has elements of constitutional orthodoxy and novelty. For instance, an obvious orthodox point is that the NSMC does not have any executive authority of its own, but rather brings together Ministers from Northern Ireland and Ireland for cooperation on matters of mutual interest.[42] While it is true that Northern Ireland Ministers are under a statutory duty to participate in meetings of the NSMC,[43] the Belfast Agreement provides that such meetings should simply enable 'those with executive responsibilities ... to develop consultation, cooperation and action within the island of Ireland ... on matters of mutual interest within the competence of the Administrations, North and South'.[44] On a traditional reading, this would emphasise the fact that Northern Ireland is a part of the UK and that sovereign and/or executive authority is exercisable only under the terms of the Northern Ireland Act 1998 (which does not grant any executive function to the NSMC). However, a more novel analysis moves beyond a focus on the NSMC's status to consider the complexities of the wider policy environment within which it functions. A part of that environment inevitably includes the influence of EU law, where the Belfast Agreement requires the NSMC to 'consider the EU dimension of relevant matters, including the implementation of EU policies and programmes ... Arrangements [are] to be made to ensure that the views of the [NSMC] are taken into account and represented appropriately at relevant EU meetings'.[45] On this wider reading,

---

[40] *Robinson* (n 8); the 'staccato' comment is at [7]. For analysis of the case (and others), see J Morison and M Lynch, 'Litigating the Agreement: Towards a New Judicial Constitutionalism for the UK from Northern Ireland' in J Morison, K McEvoy and G Anthony (eds), *Judges, Transition and Human Rights: Essays in Memory of Stephen Livingstone* (Oxford, Oxford University Press, 2008) ch 7.

[41] *Devolution: Memorandum of Understanding and Supplementary Agreements between the United Kingdom Government, the Scottish Ministers, the Welsh Ministers, and the Northern Ireland Executive Committee* ('*Memorandum of Understanding*'), para 14, available at https://www.gov.uk/government/uploads/system/uploads/attachment_data/file/316157/MoU_between_the_UK_and_the_Devolved_Administrations.pdf. For historical experience, see H Calvert, *Constitutional Law in Northern Ireland: A Case Study in Regional Government* (London, Stevens, 1968) 87.

[42] See further D Birrell, 'Intergovernmental Relations and Political Parties in Northern Ireland' (2012) 14 *British Journal of Politics and International Relations* 270.

[43] Northern Ireland Act 1998, ss 52A–52B.

[44] *Agreement reached in the multi-party negotiations*, Strand two, para 1.

[45] ibid, para 17.

the NSMC's work is thus about the imperative of coordinating decision making in a context that can transcend sovereign choices about constitutional status and/or the content of policy. Indeed, the imperative of coordination is such that a further British–Irish Agreement of 1999 created 'implementation bodies' that had been envisaged in the Belfast Agreement, and which work under the NSMC in areas that include waterways, food safety, trade and business, and the implementation of special EU programmes.[46]

The scope for EU law to cut across the work of the NSMC is reflected in paragraph 3 of Schedule 2 to the Northern Ireland Act 1998. That paragraph defines international relations (including with the EU) as an excepted matter, but excludes from that definition, inter alia, the exercise of legislative powers so far as required for giving effect to agreements or arrangements entered into by Ministers participating in meetings of the NSMC; the exercise of legislative powers so far as required for giving effect to agreements or arrangements entered into by, or in relation to the activities of, any body established for implementing policies agreed in the NSMC; and the observance and implementation of international obligations, including obligations under EU law (such observance and implementation thereby being a transferred matter). This is the closest that the Northern Ireland Act 1998 comes to recognising 'multi-layered' or 'multi-levelled' governance in the context of devolution,[47] as it potentially facilitates an interplay between UK law, Irish law, international law and EU law. However, to the extent that this may reflect some of the complexities of the Belfast Agreement, there are other features of the Act that plainly embed a much more state-centric view of sovereignty. One such feature is the absence of international legal personality for the Northern Ireland institutions under paragraph 3 of Schedule 2 to the Act, where a related Memorandum of Understanding makes it clear that 'the United Kingdom Government is responsible for international relations. The [Foreign Secretary] is responsible for the foreign policy of the [UK] ... and has overall responsibility for ... ensuring compliance with ... EU and other international obligations'.[48] This is very much at one with a centralised view of the UK constitution, and it is consistent with EU law's historical emphasis on the Member States as the responsible legal actors under the EU Treaties.[49] The sub-state nature of devolution is also

---

[46] *Agreement between the Government of the United Kingdom of Great Britain and Northern Ireland and the Government of Ireland establishing implementation bodies*, 8 March 1999. For implementation see, in the UK, Northern Ireland Act 1998, s 55, and North/South Cooperation (Implementation Bodies) (NI) Order, 1999, SI 1999/859; and, in the Republic of Ireland, the British–Irish Agreement Act, 1999. On their place in the Belfast Agreement, see *Agreement reached in the multi-party negotiations*, Strand two, paras 9–11.

[47] See N Bamforth and P Leyland (eds), *Public Law in a Multi-Layered Constitution* (Oxford, Hart Publishing, 2003) ch 1; and D Birrell and C Gormley-Heenan, *Multi-level Governance and Northern Ireland* (London, Palgrave, 2015) ch 8.

[48] *Memorandum of Understanding* (n 41) para D1.3.

[49] See, eg, Case C-103/01, *Commission v Germany* [2003] ECR I-5369; and Case C-248/12 P, *Northern Ireland Department of Agriculture and Rural Development v Commission* (CJEU, 6 March 2014). The court order can be found at http://curia.europa.eu/juris/liste.jsf?num=C-248/12&language=EN.

apparent from the manner in which EU law binds legislative and executive power in Northern Ireland—the constraints exist as statutory prohibitions rather than voluntary limitations of the kind that have been said to have been adopted by the Westminster Parliament.[50]

Paragraph 3 of Schedule 2 also makes mention of meetings of the BIC, which is a discussion forum that brings together representatives of the UK and Irish Governments, the three devolved executives, the Isle of Man and the Channel Islands, so that they might 'promote the harmonious and mutually beneficial development of the totality of relationships among the peoples of these islands'.[51] Plainly, the role of the BIC might also be analysed with reference to multi-layered governance, although a different point might be made here. In short, the BIC had a particular political significance at the time of the Belfast Agreement in so far as unionists in Northern Ireland thought it would provide a counterbalance to the 'Irish dimension' that was associated with the NSMC. While it has been argued that the BIC has since played a much broader role in terms of normalising British–Irish relations[52]—there is also a British–Irish Intergovernmental Conference that brings together 'the British and Irish Governments to promote bilateral co-operation at all levels on matters of mutual interest within the competence of both Governments'[53]—its origins remain very much tied to an 'East–West' dimension to the Northern Ireland constitution. It will be suggested in section IV on constitutional futures that that dimension may well assume a fundamental importance if—or when—debate about Northern Ireland's future focuses on the possibility of an all-Ireland constitutional settlement.

III. The Northern Ireland References: *Agnew* and *McCord*

Turning to the references in *Agnew* and *McCord*, these began as applications for judicial review brought by a group of politicians, civil society activists and non-governmental organisations (*Agnew*) and a victims' campaigner (*McCord*), who challenged the UK Government's proposed use of the royal prerogative to trigger

---

[50] *R v Secretary of State for Transport, ex parte Factortame (No 2)* [1991] 1 AC 603, 658 (Lord Bridge); *Thoburn v Sunderland City Council* [2002] EWHC 195 (Admin), [2003] QB 151, 187–89 (Laws LJ); *Pham v Secretary of State for Home Department* [2015] UKSC 19, [2015] 1 WLR 1591, [80] (Lord Mance).

[51] *Agreement reached in the multi-party negotiations*, Strand three, 'British–Irish Council', para 1. The leading commentary on the BIC remains V Bogdanor, 'The British–Irish Council and Devolution' (1999) 34 *Government and Opposition* 287.

[52] J Coakley, 'British Irish Institutional Structures: Towards a New Relationship' (2014) 29 *Irish Political Studies* 76.

[53] *Agreement reached in the multi-party negotiations*, Strand three, 'British-Irish Intergovernmental Conference', para 2.

Article 50 TEU.[54] As with the *Miller* proceedings in England and Wales, both cases raised points about, amongst other Acts, the European Communities Act 1972 ('ECA'), although those points were stayed pending the Divisional Court's ruling in *Miller*. This meant that the cases—which were heard together in the Northern Ireland High Court—centred upon five issues that were more specifically related to the Northern Ireland constitution and which were the foundation for the devolution questions that were later referred to the Supreme Court. Of these, the first was whether the royal prerogative had been displaced by 'any necessary implication' by the provisions of the Northern Ireland Act 1998 that relate to EU law, as read with the Belfast Agreement and British–Irish Agreement.[55] Much of the argument that was developed here centred upon the point that EU withdrawal would remove some constraints on the powers of the Northern Ireland Assembly and Executive and, in so doing, both narrow the scope for protecting individual rights and complicate North/South and East–West cooperation on EU matters. Rejecting that argument, Maguire J (whose judgment preceded the Divisional Court's ruling in *Miller*) held that it overstated the effects of notification under Article 50 TEU, particularly as there was, in his view, a distinction to be drawn between use of the prerogative to trigger Article 50 TEU and the manner in which legal change would subsequently occur. While the judge accepted that notification would in due course affect EU law's place within the domestic system, he emphasised that it would not have any immediate effects in domestic law, including at the level of individual rights, and that any change would be 'controlled by Parliamentary legislation'.[56] Having also examined the nature of the North/South institutions— which were said to have a remit that went beyond matters of EU law—the judge concluded that it was

> inapt for the applicants to talk in terms of notification changing the rights of individuals or of the operation of institutions … This simply will not happen … The reality is, at this time, it remains to be seen what actual effect the process of change subsequent to notification will produce. In the meantime, sections 6 and 24 of the 1998 Act will continue to apply; the North/South and East/West institutions will continue to operate; and the work of implementation bodies will go on.[57]

The second issue—which the judge addressed in the event that he was wrong about the prerogative—was whether the legislative consent convention had to be observed before any Act of Parliament could authorise notification under Article 50 TEU. Of course, this was a matter that also had implications for Scotland and Wales, and the Lord Advocate made a written intervention in the High Court and later appeared in the Supreme Court (where the Counsel General for Wales also intervened). The corresponding submissions and interventions

---

[54] Reported as *Re McCord's Application* [2016] NIQB 85.
[55] ibid, [19] and [103].
[56] ibid, [105].
[57] ibid, [107].

variously described the convention as 'constitutional' in form, and argued that it applied not just to Westminster legislation on devolved/transferred matters but also to legislation that would affect the legislative competence of the Assembly and/or the executive functions of Ministers and Departments. This led Maguire J to consider the scope of the legislative consent convention, where he assumed (but did not formally decide) that it applied only to Westminster legislation on transferred matters. Adopting that 'narrower' view of the convention,[58] he held that legislation to authorise notification would fall under international relations for the purposes of Schedule 2 to the Northern Ireland Act 1998, and that such legislation therefore could not be said to relate to transferred matters. He also noted a point that was to be central to the Supreme Court's subsequent analysis of the convention—whether it 'could, in any event, be viewed as enforceable *via* legal proceedings given its status as a convention'.[59]

The third and fourth issues—respectively, whether aspects of the Northern Ireland constitution imposed constraints on the prerogative, and whether the Northern Ireland Office was required to observe its section 75 equality duties in advance of notification—were dealt with briefly by the judge. In respect of the third issue, Maguire J thus considered that the points raised were non-justiciable and that any decision concerning notification was one of 'high policy';[60] while on the fourth issue, he held that section 75 was not engaged and that, even if it had been engaged, there were alternative (political) remedies under the Northern Ireland Act 1998.[61] This left the fifth issue—pleaded only in *McCord*—which was whether the consent principle meant that Article 50 TEU could not be triggered because a majority of the Northern Ireland electorate had voted 'remain' in the EU referendum. The corresponding argument that was advanced was that EU withdrawal would amount to a change in the constitutional status of Northern Ireland, and that any such change, without the support of the electorate, would be contrary to a legitimate expectation engendered by the Belfast Agreement and section 1 of the Northern Ireland Act 1998. It was an argument that Maguire J had little hesitation in rejecting: not only was the consent principle limited to the specific question of whether Northern Ireland should remain a part of the UK or form a part of a united Ireland, but 'any suggestion that a legitimate expectation [could] overwhelm the structure of the legislative scheme [was] not viable'.[62]

The Supreme Court's subsequent treatment of the devolution questions—which mirrored the five issues in the High Court—had a different balance.[63]

---

[58] ibid, [119].
[59] ibid, [122].
[60] ibid, [133]–[134].
[61] ibid, [143]–[146].
[62] ibid, [152]–[155].
[63] The questions were: '(i) Does any provision of the NI Act, read together with the Belfast Agreement and the British-Irish Agreement, have the effect that primary legislation is required before Notice can be given? (ii) If the answer is "yes", is the consent of the Northern Ireland Assembly required before the relevant legislation is enacted? (iii) If the answer to question (i) is "no", does any provision of the NI Act read together with the Belfast Agreement and the British–Irish Agreement operate as a restriction

This was largely because the majority in the Court had first considered the issues arising in the appeal in *Miller*, where it held that the effects of the ECA 1972 were such that the royal prerogative could not be used to give notification under Article 50 TEU.[64] For the Supreme Court, this meant that it did not need to form a definitive view on the related question of whether the Northern Ireland Act 1998, as read with the Belfast Agreement and the British–Irish Agreement, also required an Act of Parliament before notification could be given (question (i)). While the Court recognised that the Northern Ireland Act 1998 'is a very important step in the programme designed to achieve reconciliation of the communities of Northern Ireland … [and] … has established institutions and arrangements which are intended to address the unique political history of the province and the island of Ireland',[65] it limited itself to making a number of *obiter* comments about the Act and the place of EU law. The most notable of these was that it was 'unquestionably right' that the Act 'conferred [EU law-based] rights on the citizens of Northern Ireland' and that, as 'it is normally impermissible for statutory rights to be removed by the exercise of prerogative powers in the international sphere' (*Miller*), it would be 'incongruous if constraints imposed on the legislative competence of the devolved administrations … were to be removed, thereby enlarging that competence, other than by statute'.[66] However, beyond a further statement about the observance and implementation of EU obligations being a transferred matter under the Northern Ireland Act 1998—where the Court thought there might be a 'constitutional anomaly' if the prerogative could be used to change that statutory scheme[67]—the Court said nothing more about the Act and the Agreements. Nor did it engage at length with the content of questions (iii)–(v). Hence, constraints on the prerogative (question (iii)) and equality duties (question (iv)) were said to have been superseded by the need for legislation, while the consent principle (question (v)) went no further than to give 'the people of Northern Ireland the right to determine whether to remain part of the United Kingdom or to become part of a united Ireland'.[68]

Question (ii), about the legislative consent convention, in turn attracted the greater part of the Court's attention vis-à-vis the devolution issues.[69] The Court started its analysis by noting that, on its original terms, the convention means that

---

on the exercise of the prerogative power to give Notice? (iv) Does section 75 of the NI Act prevent exercise of the power to give Notice in the absence of compliance by the Northern Ireland Office with its obligations under that section? (v) Does the giving of Notice without the consent of the people of Northern Ireland impede the operation of section 1 of the NI Act?'. See *Miller* (n 2), [126].

[64] See ch 1 in this volume.
[65] *Miller* (n 2), [128].
[66] ibid, [131]–[132].
[67] ibid, [132].
[68] ibid, [129] and [133]–[135].
[69] For commentary, see J Murkens, 'Mixed Messages in Bottles: the European Union, Devolution, and the Future of the Constitution' (2017) 80 *MLR* 685, 690–94.

the UK Parliament will 'not normally legislate with regard to devolved matters without the agreement of the [relevant] devolved legislature'.[70] While the Court did not state whether Maguire J had been correct to favour a narrower view of the convention, it did note that the Scottish Parliament and Welsh Assembly had previously passed legislative consent motions in relation to Acts of Parliament that had specifically addressed their devolved powers (albeit that they had not passed motions for Acts that had affected their powers by reason of implementing changes to the competences of EU institutions).[71] This was, however, essentially an exercise in context setting, as the remainder of the ruling focused on the political nature of the convention and its resultant non-enforceability in law. In adopting that position, the Court acknowledged that judges could 'recognise the operation of a political convention in the context of deciding a legal question' and that the legislative consent convention 'has an important role in facilitating harmonious relations between the UK Parliament and the devolved legislatures'.[72] Nevertheless, the Court was ultimately of the view that, 'Judges ... are neither the parents nor the guardians of political conventions' and they 'cannot give legal rulings on [their] operation or scope, because those matters are determined within the political world'.[73] This was so notwithstanding that the convention had been written into legislation for Scotland and was about to be for Wales—that legislation was said simply to recognise 'the convention for what it is, namely a political convention ... the purpose of the legislative recognition of the convention was to entrench it as a convention'.[74]

It has already been suggested, in section I, that the Supreme Court's ruling can best be understood in terms of 'power hoarding'—what Anthony King described as 'a concentration—and usually a centralisation—of political power. Not only that ... the institutions of a power-hoarding regime are associated closely with a political culture that legitimises and reinforces the hoarding of power. The guiding normative principle ... is "winner takes all"'.[75] Of course, in the context of the references, the doctrinal basis for such hoarding was a Diceyan view of Parliamentary sovereignty,[76] which shaped the Court's ruling in two ways. The first was in its limited analysis of the status and effects of the Northern Ireland Act 1998. While the Court's approach here was influenced by pragmatism—'Because we have concluded that primary legislation is required ... The first question is ... less significant than it otherwise might have been but we address it briefly'[77]—that

---

[70] *Miller* (n 2), [138], citing the *Memorandum of Understanding* (n 41).

[71] ibid, [140], referencing, amongst others, the European Communities (Amendment) Act 2008, the Wales Act 2014, and the Scotland Act 2016.

[72] *Miller* (n 2), [146] and [151].

[73] ibid, [146].

[74] ibid, [148]–[149].

[75] King, *Does the United Kingdom still have a constitution* (n 24), 9–10.

[76] See K Ewing, 'Brexit and Parliamentary Sovereignty' (2017) 80 *MLR* 711; and G Anthony, 'Brexit and the Common Law Constitution' (2018) 24 *European Public Law* (forthcoming).

[77] *Miller* (n 2), [129].

pragmatism was clearly driven by an understanding of *Miller* as the dominant case. This inevitably meant that, once the Court had concluded that one Act of the Westminster Parliament had displaced the prerogative in relation to Article 50 TEU, there would have been little to be gained from considering whether another Act of the Westminster Parliament had that same effect. However, while this may well have had an internal logic from the point of view of Diceyan orthodoxy, it perhaps missed the fundamental point that the Northern Ireland Act 1998 is much more than a devolution Act simpliciter. The ruling, in that sense, marked a quiet retreat from *Robinson* and the constitutional promise of that earlier judgment.

The second way in which a Diceyan view shaped the Court's ruling was in its treatment of the legislative consent convention, which, in effect, rejected any idea that there might be a 'divided sovereignty' within the UK. That idea had previously gained some traction in relation to devolution in Scotland,[78] and its imagery was plainly relevant to aspects of the Northern Ireland constitution. In terms of the references and interventions, this meant that question (ii) was really a proxy invitation for the Court to re-engage with its earlier devolution case law, where it had made mention of the democratic role and legitimacy of the devolved legislatures.[79] One possible entry point for the Court here was in its statement that judges can recognise the operation of a political convention when deciding a legal question, as this arguably requires judges first to form a view about the nature and scope of any relevant convention.[80] However, this may be precisely where the orthodoxy of the Supreme Court's ruling was at its most apparent, as the Court had seemingly formed just such a view of the legislative consent convention when vouchsafing the UK Parliament's powers. To put the point differently, the Court clearly envisaged only a subordinate constitutional role for the devolved legislatures, and it limited that role by tying the convention to a bright-line distinction between the realms of law and politics. Indeed, given that the Court had earlier reasserted the UK Parliament's sovereign legal authority in respect of the Crown's prerogative powers, it was perhaps inevitable that the Court would regard the realm of law as synonymous with that very same authority. The result was that the European Union (Notification of Withdrawal) Act 2017 was enacted without any legislative consent motion(s) having been passed, and notification on foot of that Act was given on 29 March 2017.

---

[78] For divided sovereignty, see *Jackson v Attorney-General* [2005] UKHL 56, [2006] 1 AC 262, [102] (Lord Steyn). For an historical forerunner, see *MacCormick v Lord Advocate* [1953] SC 396, 411 (Lord Cooper): '[T]he principle of the unlimited sovereignty of Parliament is a distinctively English principle which has no counterpart in Scottish constitutional law'.

[79] See the cases cited in n 6.

[80] M Elliott, 'The Supreme Court's Ruling in *Miller*: In Search of Constitutional Principle' (2017) 76 *CLJ* 257, 276–77.

IV. Constitutional Futures

The remaining matter to be addressed is what this all means for Northern Ireland's constitutional future(s)—how the Northern Ireland constitution might develop as Brexit takes effect against the backdrop of the Supreme Court's ruling. Certainly, at the time of writing, it is clear that Northern Ireland's short-term future will be most immediately affected by the European Union (Withdrawal) Bill—which has also been criticised as an exercise in power hoarding[81]—and by commitments that were made in the Phase 1 agreement of 8 December 2017. While it is (of course) unknown whether there will be a final and fuller EU–UK Withdrawal Agreement, the Phase 1 agreement has emphasised that the Belfast Agreement (including the consent principle) 'must be protected in all its parts', and that specific arrangements for Ireland and Northern Ireland will be made 'irrespective of the nature of any future agreement between the European Union and United Kingdom'.[82] At its most expansive, this apparently envisages two-way regulatory alignment, in the sense that there will be neither a 'hard border' between Northern Ireland and Ireland nor any impediment to Northern Irish access to the market in Great Britain unless the Northern Ireland institutions make provision for such impediment.[83] On one reading, this would represent something akin to 'special status' for Northern Ireland both in terms of the EU *and* the UK itself, and the Scottish and Welsh Governments have already made public pronouncements about their wish to be accorded similar treatment.[84] It is thus here that the idea of 'cause and effect' that was mentioned in section I starts to find its place—increased flexibility for Northern Ireland might ultimately prompt a more general rebalancing of power within the UK, and that, in turn, might have implications for how Northern Ireland might be integrated into a united Ireland.

In terms of the European Union (Withdrawal) Bill, the potential for power hoarding results from the manner in which it proposes to retain much of EU law ('retained EU law') after 'exit day'. Here, the Bill provides for the repeal of the ECA 1972 in circumstances where a wide range of EU norms will initially remain in force and, among other things, continue to bind the devolved legislatures.[85] From a policy perspective, this approach has been said to be justified by the need 'to provide a functioning statute book on the day the UK leaves the EU … it will then be for Parliament and, where appropriate, the devolved legislatures to make any changes'.[86] However, it is in the detail about how any such changes

---

[81] The leading critique is R Rawlings, 'Brexit and the Territorial Constitution: Devolution, Reregulation and Inter-governmenal Relations', published by the Constitution Society at https://consoc.org.uk/wp-content/uploads/2017/10/Brexit-and-devolution-final-2.pdf.

[82] Joint report (n 15), paras 42 and 46.

[83] ibid, paras 49–50.

[84] See n 21.

[85] European Union (Withdrawal) Bill, cl 11.

[86] European Union (Withdrawal) Bill (Explanatory Notes), para 10.

are to be made that the Bill has attracted criticism, both more generally and as relates to devolution in particular. The more general criticisms of the Bill have focused primarily on the extent to which subordinate legislation can be used to make changes to retained EU law (including, through Henry VIII powers, to that in primary legislation), as this has been said to concentrate too much power in the hands of Ministers.[87] And those criticisms that have been made in relation to devolution have emphasised how the Bill adopts a restrictive reading of devolution that can only slow centrifugalism within the UK constitution. The concern here is that devolved powers are taken by the Bill to stand very much where they are— hence retained EU law continuing to constrain the devolved institutions—and that any post-Brexit increase in powers will be closely aligned to, if not controlled by, central government decision making.[88] It is for this reason that the Scottish Government has previously spoken of the Bill's representing a 'power-grab' that it could not support were a legislative consent motion to be moved in the Scottish Parliament (the explanatory notes for the Bill have stated that such consent will be sought).[89]

The Northern Ireland Act 1998, in turn, is given specific recognition by the Bill in so far as some Henry VIII powers cannot be used to amend or repeal the Act (though there may in any event be a query about how far a 'constitutional statute' could be subject to amendment by delegated legislation[90]). For these purposes, a distinction is apparently drawn between Henry VIII powers that might be used to deal with deficiencies in retained EU law (where the Bill expressly prohibits Ministers of the Crown from using the powers to amend or repeal the Northern Ireland Act 1998)[91] and powers that might be used to implement any final EU–UK withdrawal agreement (where the Bill is silent about amending or repealing the Northern Ireland Act 1998).[92] It is not immediately clear why such a distinction has been drawn, though it may be that it is intended to facilitate the ready implementation of any 'eleventh hour' agreement that might be reached within

---

[87] See, as regards UK Government Ministers, European Union (Withdrawal) Bill, cls 7–9; and as regards Ministers in the devolved administrations, cl 10 and Sch 2. For cautionary comments, see, eg, *European Union (Withdrawal) Bill: interim report*, House of Lords Select Committee on the Constitution, 3rd Report of Session 2017–2019, available at https://publications.parliament.uk/pa/ld201719/ldselect/ldconst/19/19.pdf.

[88] European Union (Withdrawal) Bill, cls 10–11 and Sch 2; and Rawlings (n 81).

[89] See Elliott (n 14). The explanatory notes are available at https://publications.parliament.uk/pa/bills/cbill/2017-2019/0005/en/18005en.pdf. And note that the Scottish and Welsh governments have since introduced their own 'continuity' Bills that seek to address the return of powers: see C McCorkindale and A McHarg, 'Continuity and Confusion: Legislating for Brexit in Scotland and Wales (Parts I & II)', U.K. Const. L. Blog (6th and 7th Mar. 2018) available at https://ukconstitutionallaw.org/.

[90] See, by analogy, *Thoburn v Sunderland City Council* [2002] EWHC 195 (Admin), [2003] QB 151, 187–89; and *R (Public Law Project) v Secretary of State for Justice* [2016] UKSC 39, [2016] AC 1531.

[91] European Union (Withdrawal) Bill, cl 7(6)(f). Exceptions are made for regulations that might be made by virtue of para 13(b) of Sch 7 to the Bill, or which amend or repeal para 38 of Sch 3 to the Northern Ireland Act 1998, or any provision of that Act which modifies another enactment.

[92] European Union (Withdrawal) Bill, cl 9, cl 10, Sch 2, para 21, and Sch 7, para 7.

the terms of Article 50 TEU. However, this is where the Phase 1 agreement starts to become so significant, because even if there is no final agreement for the purposes of Article 50 TEU, commitments have now been given in relation to the Irish border and protecting the wider architecture of the Belfast Agreement. As noted in section I, these will potentially require the UK Government both 'to maintain full alignment with those rules of the Internal Market and Customs Union which, now or in the future, support North–South cooperation, the all-island economy and the protection of the [Belfast Agreement]', and to ensure 'that no new regulatory barriers develop between Northern Ireland and the rest of the United Kingdom'.[93] In terms of North–South cooperation, this is expressly linked to a 'mapping exercise, which shows that North–South cooperation relies to a significant extent on a common European Union legal and policy framework', and which means that the UK Government should 'protect and support continued North–South and East–West cooperation across the full range of political, economic, security, societal and agricultural contexts and frameworks of cooperation, including the continued operation of the North-South implementation bodies'.[94] This is an approach that plainly comes close to earlier proposals about developing unique economic links between Northern Ireland and the EU,[95] although the reference to East–West cooperation corresponds with an emphasis on Northern Ireland's remaining a full economic and political part of the UK. Guarantees to that effect are an inevitable outworking of the consent principle, and at a political level they may act as a counterbalance to the possibility of sectoral 'spill-over' on foot of increased North–South cooperation (a prospect that had previously led unionists in the Northern Ireland Assembly to vote against a motion in favour of 'special status' for Northern Ireland within the EU).[96] To the extent that the Phase 1 agreement acknowledges that 'distinct arrangements' for Northern Ireland may be 'appropriate', it thus expressly provides that regulatory barriers between Northern Ireland and the rest of the UK cannot develop 'unless, consistent with the [Belfast Agreement], the Northern Ireland Executive and Assembly agree' to the emergence of such barriers.[97]

Of course, the Phase 1 agreement gives rise to many questions, not least about how far its stated aims might be reconciled with those of the European Union (Withdrawal) Bill. Although there have been a number of amendments to the Bill to the time of writing, one of its primary policy objectives remains the creation of common frameworks that will define the UK's own internal, post-Brexit market. Plainly, this is something that may be complicated by the Phase 1 agreement's

---

[93] See Joint report (n 15), para 49.

[94] ibid, paras 47–48.

[95] Doherty et al (n 17).

[96] 'MLAs vote against a motion calling for NI to be granted special status within the EU', available at http://www.bbc.co.uk/news/uk-northern-ireland-37680584. On 'spill-over', see A Niemann and P Schmitter, 'Neofunctionalism' in A Wiener and T Diez (eds), *European Integration Theory*, 2nd edn (Oxford, Oxford University Press, 2009) ch 3.

[97] Joint report (n 15), para 50.

mention of 'frameworks of cooperation' on a North–South basis, at least if Brexit takes the UK away from the Customs Union and the EU's Internal Market. Moreover, to the extent that there is a commitment to make specific arrangements for Northern Ireland in the event of no final EU–UK withdrawal agreement, this will potentially set the Northern Ireland Act 1998 far apart from the other (already asymmetrical) devolution Acts. The recent amendment of those Acts to include the legislative consent convention had marked an attempt, certainly as regards Scotland, to accommodate nationalist ambition within the framework of 'devo-max' and the continuation of the Union.[98] However, with the Supreme Court now having diminished the legal significance of the convention, and with 'devo-max' potentially meaning something very different in Northern Ireland, existing calls for flexibility for Scotland will undoubtedly grow. While it remains possible that those calls would result in a further, post-Brexit independence referendum in Scotland,[99] the current debates appear to be more immediately concerned with the need to rebalance power within the UK. At its lowest, Northern Ireland's 'cause and effect' may therefore be about devolved access to European markets; at its highest, it may grow into a dispute about nation and state and the recurring theme of divided sovereignty.

This is where federalism may be seen to offer a future option for the UK constitution. Although it is axiomatic that there are different forms of federalism, it typically incorporates a diffuse conception of sovereignty and requires 'the exclusive allocation of power by a written constitution to federal and state/provincial legislatures of co-ordinate status with each other'.[100] Historically speaking, the idea of a federal UK is not a new one, although it has previously been regarded as problematic given, among other things, the size and dominance of England.[101] England would, in that sense, remain a challenge for any contemporary federal settlement, and Rawlings, writing pre-Brexit, cautioned that 'full-form federalism' cannot provide a 'quick fix' and that there is greater potential within 'flexible federal-type responses at United Kingdom level inside a famously uncodified constitution'.[102] However, with *Miller/Agnew/McCord* suggesting that the uncodified constitution is ultimately unable to facilitate such responses, full-form federalism may well become something of a necessity. While intergovernmental relations

---

[98] On Wales, see R Rawlings, 'The Strange Reconstitution of Wales' [2018] *PL* 62.

[99] See further Aileen McHarg's contribution in ch 7 of this volume. For earlier context setting, see S Tierney and K Boyle, 'A Tale of Two Referendums: Scotland, the UK and Europe' in P Birkinshaw and A Biondi (eds), *Britain Alone! The Implications and Consequences of UK Exit from the EU* (Alphen aan den Rijn, Wolters/Kluwer, 2016) ch 2.

[100] B Hadfield, 'The Foundations of Review, Devolved Power and Delegated Power' in C Forsyth (ed), *Judicial Review and the Constitution* (Oxford, Hart Publishing, 2000) 193 and 194. On different models, see M Burgess, *Comparative Federalism: Theory and Practice* (Oxford, Routledge, 2006).

[101] R Rawlings, 'Riders on the Storm: Wales, the Union and Territorial Constitutional Crisis' (2015) 42 *Journal of Law and Society* 471, 471–74, summarising the findings of the 'Kilbrandon Commission'.

[102] ibid, 497–98.

under a federal constitution may be very similar to those at present[103]—including through use of political means to enforce conventions[104]—they would develop within a framework that would emphasise the primacy of the written constitution and how power is held on a basis of mutual self-respect between the federation's constituent parts.[105] The corresponding norms and values that might enliven the text could then include: plurinationalism and divided sovereignty (as *per* the articles of a preamble); majority voting requirements in each of the component parts on specified matters such as international relations; entrenched protection for fundamental rights (whether on the basis of the ECHR and/or a domestic bill of rights); formalised intergovernmental cooperation (where the NSMC and BIC could provide adaptable models); and secession rights (which, if triggered, would require a majority vote only within the constituent unit in question, rather than across the federation as a whole).

For Northern Ireland, the inclusion of secession rights would represent a further constitutionalisation of the consent principle, where, consistent with the Belfast Agreement, a majority vote in favour of Irish unification would take effect only if paralleled by a vote in Ireland.[106] This is very much the essence of the compromises on sovereignty that were made at the time of the Belfast Agreement—Northern Ireland is a part of the UK, but contingently so, and Irish unification can be achieved only through complementary exercises of political sovereignty in Northern Ireland and Ireland.[107] The suggestion that such fluid approaches to sovereignty might underlie a federal UK constitution is perhaps an ambitious one, but it reflects what is, post-*Miller/Agnew/McCord*, the need for mechanisms that will prevent power hoarding in the constitution.[108] Moreover, to the extent that federalism may provide a means to meet that need, it may also provide the preferred model for protecting the values in the Belfast Agreement should Northern Ireland later form part of a united Ireland. While federalism has long been discussed as one possible framework for Irish unity,[109] the Belfast Agreement clearly

---

[103] For insights into other systems, see J Poirier, C Saunders and J Kincaid (eds), *Intergovernmental Relations in Federal Systems: Comparative Stuctures and Dynamics* (Oxford, Oxford University Press, 2015).

[104] *Miller* (n 2), [141]–[143], considering *In re Resolution to amend the Constitution* [1981] 1 SCR 753.

[105] C Turpin and A Tomkins, *British Government and the Constitution*, 7th edn (Cambridge, Cambridge University Press, 2011) 212.

[106] Belfast Agreement, Annex (British–Irish Agreement), 'Constitutional Issues'; and Irish Constitution of 1937, Article 3.

[107] Cf the argument that parallel referendums amounted to an exercise of self-determination. For analysis, see C Bell and K Cavanaugh, '"Constructive Ambiguity" or Internal Self-Determination? Self-Determination, Group Accommodation and the Belfast Agreement' (1998) 22 *Fordham International Law Journal* 1345.

[108] N Walker, 'Beyond the unitary conception of the United Kingdom Constitution' [2000] *PL* 384.

[109] For earlier consideration of its potential, see D Fennell, 'Solutions to the Northern Ireland Problem: A Federal Ireland and Other Approaches' (1995) 21 *Canadian Journal of Irish Studies* 1. See, too, ch 7 of the Report of the New Ireland Forum of 1984, available at http://www.sinnfein.ie/contents/15214.

has contemporary features that lend themselves to, and may even demand, such modelling (competing ethno-national identities, recognition of rights, intergovernmental cooperation, etc). Were those features to be given further protection within a federal UK constitution (or even if they were not to be), any all-Ireland constitution may wish to draw inspiration from the wider experience of federalism. Indeed, while the Irish Constitution of 1937 has evolutionary qualities that may at least partly enable it to absorb Northern Ireland's constitution,[110] it also imports historical notions of nation and state that are arguably more uni-national than plurinational in nature.[111] Given the point, an all-Ireland constitution that is truly at one with the consent principle (and certainly its more contextual version) might need to incorporate a diffuse conception of sovereignty that guarantees equal institutional protections for Northern Ireland's two main ethno-national groups. Such protections should, again, be nested in statements about the plurinational nature of the state,[112] where recognition of shared historical and contemporary influences would elide with legal and political rights for those claiming British identity. 'Super-majorities' might be required in the state and federal legislatures for matters that impinge upon national identity; while the BIC, discussed in section II, could assume an enhanced role as an institutional bridging point to England, Scotland and Wales (however relations between those countries might be configured). European influences would also be pervasive—continued EU membership could be expected,[113] and the ECHR might be given full constitutional status as opposed to its current position within an Act of the Irish Parliament.[114]

V. Conclusion

All that, however, is speculation for the moment. While UK federalism and Irish unification may well prove to be sequential parts of Northern Ireland's future, the more pressing question for the present is how far the process of EU withdrawal can be reconciled with Northern Ireland's current constitutional values. As has been

---

[110] T Murphy and P Twomey (eds), *Ireland's Evolving Constitution 1937–1997* (Oxford, Hart Publishing, 1998); and R Humphreys, *Countdown to Unity: Debating Irish Reunification* (Dublin, Irish Academic Press, 2008).

[111] Compare D Clarke, 'Nationalism, the Irish Constitution, and Multicultural Citizenship' (2000) 51 *Northern Ireland Legal Quarterly* 100.

[112] For historical context, see G Hogan, *The Origins of the Irish Consitution, 1928–1941* (Dublin, Royal Irish Academy, 2012).

[113] 'Brexit summit: EU accepts united Ireland declaration', *The Irish Times* (29 April 2017), available at https://www.irishtimes.com/news/world/europe/brexit-summit-eu-accepts-united-ireland-declaration-1.3066569.

[114] The European Convention on Human Rights Act 2003; and R McQuigg, 'The European Convention on Human Rights Act 2003—Ten Years On' (2014) 3 *International Human Rights Law Review* 61.

seen, those values cluster around a consent principle that, if not directly engaged by the Brexit referendum (*Miller/Agnew/McCord*), has certainly been complicated by the result of that vote. In short, the consent principle's central purpose has been to accommodate competing claims to (legal and political) sovereignty through the creation of institutions that give equal recognition to those claims. While it is true that those institutions have sometimes had only a 'staccato' existence,[115] they remain premised upon the idea that sovereignty is a fluid concept rather than a rigid one.[116] For the moment, the Phase 1 agreement of 8 December 2017 contains important statements about the need to protect those institutions and their values, even if there is no final EU–UK Withdrawal Agreement for the purposes of Article 50 TEU. However, in the event that there is no such final agreement, implementation of the Phase 1 commitments may have implications not just for the aims of the European Union (Withdrawal) Bill but also for the model of sovereignty that defined *Miller/Agnew/McCord*. Should those implications include a crisis centred around legislative consent and sovereignty, *Miller/Agnew/McCord* has made it clear that only one legislature needs to authorise the final domestic legal form of Brexit. If that is how withdrawal is ultimately achieved, Brexit will have taken power hoarding to its logical—and perhaps even undemocratic—conclusion.

---

[115] *Robinson* (n 8), [7] (Lord Bingham).

[116] It has also been argued that the concept is redundant: see J Morison, '"A Sort of Farewell": Sovereignty, Transition, and Devolution in the UK' in P Leyland, R Rawlings and A Young (eds), *Sovereignty and the Law: Domestic, European and International Perspectives* (Oxford, Oxford University Press, 2014) 120.

9

The *Miller* Case
and Constitutional Statutes

SIR JOHN LAWS

I. Introduction

The relationship between the *Miller* case in the Supreme Court and the notion of a constitutional statute has something to tell us about the present and future direction of our constitution.[1] To unravel it, I must give an account of what the notion means.

The idea of a constitutional statute was advanced by me in *Thoburn v Sunderland City Council*.[2] The traditional doctrine was that there is no hierarchy of statutes; all have equal status. Turning the pages of the statute book was rather like the experience of Kipling's cat in the *Just So Stories*: all places were alike to him. I must cite quite a lengthy passage from my judgment in *Thoburn*, with which Crane J agreed:

> The common law has in recent years allowed, or rather created, exceptions to the doctrine of implied repeal: a doctrine which was always the common law's own creature. There are now classes or types of legislative provision which cannot be repealed by mere implication. These instances are given, and can only be given, by our own courts, to which the scope and nature of Parliamentary sovereignty are ultimately confided. The courts may say—have said—that there are certain circumstances in which the legislature may only enact what it desires to enact if it does so by express, or at any rate specific, provision. The courts have in effect so held in the field of European law itself, in the *Factortame* case, and this is critical for the present discussion. By this means, as I shall seek to explain, the courts have found their way through the impasse seemingly created by two supremacies, the supremacy of European law and the supremacy of Parliament.

---

[1] *R (Miller) v Secretary of State for Exiting the European Union* [2017] UKSC 5, [2017] 2 WLR 583.
[2] *Thoburn v Sunderland City Council* [2002] EWHC 195 (Admin), [2003] QB 151.

The present state of our domestic law is such that substantive Community rights prevail over the express terms of any domestic law, including primary legislation, made or passed after the coming into force of the ECA [European Communities Act 1972], even in the face of plain inconsistency between the two. This is the effect of *Factortame (No 1)* [1990] 2 AC 85. To understand the critical passage in Lord Bridge's speech it is first convenient to repeat part of ECA s 2(4):

> 'The provision that may be made under subsection (2) above includes ... any such provision (of any such extent) as might be made by Act of Parliament, and any enactment passed or to be passed, other than one contained in this Part of this Act, shall be construed and have effect subject to the foregoing provisions of the section.'

In *Factortame (No 1)* Lord Bridge said this at 140:

> 'By virtue of section 2(4) of the Act of 1972 Part II of the [Merchant Shipping] Act of 1988 is to be construed and take effect subject to directly enforceable Community rights ... This has precisely the same effect as if a section were incorporated in Part II of the Act of 1988 which in terms enacted that the provisions with respect to registration of British fishing vessels were to be without prejudice to the directly enforceable Community rights of nationals of any member state of the EEC.'

So there was no question of an implied *pro tanto* repeal of the ECA of 1972 by the later Act of 1988; on the contrary the Act of 1988 took effect subject to Community rights incorporated into our law by the ECA. In *Factortame* no argument was advanced by the Crown in their Lordships' House to suggest that such an implied repeal might have been effected. It is easy to see what the argument might have been: Parliament in 1972 could not bind Parliament in 1988, and s 2(4) was therefore ineffective to do so. It seems to me that there is no doubt but that in *Factortame (No 1)* the House of Lords effectively accepted that s 2(4) could not be impliedly repealed, albeit the point was not argued.

Where does this leave the constitutional position which I have stated? ... In the present state of its maturity the common law has come to recognise that there exist rights which should properly be classified as constitutional or fundamental: see for example such cases as *Simms* [2000] 2 AC 115 per Lord Hoffmann at 131, *Pierson v Secretary of State* [1998] AC 539, *Leech* [1994] QB 198, *Derbyshire County Council v Times Newspapers Ltd* [1993] AC 534, and *Witham* [1998] QB 575. And from this a further insight follows. We should recognise a hierarchy of Acts of Parliament: as it were 'ordinary' statutes and 'constitutional' statutes. The two categories must be distinguished on a principled basis. In my opinion a constitutional statute is one which (a) conditions the legal relationship between citizen and State in some general, overarching manner, or (b) enlarges or diminishes the scope of what we would now regard as fundamental constitutional rights. (a) and (b) are of necessity closely related: it is difficult to think of an instance of (a) that is not also an instance of (b). The special status of constitutional statutes follows the special status of constitutional rights. Examples are the Magna Carta, the Bill of Rights 1689, the Act of Union, the Reform Acts which distributed and enlarged the franchise, the HRA [Human Rights Act 1998], the Scotland Act 1998 and the Government of Wales Act 1998. The ECA clearly belongs in this family. It incorporated the whole corpus of substantive Community rights and obligations, and gave overriding domestic effect to the judicial and administrative machinery of Community law. It may be there has never been a statute having such profound effects on so many dimensions of our daily lives. The ECA is, by force of the common law, a constitutional statute.

Ordinary statutes may be impliedly repealed. Constitutional statutes may not ...[3]

Professor David Feldman has offered important and constructive criticisms of the idea of a constitutional statute and how it works in practice.[4] His observations demand close attention, not least as regards the idea's practical application. He argues that '[t]ying the "constitutional" status of legislation to fundamental rights' in the way in which I suggested in *Thoburn*[5] 'is problematic, for three reasons'.[6] The first is that the category of fundamental rights is not closed. The second is that some 'constitutional' legislation is not concerned with rights. The third is that the 'rights' aspect of my suggested test—a statute which 'enlarges or diminishes the scope of what we would now regard as fundamental constitutional rights'—is over-inclusive: '[m]ost legislation is concerned with the relationship between the state and citizens, in that it confers powers on state agencies to interfere with or regulate citizens' activities'.[7] Professor Feldman then proceeds to delineate possible alternative tests for a constitutional statute.

Professor Feldman's criticisms, and his alternative criteria, demonstrate that the application of the notion of constitutional statutes poses practical challenges. The academic response to the idea has been quite widespread, and we shall have to see how it fares in future judgments. It has not, so far as I know, been disapproved, and received what perhaps may be called a limited endorsement in the judgment of Lord Neuberger and Lord Mance in the *HS2* case:

> The United Kingdom has no written constitution, but we have a number of constitutional instruments. They include Magna Carta, the Petition of Right 1628, the Bill of Rights and (in Scotland) the Claim of Rights Act 1689, the Act of Settlement 1701 and the Act of Union 1707. The European Communities Act 1972, the Human Rights Act 1998 and the Constitutional Reform Act 2005 may now be added to this list. The common law itself also recognises certain principles as fundamental to the rule of law. It is, putting the point at its lowest, certainly arguable (and it is for United Kingdom law and courts to determine) that there may be fundamental principles, whether contained in other constitutional instruments or recognised at common law, of which Parliament when it enacted the European Communities Act 1972 did not either contemplate or authorise the abrogation.[8]

Paragraphs 58–70 of my judgment in *Thoburn*, in which I set out the notion of constitutional statutes, is referred to by Lord Neuberger and Lord Mance in the next paragraph of the judgment in *HS2*.

---

[3] ibid, [60]–[63].
[4] D Feldman, 'The Nature and Significance of "Constitutional" Legislation' (2013) 129 *LQR* 343.
[5] *Thoburn* (n 2), [62].
[6] Feldman (n 4), 345.
[7] ibid, 347–48.
[8] *R (HS2 Alliance Action Ltd) v Secretary of State for Transport* [2014] UKSC 3, [2014] 1 WLR 324, [207].

For present purposes, I would underline this observation in Professor Feldman's conclusions: 'The important point is that we cannot systematically identify constitutional legislation without a notion of the central function or functions of constitutions.'[9] With respect I am sure this is right. As I have said, I am concerned to see what the relationship between the *Miller* case and the notion of a constitutional statute has to tell us about the direction of our constitution. I should therefore touch briefly on what I see as the central function of a constitution.

The core of a constitution, as it seems to me, is that set of laws, or laws and conventions, which in a sovereign state defines the relationship between the ruler and the ruled. It must therefore include definitions of the ruler and the ruled, and of the powers and duties of each. This sits with Professor Feldman's last test or criterion for constitutional legislation: 'constitutional legislation establishes state institutions and confers functions, responsibilities and powers on them. Such legislation constitutes the state and lays out its structure'.[10] These ideas are consonant also with the first test I suggested in *Thoburn* for a constitutional statute: a statute which 'conditions the legal relationship between citizen and State in some general, overarching manner'.[11] I shall proceed in this chapter on the footing that the ECA is a constitutional statute in this sense, and cannot be impliedly repealed.

II. *Miller*

As is very well known, the *Miller* case concerned the question whether by our constitutional law the executive government was entitled to initiate or invoke Article 50 of the Treaty on European Union, notifying the UK's intention to quit the European Union (EU), without the authority of a statute. The Supreme Court, on appeal from the judgment of the Divisional Court,[12] held by a majority that a statute was required.[13] There were issues and sub-issues, but the core rationale of the majority judgment, delivered by Lord Neuberger, may I think be taken from these passages:

[B]y the 1972 Act, Parliament endorsed and gave effect to the United Kingdom's membership of what is now the European Union under the EU Treaties in a way which is inconsistent with the future exercise by ministers of any prerogative power to withdraw from such Treaties ...

In short, the fact that EU law will no longer be part of UK domestic law if the United Kingdom withdraws from the EU Treaties does not mean that Parliament contemplated

---

[9] Feldman (n 4), 357.

[10] ibid, 350.

[11] *Thoburn* (n 2).

[12] *R (Miller) v Secretary of State for Exiting the European Union* [2016] EWHC 2768 (Admin), [2017] 1 All ER 158.

[13] *Miller* (n 1).

or intended that ministers could cause the United Kingdom to withdraw from the EU Treaties without prior Parliamentary approval ...[14]

Accordingly, the main difficulty with the Secretary of State's argument is that it does not answer the objection based on the constitutional implications of withdrawal from the EU ... A complete withdrawal represents a change which is different not just in degree but in kind from the abrogation of particular rights, duties or rules derived from EU law. It will constitute as significant a constitutional change as that which occurred when EU law was first incorporated in domestic law by the 1972 Act ... It would be inconsistent with long-standing and fundamental principle for such a far-reaching change to the UK constitutional arrangements to be brought about by ministerial decision or ministerial action alone. All the more so when the source in question was brought into existence by Parliament through primary legislation, which gave that source an overriding supremacy in the hierarchy of domestic law sources.[15]

The 'constitutional implications of withdrawal from the EU' are rightly emphasised, as is the central position of the ECA. No reference to the notion of a constitutional statute appears in these paragraphs; but earlier Lord Neuberger had said:

The primacy of EU law means that, unlike other rules of domestic law, EU law cannot be implicitly displaced by the mere enactment of legislation which is inconsistent with it. That is clear from the second part of section 2(4) of the 1972 Act and *Factortame Ltd (No 2)* [1991] 1 AC 603. The issue was informatively discussed by Laws LJ in *Thoburn v Sunderland City Council* [2003] QB 151, paras 37–47.

The 1972 Act accordingly has a constitutional character, as discussed by Laws LJ in *Thoburn* cited above, paras 58–59, and by Lord Reed and Lords Neuberger and Mance in *R (Buckinghamshire County Council) v Secretary of State for Transport* [2014] 1 WLR 324, paras 78 to 79 and 206 to 207 respectively [the *HS2* case]. Following the coming into force of the 1972 Act, the normal rule is that any domestic legislation must be consistent with EU law. In such cases, EU law has primacy as a matter of domestic law, and legislation which is inconsistent with EU law from time to time is to that extent ineffective in law. However, legislation which alters the domestic constitutional status of EU institutions or of EU law is not constrained by the need to be consistent with EU law. In the case of such legislation, there is no question of EU law having primacy, so that such legislation will have domestic effect even if it infringes EU law (and that would be true whether or not the 1972 Act remained in force). That is because of the principle of Parliamentary sovereignty which is, as explained above, fundamental to the United Kingdom's constitutional arrangements, and EU law can only enjoy a status in domestic law which that principle allows. It will therefore have that status only for as long as the 1972 Act continues to apply, and that, of course, can only be a matter for Parliament.[16]

---

[14] ibid, [77]–[78].
[15] ibid, [81].
[16] ibid, [66]–[67].

III. The Primacy of EU Law?

Paragraph 81 of the majority judgment in *Miller* underlines the fact that the source of EU law's efficacy in the United Kingdom (UK) 'was brought into existence by Parliament through primary legislation'.[17] Note also these passages: '[i]t is also true that EU law enjoys its automatic and overriding effect only by virtue of the 1972 Act';[18] 'EU law in EU Treaties and EU legislation will pass into UK law through the medium of section 2(1) or the implementation provisions of section 2(2) of the 1972 Act';[19] '[the ECA] provided for a new constitutional process for making law in the United Kingdom'.[20] But so far as I can see, there is nothing which points directly to the constitutional status of the ECA; there is no express connection with the reference to the ECA's 'constitutional character'.[21] The nearest the judgment comes to a recognition that the ECA could not be impliedly repealed is to be found, I think, in paragraph 66: '[t]he primacy of EU law means that, unlike other rules of domestic law, EU law cannot be implicitly displaced by the mere enactment of legislation which is inconsistent with it.'[22] But with respect, this is itself misleading, at least if taken in isolation. It is not *the primacy of EU law* which has that legal consequence. I must return to the *Thoburn* judgment:

> There is nothing in the ECA which allows the Court of Justice, or any other institutions of the EU, to touch or qualify the conditions of Parliament's legislative supremacy in the United Kingdom. Not because the legislature chose not to allow it; because by our law it could not allow it. That being so, the legislative and judicial institutions of the EU cannot intrude upon those conditions. The British Parliament has not the authority to authorise any such thing. Being sovereign, it cannot abandon its sovereignty. Accordingly there are no circumstances in which the jurisprudence of the Court of Justice can elevate Community law to a status within the corpus of English domestic law to which it could not aspire by any route of English law itself.[23]

The reason why 'EU law cannot be implicitly displaced by the mere enactment of legislation which is inconsistent with it' is that the ECA cannot be impliedly repealed. Now, it seems unlikely that the majority in *Miller* intended in terms to hold that the efficacy of EU law in the UK is due to any autonomous, supervening status enjoyed by EU law itself. But I think it is of some importance to have in mind that that was the very proposition which the Divisional Court rejected in *Thoburn*. The argument of counsel (Eleanor Sharpston QC, now Advocate

---

[17] ibid, [81].
[18] ibid, [61].
[19] ibid, [64].
[20] ibid, [62].
[21] ibid, [66]–[67].
[22] ibid, [66].
[23] *Thoburn* (n 2), [59].

General at the Court of Justice in Luxembourg) had been that the legislative and judicial institutions of the EU may set limits to the power of Parliament to make laws which regulate the legal relationship between the EU and the UK. That was the submission confronted at paragraph 59 of my judgment.

IV. The Source of EU Law in the United Kingdom

The Supreme Court's reference to the primacy of EU law chimes with other passages in the majority judgment, which possess an almost metaphysical quality:

> In one sense, of course, it can be said that the 1972 Act is the source of EU law, in that, without that Act, EU law would have no domestic status. But in a more fundamental sense and, we consider, a more realistic sense, where EU law applies in the United Kingdom, it is the EU institutions which are the relevant source of that law ...[24]

> In our view, then, although the 1972 Act gives effect to EU law, it is not itself the originating source of that law. It is ... the 'conduit pipe' by which EU law is introduced into UK domestic law. So long as the 1972 Act remains in force, its effect is to constitute EU law an independent and overriding source of domestic law ...[25]

Contrast Lord Reed in the minority:

> [T]he effect which Parliament has given to EU law in our domestic law, under the 1972 Act, is inherently conditional on the application of the EU treaties to the UK, and therefore on the UK's membership of the EU ...[26]

> [R]ights given direct effect by section 2(1) of the 1972 Act are inherently contingent, and can be altered without any further Act of Parliament ...[27]

I think the contrast between these approaches is a distraction. They obscure more than they reveal. What are we to make of these two propositions: (i) '[W]here EU law applies in the United Kingdom, it is the EU institutions which are the relevant source of that law' (Lord Neuberger);[28] and (ii) '[T]he effect which Parliament has given to EU law in our domestic law, under the 1972 Act, is inherently conditional on the application of the EU treaties to the UK, and therefore on the UK's membership of the EU' (Lord Reed)?[29] Why are the EU institutions the relevant source of law 'in a more fundamental sense' (Lord Neuberger)? Why does the fact that EU law's domestic application is 'conditional on the UK's membership of the EU' disqualify the EU as an originating, or relevant, source of UK law (Lord Reed)?

---

[24] *Miller* (n 1), [61].
[25] ibid, [65].
[26] ibid, [177].
[27] ibid, [216].
[28] ibid, [61].
[29] ibid, [177].

I can see that there is a logical purity to the view of the minority: it points to the seeming fact that the majority appear to assume but in fact deny[30] a new rule of recognition. That, I think, is an important source of the minority's appeal to legal scholars. It seems to me, however, that this approach addresses too narrow a question. We should not lose sight of the issue that was at the heart of the case: should our constitutional law allow the executive to initiate our departure from the EU without legislative authority to that effect? Behind this question there is a larger one: how far should our constitutional law allow the executive to make or unmake domestic law?

Lord Neuberger stated:

> In the early 17th century *Case of Proclamations* (1611) 12 Co Rep 74, Sir Edward Coke CJ said that 'the King by his proclamation or other ways cannot change any part of the common law, or statute law, or the customs of the realm'. Although this statement may have been controversial at the time, it had become firmly established by the end of that century.[31]

And this is of course received doctrine. After citing further authority, Lord Neuberger added this:

> As Lord Hoffmann observed in *R (Bancoult) v Secretary of State for Foreign and Commonwealth Affairs (No 2)* [2009] AC 453, para 44, 'since the 17th century the prerogative has not empowered the Crown to change English common or statute law'.[32]

In light of these basic propositions of our constitutional law, it seems to me to be very difficult to attach critical importance to distinctions of the kind drawn in the majority and minority judgments. It is difficult, even, to fathom the basis of the distinction. The answer to the constitutional question—does the invocation of Article 50 require the authority of a statute?—cannot in my view depend on whether you choose to categorise the EU as an 'originating' or only a 'conditional' source of law in the UK. Apart from anything else, both categorisations are in a real sense true; the EU institutions are undoubtedly a source—and if you like an originating source—of UK law; equally, the application in the UK of that law is undoubtedly conditional on the UK's membership of the EU. The antithesis between these opposing positions is in the end barren, a distraction from the true question: how far should our constitutional law allow the executive to make or unmake domestic law? The core of the answer lies in Coke's principle stated in the *Case of Proclamations*. In that context, I shall come shortly to the utility of the concept of constitutional statutes.

---

[30] ibid, [60].
[31] ibid, [44].
[32] ibid, [50].

V. Delegated Legislation

But first I should draw attention to a further dissonance, if I may call it that, between *Miller* and *Thoburn*. I must cite a further passage from the majority judgment in *Miller*:

> [W]e ... do not accept the suggestion that, as a source of law, EU law can properly be compared with delegated legislation. The 1972 Act effectively operates as a partial transfer of law-making powers, or an assignment of legislative competences, by Parliament to the EU law-making institutions (so long as Parliament wills it), rather than a statutory delegation of the power to make ancillary regulations—even under a so-called Henry the Eighth clause ... The 1972 Act cannot be said to constitute EU legislative institutions the delegates of Parliament: they make laws independently of Parliament, and indeed they were doing so before the 1972 Act was passed ... A statutory provision which provides that legislative documents and decisions made by EU institutions should be an independent and pre-eminent source of UK law is thus quite different from a statutory provision which delegates to ministers and other organs of the executive the right to make regulations and the like ...[33]

In the third Hamlyn Lecture in 2013,[34] I suggested that 'European measures, so far as they are effective in this jurisdiction, possess a principal characteristic of secondary legislation: they only have force to the extent permitted by the enabling Act'. Whether or not this is right is of some importance. If the force of EU law in the UK is rightly seen as a delegation of legislative power to the European institutions by the ECA, it means that the sovereignty of Parliament was untouched by our membership of the EU. At the same time, since the delegation is on so grand a scale, the ECA may be seen as a constitutional statute *par excellence*— it 'conditions the legal relationship between citizen and State in some general, overarching manner' more than somewhat. That is why the point matters for present purposes.

I think the majority in *Miller* were wrong to repudiate 'the suggestion that, as a source of law, EU law can properly be compared with delegated legislation'.[35] The reason given by the majority—'[t]he 1972 Act cannot be said to constitute EU legislative institutions the delegates of Parliament: they make laws independently of Parliament'[36]—confuses *the fact of delegation* with *the breadth of the powers that might be delegated*. The provision made by the ECA for EU law to have effect in the UK is of course *factually* very different from any standard instance of delegated legislation. But *conceptually* it is not. The ECA authorised—revocably— the institutions of the EU as a source of law for the UK. However large the *vires*

---

[33] ibid, [68].

[34] J Laws, *The Common Law Constitution, Lecture III: The Common Law and Europe* (Cambridge, Cambridge University Press, 2014).

[35] *Miller* (n 1), [68].

[36] ibid.

thus given to the EU, that is a form of delegation. In fact the *vires* is not unlimited. Paragraph 59 of *Thoburn* shows that the ECA did not—could not—transfer to the European institutions the ultimate power of legislation for the UK.[37] Short of that, what was given was necessarily a delegated power.

My view of European measures effective in the UK as analogous to delegated legislation has been the subject of criticism, which I should by no means ignore, from Professor Mark Elliott:

> The difficulty with Laws LJ's view that EU law's status in the legal system is analogous to that occupied by secondary legislation stems from its parochialism. It is technically correct to say that, *as a matter of domestic law*, EU law applies only on the terms laid down by Parliament. Parliament is free, *as a matter of domestic law*, to repeal or amend the ECA, closing the door of the UK's legal system, wholly or partly, to the directly-effective EU law that would otherwise apply here. There is, however, a crucial difference between Parliament's capacity to curtail executive powers to enact secondary legislation and its ability to resist the application of EU law. Although—being sovereign—Parliament has unfettered domestic capacity to do each of those things, its ability to do the former in a manner that is lawful falls to be judged not only by reference to domestic, but also by reference to international, law. For the UK to resist the application of directly-effective EU law by amending the ECA might be perfectly possible, and wholly lawful, at a domestic level, but the position is otherwise on the international plane. The elegance of Laws LJ's analysis lies in its capacity to accord a pragmatic, day-to-day primacy to EU law, whilst insisting that, in theoretical terms, Parliament's sovereignty is undiminished thanks to its capacity to amend the ECA and override EU law. But the elegance of that accommodation betrays its greatest weakness: that it presents an analysis of the British constitution shorn of the international legal context in which it now falls to be understood.[38]

I hope Professor Elliott will forgive me if I suggest there is a *non sequitur* here. Of course it is right that repeal of the ECA without withdrawal from the EU on the international plane might—would (depending, theoretically, on what we did with past and future EU measures after the repeal)—put the UK in breach of its treaty obligations. But the consequence is no more nor less than this, that the grant of power to the EU institutions effected by the ECA, and its prospective withdrawal, is subject to the discipline of international law; but that, however great our duty of compliance, does not by our constitution touch the sovereignty of Parliament or the power of Parliament to grant legislative authority to the EU and thereafter to withdraw it. The international dimension to which Professor Elliott draws

---

[37] See also ibid, [67], where the majority, having referred to *Thoburn* (n 2) and *HS2* (n 8), said that 'the principle of Parliamentary sovereignty ... is ... fundamental to the United Kingdom's constitutional arrangements, and EU law can only enjoy a status in domestic law which that principle allows'. It followed, said the majority, that EU law 'will ... have that status only for as long as the 1972 Act continues to apply, and that, of course, can only be a matter for Parliament'.

[38] M Elliott, 'Is Laws LJ right to suggest that EU law is like secondary legislation?', *Public Law for Everyone*, 29 November 2013, available at https://publiclawforeveryone.com/2013/11/29/is-laws-lj-right-to-suggest-that-eu-law-is-like-secondary-legislation/.

attention does not, therefore, undermine the analogy or comparison between the status of EU law in the UK and delegated legislation. The point is important because it means, as I have said, that the sovereignty of Parliament was untouched by our membership of the EU.

The analogy is illuminated by the important circumstance that the grant of legislative authority to the EU institutions was not at large. It did not include the ultimate levers of legal power.[39] The delegation was necessarily limited. The true difference between this legal scenario and that of standard delegated legislation is that in this case Parliament lacked the power to delegate more than it did.

VI. The Impact of the Concept of a Constitutional Statute

Although Lord Neuberger acknowledged that '[t]he 1972 Act ... has a constitutional character',[40] and stated that in constitutional terms the effect of the 1972 Act was unprecedented',[41] it is by no means clear that the distinct characteristic of constitutional legislation, namely that it cannot be impliedly repealed, played any significant part in the result of the *Miller* litigation, or in the reasoning of the majority. Perhaps it did not need to: the fact that the ECA cannot be impliedly repealed is not, I think, a premise of Lord Neuberger's core conclusions at paragraph 81.

VII. Silence in Statutes

One aspect of the argument in *Miller* calls for attention in this context. The Crown argued that because the European Union (Amendment) Act 2008 and the European Union Act 2011 placed 'restrictions on the exercise of the government's foreign affairs prerogative power, it must follow that those statutes mean that other aspects of the prerogative must have been intended to have been left unfettered. *Expressio unius exclusion alterius.*'[42] Specifically, 'the two statutes specified in detail the prerogative powers which Parliament intended to control in relation

---

[39] See *Thoburn* (n 2), [59].
[40] *Miller* (n 1), [67].
[41] ibid, [60].
[42] D Howarth, 'On Parliamentary Silence', *UKCLA Blog* (13 December 2016), available at https://ukconstitutionallaw.org/.

to the EU Treaties, and ... they did not include the power to withdraw from those treaties under article 50(2)'.[43]

The majority rejected this submission: 'We do not accept this argument. The fact that a statute says nothing about a particular topic can rarely, if ever, justify inferring a fundamental change in the law'.[44] So much was echoed by Lord Reed in his dissenting judgment at paragraph 203. I will not enter at any length into the details of the Acts of 2008 and 2011. The first added the Treaty of Lisbon to the list of treaties in section 1(2) of the ECA, and made certain other provisions. The second required that any amendment of the Treaty on European Union or the Treaty on the Functioning of the European Union made by treaty must be approved by an Act of Parliament, and that a referendum must be held in certain circumstances. They may be taken to be constitutional statutes. Might that status affect the validity of the argument from silence advanced by the Crown and rejected by the Court?

As it seems to me, the constitutional status of these statutes underlines the correctness of the Court's view that their silence on Article 50, contrasted with their restrictions on prerogative power elsewhere, carries no implication that action under Article 50(2) was and remained within the prerogative power of the Crown. The important concept here is that of *implication*. A constitutional statute may not be impliedly repealed; likewise, it is not to be construed so as in effect to make or confirm a substantial provision touching the constitution by means of a rule of mere implication such as *Expressio unius exclusio alterius*. These propositions may appear to be no more than rules of construction. In fact, as I shall show, they disclose an important constitutional principle.

VIII. Constitutional Statutes: General Lessons

Overall the notion of a constitutional statute as such played little part in the *Miller* case. It might have been otherwise. If a statute 'conditions the legal relationship between citizen and State in some general, overarching manner',[45] of necessity it alters the general law of the land in some fundamental respect. That should be enough to disqualify the executive government from any entitlement to enter into the legislative field in such an area. As I have shown, Lord Neuberger cited the *Case of Proclamations*: '[T]he King by his proclamation or other ways cannot change any part of the common law, or statute law, or the customs of the realm.'[46]

---

[43] *Miller* (n 1), [107].
[44] ibid, [108].
[45] *Thoburn* (n 2), [62].
[46] *Case of Proclamations* (1610) 12 Co Rep 74.

The status of the ECA as a constitutional statute confirms and underlines Lord Neuberger's conclusion:

> It would be inconsistent with long-standing and fundamental principle for such a far-reaching change to the UK constitutional arrangements to be brought about by ministerial decision or ministerial action alone. All the more so when the source in question was brought into existence by Parliament through primary legislation, which gave that source an overriding supremacy in the hierarchy of domestic law sources.[47]

The Court—majority and minority—should not have been distracted by what I think was a barren debate as to the sense in which or the extent to which the ECA was 'relevant', 'fundamental' or 'conditional' as a source of EU law in the UK.

But there are broader lessons, though they may not spring from the pages of the *Miller* judgments. I said earlier that a constitutional statute is not to be construed so as in effect to make or confirm a substantial provision by means of a rule of mere implication; and this sits alongside the rule that a constitutional statute may not be impliedly repealed. In these respects constitutional statutes are subject to principles of interpretation that are more narrowly drawn than those applicable generally. The rationale has a certain subtlety. It is a virtue of our uncodified constitution that it has been able to evolve, with a degree of flexibility and without revolutionary disruptions, since the seventeenth century. Lord Neuberger[48] cites Dicey's well-known observation that the UK constitution is 'the most flexible polity in existence'.[49] But by contrast, it must also be right that any change to our constitutional arrangements effected by Parliament must be deliberate, clear and considered, and not the result of an approach to statutory interpretation which, by giving a large place to the effect of implication, may sometimes be little more than serendipitous. This is why tighter rules of construction are needed in the interpretation of constitutional statutes. I shall have more to say below about their rationale.

This divergence between different modes of statutory interpretation teaches us more than the need to strike a balance between constitutional flexibility and certainty. It illustrates the partnership between judiciary and legislature in maintaining the health of our constitution. The balance between flexibility and certainty is struck by the judges in formulating rules of construction; Parliament may of course stipulate particular rules of construction, but rules so stipulated fall in their turn to be interpreted by the courts. Parliament cannot, in the end, translate its own voice for the people's hearing. An Act of Parliament is words on a page. Only the common law gives it life. In *Cart*, I said this in the Divisional Court:

> [L]egislation consists in texts. Often—and in every case of dispute or difficulty—the texts cannot speak for themselves. Unless their meaning is mediated to the public, they

---

[47] *Miller* (n 1), [81].
[48] ibid, 40.
[49] AV Dicey, *Introduction to the Study of the Law of the Constitution*, 8th edn (London, Macmillan, 1915) 87.

are only letters on a page. They have to be interpreted. The interpreter's role cannot be filled by the legislature or the executive: for in that case they or either of them would be judge in their own cause, with the ills of arbitrary government which that would entail. Nor, generally, can the interpreter be constituted by the public body which has to administer the relevant law: for in that case the decision-makers would write their own laws. The interpreter must be impartial, independent both of the legislature and of the persons affected by the texts' application, and authoritative—accepted as the last word, subject only to any appeal. Only a court can fulfil the role.

If the meaning of statutory text is not controlled by such a judicial authority, it would at length be degraded to nothing more than a matter of opinion. Its scope and content would become muddied and unclear. Public bodies would not, by means of the judicial review jurisdiction, be kept within the confines of their powers prescribed by statute. The very effectiveness of statute law, Parliament's law, requires that none of these things happen. Accordingly, as it seems to me, the need for such an authoritative judicial source cannot be dispensed with by Parliament. This is not a denial of legislative sovereignty, but an affirmation of it: as is the old rule that Parliament cannot bind itself. The old rule means that successive Parliaments are always free to make what laws they choose; that is one condition of Parliament's sovereignty. The requirement of an authoritative judicial source for the interpretation of law means that Parliament's statutes are always effective; that is another.[50]

That reasoning was not overturned in the Court of Appeal or the Supreme Court, although it is perhaps interesting that in the Supreme Court Lord Phillips found it necessary to say this:

> The proposition that Parliamentary sovereignty requires Parliament to respect the power of the High Court to subject the decisions of public authorities, including courts of limited jurisdiction, to judicial review is controversial. Hopefully the issue will remain academic.[51]

I am not sure why it should remain academic.

In approaching the task of interpretation, the common law judges will apply objective standards, and these standards will condition the meaning of the laws which are the subject of adjudication. The core standards which the judges bring to the products of Parliament, as well as to the development of free-standing common law principle, are the requirements of reason, fairness and the presumption of liberty: these are central guarantees of the rule of law itself. For present purposes, however, the important point is that the court's insistence (as I would have it) on the application of narrowly drawn rules of construction to constitutional statutes—no implied repeal, no substantial provision to be derived from a rule of mere implication—itself discloses a value-laden principle. Its rationale, as I have said, is the need to ensure that any change to our constitutional arrangements effected by Parliament must be deliberate, clear and considered; that is an important constitutional principle.

---

[50] *R (Cart) v Upper Tribunal* [2009] EWHC 3052 (Admin), [2010] PTSR 824, [37]–[38].
[51] *R (Cart) v Upper Tribunal* [2011] UKSC 28, [2012] 1 AC 663, [73].

IX. Referendums

The UK's experience of membership of the EU, or rather of the bruises of leaving it, has lessons as to the use of referendums. There may be some situations, where existential change is at hand, in which the device of the referendum is justified. The vote on Scottish independence was perhaps one. But, generally, I think the use of referendums creates a potential constitutional danger. It is that the referendum appears to offer a source of democratic power which challenges the democratic power of Parliament. It creates two democratic poles, one representative—the elected legislature—and one direct—the people's vote. Lord Patten—Chris Patten—has said that referendums 'undermine Westminster'.[52]

In 1774, Edmund Burke made a famous speech to the electors of Bristol. He said this:

> [Your representative's] unbiased opinion, his mature judgment, his enlightened conscience, he ought not to sacrifice to you, to any man, or to any set of men living. These he does not derive from your pleasure; no, nor from the law and the constitution. They are a trust from Providence, for the abuse of which he is deeply answerable. Your representative owes you, not his industry only, but his judgment; and he betrays, instead of serving you, if he sacrifices it to your opinion.[53]

It is plain that Burke's speech to the electors of Bristol has matured into a constitutional principle. The difference between direct democracy and representative democracy is not merely that in the latter case the people do not literally make the laws themselves. It is also that the people's representatives are not their proxies or their delegates: they owe their constituents their judgment, not their obedience. Now, it is I think clear that the European Union (Notification of Withdrawal) Act 2017 obtained Royal Assent on 16 March with the support of many Members of both Houses of Parliament whose personal judgment was opposed to Brexit. Our Parliamentarians have given effect to what they evidently regard as an imperative mandate from the people, expressed in the referendum result. Those who voted against their better judgment as regards the merits of Brexit were, I think, caught between two democratic poles. It is noteworthy that on *Question Time* on the day of Royal Assent, 16 March, the Conservative MP Jacob Rees-Mogg (a constitutionalist, one would have thought, if ever there was one) stated that 'the fundamental point is the referendum was authoritative'.

The roller-coaster of the Brexit referendum may have made this inevitable; and it may perhaps, in the service of public tranquillity and the long-term interests of the UK, have been the right thing to do. But for MPs to treat a referendum as a mandate represents a new kind of constitutional morality. For my part, I hope it will not take root.

---

[52] BBC, *Breakfast with Frost*, 1 June 2003.
[53] Cited in PB Kurland and R Lerner (eds), *The Founders' Constitution*, vol I (Chicago, IL, University of Chicago Press, 1987) ch 13.

X. Henry VIII Powers

At the time of writing the European Union (Withdrawal) Bill (formerly trumpeted as the Great Repeal Bill) is before Parliament. Its terms have evoked much political controversy. Of course it is idle to predict what precisely the end will be, but it is surely inevitable, given the bulk and complexity of European legislation, controversies over what we should keep and what we should discard, and judicial supervision of what we keep, that there must be substantial delegated powers. The extent to which those powers will or should authorise Ministers to amend Acts of Parliament—the so-called Henry VIII clause—is uncertain, but I should have thought it must be considerable. The powers in the Bill are very wide indeed. I shall not recite them here, save to note that clause 9(2) confers a power to amend by statutory instrument the Withdrawal Act itself—a provision criticised by Lord Pannick QC: 'surely a matter for Parliament, given the constitutional significance of the bill'.[54] Whatever the Act's final shape, there are likely to be important challenges in the courts to test the powers' reach.

There is an irony in the necessity of Henry VIII powers. The *Miller* case vindicated the place of Parliament as a principal source of constitutional law, though I have with respect expressed some reservations as to some aspects of the majority's reasoning. Yet it appears that in order to give effect to the determination of Parliament that the UK should leave the EU, substantial legislative powers (whatever their final form) will in fact have to be granted to the executive; no clean break, then, between the domains of the Crown and Parliament.

XI. Conclusions

Miller was perhaps a shaky moment in the history of our uncodified constitution. The respective claims of legislature and executive to change great swathes of the laws under which we are governed were contested in the Supreme Court, against a background in which the result of the Brexit referendum laid sticky fingers on the debate. The supposed power of the people in the referendum, and the supposed power of the Crown through the prerogative, jostled to chip away at Lord Coke's principle—the Crown cannot change the common law or statute.

A battered Parliament has come through as our primary legitimate legislator upon constitutional affairs. Equally, the place of the judges as guardians of enduring constitutional principles has been illustrated and confirmed. The democratic legislature, despite its primacy *as* legislator, cannot itself occupy such a role: of necessity it reflects the changing will of the people, and that is something very

---

[54] *The Times* (7 September 2017).

different from, and sometimes antithetical to, constitutional values and principles, which develop and mature over time. These positions are underpinned by the concept of the constitutional statute, whose special rules of construction give focus and certainty to any constitutional change enacted by Parliament. The seductive and dangerous power of the referendum has been, to some extent at least, held in check. All these elements in our polity must keep their place, move in the same direction, as the pages of Brexit are turned. And our law's facility of flexible and pragmatic reaction to new challenges tells us very loudly how wise we are not to embrace a written constitution. But that would be another chapter.

10

Sovereignty, Primacy and the Common Law Constitution: What Has EU Membership Taught Us?

MARK ELLIOTT*

When the legal history of the United Kingdom's (UK's) membership of the
European Union (EU) comes to be written, it is likely to be bookended by two seminal decisions of the UK's apex court: the judgments of the Appellate Committee
of the House of Lords in *Factortame*[1] and of the Supreme Court in *Miller*.[2] Each, in
its own way, illuminates the British constitution: by grappling either with what it
meant in constitutional terms to become a Member State of the EU, or with what
that membership has entailed and what the legal and constitutional implications
of departure will be. At the heart of each case are questions about the nature and
status of EU law with respect to the UK's domestic legal system. And while *Miller*
is not, in the same way as *Factortame*, directly concerned with the doctrine of the
primacy of EU law, questions about the nature and status of EU law within the UK
legal system are nevertheless central to the issues at stake in *Miller*. Yet while the
relationship between the notions that Parliament is sovereign and that EU law has
supremacy is perhaps the most acute of the constitutional issues raised by membership, the precise nature of that relationship is still far from clear.

By introducing the construct of EU primacy into a legal system characterised
by the principle of legislative supremacy—thus creating what looks, at least a first
glance, like a classic immovable-object-meets-irresistible-force problem—EU
membership has forced UK public lawyers to think long and hard about the very
nature of the domestic legal order. But just as interesting as the *answers* that these
questions have generated is the *way* in which the questions have been confronted,

* I am very grateful indeed to Eirik Bjorge, Jack Williams and Alison Young for their invaluable
comments on an earlier draft of this chapter.

[1] *R v Secretary of State for Transport, ex parte Factortame Ltd (No 1)* [1990] 2 AC 85 ('*Factortame
(No 1)*'); *R v Secretary of State for Transport, ex parte Factortame Ltd (No 2)* [1991] 1 AC 603 ('*Factortame (No 2)*').
[2] *R (Miller) v Secretary of State for Exiting the European Union* [2017] UKSC 5, [2017] 2 WLR 583
('*Miller*').

including the degree of uncertainty that has been allowed to persist in relation to genuinely fundamental constitutional issues. In this sense, the UK's involvement with the EU shines a light on the deeply pragmatic nature of the British constitution, whereby fundamental questions are confronted only when, and to the extent that, such confrontation is strictly required. The risk, however, is that such a strong commitment to pragmatism yields—and masks—a degree of theoretical ambivalence that becomes highly problematic when hard questions arise, as they did in *Miller*.[3]

In this chapter, I explore these issues—that is, substantive questions about the accommodation of EU primacy by the domestic constitutional system and broader questions about the way in which these matters have been dealt with—in tandem. In doing so, I pay particular attention to the question whether this episode in UK constitutional history teaches only specific lessons about how EU law has been accommodated—lessons that may be of little if any relevance when or if the UK fully withdraws from the EU—or lessons of a more enduring kind that will remain pertinent long after withdrawal. I argue that it is lessons of the latter type that can be derived from attempts to understand the relationship that has existed this last half-century or so between the domestic and European legal orders. However, I argue too that the extraction of those lessons involves a degree of supposition and inference that speaks volumes about the way in which fundamental constitutional questions are (and are not) confronted in the UK. The UK's European sojourn is thus *revealing*, but only to a degree, of the substance of the domestic constitution. And, to the extent that it is *less than revealing*, the opacity that we encounter serves not simply to obscure the substance but to illuminate something more visceral: namely, a preference that can be discerned within UK constitutional adjudication, at least when it comes to the very biggest questions, for constructive ambiguity over conceptual clarity.[4]

I. *Factortame* and the British Way

The British approach to constitutionalism might best be described as one of 'make do and mend'. Problems tend to be fixed (if at all) when they arise, rather than

---

[3] For further discussion of this highly pragmatic approach, see the contribution by Paul Craig in ch 5 of this volume. This point must not be overstated. A number of the judicial discussions considered in this chapter are *obiter*, and in that sense they demonstrate a degree of curial willingness to reflect on and anticipate issues that are not yet live constitutional problems. But this does not detract from the general tendency in the UK to confront such problems only when necessary, and in a sometimes regrettably haphazard or ambiguous way.

[4] The *Miller* case is arguably a study in such ambiguity, thanks in part, but not exclusively, to its ambivalent characterisation of EU law's domestic legal status. Opinions differ about the appropriateness of the arguably less technical, more 'substantive' or 'constitutional' adjudicative approach adopted by the *Miller* majority. Compare, for instance, the contribution by Richard Ekins and Graham Gee, and that by Alison L Young, in chs 11 and 12 of this volume respectively.

being anticipated and headed off through strategic design. The fluidity of the constitution operates so as to incentivise rolling, trial-and-error reform as distinct from long-term planning. And 'what works' is prized above theoretical neatness and systematisation.[5] There can be few better, or more important, illustrations of an atheoretical approach to big constitutional questions than the judgment of the House of Lords in *Factortame (No 2)*.[6] It is perhaps easy, 30 years on, to overlook the momentousness of the step that the Law Lords took in that case when they determined that they could, and would, issue an interim injunction ordering a Minister of the Crown to disapply provisions in an Act of Parliament. But for all that time and familiarity may have served to render the path-breaking apparently mundane—consider, for instance, the low-key way in which primary legislation was disapplied in *Benkharbouche*,[7] and the casual (and questionable) way in which the Supreme Court elided the notions of disapplication and invalidity in the *HS2* case[8]—the constitutional significance of *Factortame* in truth remains undimmed.

That the *outcome* of the House of Lords' judgment in *Factortame* was and remains a legal landmark is hard to argue with. But the *reasoning* contained therein is striking for its lack of detailed engagement with the constitutional issues that were at stake.[9] It is true that in *Factortame (No 2)* Lord Bridge acknowledged, in an understatement that must make it a paradigm of the genre, 'the importance of the subject matter' of the case.[10] He also noted that the European Court of Justice's judgment that had been given in response to the preliminary reference made by the House of Lords in *Factortame (No 1)*, and which affirmed that Member States' courts can override domestic law so as to protect EU law rights, had attracted public criticism, including suggestions that 'this was a novel and dangerous invasion by a Community institution of the sovereignty of the United Kingdom Parliament'.[11] But Lord Bridge went on to say that the supremacy of EU law was 'well established in the jurisprudence of the European Court of Justice long before the United Kingdom joined the Community'; that (it followed that) 'whatever limitation of its sovereignty Parliament accepted when it enacted the European Communities Act 1972 was entirely voluntary'; and that that Act made it clear 'that it was the duty of a United Kingdom court, when delivering final judgment, to override any rule of national law found to be in conflict with any

---

[5] An obvious example is the fact that the 'West Lothian Question' was addressed not as part of the design of the devolution settlements in the late 1990s, but only when it was considered politically expedient to do so, nearly 20 years later, by amending the Standing Orders of the House of Commons to enable 'English Votes for English Laws'.

[6] *Factortame (No 2)* (n 1).

[7] *Benkharbouche v Secretary of State for Foreign and Commonwealth Affairs* [2017] UKSC 62, [2017] 3 WLR 957.

[8] *R (HS2 Action Alliance Ltd) v Secretary of State for Transport* [2014] UKSC 3, [2014] 1 WLR 324, [206] (judgment of Lords Neuberger and Mance, with which all other Justices agreed) ('*HS2*').

[9] The same is true of the House of Lords' earlier judgment in *Factortame (No 1)* (n 1).

[10] *Factortame (No 2)* (n 1), 658.

[11] ibid, 658.

directly enforceable rule of Community law'.[12] And earlier, in *Factortame (No 1)*, Lord Bridge had emphasised, again pointing the finger clearly at Parliament, that it was 'by virtue of' section 2(4) of the 1972 Act that the impugned provisions of the Merchant Shipping Act 1998 only had effect 'subject to' relevant EU law rights.[13]

All of this was doubtless a shrewd exercise in judicial politics, not least in the light of both the controversial nature of the specific issues raised by the facts of *Factortame* and the more overarching sensitivities inevitably raised by judicial prioritisation of EU law over an Act of Parliament. But what is sorely lacking in *Factortame* is any meaningful attempt to engage with the deeper constitutional questions that were necessarily in play. Lord Bridge's judgment in *Factortame (No 2)*, like the judgments of Lords Goff and Jauncey, focused squarely upon technical questions about whether interim injunctive relief was available against (Ministers of) the Crown and, if so, in what circumstances. The fact that the issuing of such relief—a step that, as is well known, the Law Lords went on to take—would precipitate the disapplication of *an Act of Parliament* was reduced to little more than part of the background to the litigation.

The fundamental constitutional questions raised by the taking of such a step, including questions about the implications for the doctrine of parliamentary sovereignty, thus went largely unconfronted. Instead, Lord Bridge, whose judgment was unique in addressing these matters *at all*, was content to underline the fact that Parliament knew what it was getting itself into when it legislated so as to enable the UK to join the EU, and that the consequences of membership—including acceptance of the EU primacy principle—flowed from that eyes-wide-open decision. The pragmatism with which this approach is shot through is so obvious that it need hardly be pointed out. Their Lordships were plainly, and doubtless sensibly, prepared to accept that Parliament had succeeded in achieving what it had set out to achieve by enacting the European Communities Act 1972 ('ECA'), and that EU law had thereby been assigned a domestic legal status consistent with the discharge by the UK of its Treaty obligations as a Member State. But as to *how*, in terms of constitutional theory, such a state of affairs was wrought, *Factortame* remained largely silent.

The occasion of the UK's departure from the EU, and the attention paid in *Miller* to constitutional questions that were barely confronted in *Factortame*, provides an opportunity to think again about these matters. In particular, it prompts reflection upon what lessons might be learned from the UK constitution's attempts over the last five decades to accommodate EU law and, specifically, a primacy doctrine that was taken by some to have sounded the death-knell of parliamentary sovereignty. However, as I argue in the remainder of this chapter, characterising what happened in that way is neither theoretically necessary nor empirically accurate.

---

[12] ibid, 658–59.
[13] *Factortame (No 1)* (n 1), 140.

That conclusion is important in itself if we are interested in how the UK constitution responded to the particular challenges posed by EU membership. But its importance is more far-reaching, for it suggests that the interaction of UK and EU law has served to illuminate aspects of the domestic constitution that are of enduring relevance, and which are thus not merely artefacts of a transitory, and soon to end, dalliance with a separate and exotic legal system.

II. Inundated by the 'Incoming Tide'?

How the relationship between UK and EU law is understood turns, at least in part, upon the perspective from which the issue is viewed.[14] In this regard, a key question is whether the relationship is to be viewed through a domestic or an EU prism. Depending on the approach that is adopted, we might conclude either that the doctrine of the primacy of EU law is something that must fit around (and which may therefore have to yield to) the sovereignty of Parliament, or that the sovereignty of Parliament has to fall into line with (and may thus have to give way to) the primacy of EU law. Neither of these perspectives is necessarily right or wrong, and there may be no one 'correct' answer to the question: 'What happens if EU and UK law conflict?' Imagine, for instance, an Act of the UK Parliament that was unambiguously and explicitly inconsistent with EU law, and which unambiguously and explicitly countermanded the priority accorded to EU law by section 2(4) of the ECA.[15] Such legislation would plainly place the UK in breach of EU law, and would produce international legal consequences for the UK qua Member State. However, it does not *necessarily* follow from any of that that the Act of Parliament in question would, as a matter of domestic constitutional law, be anything other than fully valid and enforceable. Whether the Act's incompatibility with EU law *would* have any domestic legal consequences must turn upon the position according to the constitutional law of the UK.[16] The various ways in which domestic constitutional law might have responded to the demands of EU membership can be broken down into three broad possibilities, which might be envisaged as points on a spectrum.

---

[14] I have considered this idea in more detail elsewhere: M Elliott, 'The principle of parliamentary sovereignty in legal, political and constitutional perspective' in J Jowell, D Oliver and C O'Cinneide (eds), *The Changing Constitution*, 8th edn (Oxford, Oxford University Press, 2015).

[15] These hypothetical circumstances are set out in this somewhat extreme way in order, for the time being, to put to one side questions about legislation that is other than explicitly incompatible with EU law or with the priority rule in section 2(4) of the ECA. Such questions are considered later in this chapter.

[16] Including that aspect of domestic constitutional law according to which the UK is a dualist legal system.

First, domestic law's response might have been one of intransigence. The House of Lords in *Factortame* might, for instance, have said that the EU primacy doctrine and section 2(4) of the ECA were all very well but that the primary responsibility of UK courts is to give effect to the most recent expression of Parliament's will, and that the scheme set down in the Merchant Shipping Act 1988 therefore had to be given effect whether or not it was compatible with EU law, and in spite of anything Parliament might have said in 1972 in the ECA about EU law's status vis-à-vis domestic law. But such a response would have implied a very rigid understanding of the domestic constitutional order and of the notion of parliamentary sovereignty. Enormous practical difficulties would also have ensued if UK courts had been readily willing to interpret and give effect to domestic law in ways that would place the UK in breach of its international obligation. It is therefore unsurprising—not least in the light of the already-noted deeply pragmatic approach that tends to be adopted to fundamental constitutional questions in the UK—that the House of Lords in *Factortame* did not adopt this sort of position.

If the foregoing lies at one end of our spectrum, a second possibility occupies an intermediate position. On this view, the status of EU law in the UK is still a matter of domestic constitutional law, but the latter is conceived of in terms that are flexible enough to accord to EU law at least some degree of priority over incompatible domestic legislation. This is in fact the approach that has been adopted, albeit that it amounts to a broad church, both in terms of how it falls to be *rationalised* and the *extent* of the priority that it affords to EU law. This intermediate position will thus be returned to, as its implications and theoretical basis need to be examined further.

However, before that, a third possible approach, lying at the far end of our spectrum, needs to be considered. If the first two approaches are united by their commitment to the notion that domestic law remains in the driving seat (albeit that they are distinguished by the degree of control that domestic law asserts), the third approach in effect cedes domestic control. It is important to consider this approach not only because the counterpoint it forms with the second (and more realistic) view serves to illuminate the latter, but also because the majority's judgment in *Miller* can be read as offering some support to the third view (although it will be argued it does so only ambivalently, and that this is not the best reading of the judgment). On the third view, then, the EU legal system and the primacy it enjoys are understood to have overwhelmed, or inundated, the domestic legal system: the latter has become subservient to the former; the rules of the constitutional game are laid down no longer by domestic but by EU law;[17] and EU law thus always trumps domestic law. This perspective has, on the face of it, something in

---

[17] This is not, however, to suggest that the third view goes as far as to repudiate the UK legal system's essentially dualist character, since the third view holds that the enactment of the ECA was necessary in order that EU law might enter the UK legal system in the first place.

common with the evocative language employed by Lord Denning MR in *Bulmer v Bollinger*, in which he famously said that

> when we come to matters with a European element, the Treaty [of Rome] is like an incoming tide. It flows into the estuaries and up the rivers. It cannot be held back, Parliament has decreed that the Treaty is henceforward to be part of our law. It is equal in force to any statute.[18]

However, Lord Denning went on in *Macarthys* to make it clear that he did not consider the domestic constitutional order generally, or the doctrine of parliamentary sovereignty in particular, to have been overwhelmed.[19] Although describing what would go on to become EU law as not only 'an aid to ... construction' but as an 'overriding force', Lord Denning caveated his view by saying that the courts' 'bounden duty to give priority to Community law' was 'the result of' sections 2(1) and (4) of the ECA.[20] Importantly, Lord Denning took a consequence of this to be that Parliament remained in ultimate control—not only in the sense of being able to repeal the ECA, but also in the sense of being able to depart from EU law while the ECA remained in force and while the UK remained a member of the EU. For Lord Denning, then, it followed that if Parliament deliberately sought to override EU law and said so 'in express terms', it would be 'the duty of our courts to follow the statute of our Parliament'.[21] Thus, for all that Lord Denning may have conjured the imagery of inundation, he did not in fact subscribe to the view that domestic constitutional principle had been swept aside by EU law. Indeed, far from it: for Lord Denning, the effect of EU law within the domestic legal order turned upon domestic law itself. Lord Denning thus firmly aligned himself with the second of the three approaches sketched above.

His position thus stands in stark contrast to the analysis that the Divisional Court was invited—but which it declined—to adopt in *Thoburn*, and which is perhaps the paradigm example of the third approach.[22] Counsel for the defendant urged the Court to accept that while the UK remained an EU Member State, the 'pre-accession model of parliamentary sovereignty' was of 'historical, but not actual, significance'.[23] Laws LJ understood this argument to reduce to the proposition that although the ECA had given effect to EU law within the domestic legal order, once that step had been taken EU law had become 'entrenched'.[24] Parliament, on this view, had uncorked the bottle containing the EU law genie, meaning that not only substantive EU law but also its underlying architecture, including

---

[18] *HP Bulmer Ltd v J Bollinger SA* [1974] Ch 401, 418.
[19] *Macarthys Ltd v Smith* [1979] 3 All ER 325.
[20] ibid, 329.
[21] ibid.
[22] *Thoburn v Sunderland City Council* [2002] EWHC 195 (Admin), [2003] QB 151 ('*Thoburn*').
[23] ibid, [53].
[24] ibid, [56].

the primacy doctrine, became part of UK law. And crucially, having done so, Parliament's capacity to return the genie to the bottle was (on this view) decidedly limited, unless it took the step of bringing about the UK's withdrawal from the EU.[25] The central characteristic of the analysis advanced by counsel was thus (as Laws LJ put it) that EU law was embedded within the domestic system—rendering the latter, in effect, subservient to the former—'not by virtue of any principle of domestic constitutional law, but by virtue of principles of Community law already established in cases such as … *van Gend en Loos* and *Costa v ENEL*'.[26] On this view, EU law was thus capable of having effect in and over domestic law *by virtue of EU law itself*, once the ECA had operated to allow it in. This, in turn, suggests that the role of the ECA was (to develop the metaphor introduced above) limited to the uncorking of the bottle. Once out of the bottle, however, the EU law genie was capable of standing upon its own two feet—and of standing up to UK law—without reference to the domestic legislation that had originally unleashed it.

We shall see in section III that at least some vestiges of this analysis can be found in *Miller*. First, however, it is worth observing that this way of looking at things has something in common with, even if it is not the same as, the attempt made by Sir William Wade to explain the *Factortame* decision. As is well known, Wade—seeking to rationalise the influence of EU law in a way that was consonant with his seminal, if contestable, analysis of parliamentary sovereignty[27]—resorted to the notion that *Factortame* evidenced a judicial 'revolution'. The effect was to enthrone EU law (in the place of domestic primary legislation) as the highest form of UK law, thereby shattering the doctrine of parliamentary sovereignty.[28] Where Wade's analysis parts company with that which was put to the court in *Thoburn* is as to the fundamental nature of the change that is said to have occurred. In particular, whereas the court was invited in *Thoburn* to view matters in legal terms—EU law's new status being, on this view, attributable to Parliament's having legislatively opened the way for EU law to entrench itself—Wade's explanation implies a disjunction between Parliament's legislative intervention via the ECA and the judicial response. In particular, the latter, on Wade's view, is not a straightforward result of the former, but is rather evidence of a 'revolutionary', curially-led change to the rule of recognition.

Yet, this difference notwithstanding, the two approaches have something in common. Each suggests, whether through some form of legal alchemy or a political-judicial shift of allegiance, that EU membership has entailed a shift away from (the relevant conception of) parliamentary sovereignty. On the analysis

---

[25] Although, as Laws LJ pointed out, it is not even clear that counsel's analysis left scope for Parliament to take such a step if, as contended, Parliament had succeeded in entrenching EU law.

[26] *Thoburn* (n 22), [56] (Laws LJ), citing Case 26/62, *NV Algemene Transporten Expeditie Onderneming van Gend en Loos v Nederlandse administratie der belastingen* [1963] ECR 1 and Case 6/64, *Costa v ENEL* [1964] ECR 585.

[27] HWR Wade, 'The Basis of Legal Sovereignty' (1955) 13 *CLJ* 172.

[28] HWR Wade, 'Sovereignty—Revolution or Evolution?' (1996) 112 *LQR* 568.

advanced by counsel in *Thoburn*, Parliament is taken to have legislated in a way that resulted in a diminution of its own authority: indeed, as Laws LJ observed in *Thoburn*, the logical result of counsel's analysis was that EU law's overriding force could not straightforwardly be terminated by repeal of the ECA but would end only upon UK withdrawal from the EU in a manner that was lawful *according to EU law*.[29] That seems hard to reconcile with *any* conception of parliamentary sovereignty. Meanwhile, Wade acknowledged that his reading of *Factortame* implied departure—via a 'technical revolution'[30]—from the notion of parliamentary sovereignty as he conceived of it: 'It is obvious that sovereignty belongs to the Parliament of the day and that, if it could be fettered by earlier legislation, the Parliament of the day would cease to be sovereign.'[31] What unites these two views, then, is that neither seeks to explain the implications of EU membership by reference to a pre-existing conception of parliamentary sovereignty: the view that was put to the court in *Thoburn* explicitly repudiates the 'pre-accession model' of sovereignty,[32] while Wade treats *Factortame*, in effect, as having extinguished sovereignty in the sense that he took it to have existed prior to the UK's having joined the EU.

Crucially, however, neither of these views has prevailed, at least if the case law is treated as the relevant yardstick. That case law treats the implications of EU membership as something capable of being accommodated by, rather than constituting an existential threat to, the doctrine of parliamentary sovereignty. That Wade's view has not prevailed is plain from judicial insistence that Parliament has remained sovereign throughout the UK's period of membership.[33] This suggests repudiation either of Wade's premise (ie that sovereignty is incompatible with fetters of *any* type, whether substantive or formal) or of his analysis (ie that fetters of a type that are inimical to parliamentary sovereignty have accrued by virtue of EU membership).

Meanwhile, counsel's analysis in *Thoburn* was roundly rejected by Laws LJ in that case. He instead took it to be the case that EU law had effect in the UK only because the ECA had authorised, *and continued to authorise*, such effect—and, moreover, that EU law's writ ran only to the extent, and on the terms, laid down by the ECA. Laws LJ reached this conclusion not on the ground that Parliament had chosen to withhold any greater constitutional status from EU law (although it is plain from his judgment that he found no evidence that Parliament had attempted to confer any such greater status), but because Parliament was incapable of bringing about the state of affairs postulated by counsel. 'The British Parliament,' said Laws LJ, 'has not the authority to authorise any such thing. Being sovereign,

---

[29] *Thoburn* (n 22), [57].

[30] Wade (n 28), 574.

[31] ibid, 568. Of course, this view only holds if, to begin with, we share Wade's conviction that a Parliament that is subject to any fetters—even of manner and form—is not sovereign.

[32] *Thoburn* (n 22), [53].

[33] See, eg, ibid, [59]; *Miller* (n 2), [67].

it cannot abandon its sovereignty.'[34] Laws LJ's rejection of any notion that the UK constitution has been inundated by EU law is thus clear. Indeed, for Laws LJ, it could not be any other way—for, on his view, the very architecture of the domestic system rendered it impervious to any such inundation.

The question arises, however, whether Laws LJ's analysis withstands *Miller*, or whether *Miller* requires us to think again about—and perhaps even to embrace— the analysis that was repudiated in *Thoburn*. This question arises because, in *Miller*, the majority's judgment has at least some elements in common with the view that was rejected in *Thoburn* (although it will be argued that that is not the most satisfactory reading of *Miller*). If *Miller* does in fact provide some support for that analysis, what are the broader implications? In particular, does it mean that the way in which the domestic constitution has accommodated EU law teaches us about matters that are specific to the EU law context, such that no broader lessons—lessons that might remain pertinent following departure from the EU— can be derived from this episode?

III. The Majority Judgment in *Miller*

In *Miller*, the Supreme Court considered the nature of EU law vis-à-vis domestic law at a level of detail that was sorely lacking from the judgments in *Factortame*. However, while the discussion was more thoroughgoing, the reasoning and conclusions were ambiguous. For instance, the majority allow that 'in one sense' domestic law, in the form of the ECA, 'is the source of EU law' within the domestic system, because 'without that Act, EU law would have no domestic status.'[35] Yet the majority go on to say (without repudiating it) that that analysis is not 'realistic', and that they instead prefer to treat 'the institutions of the EU' as 'the relevant source of [EU] law'.[36] But not only that: the majority go as far as to declare EU law to be 'an independent and over-riding source of domestic law',[37] such that 'the EU Treaties, EU legislation and the interpretations placed on these instruments by the Court of Justice are direct sources of UK law'.[38]

The foregoing suggests that the *Miller* majority adopt an analysis that has at least something in common with that which Laws LJ rejected in *Thoburn*. Indeed, this may be one means of reconciling elements of the majority's view that, at least prima facie, seem to be in tension with one another. Most obviously, it is difficult to see how the ECA can (on the one hand) be the lynchpin legal instrument, without which EU law 'would have no domestic status', and (on the other hand)

---

[34] *Thoburn* (n 22), [59].
[35] *Miller* (n 2), [61].
[36] ibid.
[37] ibid, [65], [80].
[38] ibid, [61].

be presented (at least implicitly) as irrelevant in the sense that EU law is a 'direct' and 'independent' source of domestic law. To invoke a metaphor that is well worn—but often, in relation to Brexit-related matters, apposite—one cannot have one's cake and eat it. Surely the EU Treaties and EU legislation cannot *depend* upon the ECA for its domestic legal status and effect while simultaneously having such status and effect *independently* of the ECA? Yet the apparent illogic of this position becomes more comprehensible if the *Miller* majority are understood to be advocating a view that assumes similar lines to those advanced by counsel in *Thoburn*. Looked at in this way, the ECA is both crucial and unimportant: crucial because, without it, EU law would never have entered the domestic legal system, and unimportant because, once EU law is here, it exerts overriding effect *as a matter of EU law*. Any dependency upon the ECA was thus a temporary state of affairs: the door needed to be unlocked, but once that moment's work was done, and once EU law infiltrated the domestic legal realm, it took on an independent life of its own. On this view, the dependence/independence paradox that the *Miller* majority appear to conjure can be resolved by understanding the majority to be proposing these mutually incompatible states of affairs not as simultaneous but as sequential phenomena.

If this was what the majority were saying in *Miller* then that would be significant for two reasons. First, it would imply an understanding of the role of EU law within the domestic sphere quite different from what had, prior to *Miller*, emerged as the dominant understanding. And, second, it would suggest that the constitutional lessons taught by EU membership were highly constricted in scope, given that, on such a view, the domestic constitutional implications of membership would turn in large part upon the peculiarities of EU law itself. Any such lessons would thus be unlikely to resonate in relation to constitutional questions having no EU dimension to them, thereby substantially limiting the likely intellectual constitutional legacy of the UK's membership of the EU.

But is the *Miller* majority really endorsing the sort of view that was repudiated in *Thoburn*? The argument can certainly be made that the majority set some store by the special characteristics of and claims made by EU law. For instance, in addition to their assertion that EU law has been constituted an 'independent' and 'overriding' source of domestic law,[39] the majority say that '*[t]he primacy of EU law* means that, unlike other rules of domestic law, EU law cannot be implicitly displaced by the mere enactment of legislation which is inconsistent with it'.[40] The majority also say, 'The EU Treaties as implemented pursuant to the 1972 Act were and are unique in their legislative and constitutional implications.'[41]

---

[39] ibid, [65].

[40] ibid, [66] (emphasis added). Sir John Laws, in his contribution in ch 9 of this volume, also notes that this statement in the majority judgment is redolent of counsel's argument in *Thoburn*, although he goes on to indicate that, on balance, 'it seems unlikely that the majority in *Miller* intended in terms to hold that the efficacy of EU law in the UK is due to any autonomous, supervening status enjoyed by EU law itself'.

[41] *Miller* (n 2), [90].

Thus, 'In 1972, for the first time in the history of the United Kingdom, a dynamic, international source of law was grafted onto, and above, the well-established existing sources of domestic law: Parliament and the courts.'[42] Such dicta at least invite the question whether similarly unique consequences could be wrought by Parliament legislating with respect to the wholly municipal plane—by, for instance, attempting to privilege a set of purely domestic legal rights—or whether the uniqueness of EU law's domestic implications are, at least in part, a function of the internal contents of and claims made by the EU legal order, as distinct from the domestic effects ascribed to norms emanating from that legal order by domestic legislation.

However, while some aspects of the majority judgment appear to exhibit sympathy with the view that was repudiated in *Thoburn*, it is difficult to reconcile that view with other aspects of the majority judgment. In this regard, it is significant that the majority are very clear that EU membership has entailed no alteration to the rule of recognition. They say that while the 'constitutional effect of the 1972 Act was unprecedented', the 'unprecedented state of affairs' that it wrought 'will last only so long as Parliament wishes' and that the ECA 'can be repealed like any other statute'.[43] Thus the majority 'would not accept that the so-called fundamental rule of recognition (ie the fundamental rule by reference to which all other rules are validated) underlying UK laws has been varied by the 1972 Act or would be varied by its repeal'.[44] This part of the majority judgment is most obviously a rejection of Wade's analysis, according to which the rule of recognition *did* change.[45] But in rejecting any suggestion of a change to the rule of recognition, the majority also adopt a position that sits very uncomfortably with that which was put forward, but dismissed, in *Thoburn*. Thus, for instance, the majority reaffirm Parliament's control of the parameters within which EU law enjoys priority, noting that 'legislation which alters the domestic constitutional status of EU institutions or of EU law is not constrained by the need to be consistent with EU law', so that '[i]n the case of such legislation, there is no question of EU law having primacy, so that such legislation will have domestic effect even if it infringes EU law'.[46] And, more generally, the *Miller* majority are uncompromising in their reaffirmation of the principle of parliamentary sovereignty which, they say, is 'fundamental to the United Kingdom's constitutional arrangements' such that 'EU law can only enjoy a status in domestic law which that principle allows'. It is hard to square this with the notion that, as counsel put it in *Thoburn*, the 'pre-accession' conception of sovereignty is of only 'historical', as distinct from 'actual', 'significance'.[47]

---

[42] ibid.
[43] ibid, [60].
[44] ibid.
[45] Wade (n 28).
[46] *Miller* (n 2), [67].
[47] *Thoburn* (n 22), [53].

The upshot is that although the majority judgment in *Miller* is ambiguous in relevant respects, the better view is that it is not consistent with any analysis that postulates EU law as having limited or transformed the notion of parliamentary sovereignty: it is explicitly incompatible with any suggestion that the rule of recognition altered, and the judgment, read as a whole, it is at least implicitly incompatible with the idea that EU law has 'entrenched' itself in the way that was suggested by counsel in *Thoburn*. It follows that if we are not to account for the domestic priority enjoyed by EU law by reference to any alteration to or displacement of the doctrine of parliamentary sovereignty, we must be able to account for EU law's domestic status by reference to that doctrine's innate and enduring characteristics. And that, in turn, suggests that whatever conclusions we draw will be conclusions that are illuminated by, but which are not limited to, the particular questions raised by domestic accommodation of the EU primacy principle.

IV. Legislative Suspension of Implied Repeal?

In *HS2*, Lord Reed said (consistently with the analysis set out in sections II and III) that questions about the extent of EU law's priority over domestic law 'cannot be resolved simply by applying the doctrine developed by the Court of Justice of the supremacy of EU law, since the application of that doctrine in our law itself depends upon the 1972 Act'.[48] But while insisting upon the relevance of the ECA is undoubtedly correct, it gets us only so far. It is tolerably clear from section 2(4) of the ECA that Parliament, in 1972, intended that EU law should have priority over at least some,[49] including some future, legislation. Observing matters from a contemporary vantage point, we know that Parliament succeeded in securing such priority for EU law. But how are we to account for this? One possibility is that section 2(4) is an entrenched provision, such that it is immune from implied repeal. And if that is how we are to account for EU law's priority then that is a point of general significance, for it may suggest that Parliament is capable of immunising statutory provisions against implied repeal whenever it wishes.

Gavin Phillipson argues that such an analysis is supported by the text of the ECA and the courts' response to it. Thus he says that the 'plain words' of section 2(4) show that Parliament attempted to 'suspend the normal doctrine of implied repeal', and that *Factortame* demonstrates that it succeeded.[50] He also notes that in

---

[48] *HS2* (n 8), [79].

[49] In *HS2* (n 8), Lords Neuberger and Mance suggest that Parliament, in enacting section 2(4) of the ECA, may not have intended EU law to have effect over *all* domestic law. This point is considered in section V.

[50] G Phillipson, 'EU Law as an Agent of National Constitutional Change: *Miller v Secretary of State for Exiting the European Union*' (2017) 36 *Yearbook of European Law* 46, 91.

Miller the majority, having observed that EU law 'not only becomes a source of UK law, but actually takes precedence over all domestic sources of UK law, including statutes', went on to refer to the 'unprecedented' constitutional effect *of the ECA*.[51] He concludes that it was Parliament that gave EU law its elevated status by legislatively rendering the doctrine of implied repeal inapplicable to the ECA. Thus, says Phillipson, 'it is clear that Parliament *can* change the rule of implied repeal—and did so in the ECA'.[52]

This analysis, however, is questionable on three grounds. First, it is hard to see what evidence there is in the text of section 2(4) of the ECA of a legislative intention to exempt it from the doctrine of implied repeal. Section 2(4) provides, in infamously Delphic terms, that 'any enactment passed or to be passed ... shall be construed and have effect subject to the foregoing provisions of this section'. In this way, section 2(4) appears to assign both interpretive weight and hierarchical priority to the directly applicable EU law given domestic effect by 'foregoing provisions' of section 2. But nowhere in section 2(4) does Parliament clearly stipulate that any hierarchical priority it confers is intended to take the form of the protection of EU law—or the protection of section 2(4) itself, and thus the requirement to give some degree of priority to EU law—from implied repeal. Indeed, the words 'shall ... have effect subject to' suggest that, for as long as the section 2(4) priority rule remains in force, domestic law that is incompatible with directly effective EU law is inapplicable, period, rather than inapplicable unless a contrary intention is manifested in express terms. It follows that to suggest, as Phillipson appears to, that the matter can straightforwardly be resolved by observing what Parliament has provided, and what the courts have done in response, is at best an oversimplification. What Parliament has provided in section 2(4) is itself ambiguous, an intention to suspend implied repeal being far from plain, while to rely upon what the courts have done in decisions like *Factortame* is merely to raise the question of *why* they did that.

Second, contrary to Phillipson's contention that the *Miller* majority endorse the idea that the ECA was placed beyond implied repeal by nothing more than an expression of parliamentary intention, the majority in fact link their conclusion regarding the extent of the ECA's susceptibility to repeal to the notion of 'constitutional legislation'. Specifically, the majority, having said that 'EU law cannot be implicitly displaced by the mere enactment of legislation which is inconsistent with it',[53] go on to say not only that '[t]hat is clear' from section 2(4) of the ECA[54] but also, in the very next sentence, that the ECA 'accordingly has a constitutional character, as discussed by Laws LJ in *Thoburn*'.[55] In this way, the majority draw a clear connection between the notion that the ECA is a 'constitutional statute' in

---

[51] *Miller* (n 2), [60].
[52] Phillipson (n 50), 92 (emphasis in original).
[53] *Miller* (n 2), [66].
[54] ibid.
[55] ibid, [67].

the sense in which Laws LJ used that term in *Thoburn* and the degree of its resistance to repeal. Indeed, the majority in *Miller* refer, with apparent approval, to the very passage in *Thoburn* in which Laws LJ says that 'Parliament cannot bind its successors by stipulating against repeal, wholly or partly, of the 1972 Act', and that it 'cannot stipulate against as to the manner and form of any subsequent legislation'.[56] Moreover, Laws LJ goes on, still in the passage referred to with approval by the *Miller* majority, to say (anticipating his discussion of 'constitutional statutes' later in the judgment) that the traditional sovereignty doctrine has 'been modified ... by the common law'[57]—a view that is hard to square with the idea that the ECA's elevated constitutional status is a function of nothing more than parliamentary intent.

Indeed, it is hard to square any of this with the notion that the *Miller* majority were endorsing the notion that Parliament straightforwardly exempted the ECA from implied repeal. But in fact—and here is the third problem with Phillipson's analysis—the *Miller* majority never actually go as far as to say that the ECA is immune from implied repeal. What the *Miller* majority actually say is that 'EU law cannot be displaced *by the mere enactment of legislation which is inconsistent with it*'.[58] The majority are thus not contending that EU law—or the ECA, which gives domestic effect to EU law—is immune from implied repeal. Rather, they are saying that EU law cannot be displaced, and that the ECA cannot be repealed or overridden, *simply by enacting legislation that is incompatible with EU law*. However, this does not mean that the ECA is immune from all repeal except express repeal. In particular, it leaves open the possibility that EU law may be displaced, and the ECA repealed or overridden, by what Laws LJ in *Thoburn* termed 'specific', as distinct from 'express', provision[59]—meaning 'words so specific that the inference of an actual determination to effect the result contended for was irresistible'.[60] It is true that Laws LJ goes on to contend that treating a provision as susceptible only to specific repeal may be inconsistent with the '*ordinary* rule of implied repeal'.[61] But this simply serves to underscore the point that questions about susceptibility to repeal are unlikely to be helpfully answered by reference to a binary distinction between express and implied repeal, the better approach being to ask whether, taken in constitutional context, Parliament has done enough to make clear its intention to override or displace whatever norm appears to be in tension with a given statutory provision. The norm in question might be a common law constitutional right, some other fundamental constitutional principle, or a 'constitutional' provision in a statute.

---

[56] *Thoburn* (n 22), [59].
[57] ibid.
[58] *Miller* (n 2), [66] (emphasis added).
[59] *Thoburn* (n 22), [62].
[60] ibid, [63].
[61] ibid. For detailed and helpful discussion of implied and specific repeal, see AL Young, *Parliamentary Sovereignty and the Human Rights Act* (Oxford, Hart Publishing, 2009) ch 2.

V. Constitutional Statutes, the Common Law and Parliament

The view that Parliament can straightforwardly immunise statutory provisions against implied repeal might be thought to stand at one end of a spectrum, where we find Parliament able to exercise full control over such matters. Laws LJ's judgment in *Thoburn* sits at the opposite end of the spectrum: while asserting that the common law can exercise control in this sphere, Laws LJ is adamant that Parliament has no part to play. On this view, it is the common law's recognition of the ECA as a 'constitutional statute' that renders it invulnerable to implied repeal, as distinct from Parliament's having legislatively shielded it from such repeal. If adopted, the characterisation of the ECA as a constitutional statute supplies a perfectly serviceable basis for explaining its capacity to ascribe priority to EU law in the face of implicitly incompatible subsequent legislation. But the prior question arises of whether, by in effect writing Parliament out of the picture when it comes to issues of this nature, Laws LJ goes too far.

The answer to that question must depend, at least in part, upon the nature of the paradigm in which we consider ourselves to be working. Although Laws LJ in his judicial capacity has professed support for the notion of parliamentary sovereignty—he tells us, for instance, that Parliament, '[b]eing sovereign, ... cannot abandon its sovereignty'[62]—it is plain from his extra-curial writings that Laws LJ's constitutional paradigm differs sharply from any that accommodates a straightforwardly orthodox conception of legislative supremacy.[63] Indeed, his judgment in *Thoburn* itself suggests that Parliament's authority is a function of, and so is subject to, the common law constitution, albeit that, at its present stage of evolution, that constitution imposes only modest restraints upon Parliament, such as that which denies it the capacity impliedly to repeal constitutional statutes. Within this paradigm, then, there is nothing jarring in the suggestion that such legislation is immune from implied repeal. Nor is there any difficulty with the notion that the doctrine of implied repeal can be modified—or, in relation to some statutory provisions, suspended—by operation of the common law but not by legislative intervention: for within the relevant paradigm the implied repeal doctrine forms part of a set of common law constitutional rules whose manipulation is beyond Parliament's (unilateral) control.

If we are prepared to buy in to Laws LJ's constitutional worldview then the logic of (the rest of) his analysis is hard to fault. If Parliament's authority is conferred by legal-constitutional rules that are fundamental and beyond legislative manipulation, the *general* attribution of the content of those rules to something

---

[62] *Thoburn* (n 22) at [59].
[63] See, eg, Sir John Laws, 'Law and Democracy' [1995] *PL* 72.

other than parliamentary intention necessarily follows, as does the *specific* proposition that legislation regarded as fundamental in common law constitutional terms is immune from implied repeal for reasons that have nothing to do with parliamentary intention. However, an alternative understanding of constitutional legislation—which is reconcilable with (a more orthodox notion of) parliamentary sovereignty—is possible. It is also preferable, for Laws LJ's analysis involves the drawing of at least three bright-line distinctions: something that, paradoxically, is an uncomfortable fit with the subtle, contextualist approach that normally characterises common law constitutional adjudication. A less stark conception of constitutional legislation enables us to reconcile it with both common law constitutionalism's more contextualist tradition *and* with a conception of parliamentary sovereignty that is more recognisable than that which Laws LJ adopts (and which is arguably not really a conception of parliamentary *sovereignty* at all).

The first distinction, of course, is between 'constitutional' and 'ordinary' statutes. On Laws LJ's view, a statute is either 'constitutional' or it is 'ordinary'. However, as David Feldman has convincingly shown, attempting to draw such a distinction is fraught with difficulty given that statutes that deal mainly with 'constitutional' matters will likely also deal with 'ordinary' matters, while statutes that deal mainly with 'ordinary' matters may also deal with 'constitutional' matters.[64] But even if we descend—as Feldman rightly argues we should—from the level of the statute itself to the level of individual provisions therein, other difficulties attend attempts to establish a distinction between the 'constitutional' and 'ordinary' categories, precisely because the distinction—even if it now bites upon provisions rather than statutes—remains in a *binary* form. This is an undeniably blunt approach, bearing in mind that not all 'ordinary' provisions are equally constitutionally (in)significant, and that the same must be true of all 'constitutional' provisions. The more meaningful, and useful, inquiry surely involves asking not the binary question of *whether* something (be it a statute or a provision therein) is 'constitutional', but a series of more discriminating questions about *why* and *in what sense* something ought to be regarded as 'constitutional', and *how relatively significant* it is judged by reference to other, including other *constitutional*, norms.

The second distinction inherent in Laws LJ's approach in *Thoburn* concerns not the *allocation* of provisions to one or other of the two categories, but the *consequences* of that allocation: namely, that the provision either is or is not susceptible to implied repeal. This, too, is problematic—for reasons that follow from the point made in the previous paragraph. If (as we surely must) we acknowledge that statutory provisions' constitutional significance cannot adequately be captured by placing such provisions in one of two boxes—respectively labelled 'constitutional' (significant) and 'ordinary' (not significant)—then neither can it be satisfactory to draw a wholly binary distinction between provisions whose constitutional status affords them a fixed degree of protection and those whose status affords no such

---

[64] D Feldman, 'The nature and significance of "constitutional" legislation' (2013) 129 *LQR* 343.

protection at all. Once it is conceded that constitutionality is a question of degree, so must it be acknowledged that the answer to that question of degree ought to sound in consequences that are correspondingly nuanced.

Third, Laws LJ's analysis erects a binary distinction between the respective roles of Parliament and the common law. On his view, whether legislation is constitutional—and hence whether legislation is subject to or immune from implied repeal—is a matter purely for the common law, and not at all for Parliament. However, that view is called into question by the Supreme Court's judgment in the *HS2* case, in which the Court considered whether section 2(4) of the ECA would require EU law to be given priority over Article 9 of the Bill of Rights. The (obiter) reasoning found in *HS2* on this point is far from unsympathetic to the notion of constitutional statutes: indeed, Lords Neuberger and Mance, with whom the other five Justices agreed, said that Laws LJ's analysis of constitutional statutes in *Thoburn* offered '[i]mportant insights' and amounted to a 'penetrating discussion'.[65] Moreover, they went on say that whereas *Thoburn* had involved a possible conflict between an 'ordinary' and a 'constitutional' statute, *HS2* concerned the relationship between what they acknowledged to be 'two constitutional instruments'.[66]

Yet in considering the relationship between those two 'constitutional instruments', Lords Neuberger and Mance did not sideline parliamentary intention. Indeed, it constituted an important aspect of their analysis—and, more generally, of their approach to the navigation of circumstances in which more than one constitutional instrument is in play. Thus they considered it to be at least—and, they implied, probably more than merely—arguable that 'there may be fundamental principles, whether contained in other constitutional instruments or recognised at common law, of which *Parliament* when it enacted the European Communities Act 1972 *did not either contemplate or authorise* the abrogation'.[67]

This suggests two things. The first is that, in line with the argument advanced above, constitutional instruments (or provisions thereof) do not form a single category and that the degree of their fundamentality, and hence the extent of their resistance to being displaced or overridden by other legislation, is variable. The second point is that in engaging with that question of degree, attention ought, where relevant, to be paid to legislative intention. Thus, on the approach adopted in *HS2*, the degree of the ECA's constitutional fundamentality—and hence its relationship with Article 9 of the Bill of Rights—fell to be determined, at least in part, by reference to whether Parliament had intended to prioritise the ECA, and so EU law, in respect of constitutional matters as fundamental as those enshrined in Article 9. This suggests that Parliament's intention as to the degree of fundamentality with which a statutory provision ought to be invested at least informs the

---

[65] *HS2* (n 8), [208].
[66] ibid.
[67] ibid, [207] (emphasis added).

court's determination of the degree of fundamentality that it is to be accorded. Indeed, there is no reason why legislative intention should not play such a role, and good reason why it should. While the UK constitution cannot properly be viewed exclusively through the prism of parliamentary sovereignty, that doctrine, together with the democratic imperative that animates it, inevitably forms part of any orthodox understanding of the constitutional order. To suggest that courts should be blind to legislative will when weighing the constitutional importance of a given provision would thus be to advocate adjudicative myopia.

It is important to recognise, however, that on this view the judicial task is not the same as that which arises if Parliament is capable straightforwardly of immunising legislation against implied repeal. The latter view implies a brittle distinction between legislation whose repeal is and is not subject to special conditions (such as the deployment of express words), while presupposing that whether a given provision finds itself in one or other of those categories is a question of nothing more than mechanical statutory interpretation. In contrast, it is argued, the better view is that resistance to repeal is a matter of degree rather than of binary categorisation, while the statutory text falls to be construed within the relevant, including the relevant constitutional, context. Looked at in this way, the debate invited by the manner and form theory—which revolves around the question whether or not legislation can be entrenched by Parliament—becomes an arid one. Meanwhile, cases that appear to reject or exhibit judicial sympathy for the possibility of legislative entrenchment need to be treated with care, not only because 'entrenchment', on this view, becomes a matter of degree, but also because whether a given statutory provision has the effect of generating resistance to repeal turns on its interpretation *in context*. In this way, the very different judicial views that can be discerned in decisions like *Ellen Street Estates*[68] and *Factortame*[69] might be considered reconcilable, given the very different circumstances of the two cases, rather than as evidence of bald disagreement.

It might be asked whether Lords Neuberger and Mance in fact go further in *HS2* by endorsing the view that questions of constitutional fundamentality, and hence resistance to legislative displacement, are *purely* a matter to be resolved by reference to parliamentary intention. But the better view is that they are not, and that to read *HS2* in this way would be to jump to an unwarranted conclusion. To substantiate this argument, it is necessary to consider the relationship—as well as the distinction—between (on the one hand) common law constitutional rights and values and (on the other hand) constitutional statutes or statutory provisions. It is plain that Article 9 of the Bill of Rights in effect *records* a constitutional principle—pertaining to the relationship between the courts and Parliament, and thus deriving from the separation of powers doctrine—that *exists* independently of the statutory provision itself. In this way, Article 9 reflects or confirms a value

---

[68] *Ellen Street Estates v Minister of Health* [1934] 1 KB 590.
[69] *Factortame (No 2)* (n 1).

whose normative roots lie deeper, in the common law constitution itself. Lords Neuberger and Mance acknowledge this in *HS2* when they observe that '[t]he common law itself … recognises certain principles as fundamental to the rule of law' (and, they might well have added, the separation of powers),[70] and that the issue under consideration in the case concerned an 'apparent conflict' between EU law (and so the ECA) and 'other principles hitherto … regarded as fundamental and *enshrined in*'—as distinct from *created by*—'the Bill of Rights'.[71] This is of a piece with the view advanced (albeit in a different context) by Lord Cooke in *Daly*, according to which 'some rights are inherent and fundamental to democratic civilised society', such that 'constitutions, bills of rights and the like respond by recognising rather than creating them'.[72] On this view, the fact that a constitutional right—or some other constitutional value or principle—is accorded statutory expression does not rob it of its 'inherent' quality. Seen thus, the degree of constitutional fundamentality to be assigned to Article 9 of the Bill of Rights is not a function of the fact that Article 9 is a provision found in a constitutional statute, or of the degree of constitutional reverence in which the Bill of Rights itself is held. Rather, its constitutional status derives, at least in large part, from the fact that it reflects a norm that sounds deeply within the common law constitution.

HS2 thus suggests that in determining the degree of constitutional fundamentality enjoyed by a given statutory provision, consideration may need to be given *both* to manifestations of parliamentary intention *and* to the extent to which the provision in question resonates with constitutional norms that exist, and are considered fundamental, independently of legislative will. However, this mode of analysis is not—as might appear at first glance—a crude amalgam of Laws LJ's constitutional statutes model (according to which the common law constitution's primacy denies any role to legislative intention in this area) and the manner and form view (which assigns Parliament unilateral authority to shield legislation from implied repeal). Rather, the approach that is inherent in *HS2*, and which reflects well-established judicial practice in contexts *not* involving constitutional statutes, amounts to a constitutional-interpretive methodology that, while not denying the sovereignty of Parliament, postulates the curial function in terms of giving effect to legislation in a way that is sensitive to dimensions of the constitutional order other than that which is captured by the notion of legislative sovereignty. Such an approach is clearly on display in a decision like *Evans*,[73] in which the Supreme Court sought to engage in a process of constitutional triangulation that accommodated the fundamental principles of sovereignty, the rule of law and the separation of powers that were in play, and in tension, in that case.[74]

---

[70] *HS2* (n 8), [207].

[71] ibid, [206] (emphasis added).

[72] *R (Daly)* v *Secretary of State for the Home Department* [2001] UKHL 26, [2001] 2 AC 532, [30].

[73] *R (Evans)* v *Attorney-General* [2015] UKSC 21, [2015] AC 1787.

[74] The decision—and, in particular, the judgment of Lord Neuberger, which subjected the relevant legislative provision to a bold form of interpretation—generated considerable controversy. For sharply

Thus it is a mistake to see constitutional statutes (or provisions) as somehow divorced from the broader approach of the common law in this area, including in contexts in which legislation is found—as in cases like *Evans*—to be in tension with unlegislated constitutional values or rights. In particular, sight must not be lost of the basic point that in a constitutional order that continues to acknowledge, but is not exhaustively defined by, a notion of legislative supremacy, the courts' ultimate responsibility is to give effect to legislation in a way that is appropriately sensitive to whatever constitutional principles are relevant in the circumstances of the case. The sovereignty of Parliament will, by definition, be *one* of those principles whenever legislative will has been manifested, but it will often not be the only principle that is in play. What this all reduces to is the importance of understanding the notion of constitutional statutes or provisions within the wider framework of the common law's treatment of fundamental rights, values and principles. That framework is resistant to the bright-line distinctions to which Laws LJ resorted in *Thoburn*, not least because not all common law constitutional rights are regarded as equally important, meaning that when such rights are in issue courts inevitably have to engage with questions of weight rather than undertaking an exercise in baldly determining whether the right is or is not 'constitutional'.[75] Once we recognise that there is no reason why a similar analytical framework cannot be applied to statute law—such that it becomes necessary to determine its constitutional 'weight', and thus the degree of its resistance to being displaced by other norms, whether found in statute or at common law—the notion of constitutional legislation becomes a more subtle and serviceable one.[76]

VI. *Factortame* and *HS2* Compared

In order to flesh out this argument, and to put it in more concrete terms, it is helpful to consider how it applies in the circumstances of two different cases—*Factortame* and *HS2*—in which questions concerning the domestic constitutional status of EU law were at stake. As pointed out in section V, constitutional statutory provisions will sometimes codify or reflect pre-existing fundamental constitutional principles, in which case the fact and degree of the provision's constitutionality fall to be understood and determined against that background. The same

contrasting perspectives, see TRS Allan, 'Law, democracy, and constitutionalism: reflections on *Evans v Attorney General*' (2016) 75 *CLJ* 38 and C Forsyth and R Ekins, 'Judging the Public Interest: The rule of law vs the rule of courts' (London, Judicial Power Project, 2015). I have addressed *Evans* in detail elsewhere: M Elliott, 'A tangled constitutional web: The black-spider memos and the British constitution's relational architecture' [2015] *PL* 539.

[75] Some, the right of access to court being perhaps the paradigm example, are accorded especial weight, and are commensurately particularly resistant to legislative displacement.
[76] Further discussion of constitutional statutes can be found in Sir John Laws' contribution in ch 9 of this volume.

cannot be said of the ECA as a whole, or of individual provisions contained in it.
No pre-existing, or inherent, domestic constitutional principle ascribes value to
UK membership of the EU, or to the notion that EU law should enjoy any degree
of priority over national law. Nor does the specific right—the right of freedom of
establishment—that was at stake in *Factortame* have any direct domestic constitutional analogue. It follows that whatever constitutional status the ECA (and so EU
law) has, it does not obviously derive from the fact that the ECA merely codifies
or reflects some inherent fundamental constitutional arrangement. At the same
time, however, the ECA does of course result in the acquisition by individuals of
legal rights—including the right at stake in *Factortame*—and general common law
constitutional principle, as expressed through the principle of legality, holds that
individual rights should not readily be taken to be displaced or removed by statute. Thus the ECA, for all that it does not enshrine institutional arrangements or
particular rights that invariably resonate with the common law constitution, does
at least resonate at a general level, in that it engages the common law constitution's
general commitment to the protection of individual rights from casual legislative
incursion.

It is evident, however, that the common law does not guard all individual rights
with equal jealousy—consider, for instance, the particular vigilance exhibited by
the common law in respect of the right of access to court[77]—and it is difficult to
account for *Factortame* by reference to nothing more than judicial acknowledgement of the common law's general aversion to the casual displacement of individual rights. It is plain, therefore, that the particular commitment exhibited in
the ECA by Parliament to EU law and the rights deriving from it must form part
of any explanation as to why *Factortame* was decided as it was. By enacting the
ECA, Parliament signalled its desire to effect a major constitutional innovation
by according domestic effect and (at least some) priority to EU law. There is no
reason why the courts should not take account of that intention when determining
the extent to which the ECA, and hence EU law, is resistant to being overridden,
repealed or otherwise displaced by other legislation. Thus, when the House of
Lords decided *Factortame*, it is entirely unsurprising that it concluded that particular legislative provisions of the Merchant Shipping Act 1988 that were merely
implicitly incompatible with EU law should not have been taken to override
section 2(4) of the ECA, with the result that the rule set out in section 2(4) continued to operate and to ascribe priority to the relevant Treaty provisions.

There is no need, however, to chalk this up as a 'win' for EU law and hence a
'loss' for parliamentary sovereignty. Absent a sufficiently clear manifestation of

---

[77] The weight attached to this right at common law is evident from cases such as *Anisminic Ltd
v Foreign Compensation Commission* [1969] 2 AC 147, *Evans* (n 73) and *R (UNISON) v Lord Chancellor*
[2017] UKSC 51, [2017] 3 WLR 409. However, judicial views are not uniform as to the right's degree
of resistance to legislative curtailment, as can be seen from the contrasting judgments of Leggatt J and
Sales LJ in (respectively) the Divisional Court and the Court of Appeal in *R (Privacy International)
v Investigatory Powers Tribunal* [2017] EWHC 114 (Admin), [2017] 3 All ER 1127 (Divisional Court);
[2017] EWCA Civ 1868 (Court of Appeal).

legislative intention, the House of Lords was at liberty to conclude that Parliament in 1988 had not intended to disturb section 2(4) of the ECA. One way of understanding this is to view it in terms of the principle that courts will, where possible, interpret different statutory provisions in a way that renders them consistent with one another.[78] As Alison Young puts it, 'When analysing conflicts between constitutional and ordinary statutes, the presumption that Parliament would not have intended to impliedly repeal earlier provisions of legislation is even stronger than that which applies to conflicts between two ordinary statutes.'[79] Viewed thus, the ECA's constitutional fundamentality—a conclusion that is rightly informed in substantial part by what was taken to be Parliament's intention in enacting the ECA—entitles courts to assume that Parliament would not casually seek to override or repeal it, and, therefore, that no intention to effect such override or repeal need be taken to exist absent very clear provision. And, of course, in *Factortame* the House of Lords was presented with no such clear provision in the Merchant Shipping Act.

The situation that the Supreme Court contemplated in *HS2* was significantly different. There, as we have already seen, the Court considered the relationship between the ECA, which it rightly considered to be a 'constitutional instrument', and (Article 9 of) the Bill of Rights, which it also, again rightly, considered to be such an instrument. However, while both instruments can properly be regarded as constitutional, the *reasons* for so characterising them diverge—and, crucially, such reasons are pertinent to their respective constitutional weights, and hence to the degree of their resistance to repeal. As noted in section V, parliamentary intention must itself be acknowledged as an important factor in relation to the ECA, given that that legislation does not enshrine constitutional values or arrangements that have any deep resonance at common law. Article 9 of the Bill of Rights, in contrast, does, meaning that its normative purchase at common law is central to the fact and degree of its constitutionality. That is not to deny that it is insignificant if such a constitutional value *also* receives legislative recognition—after all, constitutional fundamentality can only be magnified when a given arrangement, value, right or principle is both normatively resonant and democratically endorsed—but it is clearly the case that the fundamentality of the value set out in Article 9 of the Bill of Rights derives, at least in part, from something other than legislative intention. In such circumstances, the situation with which the court is faced bears some resemblance to that which arises when it has to construe (for instance) an ouster clause. The central question must, as always, be whether Parliament has evinced an intention to override the relevant constitutional value; however, the depth of the constitutional value in question may be highly influential when it comes to determining whether the relevant intention is taken to be discernible.

The difference in *HS2*, of course, is that the statute containing the potentially countervailing intention was *itself* regarded as a constitutional instrument.

---

[78] Young (n 61), ch 2; F Ahmed and A Perry, 'The quasi-entrenchment of constitutional statutes' (2014) 73 *CLJ* 514.

[79] Young (n 61), 42.

That does not fundamentally change the analytical nature of the task at hand, which remains focused upon determining whether the legislation in question (here, the ECA) ought to be read as evidence of a parliamentary intention to override the other constitutional provision/value with which it is arguably in tension. However, how that task is discharged may well be influenced by the extent of our commitment to the various overarching constitutional values that are in play. If, for instance, we consider the sovereignty of Parliament—and the commitment to (a particular form of) democracy that it signifies—to be the dominant principle of the constitution, we might expect a court to assign especial weight to the priority rule set out in section 2(4) of the ECA, such that it would discern within that provision a legislative commitment to override apparently inconsistent legislative provisions and constitutional values in most, if not all, circumstances. On this view, we would rarely, if ever, conclude that the ECA should yield to a common law constitutional value, because we would attach preponderant importance to seeing that Parliament's will, as manifested in section 2(4) of the ECA, is given maximum effect. As a result, we might conclude that a statutory provision enshrining a fundamental constitutional value should yield to section 2(4) of the ECA if, in the provision enshrining the relevant value, there is no clear evidence of Parliament's intention to invest the value with particular force. Within this paradigm, then, attentiveness to legislative intention is key, constitutional principles and values other than parliamentary sovereignty playing very much second fiddle.

In contrast, if we view the constitutional system from a different perspective—using parliamentary sovereignty not as a lens through which everything else falls to be refracted, but in terms of a rich normative order of which sovereignty is but one component part—the picture changes markedly. We might, for instance, be much less willing to read a provision like section 2(4) as enabling EU law to ride roughshod over fundamental common law constitutional values, and more inclined to treat legislation enshrining such values as enjoying a degree of fundamentality that might outstrip that which the ECA itself possesses. Within this paradigm, we would be relatively less concerned—but not unconcerned—about parliamentary intention, and relatively more concerned with the extent to which competing statutory and other norms resonate with values that are inherent in the common law constitution. These two views do not respectively accept and reject the sovereignty of Parliament. But the two views postulate that constitutional principle differently, in essence disagreeing not about its existence but about its place and meaning within the constitutional order.

VII. Lessons Learned

What all of this throws into sharp focus is the relationship between what we might think of as the *legislated* and the *innate* dimensions of the constitution. A familiar, and relatively straightforward, scenario arises when statutory provisions appear to conflict with fundamental common law rights. In such circumstances, the interpretive machinery available to the courts is well known, even if its limits are contentious. But for two reasons, the issues raised by the primacy of EU law are more complicated. First, the prospect arises of an element of the *legislated constitution* (in the form of the ECA) being in tension with *other legislation* (as in *Factortame*). Second, there is the possibility of a provision of the *legislated constitution* (as distinct from a legislative provision that does not have any special constitutional value) being in tension with another provision of the *legislated constitution*, which may or may not also relate to an *innate component of the constitutional order* (as in *HS2*). And underlying both of these issues is the further complicating factor that the distinction between the innate and legislated constitutions is a necessarily incomplete one, given that the legislated constitution derives its normative legitimacy from the innate constitution's commitment to the sovereignty of Parliament and so to the sanctity of the legislation enacted by Parliament. Questions about how the primacy of EU law has been accommodated thus throw into sharp relief the very nature of the UK constitutional order, given the intersecting issues that arise about the place within it of Parliament, the legislation it enacts and the sovereignty with which it is cloaked.

But these complexities notwithstanding, the courts' task remains one that can be straightforwardly stated, even if it cannot be similarly discharged. That task is to interpret and give effect to legislation in a way that is duly sensitive to whatever constitutional norms are in play. On this approach, faced with provisions in the Merchant Shipping Act 1988 that were incompatible with directly effective EU law, the House of Lords was right to conclude that the priority rule contained in section 2(4) of the ECA had not been displaced. It was right to do so not because, in any crude sense, the ECA was a constitutional statute and the Merchant Shipping Act was not, but because the degree of constitutional fundamentality with which the ECA was invested—including as a result of the parliamentary intention manifested in it—entitled the court to conclude that the priority assigned to EU law by the ECA was undisturbed by subsequent legislation which made no attempt explicitly, specifically or otherwise clearly to displace the priority rule. Similarly, Lords Neuberger and Mance in *HS2* were right to recognise that the ECA, notwithstanding their preparedness to characterise it as a 'constitutional instrument', need not be taken to invest EU law with priority over *all* merely impliedly incompatible domestic law. Just as the Merchant Shipping Act had to be interpreted and given effect in the light of the constitutional context of which the ECA formed an axiomatic part, so the ECA itself must be interpreted and given effect by reference to the network of (other) constitutional legislation and principle within which it is situated. The upshot is that by enacting section 2(4) of the ECA, Parliament created a potent constitutional norm that came to form part of the constitutional framework that informs the process of statutory interpretation and adjudication. But, at the same time, the constitutional norm set out in section 2(4) *itself* falls to be construed and given effect by reference to that self-same constitutional framework. In this way it is possible to understand why EU law has been assigned general priority over merely incompatible domestic legislation, while fundamental constitutional norms might simultaneously operate so as to qualify the degree of priority that section 2(4), properly construed, is to be taken to accord. The legislated and the innate constitutions thus form two parts of a single whole, the full constitutional picture becoming visible only when viewed in a suitably binocular way.

What, then, has EU membership taught us about the domestic constitution? And, in particular, has it taught us lessons that will remain pertinent following the UK's departure from the bloc? The answer to the latter question is undoubtedly 'yes': and the lessons that can be learned are not merely of enduring relevance but are ones that afford a deep insight into the nature of the UK constitutional order. One of the many paradoxes to which that constitutional order gives rise is that for all that it is famous for its flexibility, it is often understood in terms that imply a surprising degree of brittleness and rigidity. Consider, for instance, Wade's insistence that Parliament cannot privilege legislation by, for example, safeguarding it against implied repeal[80]—or the comparably categorical certainty with which proponents of the 'new view' insist that it can.[81] Or take, as another example, the way in which the debate concerning the relationship between parliamentary sovereignty and common law constitutionalism sometimes assumes an entrenched character, the implication being that each view is a threat to the other, and that a choice thus inevitably has to be made.

For reasons considered in this chapter, the constitutional questions that have arisen as a result of the UK's membership of the EU have placed matters such as these in the sharpest of relief. That has not invariably engendered clear answers. Indeed, as observed towards the beginning of the chapter, there is a good dose in this context of the atheoretical pragmatism that characterises so much of the British approach to matters constitutional. That much was readily apparent from what was—and was not—said in the *Factortame* cases 30 or so years ago, in which, it has been said, the House of Lords 'turn[ed] a blind eye to constitutional theory altogether'.[82] And while the Supreme Court majority in *Miller* engaged with questions about the nature and status of EU law more fully than the Law Lords did in *Factortame*, it can hardly be said that they provided a crystal clear account of how we ended up where we did, their analysis being, as noted in section III, shot through with ambiguity in important respects. The very fact that clarity, or theoretical neatness, has proved so elusive throughout the UK's membership of the EU is in itself telling. In particular, it highlights the pragmatic preference for 'what works' that was noted earlier, and which is so characteristic of the British approach to fundamental constitutional questions. Indeed, one senses in many

---

[80] Wade (n 27).

[81] See, eg, Sir Ivor Jennings, *The Law and the Constitution*, 5th edn (London, University of London Press, 1959); RFV Heuston, *Essays in Constitutional Law*, 2nd edn (London, Stevens and Sons, 1964).

[82] Wade (n 27), 575.

of the judgments in this area a heady whiff of *ex post* reasoning, the politically necessary outcome—that EU law is judged capable of taking priority over domestic law—being plain, with the legal analysis that delivers the requisite result sometimes coming as an afterthought.

Against that background, whatever lessons can properly be learned from this episode in British constitutional history must be taken with a pinch of salt, for any attempt to systematise, to extract general principles and to discern judicial reasoning inevitably involves a degree of inference, if not speculation. But be that as it may, it is tolerably clear that those lessons which *can* be inferred speak not (only) to the particular questions raised by the domestic status of EU law, but (also) to the nature of the UK constitution in much more general, and profound, terms. For whatever might remain uncertain, it is clear that EU law, and the primacy thereof, has been accommodated by the UK constitution on terms set by that constitution. And that, in turn, demonstrates the domestic constitutional order's capacity to acknowledge—to a previously unrecognised extent—a hierarchical ordering of norms.

In one sense, the hierarchically privileged norms are those that form directly effective EU law. But at root it is actually a provision of domestic law, in the form of section 2(4) of the ECA, that enjoys an elevated status—a status that is then borrowed by the EU norms upon which it bites. There are various ways in which that elevated status might be rationalised, including the idea that Parliament straightforwardly immunised section 2(4) against implied repeal, and the notion of constitutional statutes articulated in *Thoburn*. But both of those approaches are unwarrantedly rigid. Understanding the elevated status of section 2(4) in terms of nothing more than mechanical curial implementation of parliamentary intention is unjustified by the language of the provision and is in tension with the majority's analysis in *Miller*, which links the ECA's status to its 'constitutional character'. Meanwhile, the analysis in *Thoburn* goes too far in the other direction, treating the ECA's status as a matter that is purely for the common law constitution, such that legislative intention has no part to play. The flaw inherent within each of these views is that their respective focuses upon legislative intention and the common law results in an unduly blinkered analysis that takes insufficient account of the relationship between the legislated and the innate aspects of the constitution. Once a suitably rounded approach is adopted, the picture comes into clearer focus, the question whether EU law yields to other norms turning upon an analysis of the competing norms' constitutional weight relative to that with which the section 2(4) priority rule is itself invested. That analysis, where relevant, will entail recourse to both parliamentary intention and such unlegislated constitutional values as may be in play. None of this is antithetical to the notion of parliamentary sovereignty. The question must always be whether it is or is not consistent with legislative intention for EU law to be given effect in the circumstances of the given case. But in the course of answering that question, the court must inevitably seek to ascertain Parliament's intention by recourse not only to the statutory text, but also to the wider constitutional context.

It turns out, then, that in seeking to understand how the UK constitutional system accommodated the primacy of EU law, and the degree to which such primacy was accommodated, no single silver bullet is available. The answer, instead, lies in the subtle, and sometimes opaque, workings of the unwritten constitution: a constitution whose legislated and innate components sit in a complex relationship with one another, and whose essential nature cannot properly be appreciated unless those components are understood to comprise a single, if not always a fully cohesive, whole. That it has taken the UK legal system's interaction with the European legal order to reveal some of these truths about the domestic constitution itself is perhaps paradoxical, although it is of a piece with the British way, according to which hard constitutional questions, far from being anticipated, tend to be addressed only when necessity so demands. But now that the relevant questions have been confronted, however elliptically, the answers will remain pertinent long after the UK's membership of the EU comes to an end.

11

Miller, Constitutional Realism and the Politics of Brexit

RICHARD EKINS AND GRAHAM GEE*

I. Introduction

The *Miller* litigation was a product of the politics of Brexit. Its central legal question was fairly discrete and technical: whether the Government could use the prerogative to give notice for the purposes of Article 50 of the Treaty on European Union of the United Kingdom's (UK's) intention to withdraw from the European Union (EU), or whether statutory authorisation was required.[1] However, the political context in which this legal question arose was fraught, with sore feelings and ragged nerves shaping public debate in the months after the referendum. It is not possible to make sense of *Miller*—the genesis and framing of its legal question, the hopes that many invested in the action, the frenzied atmosphere leading up to the oral hearing in the Supreme Court, and the reasoning that led a majority of the Justices to decide against the Government—without a heavy dose of constitutional realism. This requires, above all else, seeing *Miller* for what it was: an attempt by members of the political and legal elite to use the courts to delay political action implementing the result of the referendum in the hope that, somehow, it might ultimately be possible to thwart such action.

In this chapter, we strive to pierce some of the myths and misunderstandings that have built up around *Miller*. In section II we reflect on the difficulty so many in the political and legal elite had in coming to terms with the result of the referendum.[2] This difficulty manifested itself in three powerful dynamics that

---

* We are grateful to Nick Barber, Mikołaj Barczentewicz, Timothy Endicott, John Finnis and the editors for comments on an earlier draft; the usual disclaimer applies.
    [1] *R (on the application of Miller) v Secretary of State for Exiting the European Union* [2017] UKSC 5, [2017] 2 WLR 583.
    [2] We use the term 'political elite' to refer to politicians, civil servants and—following Dennis Kavanagh—'political entrepreneurs' such as political advisers, members of think-tanks, researchers and academics for whom high-profile political activity at or near the heart of political life is part-time or a by-product of other roles. See D Kavanagh, 'Changes in the Political Class and its Culture' (1992) 45 *Parliamentary Affairs* 18, 27. 'Legal elite' denotes senior judges, leading practitioners, legal

have moulded much of the political and legal debate over the last year: namely, elite-led efforts to delegitimise the referendum; an elite-concocted narrative of 'constitutional crisis'; and sustained and scattershot attempts to use litigation to delay and disrupt the process of withdrawing from the EU. *Miller* should be understood in light of these overlapping dynamics. In section III, we consider the framing of and motivations for the *Miller* litigation, noting that it was argued in a way that was politically astute and powerful. The Supreme Court ought nonetheless to have upheld settled law and rejected the claim. Section IV examines the Court's judgment, arguing that the majority conflated constitutional practice and constitutional law, making unprincipled appeals to what they deemed *realistic* and *unrealistic*. In section V, we consider why the Court may have decided as it did, pointing to the dubious account of the separation of powers at work in the majority's reasoning. We close in section VI by reflecting on *Miller's* legacy, arguing that unless the reality of the litigation and judgment are squarely confronted, we may expect to see more ill-judged attempts to leverage judicial intervention into the political process for partisan advantage.

II. The Referendum and the Elite Cry of Rage

The result of the referendum was a shock (despite neither the Leave nor the Remain Campaigns having a decisive lead in the polls and notwithstanding the long-standing and widespread popular dissatisfaction with the UK's membership of the EU). It was especially shocking to the legal and political elite, most of whom had strongly favoured remaining in the EU, with the weeks and months after the referendum notable for the difficulty many seemed to have in accepting the voters' decision.

The public for the most part greeted the result with equanimity, with most voters who had supported continued membership appearing to view the referendum as a legitimate exercise in self-government. In this, the public exhibited a sound and reassuring democratic impulse. The contrast is notable. An elite 'cry of rage'[3] reverberated in the period after the referendum, with many striving to frustrate the process of leaving the EU (and, in some cases, to delay that process in order to increase the likelihood of being able to frustrate it). No doubt the motives varied between the politicians, lawyers and others who considered themselves as under

---

journalists and legal academics, all of whom in different ways are engaged in high-profile legal arguments that help to shape the dominant legal culture. There are overlaps between the two categories, and the membership of each is not fixed. There were political and legal elites on both sides of the referendum, but it is widely accepted that the strong preponderance of political and legal elite opinion favoured remaining in the EU. This chapter's focus is on the many members of the political elite and (especially) legal elite who sought to use the law to delay or block political action implementing the referendum.

[3] R Ekins, 'Restoring Parliamentary Democracy' (2018) 39 *Cardozo Law Review* 101.

a (dubious) 'democratic duty' to oppose Brexit.[4] Some took great care to voice their concerns about the referendum in a measured and respectful fashion, but alas many did not. Many despaired (in public and with far less restraint in private) that the conduct and result of the referendum reflected the public's ignorance, gullibility and—above all—prejudice.[5] In this, the referendum exposed not only the deep divide that ran across class, educational and generational lines,[6] but also the staggering (and troubling) disregard that many elites felt about the voters' ability to reach an informed and public-spirited assessment of the polity's governing arrangements. Many elites steadfastly refused to view the referendum as a wholly intelligible (if contestable) evaluation by the public that, on balance, the UK's long-term interests—economic, social, cultural and political—would be best served by ceasing to be part of the EU.

This elite cry of rage let loose three related and mutually reinforcing dynamics. The first was the attempt by many politicians and lawyers to delegitimise the referendum. Their objections were wide-ranging, embracing referendums in general and this referendum in particular. Referendums should have no place, it was said, in a system of representative democracy. In respect of this specific referendum, it was argued that a decision of the magnitude of leaving the EU should have required a supermajority and/or majorities in each of the four nations of the UK. The franchise for this particular referendum was also characterised as unfair, on account of the exclusion of EU nationals in the UK who would be among those most affected by any decision to leave, and because votes had not been extended to 16- and 17-year-olds.[7] A common refrain was that the referendum was advisory not merely as a matter of law, but also as a matter of constitutional practice, such that Parliament remained as free as ever—politically as well as legally—to depart from the 'advice' of the voters.[8] Lastly, motivated by a barely concealed disapproval of the result of the referendum, some argued that the decision to leave the EU was of such significance that a second referendum was required, in which voters could select between the terms of any deal that the Government negotiated on the shape

---

[4] See, eg, A Wheale, 'The Democratic Duty to Oppose Brexit' (2017) 88 *Political Quarterly* 170.

[5] Vernon Bogdanor offers an alternative view. Reflecting on the reaction of many elites to the referendum, Bogdanor comments that '[in Britain … the danger of bigotry arises not from the exercise of popular sovereignty or populism but from the intolerance of elites—many of them university-educated': V Bogdanor, 'On Popular Sovereignty' in D Galligan (ed), *Constitution in Crisis: The New Putney Debates* (London, IB Tauris & Co, 2017) 39, 43.

[6] MJ Goodwin and O Heath, 'The 2016 Referendum, Brexit and the Left Behind: An Aggregate-Level Analysis of the Result' (2016) 87 *Political Quarterly* 323. See also HD Clarke, M Goodwin and P Whiteley, 'Why Britain Voted For Brexit: An Individual-Level Analysis of the 2016 Referendum Vote' (2017) 70 *Parliamentary Affairs* 439.

[7] See, eg, Y Nehushtan, 'Why the EU Referendum's Result is Not Morally-Politically Binding', *UKCLA Blog* (5 July 2016), available at https://ukconstitutionallaw.org/.

[8] See, eg, P Eleftheriadis, 'A New Referendum is a Constitutional Requirement', *Oxford Law Business Blog* (4 July 2016), available at https://www.law.ox.ac.uk/business-law-blog/; and P Eleftheriadis, 'Constitutional Illegitimacy Over Brexit' (2017) 88 *Political Quarterly* 182.

of the UK's post-Brexit relationship with the EU, on the one hand, and remaining in the EU after all, on the other.[9]

None of these objections was persuasive. A convincing case can be made in representative democracies for occasional use of 'constitutional referendums'[10] as a tool for resolving vital questions about the long-term identity of the state, such as the UK's membership of the EU. This case has particular force whenever elite consensus works to prevent certain questions that agitate the public at large from piercing the mainstream political agenda.[11] Popular and elite assessments of the EU had diverged since the 1975 referendum. Over the same period the nature and scope of the European project had changed dramatically, and integration in particular had accelerated over the previous 25 years. Sustained discontent with European integration had been a feature of national politics for much of the last 40 years, yet 1983 was the last time that withdrawal had been advocated by a major party that enjoyed significant representation at Westminster.[12] Seen in this light, the referendum was not just an appropriate way to test whether voters continued to consent to EU membership, but perhaps the only way of doing so. Arguments that the referendum was merely advisory as a political—and not just a legal—matter were at best obtuse or at worst specious. It was true that the European Union Referendum Act 2015 did not provide for how any decision to leave the EU was to be implemented, but no one who followed the campaign or who was familiar with the relevant political context, including the background to the 2015 Act itself, could have had any doubts that the referendum was intended to settle the question of whether or not to leave.[13] Imposing a supermajority requirement for a decision to leave the EU or a requirement for a majority in each of the four nations would have broken new ground for a referendum in the UK, and would have been read rightly as an attempt to squeeze out the prospect of any change to the status quo. Any elevated threshold would also have been inconsistent with the principle of the equality of each voter. Similarly unconvincing were

---

[9] For an example of an overwrought piece that attempts to delegitimise the referendum on multiple grounds before calling for a second referendum that could arrive at 'the appropriate answer', see L Blom-Cooper, 'The Referendum of 23 June 2016: Voting on Europe' [2017] *PL* (Brexit Special Issue) 2, 9 ('Second thoughts, as other EU members have found, may produce appropriate answers').

[10] See generally S Tierney, *Constitutional Referendums: The Theory and Practice of Republican Deliberation* (Oxford, Oxford University Press, 2012).

[11] See generally R Ekins, 'The Value of Representative Democracy' in C Charters and D Knight (eds), *We the People(s): Participation in Governance* (Wellington, Victoria University Press, 2011) 29, 48.

[12] Some might quibble with this and suggest instead that only a small section of the public ranked discontent with EU membership as amongst their main political priorities. It is difficult to deny, however, that discontent has been a central theme of the UK's membership of the EU, with a strong streak of scepticism a long-standing current in political discourse about the EU, albeit with the levels of discontent unevenly distributed across the UK. The literature on the tradition of Euroscepticism in UK politics is large, but useful overviews include: A Gamble, 'Better Off Out? Britain and Europe' (2012) 83 *Political Quarterly* 468; and O Daddow, 'Margaret Thatcher, Tony Blair and the Eurosceptic Tradition in Britain' (2013) 15 *British Journal of Politics and International Relations* 210.

[13] It was clear throughout the parliamentary debates on the 2015 Act that the referendum was intended to give voters the final say on whether the UK should remain in the EU.

arguments that the franchise was unfair.[14] The franchise replicated that adopted in general elections, which was prudent given that any departure from this might have been interpreted as an underhand attempt to stack the deck in favour of the status quo.[15] More generally, the time for raising objections such as these—and particularly arguments about the need for a second referendum—was before the referendum was held. There might have been a reasonable case to be made for sequential referendums—the first on whether or not to leave and a second on the terms of leaving—but only if provision for this had been made in advance, not as an *ex post facto* attempt by elites to upend the result of the referendum.

A narrative of 'constitutional crisis' developed alongside the elite-led attempts to delegitimise the referendum, and this was the second dynamic unloosed by the elite cry of rage.[16] On this view, the referendum triggered a constitutional crisis[17] (or, in some of the more sophisticated accounts, had laid bare fissures within and between the nations of the UK that will likely over time, and possibly a very short time, precipitate a constitutional crisis).[18] This crisis narrative encompassed four overlapping themes. First, the referendum revealed deep fractures within a constitution that had traditionally commanded broad consensus that traversed ideological, geographical and socio-economic lines. Second, the referendum had catapulted to the top of the political agenda questions that risked fermenting division within—and ultimately the break-up of—the territorial constitution; questions, for example, about the future of the land border with the Republic of Ireland, and questions about the allocation of repatriated powers between central and devolved tiers of government.[19] Third, the constitution lacked the sort of clear and principled constitutional law needed to address questions such as these[20] and, more generally, to manage political and legal change of the scale and complexity involved in leaving the EU. The domestic processes for withdrawal would be shaped instead by politics, with the risk that constitutional practice untamed by constitutional law would enable a power-hungry central executive to sideline the

---

[14] Cf J Shaw, 'The Quintessentially Democratic Act? Democracy, Political Community and Citizenship In and After the EU Referendum of June 2016' (2017) 37 *Journal of European Integration* 559.

[15] The question of whether to extend the franchise to EU citizens and 16- to 17-year-olds featured prominently in the parliamentary debates on the 2015 Act, but Parliament chose to adopt the franchise used in general elections. A legal challenge to the terms of the franchise was dismissed: *Shindler v Chancellor of the Duchy of Lancaster* [2016] EWCA Civ 469, [2017] QB 226.

[16] The language of constitutional crisis had been building in the months leading up to the referendum; see, eg, V Bogdanor, *The Crisis of the Constitution: The General Election and the Future of the United Kingdom* (London, Constitution Society, 2015).

[17] See, eg, D Galligan (ed), *Constitution in Crisis: The New Putney Debates* (London, IB Tauris & Co, 2017); and AC Grayling, *Democracy and Its Crisis* (London, Oneworld, 2017).

[18] See, eg, S Douglas-Scott, 'Brexit, Article 50 and the Contested British Constitution' (2016) 79 *MLR* 1019, 1038; and M Loughlin, 'The End of Avoidance: The UK Constitutional Crisis', *London Review of Books* (28 July 2016).

[19] For a clear-headed and sophisticated discussion, see A McHarg and J Mitchell, 'Brexit and Scotland' (2017) 19 *British Journal of Politics and International Relations* 1.

[20] See, eg, F Matthews, 'Whose Mandate Is It Anyway? Brexit, the Constitution and the Contestation of Authority' (2017) 88 *Political Quarterly* 1.

UK Parliament and the devolved institutions. Lastly, the constitution was about to take a step back into an age of unreason by eschewing the stable legal framework of the EU and returning to the permissive national legal framework that had existed prior to 1972. This was only the first such step: over time other progressive pillars of the constitution, such as the Human Rights Act and the European Convention on Human Rights (ECHR), would be targeted by the reactionary forces that successfully campaigned for withdrawal from the EU. Running throughout this narrative of crisis was concern about the constitution's capacity to manage the radical change involved in unpicking political and legal relations with the EU and a fear of 'the coming constitutional instability'.[21] But for many in the political and legal classes, this genuine concern was very difficult to disentangle from a deep and personally felt disappointment that the referendum had mandated radical constitutional change that not only disturbed the status quo, but also departed from their preferences.

In the aftermath of the referendum, this crisis narrative was never too far from the surface in debates about the implications of and process for leaving the EU.[22] However, the language of crisis is cheap,[23] and much of the post-referendum narrative was (as Levinson and Balkin put it in a different context) 'the equivalent of pounding the table and marking one's upset about some state of affairs in the world'.[24] In any case, there was no constitutional crisis.[25] There were abnormally high levels of political change and uncertainty, a partial consequence of the confluence of the Prime Minister's resignation the morning after the referendum and a failed coup against the Leader of the Opposition. New political territory was being entered: the process of leaving the EU would be overseen by a Parliament that strongly favoured the UK's continued membership. This mismatch between elite and popular assessments of European integration gave rise to various complications, including the lack of adequate contingency work by the civil service in the event that the voters voted to leave the EU. The months following the referendum had also heightened tensions between the UK Government and the devolved administrations, and the Scottish Government in particular (but, once again, the public showed greater forbearance in so far as one of the consequences of the referendum was to temper enthusiasm for Scottish independence,

---

[21] P Eleftheriadis, 'The Coming Constitutional Instability' [2017] *PL* 347.

[22] Invoking the language of crisis was not confined to those elites who were opposed to or concerned by the referendum result. Notably, *The Daily Mail* warned in November 2016 that the Divisional Court's decision in *Miller* 'could trigger [a] constitutional crisis', although it is at least arguable that a genuine crisis would have resulted from the House of Commons or House of Lords defying the referendum result by refusing to pass legislation authorizing ministers to give notice under Article 50. It is also true that one might expect tabloid newspapers to be more sensationalist in their use of language than, for example, legal academics. See *Daily Mail*, 'Enemies of the People' (4 November 2016).

[23] See generally C Hay, 'A Crisis of Politics in the Politics of Crisis' in D Richards, M Smith and C Hay (eds), *Institutional Crisis in 21st Century Britain* (Basingstoke, Palgrave, 2014) 60, 77.

[24] S Levinson and J M Balkin, 'Constitutional Crises' (2009) 157 *University of Pennsylvania Law Review* 707, 714.

[25] ibid.

at least in the short term). All of this could perhaps be said to have amounted to a *political* crisis, but it falls short (indeed, in our view, very significantly short) of a *constitutional* crisis.[26] Such a crisis occurs principally where a constitution no longer makes politics possible; where serious failures within the constitutional architecture prevent politics addressing political uncertainty, change and conflict. A crisis, in other words, involves a serious breakdown of the constitutional order. This might arise where disputes cannot be resolved within the existing framework, or where key actors no longer adhere to the rules of the constitutional game.[27]

There had been no such breakdown in the UK. Holding the referendum was an intelligible response to the diverging elite and popular assessments of the EU,[28] and in its aftermath the Government was rightly intent on implementing the voters' decision to leave. The governing apparatus has been tested in numerous ways since June 2016, and at various junctures the machinery of government has not always looked like a beacon of excellence. But there has been no rupture in basic constitutional processes. The constitution in action had enabled the governing institutions to grapple with the novel, complex and challenging questions to which leaving the EU gives rise, although of course assessments will differ as to the soundness of the answers proffered to those questions. In saying all of this, we do not mean to downplay the scale of the challenges presented by leaving the EU. The challenges for the governing institutions are not merely political and legal but cultural (adjusting to governing processes leavened by the removal of a supranational legal framework) and organisational (recruiting civil servants with new skill-sets, reallocating officials to new jobs, and creating and staffing in short order a new department of state). We also do not deny that there have been episodes since the referendum where this or that actor has tried to stretch constitutional practice. We also acknowledge that there remain thorny questions still to be addressed, most notably questions relating to Northern Ireland. Our claim is simply that the crisis narrative was the concoction of panicked elites; the constitution has to date enabled politics to work in established ways and through settled processes, and in so doing has provided sufficient political stability to absorb the shock of the referendum result. For some, this might seem like a cavalier or complacent reading of the reverberations caused by the referendum, one that puts too much confidence in the traditional constitution to accommodate the unpredictable political forces unleashed by leaving the EU. However, in our view, precipitately invoking a narrative of crisis poses serious risks to the constitutional order. It distorts how political and legal actors discharge their constitutional functions—perhaps even

---

[26] Aileen McHarg offers a measured account, arguing that there was a political crisis in the months following the referendum, but that it remains an open question whether this might engender a constitutional crisis: A McHarg, 'Navigating Without Maps: Constitutional Silence and the Management of the Brexit Crisis' (2018) *ICON* (forthcoming).

[27] KE Whittington, 'Yet Another Constitutional Crisis?' (2002) 43 *William & Mary Law Review* 2093.

[28] Plainly views differ on whether the referendum was either necessary or desirable: cf P Craig, 'Brexit: A Drama in Six Acts' (2016) 41 *EL Rev* 447 and H Thompson, 'Inevitability and Contingency: The Political Economy of Brexit' (2017) 19 *British Journal of Poliitics and International Relations* 434.

motivating them to neglect or betray their responsibilities—which risks bringing about the very crisis it aims to answer.

These two dynamics—the elite critique of the referendum's legitimacy and the elite-contrived narrative of constitutional crisis—fuelled a final and related dynamic: the repeated attempts to initiate litigation to delay or disrupt the process of leaving the EU. The *Miller* litigation was only the most high-profile of a number of attempts to relocate the politics of Brexit from the political realm to the legal arena. Other attempts included: a case brought in parallel to *Miller* asking whether the Northern Ireland Act 1998 had abrogated the Government's prerogative to give notice under Article 50;[29] the unsuccessful attempt by an English barrister to litigate in Dublin the question of whether notice under Article 50 was revocable, where the ultimate goal was to engineer a preliminary reference by the Irish High Court to the Court of Justice of the EU; and the threat hanging over the Government of litigation to secure the release of studies on the economic impact of the UK's leaving the EU. Two further sets of legal proceedings are underway at the time of writing. The first is a case before the Court of Session, where a group of Scottish MPs, MEPs and MSPs—coordinated by the same English barrister behind the Dublin litigation—seeks a reference to the Luxembourg Court about whether the UK can unilaterally revoke its notice under Article 50. The second is in the High Court, where the claimant argues that the European Union (Notification of Withdrawal) Act 2017 does not include a formal 'decision' to leave the EU as required under Article 50. The first is arguable (if difficult to square with *Miller* itself), but the second is not and should be dismissed out of hand. Some legal academics have been industrious in dreaming up other outlandish and—to be frank—legally absurd ways of attempting to upend the voters' decision to leave the EU. Philip Allott, for example, proposed that the courts could conclude that departing the EU was unlawful on the grounds that holding the referendum was not in the public interest and its ultimate result was unreasonable.[30] Equally lacking any legal foundation was Yossi Nehushan's contention that it would be unlawful for the Prime Minister to take the referendum's result to be morally authoritative, and that instead the courts should require her to treat the referendum as merely advisory and to consider it alongside the factors that weigh against withdrawal.[31] Perhaps the high-water mark of this hyperactivity amongst the legal class was a letter in July 2016 to the Prime Minister signed by 1,054 barristers, purporting to reconcile 'the legal, constitutional and political issues' that arose from the referendum by proposing 'a Royal Commission or an equivalent independent body to receive evidence and report, within a short, fixed timescale, on the benefits, costs

---

[29] *Re McCord's Application* [2016] NIQB 85, [2017] 2 CMLR 7.
[30] P Allott, 'Forget the Politics—Brexit May Be Unlawful', *The Guardian* (30 June 2016).
[31] Y Nehushtan, 'Why is it Illegal for the Prime Minister to Perceive the EU Referendum's Result as Morally-Politically Authoritative?', *UKCLA Blog* (11 July 2016), available at https://ukconstitutionallaw.org/.

and risks of triggering Article 50 to the UK as a whole, and all of its constituent populations'.[32] This letter garnered press headlines but no political traction; it was emblematic, however, of the extent to which many in the legal class sought to conceal their own preferences for continued membership of the EU in the finery of (weak and ill-founded) 'legal analysis'. The *Miller* litigation should be understood in the light of the wider pattern of lawyerly hyperactivity relating to Brexit; hyperactivity that preceded *Miller* and which has continued in its wake. As we explain in the next section, *Miller* differed from some of the other more fanciful legal analyses proposed in the aftermath of the referendum because it presented an arguable legal question that the claimants crafted in a politically potent fashion.

III. Politics by Other Means? Framing Strategic Litigation

The litigation in *Miller* was framed around a focused and technical question of constitutional law: whether the Government could use the prerogative to give notice of the UK's intention to leave the EU for the purposes of Article 50. The claimants submitted that fresh legislation was required to authorise the Government to initiate the Article 50 process, and relied on two main arguments to support this. First, the European Communities Act 1972 ('ECA') creates statutory rights that can only be diminished or abrogated by another statute. The triggering of Article 50 would lead to the UK's leaving the EU, which would necessarily frustrate or erase these statutory rights. Since only an Act of Parliament can abrogate statutory rights, a statute was required to authorise Ministers to trigger Article 50. Second, the ECA's purpose was to provide for the UK's membership of the EU and to give effect in domestic law to the EU Treaties. Triggering Article 50 would put in motion a chain of events that would culminate in leaving the EU and the Treaties' ceasing to have effect in the UK, thereby rendering the ECA an empty shell and frustrating its purpose. It was settled constitutional law that the Government cannot use its prerogative powers to frustrate a statute, and thus a statute was required to authorise Ministers to issue the Article 50 notice. The claimants contended in the alternative that the ECA and subsequent statutes relating to the EU had impliedly abrogated the Government's prerogative to withdrawn from the EU Treaties.

The claimants' arguments were cleverly crafted but legally unsound, for the reasons noted in section IV, not least because they mistook the contestable requirements of constitutional practice (ie what good practice and political prudence require in a constitution such as the UK's) for the requirements of constitutional

---

[32] 'In Full: The Letter From 1,000 Lawyers to David Cameron Over EU Referendum', *The Independent* (10 July 2016).

law (ie what is required as a matter of law).[33] Although legally flawed, the claimants' arguments were a beguiling blend of tradition, prudence and politics, which was astute and powerful in political terms. The litigation was framed not as an attempt to flout the referendum but as vindicating traditional principles, most notably representative democracy and parliamentary sovereignty. By arguing that only an Act of Parliament could authorise Ministers to invoke Article 50, the claimants depicted themselves as insisting only on lawful processes that would safeguard Parliament's role in this momentous constitutional change. Echoing throughout the claimants' submissions was the claim that for Ministers to initiate the Article 50 process without statutory authorisation would be the sort of executive overreach traditionally subject to parliamentary resistance and judicial checks. It is easy to forget, especially following the 2017 General Election, the degree to which this resonated with concerns widely held by elites in the months after the referendum that Theresa May led an overbearing government that faced no credible opposition inside Parliament from a Labour Party distracted by its own internal schisms. What is more, the claimants' arguments overlapped with what many viewed as sound constitutional practice and political prudence. Even putting to one side any supposed legal requirement, it was arguable that, as a matter of constitutional practice and political prudence, Ministers should have invited Parliament to signify its support for the triggering of Article 50, whether by way of primary legislation or a resolution of each chamber.[34] Or to put this more bluntly: the litigation was intended, and widely thought, to place in a political bind those who believed that leaving the EU would lead to the reinvigoration of parliamentary sovereignty in a constitution freed from the constraints of EU law. Such Brexiteers might have felt instinctively suspicious of the litigation, yet found appealing its emphasis on giving Parliament the final decision whether and when to initiate Article 50.

The litigation was presented as an attempt to affirm parliamentary sovereignty and to avoid Ministers exceeding their lawful powers, but a realpolitik reading would see it as a subtle legal strategy that was seized on (and perhaps also concocted by) elites to delay or frustrate (or to delay in the hope of frustrating) the referendum result.[35] Indeed, whatever the litigants' actual motivations, the *Miller* litigation was 'undoubtedly perceived [at least by many] ... as an attempt to prevent or to delay Brexit'.[36] Motivations are complex of course, and may not always be fully understood by those who act on them. Still, it would be unsurprising if the political preferences of those most invested in the referendum tracked their

---

[33] See generally R Ekins, 'Constitutional Practice and Principle in the Article 50 Litigation' (2017) 133 *LQR* 347.

[34] See House of Lords Select Committee on the Constitution, *The Invoking of Article 50*, HL44 (13 September 2016).

[35] Some might suggest that the salient question was not why the claimants brought the action, but why the Government contested it. See, eg, P Craig, 'Brexit, A Drama: The Interregnum' (2017) 35 *YEL* 1.

[36] McHarg (n 26).

support for (or opposition to) this litigation. The lead claimant, Gina Miller, described the litigation as about 'process not politics', but it bears noting that she was an active supporter of the Remain Campaign who described herself as having felt 'physically sick' on learning of the voters' decision to leave,[37] and who in the 2017 Election led a tactical voting initiative designed to empower candidates who might vote against the Government's deal with the EU.[38]

Litigation was clearly an intelligent way, and perhaps the only realistic way, to delay the triggering of Article 50. Reflecting a year on from their influential blog-post that was the intellectual genesis for the litigation,[39] Nick Barber, Tom Hickman and Jeff King acknowledge that delay was a factor that led them to explain why, in their view, legislation was required before Article 50 could be triggered. As they saw it, the requirement to legislate would slow down the process of initiating Article 50 'at a time of political crisis within the UK', and therefore 'provide much needed breathing space for political actors'.[40] Delay would be in the national interest since it would allow the Government more time to determine its negotiating position, as well as providing an opportunity to obtain commitments from the EU and other Member States concerning the substance and process of the UK–EU negotiations.

If delay is an admitted reason for litigation then it is important to acknowledge that, for many,[41] the attraction of delay must also have been that it made it space for the UK to reverse course; if, for example, the economy soured, encouraging public opinion to turn against withdrawal. Initiating the litigation itself generated delay. As importantly, if successful, litigation promised much more delay: the parliamentary process takes time, and overcoming opposition in the House of Lords by way of the Parliament Acts 1911 and 1949 might take at least a year. The litigation was never directly going to frustrate implementation of the referendum result, notwithstanding some of the wilder legal arguments noted in section II, for the courts clearly had no authority to rule as much. However, the litigation promised to (and in the end did) pass the decision whether or not to trigger Article 50 to MPs and peers, the overwhelming majority of whom had favoured the UK's

---

[37] J Llewellyn Smith, 'One Woman's Lonely Battle to Prevent A Rush for the Brexit', *The Times* (15 October 2016).

[38] D Roberts, 'Gina Miller to Launch Tactical Voting Initiative Against Hard Brexit', *The Guardian* (19 April 2017).

[39] NW Barber, T Hickman and J King, 'Pulling the Article 50 Trigger: Parliament's Indispensable Role' *UKCLA Blog* (27 June 2016), available at https://ukconstitutionallaw.org/.

[40] NW Barber, T Hickman and J King, 'Reflections on *Miller*' (2016–17) 8 *UK Supreme Court Yearbook* 212.

[41] Not for all: Jeff King, writing after the Divisional Court's judgment, explicitly states that it would be politically illegitimate for Parliament to block on second reading a bill authorising the triggering of Article 50, that there is a political duty on the Government and Parliament to commence negotiations for exit from the EU in good faith and, relatedly, that any bill should not be loaded with conditions that would make Brexit practically impossible. If Parliament wishes to block Brexit, he says, it must do so openly. See J King, 'What Next? Legislative Authority for Triggering Article 50', *UKCLA Blog* (8 November 2016), available at https://ukconstitutionallaw.org/.

remaining a member of the EU and some of whom were openly contemplating defying the referendum. In this way, the ensuing delay could be used to ramp up the pressure on Parliament to buck the will of the voters. Politically motivated litigation is far from unusual, of course, and the motives of the litigants or those who were supportive of them are not strictly relevant to how the Supreme Court should have discharged its role. But it is reasonable to reflect frankly on the reasons why litigation was probably undertaken in order to grasp its constitutional significance and, relatedly, the importance attached to it by many in public life.

IV. Constitutional Law and Constitutional Practice in the Supreme Court

The Supreme Court upheld the claim and ruled that fresh legislation was required to trigger Article 50. This would have been an unobjectionable ruling if it had been truly required by law. But in fact the judgment is legally unsound, as this section documents. Few notice, but strictly the Court did not take up the claimants' sweeping claims about the frustration of rights. Those claims were obviously problematic, for EU legal rights are not statutory rights. Parliament has never enacted the rights in question, but has instead made provision for rights in international law to have force in domestic law: EU legal rights in domestic law are treaty-based rights, not ordinary statutory rights; they depend for their force on the enabling statute *and* on their standing in international law. The Government lacks authority to set aside the ECA or to declare that EU legal rights in UK law are to be set aside. But it does not follow from this that the Government may not exercise the prerogative to change the position in international law, which in turn changes domestic law in accordance with the terms of the enabling statute itself.

John Finnis analysed treaty-based rights in a series of papers for Policy Exchange's *Judicial Power Project*,[42] which the Government relied on in argument before the Court. Elaborating and clarifying a line of argument that the Government introduced, but mishandled, before the Divisional Court, Finnis explored the parallel with double-tax treaties, a parallel established well before 1972.[43] Treaty-based rights rest on two bases: statute and treaty. An asymmetry exists in how treaty-based rights are introduced into domestic law and the manner in which they are terminated. They cannot be introduced into domestic law without both legislation and prerogative, but they can be terminated by prerogative

---

[42] J Finnis, 'Terminating Treaty-Based UK Rights', *Judicial Power Project* (26 October 2016); and J Finnis, 'Terminating Treaty-Based UK Rights', *Judicial Power Project* (2 November 2016).

[43] Finnis focused on s 2 of the Taxation (International and Other Provisions) Act 2010, but noted that substantially identical provisions could be found in earlier taxation legislation, including in examples prior to 1972.

alone, including via the exercise of termination rights within the relevant treaty itself. This asymmetry follows from the scheme of the legislation, which makes domestic law turn on the position at international law. Plainly, the constitutional significance of the treaty-based rights arising under double-tax treaties is relatively muted, at least as compared with EU legal rights under the EU Treaties. But it is this fact that makes the parallel instructive, in so far as thinking about double-tax treaties renders the interplay between prerogative and legislation in the context of treaty-based rights clearer. The point is not that treaty-based rights are somehow unimportant, as Sionaidh Douglas-Scott wrongly assumed Finnis to be suggesting,[44] and so ought to be liable to be destroyed without parliamentary debate. Rather, Parliament has made provision for these rights to have this particular foothold in domestic law, which entails that the Government is able to take action in the international realm that results in changes in domestic law, changes which Parliament itself intends and authorises by virtue of the scheme of the legislation in question. (Contrast cases in which Parliament chooses to incorporate international obligations directly into statute, such that changes in international law do not in turn change domestic law.) The Government remains answerable to Parliament for its actions. Parliamentary debate, or the threat of debate, may stop a proposed course of action, but legislation is not required. The Court did not properly consider the double-tax parallel. The majority dismissed it in short order,[45] noting that the parallel had not been explored in oral argument (but it was made out clearly in written submissions, which included responses to all counter-arguments identified by claimants' counsel). The majority merely asserted that the parallel had been answered in unspecified ways and with unspecified arguments by unnamed third parties. This is not the careful attention to logically make-or-break, decisive detail that one might reasonably expect from eight judges in an important and high-profile case.[46]

Still, the majority clearly saw that EU legal rights are not ordinary statutory rights and that they can and do change without parliamentary involvement, for the content of EU legal rights is a question of EU law.[47] However, the majority went on to say that the constitutional processes by which UK law is made can only be changed by Parliament, and that using the prerogative to withdraw from the Treaties would amount to the executive's unilaterally removing a source of domestic law. This would 'effect a fundamental change in the constitutional arrangements of the [UK]'[48] by 'cut[ting] off [this] source of law entirely'.[49]

---

[44] S Douglas-Scott, 'Brexit and the British Constitution: An Update on Sionaidh Douglas-Scott, "Brexit, Article 50 and the Contested British Constitution" (2016) 79(6) *MLR* 1019–40' [2017] *MLR Forum* 004, 3, available at http://www.modernlawreview.co.uk/brexit-british-constitution/.

[45] *Miller* (n 1), [98].

[46] For a biting critique of the intellectual rigour of the majority's reasoning, see M Elliott, 'The Supreme Court's Judgment in *Miller*: In Search of Constitutional Principle' (2017) 76 *CLJ* 257.

[47] *Miller* (n 1), [62].

[48] ibid, [78].

[49] ibid, [79].

The majority proceeded to assert that fundamental constitutional change (of this kind?) requires legislation. They rejected the argument articulated by Lord Reed in dissent, namely, that withdrawal effected by executive action changes the international legal position, to which the Act then gives effect.[50] As we see it, the majority's argument turned on a deeply confused account of how EU law is received in domestic law.

The majority recognised, of course, that EU law's standing in domestic law turned entirely on the ECA, hence the rule of recognition had not been changed,[51] but, remarkably, added that 'in ... a more realistic sense where EU law applies in the [UK], it is the EU institutions which are the relevant source of that law'.[52] Likewise, it was said to be 'unrealistic to deny that, so long as that [ECA] remains in force, the EU Treaties, EU legislation and the interpretations placed on these instruments by the Court of Justice are direct sources of UK law'.[53] This emphasis on what the majority regarded as *unrealistic* led the majority to the extraordinary conclusion that the ECA constitutes EU law as 'an independent and overriding source of domestic law'.[54] The majority also asserted that the ECA 'effectively operates as a partial transfer of law-making powers, or an assignment of legislative competences, by Parliament to the EU lawmaking institutions'.[55] In the same paragraph the Court refers to passages quoted in Lord Reed's dissent from *Van Gend en Loos*[56] and *Costa v ENEL*.[57] According to the majority, those passages 'demonstrate that rules which would ... normally be incompatible with UK constitutional principles, became part of our constitutional arrangements as a result of the ECA and the 1972 Accession Treaty for as long as the ECA remains in force'.[58]

The references to what is *realistic* or *unrealistic* indicated that the majority had abandoned principled legal analysis.[59] The position the Court adopted was incoherent on its own terms and inconsistent with settled law: EU law is not an independent, overriding or direct source of UK law.[60] The effect of EU law in the UK is radically dependent on the ECA, and hence neither independent nor direct: EU law does not override other sources of law as such, but rather takes effect notwithstanding inconsistency with other legal propositions, in accordance with the terms of section 2(1) and (4) of the ECA, to the extent that subsequent Acts take

---

[50] ibid, [217], per Lord Reed.
[51] ibid, [60].
[52] ibid, [61].
[53] ibid.
[54] ibid, [65].
[55] ibid, [68].
[56] Case C-26/62 *Van Gend en Loos* [1963] ECR 1, 12.
[57] Case C-6/64 *Costa v ENEL* [1964] ECR 585, 593.
[58] *Miller* (n 1), [68].
[59] For discussion of the absence of principled legal analysis in the majority's reasoning, see M Elliott, 'Judicial Power and the United Kingdom's Changing Constitution' (2017) 36 *University of Queensland Law Journal* (forthcoming).
[60] R Ekins, 'Legislative Freedom in the United Kingdom' (2017) 133 *LQR* 582.

for granted and thus maintain this rule of priority.[61] As Lord Reed notes in his dissent, section 2(1) 'enables EU law to be given direct effect in our domestic law, but within a framework established by Parliament, in which parliamentary sovereignty remains the fundamental principle'.[62] As he explains later on in his dissent, '[s]ince EU law has no status in UK law independent of statute, it follows that the only relevant source of law has at all times been statute'.[63] Parliament cannot *transfer* its law-making powers to any other institution; it can only give effect to some other institution's acts. Further, the UK, like many other Member States, has *never* accepted the Court of Justice's self-understanding. In affirming that the status of EU law is dependent on a continuing statutory basis, section 18 of the European Union Act 2011 makes this clear, as indeed do dicta from the Supreme Court's decisions in *Pham*[64] and *HS2*.[65] In *Miller*, the majority's 'realism' led them to contrive a deeply mistaken account of how EU law takes effect in domestic law.[66]

The reception of EU law in UK law depends on the ECA *and* the Treaties, which entails that the continuing effect of EU law in domestic law expires either if the ECA is repealed, or if the Treaties cease to apply to the UK. The ECA *might* have limited the Government's power to withdraw from the Treaties, but if it did not then the Government may set in motion Article 50's provisions for bringing the application of the Treaties to the UK to an end. As Lord Reed made clear, the ECA 'simply creates a scheme under which domestic law reflects the UK's international obligations, whatever they may be'.[67] Lord Reed noted that the ECA came into force before the Treaties were ratified, such that for a time there were no Treaties to which the ECA applied and it introduced no new legal rights into our law.[68] In answer to Lord Reed, the majority suggested that

> by the 1972 Act, Parliament endorsed and gave effect to the UK's future membership of the European Union, and this became a fixed domestic starting point. The question is whether that domestic starting point, introduced by Parliament, can be set aside, or could have been intended to be set aside, by a decision of the UK executive without express Parliamentary authorisation.[69]

The majority raise an arguable point about the intention of the ECA.[70] However, what bears emphasis is that the ECA does not commit the UK to membership of

---

[61] R Ekins, 'Constitutional Practice and Principle in the Article 50 Litigation' (2017) *133* LQR 347, 349.

[62] *Miller* (n 1), [183].

[63] ibid, [227].

[64] *Pham v Secretary of State for the Home Department* [2015] UKSC 19, [2015] 1 WLR 1591.

[65] *R (HS2 Action Alliance) v Secretary of State for Transport* [2014] UKSC 3, [2014] 2 All ER 109.

[66] See AL Young's contribution in ch 12 of this volume for further discussion of what might be meant by a 'realistic' interpretation.

[67] *Miller* (n 1), [217].

[68] ibid, [192].

[69] ibid, [82] and [77].

[70] See generally M Barczentewicz, '*Miller*, Statutory Interpretation, and the True Place of EU Law in UK Law' (2017) *PL* (Brexit Special Issue) 10, 14–16.

the EU. Indeed, it did not even require entry into the EEC, as it then was.[71] The ECA's long title is '*an Act to make provision in connection with the enlargement of the European communities*', not an Act to make provision *for* such enlargement, as some have wrongly said.[72] Nor does the ECA in any other way purport to bring about this enlargement, as the Divisional Court mistakenly suggested.[73] More generally, the majority misunderstood the ECA. The structure of the ECA is that *if and when* defined treaties come into force or change internationally, domestic law changes too. Changes in domestic law might follow from executive action (whether on or under the Treaties) and need not involve legislation. While section 1(2) requires primary legislation to amend the Act to recognise major new treaties, section 1(3) recognises ancillary treaties that are declared as such by Order in Council and supported by a resolution of each House.[74] This is a scheme for parliamentary control, but not a scheme that requires primary legislation for the scope of effective EU law (including any or all of the EU Treaties that have come into force) to change.

The crux of the majority judgment in *Miller* was a striking and unsubstantiated assertion that withdrawal from the Treaties would be a constitutional change that cannot be for Ministers alone. Such a momentous constitutional change, the majority claimed, could only be effected through legislation. The majority noted that withdrawing from the EU would be as significant a change as that which occurred when the ECA had first incorporated EU law into domestic law.[75] They further noted that once notification of withdrawal is given to the EU under Article 50, this change will occur irrespective of whether Parliament repeals the ECA. It was in this light that the majority asserted that 'It would be inconsistent with long-standing and fundamental principles for such a far-reaching change to the UK constitutional arrangements to be brought about by ministerial decision or ministerial action alone.'[76] The majority continued by saying:

> We cannot accept that a major change to UK constitutional arrangements can be achieved by ministers alone; it must be effected in the only way that the UK constitution

---

[71] *Miller* (n 1), [193]–[195].

[72] The long title is wrongly stated in the blog-post which was the intellectual inspiration for the *Miller* litigation: Barber, Hickman and King (n 39). It was also wrongly re-stated in J King and N Barber, 'In Defence of Miller', *UKCLA Blog* (22 November 2016), available at https://ukconstitutionallaw.org/. For discussion of the relevance of the long title, as correctly stated, see J Finnis, 'Brexit and the Balance of Our Constitution', *Judicial Power Project* (2 December 2016); and M Barczentewicz, 'The Core Issue in *Miller*: The Relevance of Section 1 of the 1972 Act', *Judicial Power Project* (4 January 2017), available at http://judicialpowerproject.org.uk/.

[73] *R (Miller) v The Secretary of State for Exiting the European Union* [2016] EWHC 2768 (Admin), [62], [66] and [93].

[74] Barczentewicz (n 70), 16–23.

[75] However, the ECA had no constitution-changing effect before the accession treaty went into force, a point that is omitted from the majority's judgment, as noted ibid, 15. Further, even after the treaty came into force, the ECA, while no doubt constitutionally significant, made no change to the fundamentals of the UK constitution: J Finnis, 'Postscript' in R Ekins (ed), *Judicial Power and the Balance of Our Constitution* (London, Policy Exchange, 2017) 157, 160–62, available at http://judicialpowerproject.org.uk/publications/.

[76] *Miller* (n 1), [81].

recognises, namely by Parliamentary legislation. This conclusion appears to us to follow from the ordinary application of basic concepts of constitutional law to the present issue.[77]

The majority cited no authority for these propositions. The reason for the lack of authority is very simply stated: there is none. No principle of the UK constitution—or of UK constitutional law in particular—requires that major change must be realised by primary legislation.[78] The history of the UK's membership of the EU illustrates the point. Entry into the EU Treaties was an act of immense significance. But it was neither required nor authorised by legislation and was, in law, an exercise of the prerogative. It is true that Parliament by resolution approved in principle the entry into the Treaties, with the ECA subsequently enacted to make provision in connection with the Treaties in due course. This is not the same, however, as requiring ratification of the Treaties, and likewise is not the same as withdrawal. If Parliament chooses to make major legal consequences turn on the power of Ministers to change UK obligations in international law then Ministers may make very significant decisions, and so it is with the ECA.

In asserting (without evidence) that significant constitutional change in the UK can only be effected via legislation, the majority ran together what may or may not be good constitutional practice with what is valid constitutional law. Several points later on in the judgment confirm that the majority confused the two (or possibly abandoned the latter to secure their perception of the former). The first is the assertion that it is implausible to say that Ministers could have withdrawn the UK from the Treaties on or after the ECA came into force, with or without the referendum or even in defiance of a popular vote to remain.[79] Strikingly, the majority noted that 'it would clearly be appropriate' for withdrawal from the Treaties to be a power that did not exist unless and until Parliament explicitly accorded it to Ministers.[80] The majority also remarked later, albeit without relying on the point, that because withdrawal will necessitate much legislation, there is 'a good pragmatic argument' that Ministers should not impose this burden on Parliament without prior authorisation by statute, all of which confirmed for the majority the scale of the change, and thus 'the constitutional propriety of prior Parliamentary sanction'.[81] The majority addressed the counter-argument that Ministers would of course be accountable for their exercise of the prerogative, dismissing it as 'a potentially controversial argument constitutionally'.[82] It is true that ministerial accountability is not a reason to be cavalier about the scope and legal limits of executive power, but what the majority fail to recognise is the relevance (or constitutional

---

[77] ibid, [82].

[78] As Mark Elliott notes, the majority's proposition 'lacks support in authority, imports into the law a novel and highly imprecise criterion by which prerogative power is delimited and rests upon normative constitutional foundations that are unarticulated and arguably absent': Elliott (n 46), 258.

[79] *Miller* (n 1), [91]. See also Douglas-Scott (n 18), 1029.

[80] *Miller* (n 1), [92].

[81] ibid, [100].

[82] ibid, [92].

importance) of responsible government. The Government's accountability to Parliament, and especially to the House of Commons, is a vital restraint on its powers, including, for example, its undeniable legal power to commit the UK to war with any or all other EU Member States. This then is the answer to the majority's scepticism about withdrawal from the EU apart from or in defiance of the referendum result. It would not be constitutionally improper for the Government to trigger Article 50 if supported by the House of Commons, if, say, it had contested an election on a manifesto commitment to withdrawal. It would be politically unthinkable for the Government to propose to initiate the Article 50 process in defiance of a popular vote to remain, and the House of Commons would ensure as much. It might be contended that this would be unlawful in any event in view of voters' legitimate expectation that Ministers would implement the outcome of the referendum. But it would be much better to say that the referendum's outcome should be honoured, and if the Government proposed otherwise it would have to explain itself to the Houses of Parliament and the electorate. It is the principle of responsible government that renders intelligible the scheme that Parliament enacted in 1972, and took for granted and extended in subsequent legislation.[83] Recognising the relevance and force of this principle avoids the rash assumption that legal disability is required to prevent the misuse of executive power.

On our reading, the majority's conclusion—that the prerogative does not extend to triggering Article 50 and withdrawal from the Treaties—was driven by presuppositions about what is and is not constitutionally proper. The presuppositions are not well made, and are contestable at best. More to the point, they do not support the Supreme Court's conclusions about the law. It is almost too obvious a point to state, but clearly bears emphasis: the Court does not have authority to enforce constitutional principle writ large. Its authority is confined to law, a point on which the majority quite properly relied in dismissing the challenges arising from the devolutionary settlements.[84] The only plausible legal ground on which *Miller* could rest is that the ECA impliedly limited the exercise of the prerogative to withdraw from the Treaties. This is a question ultimately about Parliament's intention in 1972, to be answered by attending to the context of the ECA's enactment. The assertion that Parliament simply must have intended to oust the prerogative is ungrounded and does not cohere with the interplay between executive and legislative action in taking the UK into the EEC. It implausibly attributes the EU's legal self-understanding to the 1972 Parliament. The majority also turned the idea of legality on its head, asserting first that one cannot attribute to Parliament 'the notion that it was clothing ministers with the far-reaching and anomalous right to use a treaty-making power to remove an important source of domestic law and important domestic rights'[85] and later that '[t]he fact that a statute says

---

[83] On this point, see Barczentewicz (n 70), 17.

[84] For a different view, see C McCrudden and D Halberstam, '*Miller* and the Northern Ireland: A Critical Constitutional Response' (2017) 8 *UK Supreme Court Yearbook* 299.

[85] *Miller* (n 1), [87].

nothing about a particular topic can rarely, if ever, justify inferring a fundamental change in the law'.[86] Yet it was the majority that took the silence of the ECA to have effected a fundamental change, namely, abrogation of the government prerogative of making and unmaking treaties. Parliament did not clothe Ministers with anomalous authority in enacting the ECA. Rather, Parliament avoided anything suggesting intent to abrogate the prerogative, the continuing exercise of which it took for granted, as subsequent Acts confirm, with Ministers always remaining accountable to Parliament when exercising the prerogative.

V. Who Guards the Constitution?

Miller is remarkable, but not in a good way. Eight of 11 Supreme Court Justices commit themselves to a judgment that perceives, at least in part, the central flaw in the claimants' case, but nonetheless gives judgment in their favour by adopting an incoherent, incompletely reasoned and unprincipled account of EU law's standing in UK law. Their judgment conflates constitutional propriety (itself misunderstood) with constitutional law, and in so doing departs from the rule of law and, finally and in consequence, misconstrues the ECA. The judgment is constitutionally confused, unnecessary and dangerous. It risked exposing the Justices to political criticism, and could have been hazardous for their reputation and the rule of law.

But why did the Court decide in this way? The judgment betrays an ambition to superintend constitutional practice rather than to uphold constitutional law. The majority reason that in our constitution, it should be Parliament rather than the Government that decides that the UK should withdraw from the Treaties. It then transmutes this (contestable) proposition about constitutional practice into a rule of constitutional law, which it attributes to the Parliament that enacted the ECA. What is more, the Court's claim is not just that the Government must seek express authorisation from the Houses of Parliament, or at least the Commons, before triggering Article 50, say by a resolution, but that the decision to trigger must be authorised by a statute. (A resolution had of course been adopted by the House of Commons on 7 December 2016.) Within the logic of their own reasoning, the majority have no choice but to insist on legislation, rather than resolution, because to be satisfied by the latter would have made it clear that parliamentary support is not a legal requirement. More importantly, parliamentary control is not for judges to secure. The Supreme Court is not the guardian of the constitution, somehow charged with spurring the political authorities to do their constitutional duty. The Court betrays its own responsibility when its acts in such a way.

---

[86] ibid, [108]. See also ibid, [86].

Not everyone appreciates this. It is all too common for lawyers to speak unthinkingly of the Justices as 'the guardians of the constitution', as indeed Lady Hale did in an ill-judged speech in Malaysia shortly after the Divisional Court's decision in *Miller*.[87] True, the majority (including Lady Hale) seemed to distance themselves from such grandiose thinking when saying, rightly, that 'judges are neither the parents nor the guardians of political conventions'.[88] But this welcome discipline did not inform the balance of the Court's judgment, where its view of constitutional practice was refashioned into an enforceable point of constitutional law.[89]

Or to put this point differently: the litigation succeeded because the Supreme Court took up the claimants' implicit invitation to serve as the guardian of the constitution by protecting a browbeaten Parliament from an over-mighty executive. To fulfill its guardianship function, the Court—on this thinking—had to disable the executive from initiating the withdrawal process without Parliament's assent to primary legislation. Intervening without any legal basis in the relationship between the Houses of Parliament and the Government was a misuse of the Court's jurisdiction. The decision also provides further evidence that many of our leading judges do not have a good grasp of the nature and dynamics of that relationship. That relationship is animated by the principle of responsible government, framed by constitutional convention, and is the site of complex political and electoral dynamics. It is not true that unless an Act of Parliament is required to trigger Article 50, the Government would be free from parliamentary control. It is also a serious over-simplification to suggest that the Government's duty is to act on direction from the Houses of Parliament. The Government is drawn from and can at any point be unseated by the Commons. But it is constitutionally entitled to frame and execute its policy, which (other) parliamentarians are able to scrutinise, critique or oppose. It is true that the Government initially refrained from inviting the Houses of Parliament to express their support for Article 50 to be triggered, whether by resolution or by legislation, perhaps because it feared that one or other chamber, or possibly both, might obstruct its policy of honouring the referendum. This may have been unwise, or it may have been an intelligent response to the politics of the moment, of which the narrative of constitutional crisis and attacks on the legitimacy of the referendum chronicled earlier in this chapter formed major parts. In any case, the Houses of Parliament were not passive bystanders: they had the capacity, which they used, to question the Government's approach, both on process and substance. The rhetoric about the litigation saving Parliament from being sidelined is simply misleading (and misunderstands the executive-legislative

---

[87] Lady Hale, *The Supreme Court: Guardian of the Constitution*, Sultan Azlan Shah Lecture (9 November 2016). See also Lord Mance, 'The Role of Judges in a Representative Democracy', Lecture given during the Judicial Committee of the Privy Council's Fourth Sitting in The Bahamas (24 February 2017) para 32.

[88] *Miller* (n 1), [146].

[89] For a critical take on the Supreme Court's handling of conventions in *Miller*, see Alieen McHarg's contribution in ch 7 of this volume. See also McCrudden and Halberstam (n 84).

relationship), as is the subsequent complaint that Parliament squandered the opportunity which the courts (and the claimants) secured for them. *Miller* is alas not the first (and at this rate will be far from the last) case in which senior judges fail to understand responsible government, and either fail to respect, or attempt to compensate for perceived deficiencies in, political accountability.[90]

In any case, it is beyond artificial to treat this case as if the Government somehow decided to trigger Article 50 in a fit of pique. If, as we suggest, the majority were concerned with optimal constitutional practice—or, to use language adopted by the majority, if constitutional 'realism' is the focus—then the referendum matters. The Court sets this aside as irrelevant. If, in the rest of its judgment, the Court had hewed closely to settled law, leaving both the prerogative unimpaired and the significance of the referendum to the free flow of political argument between the political authorities and the electorate, this would have been an unobjectionable analysis. However, the majority are inconsistent in their interest in and recourse to constitutional realism: certain aspects of constitutional practice are plucked out as relevant in order to offer a realistic analysis, whilst other things are ignored. This can be seen in the odd conception of the status of EU law within the UK, even if the majority have somehow persuaded themselves that their (novel and incoherent) account is legally sound. It is especially evident in the majority's assertions about the importance of withdrawal and the importance of Parliament rather than the Government making a decision of this magnitude. What about the electorate itself, which Parliament had invited to decide the *question* by way of the referendum established by the European Union Referendum Act 2015? The point is not that that Act authorises the triggering of Article 50. It does not. But the referendum was the means that Parliament chose to settle the question of whether or not to withdraw.[91] In proposing to trigger Article 50 the executive acted in reliance on the electorate's decision, which rather upends the Court's framing of the question as whether Parliament or Government should decide. Lastly, those disappointed claimants who relied on the devolution settlements might reasonably ask why constitutional realism is good for some claimants but not for them.[92] In short, the Court's asymmetric constitutional realism is a major problem: the preferences and dispositions of some are privileged by the judgment.[93]

---

[90] For discussion of other recent examples, see JNE Varuhas, 'Judicial Capture of Political Accountability', *Judicial Power Project* (6 June 2016).

[91] *Miller* (n 1), [214]. As Lord Reed put it, 'in enacting the 2015 Act, Parliament considered withdrawal from the EU, and made the holding of a referendum part of the process of taking the decision under article 50(1). It laid down no further role for itself in that process'.

[92] *Miller* involved an appeal not only from the Divisional Court of the High Court of England and Wales, but also from a series of cases in Northern Ireland. McCrudden and Halberstam offer a scorching critique of how the Supreme Court handled the legal issues arising from the latter cases. Part of their critique relates to the Court's failure to appreciate (what they regard as) the reality of the constitutional nature of the devolution arrangements, especially (although not exclusively) as concerns Northern Ireland: McCrudden and Halberstam (n 84).

[93] For a somewhat similar discussion framed in terms of the majority's inconsistent reliance on 'form and 'substance', see P Daly, '*Miller*: Legal and Political Fault Lines' [2017] *PL* (Brexit Special Issue)

Timothy Endicott, as stern a critic of the judgment as any, speculates about whether it might nevertheless be possible to rationalise *Miller* as a justified constitutional innovation, like others before it.[94] There have been times in the UK's long constitutional tradition after all when the courts have helped to secure constitutional principle by changing the law of the constitution. This was not such a time (and indeed the claimants and judges disavow any such ambition, insisting that it was simply application of settled law). Courts ought not to be innovating in this way. Recall what innovation in a high-stake and politically salient case involves: exposure to fierce (and likely justified) political criticism for departing from settled law. In any case, as Endicott points out, the judgment serves no grand principle. It is at best an exercise in formality, in which courts demand sanctification of a major decision. Requiring an Act of Parliament before Article 50 is triggered does not correct a shortcoming in our constitutional arrangements, and stands in poor comparison to the great cases of earlier times.

Still, the echo of history is at work in the judgment. Writing shortly after the Divisional Court's decision, one of us observed that

> [t]he temptation for the Justices will be to abandon the law under the guise of apparent continuity with constitutional history. This whole litigation has been an exercise in tempting the courts. There are reasons to hope that in the end a majority will resist the temptation.[95]

The claimants—and their many supporters in the press, Bar and academy—played up the opportunity for the courts at a time of supposed constitutional crisis to stand with their illustrious forebears, once again defying executive abuses to vindicate the privileges of Parliament, not to mention the doctrine of parliamentary sovereignty. The 'stubborn stain theory' of executive power, as Endicott terms it,[96] is much in evidence, where the executive is taken to be the wicked stepmother of the constitution, with any and all restrictions imposed on it being to the good.[97] However, it flatters the Justices to present them as a bench of latter-day Edward Cokes resisting King James. References in public debate to the 'ancient'

73, 74 ('on the juridical effect of triggering art 50, substance trumped form, but when it came to the impact of triggering art 50 on the devolution arrangements, form trumped substance; the "constitutional" nature of the [ECA] weighed heavily in the balance, but other constitutional innovations, such as referendums and devolution, exerted next to no weight at all').

[94] T Endicott, 'Gina Miller's Case and the Principles of Our Constitution' (2017) 8 *UK Supreme Court Yearbook* 259.

[95] R Ekins, 'A guide to the Supreme Court justices', *Spectator* (3 December 2016).

[96] T Endicott, 'The Stubborn Stain Theory of Executive Power: From Magna Cara to *Miller*', *Judicial Power Project* (7 September 2016).

[97] Emblematic of the hold of 'the stubborn stain' theory is Douglas-Scott's bemused query about how the judgment in *Miller* can be thought to be a judicial power-grab if it does not undermine legislation or take power from the legislature. The answer is that the Court has blocked the Government from exercising its lawful powers, and thus delivering on its undertaking to the electorate. See Douglas-Scott (n 44), 3.

royal prerogative, complete with clanking chains, were a parody of the true state of affairs. The Government was not arbitrary, imperious or unaccountable, and the prerogative power to conduct foreign policy is neither mysterious nor disreputable. Indeed, in this context, the Government was acting in pursuit of the constitutional obligation entailed by the referendum, and stands in favourable contrast to the MPs, peers and others who contemplated defying its outcome. As we explained earlier, the *Miller* litigation was designed to disrupt, if only through delay, the Government's intention to honour the undertaking (which was Parliament's as much as the Government's) to voters to give effect to their decision that the UK should leave the EU.

The Supreme Court's eventual judgment was not unexpected, and of course explains the reasons on which it is based. Our preceding commentary suggests how that reasoning should be understood. However, more can be said about how the Court ended up deciding as it did, and this reflection is useful in evaluating the judgment and in determining what its legacy for our constitution may be. We have already noted that the litigation arose in the febrile atmosphere after the referendum, in which an enraged minority (disproportionately represented in the media, the law and the academy) flailed about in desperate search of a way to spike the referendum's guns. Unsurprisingly, the litigation served as a lightning-rod (and a reservoir of hope) for efforts to stop Brexit in its tracks. Its success seemed to offer the only salient, if far-fetched, means so to do. Some of the Justices might have shared these hopes, but we very much doubt that they ruled against the Government in order to stop Brexit (not least since it was clear that this was a forlorn hope when—coincident with the third day of the oral hearing before the Supreme Court—MPs adopted a resolution backing withdrawal by 448 to 75). But some of them might have viewed a defeat for the Government as a salutary blow against the Brexiteers, exposing their alleged hypocrisy in abandoning parliamentary sovereignty when convenient. They may also have shared the perception that the UK constitution was in (or on the precipice of a) crisis. Here, the vehement media criticism of the Divisional Court's judgment, together with the frenzied overreaction of the legal community to the Lord Chancellor's supposed failure to respond adequately to it,[98] was likely relevant in stiffening the resolve of the Justices to defend their colleagues and defy the rabble-rousers. Similarly, the legal reaction to the substance of the Divisional Court's judgment is important as well, for many lawyers and commentators began to speak of the judgment as irrefutable, and to characterise the Government's appeal as hopeless. If the Divisional Court had ruled against the claimants it would have been more difficult for the Supreme Court to go astray. Finally, the resolution of the Commons that coincided with the hearing suggested that defeat in the Supreme Court would be unlikely to frustrate the triggering of Article 50, since Ministers would be able to secure fresh

---

[98] See generally G Gee, 'A Tale of Two Constitutional Duties: Liz Truss, Lady Hale and *Miller*', *Judicial Power Project* (28 November 2016).

legislation if need be. This lowered the political salience of the litigation, which may have made the Court less responsible in ruling that legislation was required.[99]

VI. Notes on the Next 'Crisis'

The Supreme Court was wrong to rule that the Government had no legal power to trigger Article 50. However, the Government accepted the Court's ruling with no public fuss, and moved swiftly to introduce a Bill in Parliament. The Bill was narrowly cast, comprising only two sections that empowered the Prime Minister to give notice to the EU under Article 50 and made clear that this power was not subject to any other enactment.[100] The resulting Act in one sense reversed the outcome of *Miller*, restoring the antecedent legal position in which the Government had the authority to trigger Article 50. Of course one can equally say that the Act could not and did not reverse *Miller*, for the whole point of that judgment (in law) was to hold that an Act was required, and the judgment did not specify the form legislation would have to take to authorise withdrawal. The narrowness of the European Union (Notification of Withdrawal) Act 2017 disappointed many, not least those who hoped that, duly empowered, Parliament would refuse to support withdrawal, or at least impose onerous preconditions and/or make provision for a second referendum. Yet despite some lawyers hinting otherwise,[101] it would have been outrageous, and unlawful, for the Supreme Court to dictate to Parliament the terms on which it had to proceed to manifest an intention to authorise the Government to begin withdrawal.

Still, the Supreme Court's judgment in *Miller* had more constitutional significance than its swift legislative disposition might imply. It changed the nature of the exchange between the Government, Lords and Commons, forcing it to take the form of deliberation about a bill, rather than a more open-ended debate culminating in a resolution. Many amendments were moved by MPs and peers, including some wrecking amendments. The Commons decisively supported a narrowly cast bill, and did so in the face of initial resistance from the House of Lords. Indeed, the main implication of *Miller*, as was clear throughout the litigation, was the empowerment of the Lords, making its assent necessary for Article 50 to be triggered and

---

[99] On our reading, the Court was reckless when disposing of the central question in *Miller*, when deciding whether legislation was required to authorise the initiation of the Article 50 process, but much more responsible in its treatment of the potentially explosive devolution claims.

[100] European Union (Notification of Withdrawal) Act 2017, s 1(2).

[101] In an exceptionally ill-advised comment shortly after the Divisional Court's judgment and when it was known that the Government intended to appeal to the Supreme Court, Lady Hale had suggested in the context of the *Miller* litigation that '[a]nother question is whether it would be enough for a simple Act of Parliament to authorise the government to give notice, or whether it would have to be a comprehensive replacement for the 1972 Act'. This question had not featured in the Divisional Court's judgment or the claimants' submissions. Lady Hale (n 87), 12.

giving peers the power to delay withdrawal by up to a year, if the Parliament Acts 1911 and 1949 had to be invoked. The Commons kept faith with the resolution of 7 December and with the outcome of the referendum, and was unwilling to accept amendments proposed by the Lords—and in the end the Lords too assented. Seen in light of these developments, the outcome of the *Miller* litigation was in a sense happy. The Court's judgment introduced merely the possibility, not the reality, of delay or frustration of withdrawal from the EU. The judgment might easily have been received in a very different temper, with the electorate asking why the Court was lending its authority to a scheme to keep the UK within the EU. (It is likely that the fact that three judges dissented helped minimise damage to the Court's reputation.) The Court acted wrongly, but otherwise the constitution worked: the Government responded swiftly, the Commons was politically responsible, and the Lords acknowledged the primacy of the Commons. If the Lords and the Commons had acted otherwise, the judgment would have been momentous and might very well have invited withering (and justified) political criticism, possibly culminating in a genuine crisis. Something similar can be said for the General Election that took place a few months later, in which the overwhelming majority of the newly returned House of Commons were elected on manifesto commitments to honour the referendum, to withdraw from the EU and to bring free movement to an end. These political dynamics further confirm, if there was any doubt, the shallowness of all of the loose talk about a constitutional crisis and the subversion of parliamentary sovereignty. Rather, a referendum for which Parliament made provision in 2015 is being taken seriously by the UK's representative institutions and electors.

However, there is a sting in the tail. The dynamics unleashed in the post-referendum elite cry of rage, and from which the *Miller* litigation emerged, have not altogether receded. Lawyers continue to threaten all manner of outlandish lawsuits when the twists and turns of parliamentary and electoral politics seem to them inauspicious. Strictly speaking, the various lawsuits could be viewed as lawyers advising clients on questions put to them, and in so doing merely opining on the merits of possible litigation. This analysis stretches credulity. Much (and perhaps most) of the legal posturing is politically motivated, and many (and perhaps most) of the prominent lawyers involved are willing participants in this dynamic, initiating (threats of) litigation, coordinating various legal proceedings, and acting pro bono or for reduced fees in exchange for political access and impact. The strategic threat of litigation is constitutionally problematic. Consider the so-called 'Three Knights' Opinion', published by eminent lawyers in February 2017 while the Bill providing for notification under Article 50 was under consideration.[102] The Opinion asserts that the Bill then before Parliament was incapable of authorising the UK's withdrawal from the EU as a matter of UK law. The argument was

---

[102] D Edward, F Jacobs, J Lever, H Mountfield and G Facenna, 'Opinion in the Matter of Article 50 of the Treaty on European Union' (10 February 2017), available at https://www.bindmans.com/uploads/files/documents/Final_Article_50_Opinion_10.2.17.pdf.

two-fold: first, the Bill did not specify which rights were to be abrogated and, therefore, under the principle of legality, it should not be interpreted to bring to an end the effect of any EU legal rights in UK law; second, and more fundamentally, no statute could authorise withdrawal at this stage because the shape of any UK–EU deal was unknown and Parliament must legislate expressly to authorise the terms of any withdrawal. Neither limb to the Opinion is at all persuasive. The 2017 Act, as it now is, clearly authorised Article 50 to be invoked, as it subsequently was in March 2017, and in due course the EU Treaties will cease to have effect in the UK. The Opinion seriously misconstrues the principle of legality (as, in quite a different way, did the majority in *Miller*), posits an absurd reading of Parliament's intention in enacting the 2017 Bill and is flatly at odds with the premise of *Miller* that triggering Article 50 will in due course lead to the termination of EU legal rights. So the Opinion is hopeless, despite the eminence of its authors, and should be rejected.[103] Yet it is nonetheless being deployed in parliamentary politics, with some MPs and others warning the Government, and other MPs, of the risks of a replay of *Miller* if the right type of legislation is not forthcoming.

In a recent article, Helen Mountfield QC (one of the authors of the Opinion, who was also one of the barristers in *Miller*) reflected on other legal consequences of the judgment.[104] She speculates about the likelihood of legal challenges to the exercise of the prerogative to withdraw from the ECHR or to commit the UK to international treaties that call for domestic legal change.[105] These would be far-reaching changes to our constitutional arrangements. They are not spelled out in *Miller*, which might very well be limited, on its own terms, to the specific context of EU law's reception. The judicially-divined principle on which the judgment is grounded—the constitutional importance of withdrawal from the EU—is at best uncertain. Mountfield is doubtless right that *Miller* encourages future litigation. Whether such litigation would succeed may depend on the extent to which the Bar, bench and academy remain in a state of alarm, and whether the shortcomings of the majority's reasoning in *Miller* are frankly acknowledged, not least by the legal community itself. However, the process of withdrawal from the EU is far from straightforward, and the legal and political culture that gave rise to the *Miller* litigation and the Supreme Court judgment may not be spent. In which case, there is a real risk that the post-referendum dynamics may run and run, with lawyers leveraging judicial process for political advantage and the courts failing to heed Lord Reed's sage admonition that 'the legalisation of political issues is not

[103] For critiques of the Opinion, see M Elliott, '"The Three Knight's Opinion": A Response', *Public Law for Everyone* (17 February 2017); and M Barczentewicz, 'The Principle of Legality and EU-Withdrawal Statute', *UKCLA Blog* (21 February 2017), available at https://ukconstitutionallaw.org/.

[104] H Mountfield, 'Beyond Brexit: What does Miller Mean for the UK's Power to Make and Break International Obligations?' (2017) 22 *Judicial Review* 143.

[105] See also G Phillipson and A L Young, 'Would Use of the Prerogative to Denounce the ECHR "Frustrate" the Human Rights Act? Lessons from *Miller*' [2017] *PL* (Brexit Special Issue) 150.

always constitutionally appropriate, and may be fraught with risk, not least for the judiciary'.[106]

VII. Conclusion

There was nothing close to a constitutional crisis in the sequence of decisions by which Parliament provided for a referendum on membership of the EU, the electorate voted for withdrawal, and the Government undertook to trigger Article 50 and begin the process of leaving the EU. The constitution is open to radical politics and often relies on political discipline, rather than legal disability, to restrain abuse of power. For some, one of the primary virtues of EU membership has been precisely to overlay this scheme with hard-edged legal control. Many lawyers and others were dismayed by the way in which the traditional constitutional scheme (with its latent potential for radical politics) was being used to unpick the UK's membership of the EU. The *Miller* litigation is an episode in the politics of Brexit, part of an elite-led rearguard action waged against implementation of the referendum. The majority's judgment cannot be properly understood apart from the political character and context of the litigation, and the related crisis of confidence in our constitutional order on the part of many in public life.[107] The judgment did not itself cause a crisis, but it might easily have provoked serious and sustained tensions if the political context had been different. Indeed, the mostly calm and patient reaction of Ministers and other elected politicians to the legal proceedings in *Miller* is commendable, and a sharp contrast with the post-referendum panic of many others in politics, the legal profession and the academy. Judges are on safe ground when they hew close to the law; when they depart from law, or extend it in novel ways, they expose themselves to political criticism. The Supreme Court's judgment was very weak and should be remembered as such. Misunderstanding of and lack of respect for the political constitution is at the heart of *Miller*. If judges and others fail to recognise these shortcomings we may be doomed to witness further attempts to misuse the law to gain advantage in the political process.

---

[106] *Miller* (n 1), 240.
[107] For a markedly different account of the political character of the *Miller* litigation that defends the majority's judgment in what is depicted as a 'landmark' case, see P Craig, 'Epilogue: *Miller*, the Legislature and the Executive' in S Juss and M Sunkin (eds), *Landmark Cases in Public Law* (Oxford, Hart Publishing, 2017) 305.

12

Miller and the Future of Constitutional Adjudication

ALISON L YOUNG*

It is hard to deny that the *Miller* decision raised the profile of constitutional adjudication in the United Kingdom (UK). Not only did it merit consideration by the then full set of 11 Justices of the Supreme Court, but it prompted global as well as national media coverage. This was combined with the use of crowd-sourcing to fund some of the applicants, in addition to coverage in blog posts, which were perused by the general public in addition to their usual academic audience. This chapter is not the place to discuss the merits of this coverage. Rather, it asks a deeper question as to the place of the *Miller* decision as regards the role of the judiciary in the UK constitution. In particular, it looks at the extent to which the majority of the Supreme Court adopted a different approach to legal reasoning, focusing in particular on the extent to which this provides further evidence to support the growing perception that courts are not just guardians of the law, but are also guardians of the constitution.[1]

This chapter will argue that the *Miller* decision provides evidence of the adoption of a more constitutional approach to adjudication. This can be seen, in particular, in the adoption by the majority of a more 'fundamental' or 'realistic' approach to statutory interpretation, in the reference by the majority to broad constitutional principles and in the way in which the Court was willing to adopt a more abstract form of constitutional reasoning, both through holding a judicial

* The author would like to thank Gavin Phillipson for comments on an earlier draft.
[1] See, eg, Lady Hale, 'The Supreme Court: Guardians of the Constitution' (9 November 2016), available at https://www.supremecourt.uk/docs/speech-161109.pdf, and 'The United Kingdom Constitution on the Move' (7 July 2017) available at https://www.supremecourt.uk/docs/speech-170707.pdf; Lord Neuberger, 'The UK Constitutional Settlement and the Role of the UK Supreme Court' (10 October 2014), available at https://www.supremecourt.uk/docs/speech-141010.pdf, and 'The constitutional role of the Supreme Court in the context of devolution in the UK' (14 October 2016), available at https://www.supremecourt.uk/docs/speech-161014.pdf, and 'The Role of the Supreme Court Seven Years on—Lessons Learnt' (21 November 2016), available at https://www.supreme-court.uk/docs/speech-161121.pdf; Lord Mance, 'The Role of Judges in a Representative Democracy' (24 February 2017), available at https://www.supremecourt.uk/docs/speech-170224.pdf.

review hearing before a definitive decision had been made and through its assessment of the assumptions surrounding the expressed will of the Government to use the prerogative to trigger Article 50.[2] However, it is important to recognise both that this approach is not novel and that the decision of the majority respected the division of power between the legislature and the judiciary. This was illustrated both in the care the Supreme Court took when determining the legal question to be answered by the Court and in the way in which the Court analysed the Sewel Convention.

Nevertheless, this chapter does recognise the difficulties that arise as the Supreme Court takes on the role of a constitutional court and the Justices of the Supreme Court become guardians not just of the law, but also of the constitution. This is not to argue that the Justices of the Supreme Court are acting in an illegitimate manner either more generally, or specifically in the *Miller* decision. Rather, this chapter will argue that more justification should have been provided for why the majority adopted their approach in *Miller*, focusing more specifically upon the impact of the constitutional nature of the decision in question and, more particularly, how the issues in *Miller* were more akin to issues of abstract constitutional review. It will be argued that a better means of resolving such issues in the future would be either to use section 4 of the Judicial Committee Act 1833, or to develop a similar reference procedure to the Supreme Court.

The first section of the chapter discusses the adoption by the majority of the Supreme Court of a 'fundamental' or 'realistic' reading of the European Communities Act 1972 ('ECA'). It will argue that it is difficult to determine precisely what the majority meant by their use of these terms. However, the best interpretation would appear to be that the majority were more concerned with providing an interpretation of the impact of the ECA as this would be understood by those who have rights and obligations under European Union (EU) law on which they rely on a regular basis, as opposed to providing a more technical or legalistic account of the impact of the Act. There would also appear to be a difference of emphasis of distinct aspects of the constitution between the opinions of the majority and the minority. Whilst the terminology may appear to be new, the approach is not. Moreover, the decision in *Miller* has less of an impact on the perceived modification of the role of the judiciary, given that statutory interpretation is used in this case not to determine the content of the law, but to determine how a legal principle should apply to a set of circumstances when those circumstances include the interpretation of legislation.

---

[2] In response to the High Court judgment, I argued that there was evidence of a distinction between 'form' and 'substance', see AL Young, 'R *(Miller) v The Secretary of State for Exiting the European Union* [2016] EWHC 2768 (Admin): Constitutional Adjudication: Reality over Legality?', *UKCLA Blog* (9 November 2016), available at https://ukconstitutionallaw.org/. See also P Daly, *Miller*: Legal and Political Fault Lines' [2017] *PL* (November Supplement Brexit Special Extra Issue) 73.

The second section will examine the argument that the Supreme Court in *Miller* reasoned in a different manner, adopting a more deductive as opposed to inductive approach, drawing on broad constitutional principles rather than providing a close analysis of a series of earlier cases, developing the law in an incremental manner. The section will argue that, whilst the Supreme Court in *Miller* may have adopted an approach that is relatively more deductive than inductive when developing the principle that major constitutional change should be enacted through legislation as opposed to Ministerial order, this approach is similar to that adopted in other cases of the House of Lords or the Supreme Court that have had to reason more from first principles given the relative lack of prior authority. Moreover, this approach may be more justified when the decision is taken by a larger as opposed to smaller panel in the Supreme Court.

The third section investigates the extent to which *Miller* can be understood as a form of 'moot' constitutional issue, arising before a decision is made, and whether this represents a novel approach to constitutional litigation. It will argue that whilst there is a growing number of challenges that are brought at an earlier stage of the decision-making process of the administration, these challenges are by no means novel. In addition, it will argue that although this may mean that courts have to take account of possible future courses of action, the approach of the majority in *Miller* is best understood as an adoption of a constitutional precautionary principle, where courts err on the side of caution and declare an action unlawful if it is possible that illegality could arise in the future when the constitutional consequences of this illegality are particularly high.

The last section examines how the Supreme Court's approach to devolution was based upon the adoption of a strong division between 'law' and 'politics', suggesting that the Court was less rather than more willing to adopt a 'fundamental' or 'realistic' approach to constitutional adjudication. The conclusion will analyse whether a better outcome could have been reached had the Supreme Court been able to provide a pre-emptive constitutional opinion on the existence of the prerogative power, rather than providing a legal judgment.

I. A 'Fundamental' or 'Realistic' Approach to the European Communities Act 1972

In one sense, of course, it can be said that the 1972 Act is the source of EU law, in that, without that Act, EU law would have no domestic status. But in a more fundamental sense and, we consider, a more realistic sense, where EU law applies in the United Kingdom, it is the EU institutions which are the relevant source of that law.[3]

---

[3] *R (Miller) v Secretary of State for Exiting the European Union* [2017] UKSC 5, [61].

The paragraph cited above provides the clearest evidence of the adoption by the majority of the Supreme Court of a different approach to the interpretation of legislation, adopting a 'fundamental' or 'realistic' interpretation of the ECA. This would appear to be a novel approach to statutory interpretation, suggesting a radical change in departure for the Supreme Court when dealing with constitutional adjudication. However, when we investigate the differences between the reasoning of the majority and the minority, it is hard to regard the majority as adopting a wholly novel approach to statutory interpretation. Although the use of the words 'fundamental' and 'realistic' may be novel, their approach is similar to that adopted in other constitutional cases. Moreover, to the extent that there is any difference in approach, it is justified given the novel situation which arose in *Miller*.

In order to explain how the approach of the majority has made little, if any, change to the approach of courts to constitutional adjudication, we need to determine what is meant by interpreting legislation in a 'fundamental' or 'realistic' sense. The provision over which the majority and minority divided is section 2(1) of the ECA, which states:

> All such rights, powers, liabilities, obligations and restrictions from time to time created or arising by or under the Treaties, and all such remedies and procedures from time to time provided for by or under the Treaties, as in accordance with the Treaties are without further enactment to be given effect or used in the United Kingdom shall be recognised and available in law, and be enforced, allowed and followed accordingly ...[4]

Lord Reed regarded this as being conditional in structure—that is, it took the following form:

> All such [*members of a specified category*] as [*satisfy a specified condition*] shall be [*dealt win in accordance with a specified requirement*].[5]

As applied to section 2(1), the 'members of a specific category' are the rights, powers, liabilities and obligations created 'from time to time' by the Treaties, along with their corresponding remedies and procedures, which also arise 'from time to time'.[6] These rights and liabilities are 'to be recognised and available in law',[7] provided that they 'satisfy a specified condition'—that these rights, powers, liabilities and obligations are to be given legal effect without further legal enactment, in accordance with the Treaties.[8] In short, the only EU rights, powers, obligations and liabilities that are to be given effect in UK law are those arising from the EU Treaties to which the UK has adhered. According to Lord Reed's interpretation, these Treaties vary 'from time to time' according to an exercise of prerogative

---

[4] ECA, s 2(1).
[5] *Miller* (n 3), [184] (original emphasis).
[6] ibid, [186].
[7] ibid, [188].
[8] ibid, [189].

powers in relation to EU Treaties. Consequently, '[i]f the Treaties do not apply to the UK, then there are no rights, powers and so forth which, in accordance with the Treaties, are to be given legal effect in the UK'.[9] If the prerogative is used to withdraw the UK from the EU, this does not remove domestic rights or alter domestic law. Rather, the legislation continues to incorporate the UK's obligations under EU law as they arise 'from time to time'. The difference is that, post Brexit, the rights, powers, liabilities and obligations will have changed from those in place at the time prior to Brexit. They will be removed if the UK leaves with no withdrawal agreement in place, or be replaced with whatever rights, powers, liabilities and obligations emerge from the withdrawal agreement between the UK and the EU.

It is important to recognise that when reaching the opposite conclusion, the majority of the Supreme Court did not reject the 'ambulatory' nature of section 2(1), with its recognition that Treaty obligations will modify from time to time.[10] The majority also did not conclude that *all* EU law rights and obligations are incorporated into domestic law. The ECA only incorporates those rights, obligations, powers and liabilities that are 'capable of being given effect' in the UK, or which can be 'used' or 'enjoyed' in the UK. That is those which, as a matter of EU law, have 'direct effect', meaning that they are capable of creating rights and obligations in UK law without any further means of implementation by UK law.[11] Section 2(1) was required in order to ensure that the UK could adhere to its obligations under EU law, including the ability to ensure that, as these obligations were modified through acts of the EU institutions, these provisions could become part of domestic law. Where disagreement arose was as to whether the wording of section 2(1) necessarily included the implication that the prerogative could be used to withdraw the UK from the EU. For the majority, this was not the case. Section 2(1) was intended to enable the UK to uphold its international obligations of EU membership.[12] It was not intended to enable the prerogative to be used to withdraw the UK from its international law obligations, given that this would incur a large constitutional change, modifying the structure of the UK constitution by removing a source of law.[13]

Whilst we can set out the difference in approach between the majority and the minority, it can be difficult to pinpoint precisely what is meant by the 'fundamental' or 'realistic' sense in which the ECA is being interpreted. There are at least three possible interpretations, none of which appears to be wholly persuasive. First, it could be argued that a 'fundamental' or 'realistic' interpretation is not concerned

---

[9] ibid, [191].

[10] ibid, [74]–[76].

[11] ibid, [76].

[12] See G Phillipson, 'EU Law as an Agent of National Constitutional Change: Miller v Secretary of State for Exiting the European Union' [2017] *Yearbook of European Law* 1, 17.

[13] Miller (n 3), [79]–[81].

with textual analysis. Whilst Lord Reed adopts an approach that pays close attention to the specific wording of section 2(1), the approach taken by the majority is
more 'realistic' as it focuses less specifically on the text of section 2(1). However,
this is difficult to square with other elements of the approach of the majority of
the Supreme Court. Although Lord Reed focuses on the wording of section 2(1),
there is nothing specific in the wording of this section that sets out its conditional
nature as expressed by Lord Reed. This is Lord Reed's restructuring of the provisions of the legislation in order to support his interpretation of the provision. The
majority interpret section 2(1) differently not because they fail to focus on the
wording of section 2(1), but because they interpret its provisions in a dissimilar
manner.[14]

Nor is it the case that the majority do not pay close attention to the specific
wording of section 2(1). The phrase 'from time to time' is used to characterise
'rights, powers, liabilities, obligations and restrictions' that are 'created by or arising under the Treaties' and 'remedies and procedures' that are 'provided for by or
under the Treaties'. For the majority, this refers to EU law, created by the EU institutions, whose provisions modify from time to time. There is no specific reference
to 'Treaties' that are provided for 'from time to time'. Instead, the list of 'Treaties'
is found in section 1(2) of the ECA, with section 1(3) of the Act setting down how
new Treaties are to be added to the list of Treaties found in section 1(2).[15]

Second, it could be argued that a 'realistic' or 'fundamental' interpretation is
one that pays more attention to the purpose of legislation, perhaps doing so in
a more abstract manner. As such, we would expect to see evidence in *Miller* of
the majority's referring to the purposes of the ECA, with Lord Reed paying less
attention to purpose. However, this is not the case. Lord Reed does examine the
purpose of section 2(1), characterising it as according direct effect to provisions
of EU law—that is, enabling those provisions which have direct effect to be relied
upon in national courts, without the need for further implementation measures
from the UK. This is incompatible with the UK's adoption of dualism. Section 2(1)
resolves this conundrum.[16] More generally, the ECA, and section 2(1) in particular, is designed to ensure that the UK adheres to its international obligations,
now including its international obligations under EU law; 'the 1972 Act creates a
scheme under which the effect given to EU law in domestic law exactly matches
the UK's international obligations, whatever they may be'.[17]

The majority also focus on the purpose of the ECA. Where the difference lies
is in the assessment of that purpose. For the majority, the ECA does not just 'give
effect to treaties by prescribing the content of domestic law in the areas covered

---

[14] Phillipson (n 12), 18–21, reaches the same conclusion, reinforcing this through an analysis of
Lord Reed's interpretation of the European Parliamentary Act 2002.

[15] *Miller* (n 3), [84].

[16] ibid, [182]–[183].

[17] ibid, [189].

by them'.[18] Rather, the ECA also 'authorises a dynamic process by which, without further primary legislation … EU law not only becomes a source of UK law, but actually takes precedence over all domestic sources of UK law, including statutes'.[19] Its purpose is not only to adhere to the UK's international law obligations, but also to facilitate a constitutional change, adding a new source of law that, in certain circumstances and subject to certain conditions, takes precedence over UK law, including primary legislation.

This analysis naturally leads on to the third possible way of defining a 'fundamental' or 'realistic' interpretation; an interpretation that pays greater regard to background constitutional principles. As such, we would expect the reasoning of the majority to contain multiple references to constitutional principles, with less attention being paid to constitutional principles by the minority. The reasoning of the majority is shot through with references to the constitutional impact of the ECA as creating a new source of law, as well as to the Act's possessing a 'constitutional character'.[20] The majority are also careful to pay attention to the deeper underlying principles of the constitution, particularly parliamentary sovereignty,[21] which the Court sees as reflected in the UK's dualist approach to international law, in addition to underpinning the control over prerogative powers.[22] Lord Reed, in his dissent, is also clear in his acceptance of 'the importance in our constitutional law of the principle of Parliamentary supremacy',[23] and of the UK's dualist approach to international law.[24] If a difference in reasoning occurs, it is not because there is a greater or lesser reference to fundamental principles of the constitution, or even to the relative weight of these principles, rather it lies in how these principles influence the interpretation of the ECA.

Having rejected these possible explanations of what it means to adopt a 'realistic' or 'fundamental' approach to determining the meaning of the ECA, one may be forgiven for thinking that the reference to these terms does nothing to distinguish the approach adopted by the majority from that of the minority, let alone justify the adoption of a more or less 'realistic' or 'fundamental' reading of the ECA. The distinction is subtle, and is really one of emphasis. If the majority is looking to a 'fundamental' sense of the Act, it is because it is focusing more on understanding the constitutional importance and impact of the Act. Whilst the Act may have been intended to ensure that the UK adhered to its obligations under EU law, the reality of membership of the EU, as understood from the perspective of UK citizens subject to obligations, rights, powers and immunities under EU

---

[18] ibid, [60].

[19] ibid.

[20] ibid, [67]. For a further discussion of the constitutional character of the Act, see the contribution of Sir John Laws in ch 9 of this volume.

[21] *Miller* (n 3), [43]–[59].

[22] ibid.

[23] ibid, [177].

[24] ibid, [182]–[184].

law, is reflected in the understanding of viewing EU law as a distinct source of law, made by the EU institutions, whose provisions flowed into the UK through the pipeline of the ECA. Whilst the wording of the Act may suggest that it can be read as providing for EU law rights, conditional on the scope of those rights as determined by the exercise of prerogative powers to join and leave EU Treaties, this fails to consider the real impact of the Act. For the average individual not versed in the intricacies of EU law and the ECA, EU law provides a separate set of rights and powers, which will be removed upon withdrawal, unless measures are taken to provide for a distinct incorporation of these provisions into UK law. The majority adopt a 'realistic' approach through adopting the perspective of that well-known legal fiction—the man, or woman, on the Clapham omnibus. The minority focus more on the technical, legal mechanisms.[25]

Having already recognised that it may be difficult to pinpoint what is meant by adopting a 'realistic', and especially a 'fundamental' reading of the ECA, it becomes equally difficult to predict the extent to which this reading of legislation has changed existing approaches to the interpretation of legislation—of a constitutional nature or otherwise[26]—and how far this approach will be adopted in future. Whilst the reference to 'realistic' or 'fundamental' senses of legislation may be novel, there are examples of cases where the Supreme Court has adopted a reading of legislation, based on background constitutional principles, which could be regarded as placing more emphasis on background principles than on textual requirements. This is found in particular where courts apply the principle of legality, which is used to read down broad legislative provisions to ensure that they do not contravene fundamental constitutional principles. Courts presume that Parliament would not wish to legislate contrary to fundamental principles of the common law unless it specifically, clearly and precisely expressed its intention to do so. General words granting broad powers are insufficient to restrict, or grant the power to restrict, fundamental principles of the common law.[27] A similar principle applies to the interpretation of Henry VIII clauses, which empower the executive to enact measures that modify or amend primary legislation. The broader the scope of the power, the more likely it is that the courts will find that an exercise of the power according to the literal meaning of the Henry VIII clause was nevertheless not authorised by the legislature, particularly as regards the use of a Henry VIII clause to contradict a fundamental principle of the common law.[28]

---

[25] Phillipson (n 12), 12–14. See also T Poole, 'Devotion to Legalism: On the Brexit Case' (2017) 80 *MLR* 696.

[26] For a more detailed discussion of this issue, see the contribution of Sir John Laws in ch 9 of this volume.

[27] *R v Secretary of State for the Home Department, ex parte Leech* [1999] QB 198; *Pierson v Secretary of State for the Home Department* [1998] AC 549; *R v Secretary of State for the Home Department, ex parte Simms* [2000] 2 AC 115; *Ahmed v Her Majesty's Treasury* [2010] UKSC 2, [2010] 2 AC 534; *R (Unison) v Lord Chancellor* [2017] UKSC 51, [2017] 3 WLR 409.

[28] *R (Public Law Project) v Lord Chancellor* [2016] UKSC 39, [2016] AC 153; *R (Ingenious Media) v Revenue and Customs Commissioners* [2016] UKSC 54, [2016] 1 WLR 4164; and *Miller* (n 3), [68].

Given these other principles of interpretation, which emphasise the importance of background constitutional principles, it is difficult to see the approach adopted in *Miller* as one that is either wholly novel, or which goes beyond an emerging trend. This is particularly true when we examine one of the most striking examples of the application of the principle of legality, the judgment of Lord Neuberger, with the agreement of Lords Kerr and Reed, in *R (Evans) v Attorney-General*.[29] One of the issues arising for the Supreme Court was the interpretation of section 53 of the Freedom of Information Act 2000, which empowered certain individuals—in this instance the Attorney-General—to override an enforcement notice issued under the Freedom of Information Act through issuing a certificate confirming that the individual had on 'reasonable grounds' concluded that there was no requirement to disclose this information. Lord Neuberger concluded that this provision should be read in line with background constitutional principles, in this instance two aspects of the rule of law. First, that a court decision is binding between the parties and cannot be reversed by executive order and, second, that executive decisions should be subject to judicial review.[30] By issuing a certificate in *Evans*, the Attorney-General was reversing the decision of the Upper Tribunal, which was legally recognised as having the same status as the High Court. As such, the broad provision of 'reasonable grounds' in section 53 should be interpreted more narrowly, to ensure the maintenance of background constitutional principles, and could not be equated to a general power to issue a certificate to reverse the decision whenever the executive takes an opposite view to that reached by the Upper Tribunal.[31] Rather, 'reasonable grounds' would only exist when there was a 'material change of circumstances since the tribunal decision', or where 'the decision of the tribunal was demonstrably flawed in fact or in law'.[32]

Lord Neuberger did not give the only judgment in the case. Lord Mance, with the agreement of Lady Hale, reached the same outcome as Lord Neuberger, but for different reasons. He would have allowed the Attorney-General to reverse the decision of the Upper Tribunal if he had been able to provide reasons for the 'reasonable grounds' for reversing the decision, subject to these reasons withstanding judicial scrutiny. However, Lord Mance concluded that the reasons provided by the Attorney-General were insufficient.[33] Lord Hughes, with the agreement of Lord Wilson, dissented, concluding that it was not possible to read section 53 in the manner suggested by either Lord Neuberger or Lord Mance, as the plain words

---

[29] *R (Evans) v Attorney-General* [2015] UKSC 21, [2015] 2 WLR 813.
[30] ibid, [52].
[31] ibid, [59] and [69]–[70].
[32] ibid, [71].
[33] Recently, the Court of Appeal regarded the opinion of Lord Mance as the ratio to be followed by lower courts in *Lukasz Roszkowski v Secretary of State for the Home Department* [2017] EWCA Civ 1893. See R Craig, 'The Fall Out from *Evans*: Positioning *Roszkowski* and *Privacy International* in a Post-*Evans* Constitutional Landscape', *UKCLA Blog* (8 and 9 December 2017), available at https://ukconstitution-allaw.org/.

of the legislation clearly would permit the executive to override the decision of the tribunal when the executive had reasonable grounds to do so.[34]

Evans also provides a clear example of the occurrence of divergent judicial opinions because of different emphasis being placed upon background constitutional principles and legal texts, again demonstrating that although the use of 'fundamental' and 'realistic' may be novel, this approach to statutory interpretation is similar to approaches taken in earlier cases. Lord Neuberger expressly states in his judgment that he reaches a different conclusion because he places 'considerably greater reliance … on the implication of the constitutional principles' of the rule of law, specifically that decisions of courts should be binding between the parties and that the executive should be subject to judicial review.[35] This reliance means that Lord Neuberger is not convinced that the wording of section 53 is sufficiently precise to demonstrate that Parliament has clearly confronted the extent to which this provision undermines the rule of law. Nor does the section clearly express Parliament's specific intention to undermine this fundamental constitutional principle.[36] Lord Hughes places more emphasis on the wording of the legislation. He agrees that constitutional principles support both Lord Neuberger's claims, that decisions of courts should bind the executive and that the executive should be subject to judicial review, such that any intention to overrule these provisions should be made explicit. However, for Lord Hughes, the specific wording of the legislation does make the intention of Parliament explicit; 'Parliament has plainly shown' its intention to empower the Attorney-General to countermand the decision to disclose information;[37] this is clearly 'a matter of the plain words of the statute'.[38] For Lord Hughes, Lord Neuberger and Lord Mance's construction of the legislation is 'too highly strained', departing too greatly from the meaning of legislative provisions, and therefore should be rejected.[39]

The decision in *Evans* also illustrates how differences in approach may depend upon a different understanding of constitutional principles, in a manner similar to our refinement of the difference between the 'fundamental' and 'realistic' reading of the ECA and the reasoning of the minority in *Miller*. In *Evans*, Lord Hughes and Lord Neuberger place different emphases on distinct components of the rule of law. Lord Neuberger prioritises the requirements of the rule of law that the executive should be subject to the law and that decisions of the courts should be binding between the parties. Lord Hughes does not reject these elements of the rule of law, and even concludes that '[t]he rule of law is of the first importance'.[40] However, he also states that 'it is an integral part of the rule of law that courts give effect

---

[34] Phillipson (n 12), 40–42, reaches a similar conclusion.
[35] *Evans* (n 29), [90].
[36] ibid.
[37] ibid, [154].
[38] ibid, [155].
[39] ibid.
[40] ibid, [154].

to Parliamentary intention. The rule of law is not the same as a rule that courts must always prevail, no matter what the statute says.'[41] Moreover, Lord Hughes supports his conclusion through an analysis of the practical difficulties that might arise if the courts were to interpret section 53 in the narrow manner suggested by Lord Neuberger. In particular, he is concerned that, given the short time limit available to issue a certificate, Lord Neuberger's requirements would be almost impossible to satisfy, or would merely replicate the appeal rights available to the executive from a decision of the Upper Tribunal, essentially making the provisions of section 53 devoid of application.[42] Not only does Lord Neuberger disagree with this assessment, but he also prioritises the maintenance of constitutional principles over these practical difficulties.[43]

This example demonstrates that *Miller* does not provide a strikingly novel manner of reading legislation. It merely adds more grist to the mill for those who wish to argue that UK courts are interpreting legislation in a manner that indirectly undermines a particular conception of the sovereignty of Parliament given that the sole concern of the court is not to determine the 'will of Parliament' when interpreting legislative provisions; or, alternatively, that they are interpreting legislation in a manner that upholds their proper constitutional role as guardians of the rule of law and of the constitution. This would suggest that the impact of *Miller* on future cases concerning legislative interpretation will be minor. It is merely yet another example of the importance of background constitutional principles; a further illustration as to how a different emphasis on the specification and the relative importance of competing constitutional principles can play a decisive role.

Moreover, we can argue further that *Miller* may have less importance given its narrower application. This is because the legislation in *Miller* was being interpreted for a purpose different from that discussed in *Evans*. In *Evans*, legislation was being interpreted in order to determine whether an action of the Attorney-General was within the scope of his powers. Statutory interpretation was needed to determine the scope of the law—the extent of the legal power granted to the executive. Once determined, this was applied to determine whether the action of the Attorney-General, to issue a certificate reversing the decision of the Information Tribunal, was within the scope of his legal powers. In *Miller*, the legal principle applying in the case stemmed not only from the interpretation of the ECA, but also from principles of the common law determining the extent to which the common law restricted the scope of prerogative powers—that they did not extend to abrogating legislation, modifying the common law, including rights, or frustrating legislation. Once the legal principle was determined, it was then applied to the prerogative power of foreign affairs, specifically to determine whether the

---

[41] ibid.
[42] ibid, [156].
[43] ibid, [90].

prerogative extended to include withdrawal from the EU Treaties. This required an interpretation of the ECA, in order to determine whether withdrawing from the EU Treaties would modify domestic law, remove statutory rights or frustrate the provisions of the ECA, with the majority and minority reaching different conclusions on this point.

Whilst this may seem an overly pedantic distinction, it is important to recognise the distinct nature of the interpretation of the ECA in *Miller* given that this has implications for the legitimacy of the use of constitutional principles by the judiciary. Criticisms are made of the decision in *Evans* due to its impact on parliamentary sovereignty and on the rule of law.[44] In particular, it is argued that the Supreme Court contradicted the will of Parliament through the way in which the interpretation of Lord Neuberger, in particular, effectively made it impossible for the Attorney-General to issue a certificate, it being very difficult in the time frame to demonstrate a change in circumstances, or that the decision was demonstrably flawed in fact or in law. Moreover, the latter could give rise to a possible appeal against the decision of the tribunal, meaning that a certificate would not be needed to achieve the same end. Also, 'strained' legislative interpretations are problematic in terms of legal certainty, given that it may be hard to predict how legislation will be interpreted in the future. As these interpretations determine the scope of the law, this gives rise to problems as regards the upholding of the ideal of the rule of law.

However, these criticisms have less of an impact when statutory interpretation is used not to determine the scope of the law but as part of an assessment of the application of a legal principle to particular facts. This is particularly true as regards the problems posed for legal certainty. The interpretation of the ECA in *Miller* provides an answer to a specific question regarding the scope of prerogative powers: would the Act be frustrated or changed were the UK to use the prerogative to trigger Article 50? It does not provide a new interpretation of legislation that applies beyond its application to the specific facts before the court. When interpreting the Act in this way, the court is not contradicting the will of Parliament as to its desire to enact a specific outcome in the law, which is partially undermined by the interpretation of a legislative provision by the court. Rather, the court is interpreting legislation in order to determine whether it would be frustrated or modified by an exercise of prerogative power. If so, it is not the case that the legislature's will to achieve a particular outcome has been thwarted. Rather, the executive's will to achieve a specific outcome through the use of prerogative power has been prevented; instead this outcome has to be achieved through Parliament enacting legislation to empower the executive to act. If conditions are placed upon the power of the executive to act, they will be placed by the legislature and not by the court.

---

[44] M Elliott, 'A Tangled Constitutional Web: The Black-Spider Memos and the British Constitution's Relational Architecture' [2015] *PL* 539. *Cf* TRS Allan, 'Law, Democracy and Constitutionalism: Reflections on *Evans v Attorney General* (2016) 75 *CLJ* 38.

The 'fundamental' or 'realistic' approach taken to legislative interpretation in *Miller* is not an example of a new approach to legislative interpretation that is far removed from earlier case law. Rather, it is best understood as yet another example of a growing number of cases in which legislation is required to be construed against background constitutional principles. In addition, it can be argued that the approach adopted in *Miller* is easier to justify than that taken by the Supreme Court in other recent cases of constitutional importance. This is because, in *Miller*, the Court was not interpreting legislation in order to provide a definitive account of the meaning and scope of the law as found in a legislative provision. Rather, the Court was interpreting legislation in order to determine the application of a different legal principle—that general prerogative powers do not include a power to modify legislative provisions, remove statutory rights or frustrate legislation.

II. The Use of General Principles of Constitutional Law

We cannot accept that a major change to UK constitutional arrangements can be achieved by ministers alone; it must be effected in the only way that the UK constitution recognises, namely by Parliamentary legislation. This conclusion appears to us to follow from the ordinary application of basic concepts of constitutional law to the present issue. [45]

The previous section discussed how the majority interpreted the provisions of the ECA differently from the interpretation of the minority, focusing in particular on the reference of the majority to the major constitutional change that would arise were the UK to leave the EU. This interpretation also influenced the majority's conclusion that it would be contrary to the 'basic concepts of constitutional law' for Ministers to effect such a large constitutional change as would occur were the UK to leave the EU. A major change to the UK constitutional arrangements should occur through the actions of parliamentary legislation, not through the actions of Ministers acting alone. This section will argue that it is not the case that the Supreme Court invented a constitutional principle with no connection to earlier case law or other constitutional principles. However, it will argue that the majority of the Supreme Court reasoned in a more deductive as opposed to inductive manner. Again, this is not a completely novel situation. The Supreme Court has reasoned in this manner in other case law, showing that *Miller* merely adds a further example of an emerging approach to constitutional adjudication.

---

[45] *Miller* (n 3), [82].

The approach of the majority has been criticised for failing to explain the origins of the 'basic concepts of constitutional law', particularly through failing to reference specific earlier case law that establishes these 'basic concepts'.[46] However, it can be argued that the majority do give their account of the basic concepts of UK constitutional law. In particular, there are references to the principle of parliamentary sovereignty throughout the judgment of the majority.[47] Moreover, the majority judgment explains how other provisions of English law derive from parliamentary sovereignty. This explains why it is that the courts may develop the common law, but may not develop or interpret the common law in a manner incompatible with statutory provisions;[48] why the executive has to act within the powers conferred by legislation and the common law;[49] why the UK adopts a position of dualism in international law, requiring Parliament to enact legislation to incorporate international law obligations into domestic law;[50] and the limits placed upon the scope of prerogative powers.[51] Parliamentary sovereignty is maintained through the fact that it was the will of Parliament, expressed in the provisions of the ECA, that enabled directly effective provisions of EU law to have supremacy.[52] Moreover, it provides a limit as to the extent to which the principle of the supremacy of EU law applies in UK law.[53] The principle that a major constitutional change has to occur through legislation as opposed to the actions of a Minister alone can also be seen to derive from the principle of parliamentary sovereignty. Parliamentary sovereignty implies that Parliament is the most important institution in the constitution, and that legislation is the most important source of law in the UK constitution—even more important than EU law, given that directly effective provisions of EU law are only able to disapply legislation because another piece of legislation, the ECA, provides for this effect. It would also appear to follow from this, therefore, that a major legal constitutional change should be enacted by Parliament and not by the executive acting alone.[54]

In addition, three main themes running through the judgment explain why the majority concluded that leaving the EU would give rise to a major constitutional change, meaning that such change should only occur through legislation and not through a Ministerial order. First, the majority argue that the ECA

---

[46] M Elliott, 'The Supreme Court's Judgment in *Miller*: in search of constitutional principle' (2017) 76 *CLJ* 257, 263–68.

[47] In particular *Miller* (n 3), [41] and [43].

[48] ibid, [42].

[49] ibid, [45].

[50] ibid, [57].

[51] ibid, [44], [48], [50] and [51].

[52] For a more detailed discussion of the impact of *Miller* on sovereignty, see Mark Elliott's contribution in ch 10 of this volume.

[53] *Miller* (n 3), [67].

[54] I am grateful to Gavin Phillipson for pointing out that this principle can only apply to legal modifications of the constitution. See Phillipson (n 12), 31– 48.

provides for a new source of law—law enacted by the EU institutions, which is incorporated into domestic law through the pipeline of the ECA.[55] Second, EU law is a source of a large number of rights in UK law. Withdrawal from the EU would lead to the removal of at least some of those rights.[56] Third, the majority recognised that the ECA ensured that the UK upheld its obligations in EU law to provide for the supremacy of directly effective provisions of EU law. This extends to the ability to disapply legislation that is not compatible with directly effective EU law.[57] As such, a principle that would 'normally be incompatible with UK constitutional principles became part of our constitutional arrangements as a result of the 1972 Act and the 1972 Accession Treaty for as long as the 1972 Act remains in force'.[58] The ECA brought about a major change to the constitution. Consequently, reversing the UK's membership of the EU would bring about a similar major constitutional change.[59]

In this sense, therefore, it is not necessarily the case that the Supreme Court failed to provide any justification for the principle that major constitutional changes should occur through legislation and not by actions of the executive. Nevertheless, there are two potentially novel ways in which the majority of the Supreme Court reached this conclusion. First, it used a different process of reasoning. The common law often reasons in an inductive manner, deriving general principles from a series of specific cases which reached particular conclusions on their own facts. The majority of the Supreme Court appear to have used a process of reasoning more akin to deductive reasoning, finding a general principle of law which they apply to the specific facts of *Miller*. Second, the Court argues that the conclusion 'appears to follow from' the basic concepts. This does not just illustrate how the Court applies a deductive approach to reasoning, but also demonstrates that there is not, perhaps, a clear answer to the question. It does not 'follow' but only 'appears to follow', suggesting a looser chain of causation. Is this loose approach to reasoning a new direction and, if so, how far is this restricted to the specific situation in *Miller*, or could it be applied to other situations in the future?

The difference in the process of judicial reasoning in *Miller* used to generate the principle that major constitutional change has to occur through legislation and cannot occur through mere Ministerial order can be contrasted with the way in which English common law has given rise to two doctrines that were referred to in the *Miller* judgment: the principle of legality[60] and the development of constitutional statutes, or statutes with a constitutional character.[61]

---

[55] *Miller* (n 3), [61]–[62] and [86].
[56] ibid, [86].
[57] See, most recently, *Benkharbouche v Secretary of State for Foreign and Commonwealth Affairs* [2017] UKSC 62, [2017] 3 WLR 957.
[58] *Miller* (n 3), [68].
[59] ibid, [86].
[60] ibid, [87].
[61] ibid, [67].

The *Miller* decision refers to the statement of Lord Hoffmann in *Simms*, which focuses on the constitutional importance of the principle of legality, explaining in particular how this principle ensures that whilst Parliament can legislate contrary to fundamental rights, it has to do so in clear, specific and precise words, thereby ensuring that Parliament 'must squarely confront what it is doing and accept the political cost'.[62] The principle of legality, however, derives from earlier case law focusing on principles of interpretation and the application of the doctrine of ultra vires. This history of cases shows an incremental approach to the development of the principle of legality, drawing on past case law to help support statements of legal principle.

Leech is often cited as one of the first cases providing support for the principle of legality, despite there being no mention of the principle of legality by name in the case.[63] In *Leech* the issue arose as to the legality of a rule made under section 47 of the Prison Act 1952, which authorised the Secretary of State to make rules for the regulation of prisons. The Secretary of State used this power to enact prison rule 33(3), empowering prison governors to read or examine letters and communications received from and sent to prisoners, including the power to stop such letters and communications. It was argued that this rule should not cover the sending of letters from prisoners to their legal representatives. Lord Steyn approached this issue as one of vires, determining whether the legislation empowered the making of a rule with the breadth and scope of application of rule 33(3).[64] This required the Court to examine whether the legislation contained an implied power to enact provisions which would interfere with rights and civil liberties. Before carrying out this investigation, Lord Steyn stated that '[i]t can fairly be said that the more fundamental the right interfered with, and the more drastic the interference, the more difficult becomes the implication'.[65] Lord Steyn does not provide any specific authority for this statement, arguably reasoning from general principles in a manner similar to the approach of the majority in *Miller*. However, later on in his judgment, Lord Steyn refers to previous cases interpreting prison rules, which concluded that the broad legislative provision of the 1952 Act did not authorise rules to interfere with prisoners' rights of access to the courts[66] or access to a solicitor.[67]

Similarly, in *Pierson*, Lord Browne-Wilkinson finds support for his approach in academic commentaries on statutory interpretation, in addition to previous case law.[68] This then leads him to the conclusion that

> [f]rom these authorities I think the following proposition is established. A power conferred by Parliament in general terms is not to be taken to authorise the doing of acts

---

62 *Simms* (n 27), 131.
63 *Leech* (n 27).
64 ibid, 208.
65 ibid, 209.
66 *Raymond v Honey* [1983] 1 AC 1.
67 *Anderson's Case* [1984] QB 778.
68 *R v Secretary of State for the Home Department, ex parte Pierson* [1998] AC 539, 573–75.

by the donee of the power which adversely affect the legal rights of the citizen or basic principles on which the law of the United Kingdom is based unless the statute conferring the power makes it clear that such was the intention of Parliament.[69]

Lord Browne-Wilkinson may be tentative in his expression of this principle, in a manner similar to that found in *Miller*, but he bases the foundation of this principle on previous case law and commentaries on statutory interpretation, citing these examples to support his assertion.

Laws LJ's judgment in *Thoburn* provides the authority both for the establishment of the separate category of constitutional statutes, and for the assertion that constitutional statutes are not subject to the doctrine of implied repeal.[70] However, it is not the case that Laws LJ asserted this proposition with no authority. Rather, he relies on the fact that the common law has created prior exceptions to the doctrine of implied repeal, focusing in particular on the outcome in *Factortame*.[71] In addition, he draws support for the existence of constitutional statutes, and the inability for such statutes to be subject to the doctrine of implied repeal, from the case law discussed above concerning the establishment of the existence of constitutional or fundamental principles of the common law. If there can exist a hierarchy amongst principles of the common law, with constitutional or fundamental principles of the common law being more important than other principles of the common law, then it follows that the courts 'should recognise a hierarchy of Acts of Parliament: as it were "ordinary" statutes and "constitutional" statutes'.[72] In a similar manner to the principle of legality, '[f]or the repeal of a constitutional Act or the abrogation of a fundamental right to be effected by statute, the court would apply this test: is it shown that the legislature's *actual*—not imputed, constructive or presumed—intention was to effect the repeal or abrogation'.[73] The existence of constitutional statutes is derived from a series of developments of cases in the common law, leading to the establishment of a new principle.

The approach of the Supreme Court in *Miller* can be clearly contrasted with the approach adopted by earlier courts when determining both the principle of legality and the establishment of constitutional statutes. However, although this illustrates a difference in approach, it does not demonstrate a unique approach. Examples can also be provided where the House of Lords or the Supreme Court has also reasoned in a more deductive manner, drawing a specific application from a general principle of the constitution. This is particularly true of the case law concerning parliamentary sovereignty and the rule of law in the UK constitution. For example, Lord Steyn famously stated in *Jackson* that the classic account

---

[69] ibid, 575.
[70] *Thoburn v Sunderland District Council* [2002] EWHC 195 (Admin), [60].
[71] In particular the statement of Lord Bridge in Case C-213/89 *R v Secretary of State for Transport, ex parte Factortame (No 2)* [1991] 1 AC 603, 658–59.
[72] *Thoburn* (n 70), [62].
[73] ibid, [63].

of parliamentary sovereignty found in the work of Dicey 'can now be seen to be out of place in the modern United Kingdom', suggesting further that there may be constitutional fundamentals that cannot be abolished by legislation.[74] Lord Hope in the same case also recognised that sovereignty was no longer absolute,[75] drawing on these arguments in *AXA General Insurance* to justify his conclusion that there were common law limits on the legislative powers of the Scottish Parliament in addition to the limits found in the provisions of the Scotland Act 1998.[76] Lord Hope realises that he cannot draw on prior legal authorities to determine the content of the control of the common law over legislation, given that this was not a question that could be entertained by English courts when faced with the principle of parliamentary sovereignty applied to the Westminster Parliament, meaning that the issue 'has to be addressed as one of principle'.[77] Nevertheless, Lord Hope still referred to some principles in order to conclude that controls over democratic law makers should be less stringent than those over non-democratic law makers, leading to the conclusion that the courts could not apply the standards of rationality, unreasonableness or arbitrariness to Acts of the Scottish Parliament.[78]

In a similar manner, the statements of Lord Neuberger and Lord Mance in *HS2* appeal to broad expressions of constitutional principle when determining the extent to which principles of directly effective EU law override national law.[79] Their conclusion that

> [i]t is putting the point at its lowest, certainly arguable (and it is for the United Kingdom law and courts to determine) that there may be fundamental principles, whether contained in other constitutional instruments or recognised at common law, of which Parliament when it enacted the European Communities Act 1972 did not either contemplate or authorise the abrogation …[80]

resembles the broad statement in *Miller*, both in terms of its content and in terms of its apparent assertion, without drawing on an incremental development of the case law. The authority for this conclusion stems from their analysis of the nature of the UK constitution, the development of constitutional instruments—including constitutional statutes—and fundamental principles of the common law.[81]

When analysed against this context, *Miller* is not a startling new method of reasoning in constitutional cases. Rather it is part of a chain of cases of constitutional importance where the judiciary have made broad statements of constitutional principle, drawing on characterisations of the UK constitution.

---

[74] *R (Jackson) v Attorney-General* [2005] UKHL 56, [2006] 1 AC 262, [102].
[75] ibid, [103].
[76] *AXA General Insurance Ltd v Lord Advocate* [2011] UKSC 46, [2012] 1 AC 868, [47].
[77] ibid, [48].
[78] ibid, [52].
[79] *R (HS2 Alliance) v The Secretary of State for Transport* [2014] UKSC 3, [2014] 1 WLR 324.
[80] ibid, [207].
[81] ibid.

The difference between inductive and deductive reasoning in these constitutionally important cases is best understood as a matter of degree. We can point to a series of incremental, or not so incremental, developments in the case law before the establishment of the principle of legality and of the distinction between 'constitutional' and 'ordinary' statutes. These principles in turn are used as evidence of the changing nature of the doctrine of parliamentary sovereignty, which is then relied upon in *Jackson* and *AXA*. The broad statements of constitutional principle in *HS2* also rely on the development of constitutional statutes and of fundamental principles of the common law.

In a similar manner, we can argue that the broad statement of constitutional principle in *Miller*—that major constitutional change should occur through legislation and not merely through the decisions of a member of the executive— also rests on our understanding of the nature of the UK constitution, developments in the current understanding of the nature of parliamentary sovereignty, the hierarchy between constitutional and ordinary statutes, and the development of fundamental principles of the common law. After all, if clear and specific words are needed to repeal constitutional legislation, or to modify fundamental principles of the common law, this stems from an understanding that Parliament is sovereign, and may enact these changes but must do so fully aware of the political cost of doing so. In a similar manner, major constitutional changes should occur from acts of Parliament, facing up to the political costs of making these changes, and should not occur through actions of the Minister alone without the same higher political cost that might accompany such a change were this to occur through clear legislative enactment or specific legislative authorisation.

Moreover, even though there is more evidence of the majority's reasoning from first principles in *Miller* than in the other examples discussed above, this is justified both by the novelty of the issue raised before the Supreme Court and by the composition of the Supreme Court. As recognised in *Keyu*, there are some changes to the law that have implications that are 'profound in constitutional terms' and which are 'very wide in applicable scope', which require argument before a panel of nine as opposed to a panel of five members of the Supreme Court.[82] A similar correlation can be drawn between judgments that rely more on first principles and those which rely more on incremental developments of the common law. There is more of a tendency to make broad statements of constitutional principle when there is a larger judicial panel. For example, there was a seven-member panel of the Supreme Court in *AXA* and *HS2*, and a nine-member panel of the House of Lords in *Jackson*. *Miller*, as is well known, is the first case to be heard with what was, at the time, a full complement of 11 Justices of the Supreme Court. We may expect the judiciary to draw more on general statements of constitutional principle in these cases than in cases that do not attract the same membership, given there is not the same profound constitutional implications of the judgment.

---

[82] *R (Keyu) v Secretary of State for Foreign and Commonwealth Affairs* [2015] UKSC 69, [2015] 3 WLR 1665, [132].

Miller may provide evidence of a more deductive as opposed to inductive approach to legal reasoning. However, again, there is evidence of the Supreme Court's having used broad sweeping principles in other cases prior to *Miller*. In addition, we have recognised that the Supreme Court is more likely to reason in a deductive as opposed to an inductive manner when faced with novel issues of constitutional importance. In these cases, it is also common for the Court to be composed of more than the usual five Justices. *Miller* may have larger constitutional consequences than these earlier cases, but its approach fits with earlier case law.

III. Abstract Constitutional Adjudication in All But Name?

> If ministers give Notice without Parliament having first authorised them to do so, the die will be cast before Parliament has become formally involved. To adapt Lord Pannick's metaphor, the bullet will have left the gun before Parliament has accorded the necessary leave for the trigger to be pulled. The very fact that Parliament will have to pass legislation once the Notice is served and hits the target highlights the point that the giving of the Notice will change domestic law: otherwise there would be no need for new legislation.[83]

The litigation in *Miller* was also unusual in terms of the timing of the application for judicial review, in addition to the way in which the Court had to adjudicate not only as regards facts that were known, but also as regards possible future consequences. This meant that the type of challenge brought looked more like a challenge for abstract as opposed to specific constitutional review. Specifically, it was a challenge as to the potential legality of a future course of action, as opposed to a challenge as to the legality of an action that had already occurred. Unlike other constitutional systems that do permit pre-emptive challenges to the constitutionality of legislation, the UK constitution does not include a general ability for legislative or governmental acts to be reviewed by the courts before they are enacted.[84] It does include a specific reference procedure as regards the validity of legislation enacted by the devolved legislatures.[85] However, this would not include the type of challenge that took place in *Miller*—that is, a challenge to a letter, written by the Government, in response to a letter written to the Government requesting information as to the legal power the Government would use to trigger Article 50.

---

[83] *Miller* (n 3), [94].

[84] See, eg, Article 61 of the French Constitution, sections 79–80 and sections 121–122 of the South African Constitution, and section 53 of the Supreme Court Act 1982 in Canada.

[85] Scotland Act 1998, s 33; Governance of Wales Act 2006, s 112; and Northern Ireland Act 1998, s 11.

Not only was this a challenge brought earlier than usual public law challenges, but it also required the Court to reason in a more abstract and speculative manner. The Court was looking at whether it *would be* the case that the prerogative *would be used* to modify domestic law and remove domestic rights, rather than investigating whether the Government *had removed* rights and modified domestic law by prerogative powers. To apply Lord Pannick QC's analogy, referred to in the quotation at the beginning of this section, the Ministers would be 'pulling ... the trigger which causes the bullet to be fired, with the consequence that the bullet will hit the target and the Treaties will cease to apply'.[86] The Court was examining whether the Government had the power to pull the trigger, regardless of whether later on Parliament would intervene to authorise a removal of rights, assuming that the trigger would lead to the removal of rights regardless of whether Parliament acted or not; to examine the legality in December 2016 of a series of future actions that would take place in 2017 to 2018. Does this mark a move to a more abstract form of pre-emptive judicial review?

Miller does provide an example of judicial review of a decision as to future governmental conduct, as opposed to past conduct. However, it is important to recognise that there are other examples of judicial review's being carried out in this manner. For example, in *Public Law Project*, the Supreme Court investigated the legality of a draft Order, laid before Parliament by the Lord Chancellor, which effectively provided for a residency test for those wishing to obtain legal aid.[87] By bringing a challenge to the draft Order, the Court was able to determine whether the draft Order was within the statutory powers conferred on the Lord Chancellor before the Order became law, effectively achieving a form of pre-legislative scrutiny for delegated legislation. Nor would it be accurate to argue that this form of quasi pre-emptive scrutiny is a relatively new invention of English law. In *R v Electricity Commissioners, ex parte London Electricity Joint Committee*, for example, the Court of Appeal heard an action for judicial review of a draft Order enacted under section 7 of the Electricity (Supply) Act 1919.[88] Moreover, in agreeing to hear the action for judicial review, the Court of Appeal was not willing to entertain the argument that judicial review should not be allowed given that the draft Order in question was subject to the affirmative resolution procedure, meaning that the legislation had given Parliament the job of checking the draft Order, not the court. The Court of Appeal rejected this argument by focusing on how, whilst Parliament is there to scrutinise the content and the policy of the legislation, the courts still had to determine whether the Order was within the power of the Electricity Commissioners granted to them by the 1919 Act. In addition, in reaching its conclusion, the Court drew

---

[86] *Miller* (n 3), [36], quoting the argument of Lord Pannick QC.
[87] *R (Public Law Project) v Lord Chancellor* [2016] UKSC 39, [2016] AC 1531.
[88] *R v Electricity Commissioners, ex parte London Electricity Joint Committee* [1924] 1 KB 171.

on *Byerley v Windas*, a case decided in 1826, with regard to the writ of prohibition.[89] This seems to suggest that whilst the early nature of the challenge in *Miller* may appear to be distinct, it is not novel. Moreover, each of these authorities recognised the advantages that may accrue from hearing argument at an earlier stage, determining the legality of prospective powers as opposed to facing later case law, which may require administrative delegated legislation, or administrative action, to be struck down as beyond the scope of the administration's powers. If accommodation is to be made for these earlier challenges, it is to be found in the modification of the remedy that should be applied, as opposed to an outright rejection of the ability for such challenges to be brought.

What is more novel, and potentially more problematic, is the nature of the assumption on which Lord Pannick QC's analogy was based. These problems are evident from Lord Carnwath's dissent.[90] As Lord Carnwath points out, when an individual fires a gun, there is not normally a two-year time gap between the pulling of the trigger and the bullet's hitting its target. Whilst this may seem an odd distinction to draw, it is important as regards the actions of Parliament that may occur during this time. Whilst there may be no time to put in place measures to protect the intended victim of a gunshot—despite many a film's suggesting to the contrary—there is time in between triggering Article 50 and leaving the EU for legislation to be enacted by Parliament in order to authorise the removal of rights or the modification of domestic law. There is also time for Parliament to enact legislation to maintain EU law, as it is currently in the process of doing,[91] and as was expressed by the Government as its intention prior to the *Miller* litigation in the Supreme Court.[92] For Lord Carnwath, this meant that the assumption on which the majority's case rested—that the triggering of Article 50 would automatically lead to a modification of domestic law—had effectively amended the long-standing legal principle that prerogatives do not extend to include a power to modify domestic law, to frustrate legislation or to change rights. Instead, the majority were effectively applying a different legal principle—that 'the prerogative does not extend to any act which will necessarily lead to the alteration of the domestic law, or of rights under it, *whether or not that alteration is sanctioned by Parliament*'.[93] If Lord Carnwath is right, then the decision of the majority in *Miller* cannot rest on a novel application of long-standing, if perhaps not frequently used, provisions relating to the extent of prerogative powers.

Lord Carnwath is right to point out the problems with the bullet analogy used by Lord Pannick QC. However, this is not best understood as a modification of the requisite provisions of constitutional law. Rather, it is recognising the difficulties

---

[89] *Byerley v Windas* (1826) 5 B and C 1, 108 ER 1.

[90] *Miller* (n 3), [263]–[264].

[91] European Union Withdrawal Bill 2017–9.

[92] HC Deb 10 October 2016, vol 615, cols 40–41, referred to by Lord Carnwath in *Miller* (n 3), [263].

[93] *Miller* (n 3), [264] (emphasis added).

that can arise when applying judicial review at the pre-emptive stage, determining prospective as opposed to retrospective legality. The Court was examining whether the prerogative power of foreign affairs extended to include the power to trigger Article 50, starting the process of leaving the EU. The prerogative would not extend to include any ability to modify domestic law, alter domestic rights or frustrate legislative provisions. When determining whether Article 50 would modify domestic law, alter rights or frustrate legislative provisions, the Court was aware of the possibility that legislation might be enacted in the future to modify domestic law or remove rights. However, given the pre-emptive nature of this action for judicial review, it was not clearly the case that Parliament *had* so legislated, or that it *would* so legislate in the future. As such, the Court was faced with a choice of two possible assumptions: an assumption that Parliament would legislate to modify domestic law and remove rights; or an assumption that Parliament would not legislate to modify domestic law and remove rights. It could either choose between these assumptions, or choose to argue that, if there is potential illegality according to either assumption, then this is sufficient to justify the conclusion that triggering Article 50 would not be within the scope of the prerogative power.

There are at least two clear justifications for adopting the position that any potential illegality should be checked by the Court. If the Supreme Court were to assume that legislation would be enacted, but this later proved not to be the case, then it would be highly likely that future litigation would arise, after the UK had left the EU. Applying the legal principles established in *Miller*, this would give rise to a situation in which the prerogative alone had been used to remove rights, modify domestic law and frustrate the ECA. However, it would be impossible for the Court to do anything at that stage to prevent that illegality. It would not be possible for the UK courts alone to prevent the UK from leaving the EU, this being governed by EU law and international law.

Second, if the Court were to assume that Parliament would act, and Parliament did not enact legislation, the Court might be perceived as either directly or indirectly requiring Parliament to enact legislation, breaching parliamentary privilege and parliamentary sovereignty. This could arise directly, were we to be facing the situation where the UK left the EU with no deal and no legislation. In this circumstance, a legal challenge might be brought to require Parliament to enact legislation to authorise the removal of rights. Even if no litigation were brought, the Court's assumption that Parliament would enact legislation might create indirect pressure on Parliament to ensure that legislation was enacted. This is because the Court's judgment had made it clear that legislation was needed in order to remove rights. In short, the Supreme Court was faced with a choice between two assumptions. To assume that Parliament would act could potentially challenge parliamentary sovereignty and parliamentary privilege, or potentially condone future illegality. To assume that Parliament might not act, however, would ensure that Article 50 was definitely triggered in the legally correct manner. When faced with this choice of assumptions, the wisest choice is to err on the side of caution. If either of the possible assumptions on which the decision could be based was to lead to potential illegality, it should be declared at the time the legal challenge was brought to prevent possible irreparable future illegality or the perpetuation of legal uncertainty.

Understood in this manner, is the Supreme Court adopting a novel, abstract approach to constitutional litigation? Although it could be argued that the Supreme Court is almost carrying out an abstract hearing, or a reference as to legality or constitutionality, this is not what arose in *Miller*. Nor would it be entirely novel for the Justices of the Supreme Court to answer an abstract question as to constitutionality, the Justices also being members of the Privy Council, which has the power to give opinions on matters referred to it by the executive, or following a motion of the House of Commons requesting the executive to raise this matter.[94] In these instances, the Privy Council provides a non-legally binding opinion, the reference determining legal questions but not providing legal solutions.[95] When petitioned in this manner, the Privy Council is careful to ensure that it only determines the legal issue before the court. For example, in *Reference re the Parliamentary Privilege Act 1770*, the Privy Council was careful to ensure that it only determined whether the 1770 Act, allowing legal suits to be brought against Members of Parliament (MPs), applied to all legal suits, or only to those addressed to MPs in their personal capacity and not in relation to proceedings in Parliament. The Privy Council was particularly careful to ensure that it did not determine whether the act—a letter written by an MP to the London Electricity Board—amounted to a proceeding in Parliament or not.[96]

A better understanding of the approach of the Supreme Court is that when courts are dealing with cases that have clear constitutional significance, or where there may be fundamental constitutional consequences of the decision, they will err on the side of caution, adopting interpretations of the law that are more able to minimise the potential constitutional repercussions of their decision. In *Miller*, this was achieved through ensuring that, should either assumption lead to the potential for a prerogative power to alter domestic law, remove rights or frustrate legislation, legislation would be required to empower the Minister to trigger Article 50. The Court is erring on the side of caution to ensure legality and constitutionality, particularly given the large constitutional repercussions of an unlawful triggering of Article 50.

Nor is this approach entirely novel. In *Robinson*, the House of Lords was arguably prepared to go even further.[97] Section 16 of the Northern Ireland Act 1998 provided that, following elections for the Northern Ireland Assembly, the

---

[94] Judicial Committee Act 1833, s 4. See *In Re Parliamentary Privilege Act 1770* [1958] AC 331.

[95] See, eg, *Re Baronetcy of Pringle of Sitchell* [2016] UKPC 16, determining whether the presumption of the legitimacy of heirs can be rebutted by DNA evidence; and *In re Piracy Jure Gentium* [1934] AC 586, determining whether robbery was a necessary component of the offence of piracy.

[96] *In re Parliamentary Privilege Act 1770* (n 94). See also SA de Smith, 'Parliamentary Privilege and the Bill of Rights' (1958) 21 *MLR* 465.

[97] *Robinson v Secretary of State for Northern Ireland* [2002] UKHL 32, [2002] NI 390.

Assembly had a period of six weeks to elect the First Minister and the Deputy First Minister. Whilst section 16 was silent on what should happen were the election not to take place within the six-week period, section 32(3) of the Act stated that if the six-week period were to come to an end without the election of a First Minister and a Deputy First Minister, the 'Secretary of State shall propose a date for the poll for the election of the next Assembly'. An election for the First Minister and Deputy First Minister having failed within the six-week period, a successful election was made outside of this period. Nevertheless, the Secretary of State did not propose a date for an immediate re-election of the Assembly, instead arguing that he had no reason to alter the date of the poll of the next election from that set out under the fixed-term period established in the Northern Ireland Act 1998. By adopting a more purposive approach, focusing on the impact on democracy and stability in Northern Ireland, the House of Lords interpreted the Northern Ireland Act 1998 in a manner that was likely to avoid a potential constitutional crisis and promote constitutional stability. The regard to the constitutional background was influential as to the choice between competing interpretations of the 1998 Act. It is potentially less problematic for the Supreme Court in *Miller* to rest its decision on a factual assumption which aims to minimise future illegality than for the House of Lord in *Robinson* to choose to interpret a legislative provision in a manner which minimises future constitutional instability.

Whilst *Miller* may appear to provide for a form of abstract constitutional review, resting on assumptions that may not reflect future reality, this is not an example of a particularly novel or a particularly problematic form of constitutional review. Rather, it is part of a chain of decisions where the Privy Council, the House of Lords and the Supreme Court have had to determine issues of constitutional importance. In taking these decisions, or providing opinions under the provisions of the 1833 legislation, the Justices of the Supreme Court, whether acting as members of the Judicial Committee of the Privy Council or of the highest court, have been careful to take decisions that aim to avoid future constitutional problems and avoid constitutional instability, whilst also being careful to ensure that they do not transgress the proper bounds of their powers.

IV. The Sewel Convention:
An Overly Narrow Approach?

Judges therefore are neither the parents nor the guardians of political conventions; they are merely observers.[98]

In addition to determining whether the prerogative power of foreign affairs included the power to trigger Article 50, the Supreme Court was asked to

---

[98] *Miller* (n 3), [146].

determine whether, if legislation were needed to empower the executive to act, this would require a legislative consent motion, obtaining the consent of the devolved legislatures.[99] The case for a legislative consent motion was predominantly based upon, but not limited to, the Sewel Convention. In addition, reliance was placed upon section 2 of the Scotland Act 2016, which inserted section 28(8) into the Scotland Act 1998, which states that 'it is recognised that the Parliament of the United Kingdom will not normally legislate with regard to devolved matters without the consent of the Scottish Parliament'. All of the Justices of the Supreme Court concluded that the Sewel Convention, as a constitutional convention, should not be enforced by the courts.[100] Moreover, as the Scotland Act 'recognises' the Convention, as opposed to specifically incorporating this into legislation, this was indicative of an intention to entrench the Sewel Convention as a convention, as opposed to an intention to give the Convention legal force.[101] Is this an example of the Court's adopting an overly formalistic as opposed to realistic approach? If so, does this undermine or add to our conclusion that, although *Miller* may appear to adopt a novel approach to constitutional adjudication, its approach fits with earlier case law?

It could be argued that it was not really possible for the Court to be more 'realistic', or more constitutional, in its approach when determining whether the Sewel Convention imposed a legal obligation on Westminster to obtain the consent of the devolved legislatures. The specific use of the word 'recognises' is distinct from other instances in which there is evidence of a convention's being placed on a statutory footing. Where legislatures have incorporated conventions into legislation before, they have done so through including an obligation in legislation which mirrors that found in the convention. For example, section 20 of the Constitutional Reform and Governance Act 2010 replicates the Ponsonby Rule requiring Treaties to be laid before Parliament, subject to the negative resolution procedure, before ratification. In a similar manner, it is hard to see how the Supreme Court could have gone further without contravening a long line of cases recognising that courts are not able to enforce constitutional conventions.[102]

---

[99] For a more detailed discussion of these issues and the ensuing constitutional consequences, see the contributions of Gordon Anthony and Aileen McHarg in chs 8 and 7 of this volume respectively.

[100] *Miller* (n 3), [141]–[145].

[101] ibid, [149].

[102] *Madzimbamuto v Lardner Burke* [1969] 1 AC 645; *Attorney- General v Jonathan Cape* [1976] 1 QB 752; *In re Resolution to Amend the Constitution* [1981] 1 SCR 753 (Canadian Supreme Court). See also C Munro, 'Laws and Conventions Distinguished' (1975) 91 *LQR* 218; D Feldman 'Constitutional Conventions' in M Qvartup (ed), *The British Constitution: Continuity and Change: Festschrift in honour of Vernon Bogdanor* (Oxford, Hart Publishing, 2013) 93; M Elliott, 'Parliamentary Sovereignty and the New Constitutional Order: Legislative Freedom, Political Reality and Convention' (2002) 22 *Legal Studies* 340; J Jaconelli, 'Do Constitutional Conventions Bind?' (2005) 64 *CLJ* 149; RB Taylor, 'Foundational and regulatory conventions: exploring the constitutional significance of Britain's dependency upon conventions' [2015] *PL* 614; and NW Barber, *The Constitutional State* (Oxford, Oxford University Press, 2010) ch 6.

Nevertheless, it might have been possible for the Supreme Court to have gone further than it did, providing further evidence for the fact that *Miller* is not an example of a radically novel approach to constitutional adjudication. For example, although it is hard to see how the Court could have regarded the Scotland Act 2016 as placing the Sewel Convention on a legal footing, it might have been open to the Court to provide an answer to the legal question of whether Westminster was legislating on a devolved issue or not. This is a legal issue which the courts do determine, and have determined, when ascertaining whether the devolved legislatures are acting with the scope of their devolved powers. Whilst the definition of 'normally' may be regarded as too political for court enforcement,[103] it might have been possible for the Court to provide some of the criteria regarding when it may not be normal for legislative consent to be obtained, for example when faced with urgent legislation or a national emergency. Providing these criteria might not have breached Article 9 of the Bill of Rights 1689 if the Court was merely providing legal boundaries and was not questioning the behaviour of either Westminster or a devolved legislature. It could also have regarded the Sewel Convention as forming part of the constitutional requirements of Article 50, such that EU law would require that the Convention be adhered to.[104] Moreover, it could be possible for Parliament or the executive to use the procedure of the Judicial Committee Act 1833, referring a question to the Privy Council, in a manner similar to the reference regarding the Parliamentary Privilege Act 1770.[105]

Further, it might have been possible for the Court to have indirectly, as opposed to directly, enforced the Sewel Convention. The Supreme Court in *Miller* does recognise the constitutional importance of conventions, including recognising in particular that '[t]he Sewel convention has an important role in facilitating harmonious relationships between the UK Parliament and the devolved legislatures'.[106] It might have been open for the Supreme Court to have gone further, recognising that Westminster's legislating without consent on a devolved matter, when it would normally obtain consent, would be unconstitutional, if not unlawful, because it would undermine the harmonious relationship between Westminster and the devolved legislatures. The Canadian Supreme Court was willing to do so, albeit on an issue which came to the Court through the reference procedure rather than through judicial review.[107] Given the reference procedure,

---

[103] Lady Hale, 'The UK Constitution on the Move' (n 1).

[104] A McHarg, 'The Devolution Implications of the *Miller* decision', available at https://judicialpowerproject.org.uk/aileen-mcharg-the-devolution-implications-of-the-miller-decision/, posted 6 December 2016.

[105] *In re Parliamentary Privilege Act 1770* (n 94). Sir Louis Blom-Cooper suggests that this procedure should be used in order to determine the legal response to the Brexit referendum. See L Blom-Cooper, 'The referendum of 23 July 2016: voting on Europe' [2017] *PL* (November Supplement Brexit Special Extra Issue) 1.

[106] *Miller* (n 3), [151].

[107] *In re Resolution to Amend the Constitution* [1981] 1 SCR 753 (Canadian Supreme Court).

the opinion of the Canadian Supreme Court was not a legally binding judgment, although it carried significant weight, indirectly enforcing the political obligations placed on the Canadian Government by constitutional conventions. In a similar manner, the Supreme Court in *Miller* was only asked to issue a declaration, not to quash a decision or measure. Given that the Supreme Court was willing to entertain an earlier challenge than one might expect, and reason from assumptions that might have been more justified in a form of abstract constitutional review, the Court could perhaps have also justified determining that it would have been unconstitutional, if not unlawful, for Westminster to enact the European Union (Notification of Withdrawal) Bill without the consent of the devolved legislatures.

If the Supreme Court had taken this stance, this might have helped to alleviate some of the growing tensions between Westminster and the devolved legislatures. The explanatory notes to the European Union (Notification of Withdrawal) Bill made it clear that the Bill did 'not contain any provision which gives rise to the need for a legislative consent motion in the Scottish Parliament, the National Assembly for Wales or the Northern Ireland Assembly'.[108] This conclusion was reached as the *Miller* decision confirmed that 'the devolved legislatures do not have a veto on the UK's decision to withdraw from the EU'. Whilst *Miller* made it clear that the devolved legislatures did not have a legal veto, no specific conclusion was reached as to the existence of a political veto. If the Supreme Court had been willing to go further, this might have encouraged more interaction between Westminster and the devolved legislatures. It might also have helped to smooth negotiations currently taking place at the inter-governmental level in the Joint Ministerial Committee on European Negotiations.[109]

V. Conclusion

It is hard to deny that the Supreme Court's decision in *Miller* will take its place in constitutional history, standing with other key cases that are interpreted as providing a definitive account of aspects of the UK's constitution. It is also hard to deny the assertion that in *Miller*, as well as in these other key constitutional cases, the Justices of the Supreme Court were acting not just as guardians of the law but also as guardians of the constitution. It is also hard to refute the claim that the majority in *Miller* adopted an approach to the case that focused more on background constitutional principles than on a close textual analysis of the wording of the ECA 1972. However, this assertion needs to be tempered by the recognition that both textual analysis and background constitutional principles played

---

[108] 'European Union (Notification of Withdrawal Bill) Explanatory Notes', Bill 132-EN 56/2, available at https://www.publications.parliament.uk/pa/bills/cbill/2016-2017/0132/en/17132en.pdf.

[109] See Joint Ministerial Committee Communiqué: 24 October 2016, available at https://www.gov.uk/government/publications/joint-ministerial-committee-communique-24-october-2016.

a role in the majority and in the minority judgments, with difference between them being more a matter of degree and choice of background constitutional principle. It is also clear that the majority were more willing to reason from first principles, adopting a more deductive as opposed to inductive reasoning process, acting on assumptions that were more suited to abstract constitutional reasoning given the quasi pre-emptive manner in which the decision in *Miller* came to the Supreme Court. Nevertheless, this approach to constitutional adjudication is not completely novel. Nor is it the case that the Court was willing to adopt a role as the guardian of all aspects of the constitution, refraining from enforcing the Sewel Convention even when it might have been possible for the Supreme Court to have placed greater stress on its constitutional importance, or to have more clearly recognised how acting in breach of the Convention may be unconstitutional if not illegal. If *Miller* is a shift to the recognition of the courts as 'guardians of the constitution', it is clearly one where the courts see their role as to protect the 'legal' and not the 'political' constitution—despite the difficulties that exist when drawing a line between the two.

Nevertheless, the decision of the majority is criticised for going too far, straying too far from the law towards a role which guards constitutional principles, even when they are not fully recognised as legal principles.[110] In defending the approach of the majority, this chapter has explained how the decision in *Miller* was nearer to an example of abstract constitutional review rather than a specific action of judicial review. This suggests a different potential impact of *Miller* on constitutional adjudication. If the Supreme Court is to develop its role as a guardian of the constitution in addition to that of guardian of the law, it may be helpful for legislation to be enacted to allow for a reference procedure to the Supreme Court, in a manner similar to the reference procedure for delegated legislation and to the reference procedure before the Privy Council under section 4 of the Judicial Committee Act 1833, or that found in the devolution legislation. Such a procedure would enable the Supreme Court to reason in a more abstract constitutional manner when asked to advise on the potential constitutionality of future actions of the Government. Such a procedure might have provided a better means of resolving the issues in *Miller* than the use of assumptions as to future conduct, or what might appear to be abstract reasoning with less clear legal justification. It might also have paved the way for the Supreme Court to have provided a more detailed evaluation of the constitutionality of enacting legislation in breach of the Sewel Convention. The development of such a procedure would be a better future legacy of the *Miller* litigation, enabling the courts to play a role in the defence of the constitution without accusations that they are transgressing their proper constitutional role.

---

[110] See, eg, Elliott (n 46); M Barczentewicz, 'Miller, Statutory Interpretation and the True Place of EU Law in the UK' [2017] *PL* (November Supplement Brexit Special Extra Issue) 10; R Ekins, 'Constitutional Practice and Principle in the Article 50 Litigation' (2017) 133 *LQR* 347; and J Grant, 'Prerogative, Parliament and Creative Constitutional Adjudication: Reflections on Miller' (2017) 28 *King's Law Journal* 35.

INDEX